THE COMPLETE WORKS OF
FRANCIS A. SCHAEFFER
A CHRISTIAN WORLDVIEW

VOLUME TWO

A Christian View of the Bible As Truth

THE COMPLETE WORKS OF
FRANCIS A. SCHAEFFER

A CHRISTIAN WORLDVIEW

VOLUME TWO
A Christian View of the Bible As Truth

CROSSWAY BOOKS ● WESTCHESTER, ILLINOIS
A DIVISION OF GOOD NEWS PUBLISHERS

THE COMPLETE WORKS OF
FRANCIS A. SCHAEFFER
A CHRISTIAN WORLDVIEW

Preface to Volumes I–V

We are reediting and republishing the twenty-one books written by me between 1968 and 1981. Various people asked for this, so that they would be available in permanent form. I agreed to the work involved in it because we have found that all the books are contemporary for the 1980s. We think they are more contemporary now than when they were first published.

These books are now published as five hardback volumes. Thus, all my printed work which is in book form will be available in five companion volumes.

Much reediting has gone into this. They are the same books, yet brought up to date and clarified where time has shown they need clarification.

A section of *The God Who Is There* which seems to have been rather widely discussed and, it seems to me, at times misunderstood and misstated has been what is sometimes called "Schaeffer's apologetics." This section is enlarged as an added appendix on pages 175-187 of Volume I of this series.

All the books are to be read and understood together (along with my wife Edith's books). They together are a unit.

They were written to be read and useful to both Christians and non-Christians. Time has proved this to be the case far beyond our hopes.

They were not written to be only used on the academic scene, though they have been used there, but also for the less academic— though, of course, we realize that they do take care and study and are not popular reading to be pursued while dozing in an armchair. Some have thought the terminology difficult, but I have letters from many parts of the world saying that it was the use of this terminology that for them showed that Christianity has something to say to twentieth-century people, and that it was this terminology which was the bridge which caused them to study the books and to be helped by them. We have tried to make the terminology easier where possible.

The Bible translations have been maintained as they were in the original editions: that is, the *King James* in the earlier books, and the *New International Version* in *Whatever Happened to the Human Race?* and *A Christian Manifesto*.

Another choice to be made was whether to leave the word *man*, as designating men and women, or go to the recent usage of indicating in each case that *she* or *he* is meant. When the earlier books were written, this was not a problem. In my later books the newer way of speaking and writing has been used. However, bringing the earlier books in line in this regard would have been a horrendous task. Please therefore forgive me, anyone who would be disturbed, and please read the usage in the older accepted way. I would be overwhelmingly sorry if anyone would be "put off." Please read it as "man" equaling a human being and all human beings—whoever you are—women and men, children and adults.

The basic trilogy has been: *The God Who Is There, Escape From Reason,* and *He Is There and He is Not Silent.* All the others fit into these as spokes of the wheel fit into the hub.

The early books broke ground in calling for the Lordship of Christ in the arts—art, literature, cinema, philosophy and so on. *How Should We Then Live?, Whatever Happened to the Human Race?* and *A Christian Manifesto* bring this body of thought forward into the area of a Christian's duty, under the Lordship of Christ, in the whole of life as a citizen, especially in the area of law, government, and standing for a high view of human life.

We have been overwhelmed at the way these books have been used over such a wide spectrum of kinds of people and geographically. I can truly say it has brought us to awe and worship. These new five volumes are now published in the hope that they too will be so used.

To make these present volumes more useful for some, at the end of each volume there is a list of translations in the various countries and the publishers for the books in that volume.

This venture would not have been possible without the hard work and wisdom of Dr. Jeremy Jackson and Ranald Macaulay who gave me their suggestions. I thank them profoundly.

Francis A. Schaeffer, 1982

Contents

BOOK FOUR: BASIC BIBLE STUDIES

BOOK FIVE: ART AND THE BIBLE

GENESIS IN SPACE AND TIME

Preface

The battle for a Christian understanding of the world is being waged on several fronts. Not the least of these is biblical study in general, and especially the question of how the opening chapters of the Bible are to be read. Modern writers commenting on the book of Genesis tend to treat the first eleven chapters as something other than history. For some, this material is simply a Jewish myth, having no more historical validity for modern man than the Epic of Gilgamesh or the stories of Zeus. For others, it forms a prescientific vision that no one who respects the results of scholarship can accept. Still others find the story symbolic but no more. Some accept the early chapters of Genesis as revelation in regard to an upper-story religious truth, but allow any sense of truth in regard to history and the cosmos (science) to be lost.

How should these early chapters of Genesis be read? Are they historical and if so, what value does their historicity have? In dealing with these questions, I wish to point out the tremendous value Genesis 1—11 has for modern man. In some ways these chapters are the most important ones in the Bible, for they put man in his cosmic setting and show him his peculiar uniqueness. They explain man's wonder and yet his flaw. Without a proper

3

understanding of these chapters we have no answer to the problems of metaphysics, morals or epistemology, and furthermore the work of Christ becomes one more upper-story "religious" answer.

Although I have often made deliberate changes in this new edition, I have used the King James Version throughout the book. Occasionally where the American Standard Version (ASV) is helpful, I have quoted from it.

I would like to thank Professor Elmer Smick, a friend of many years, who read the manuscript and offered helpful suggestions. Any errors are certainly my own.

Francis A. Schaeffer

CHAPTER ONE

Creation

The subject of this book is the flow of biblical history. Our focal passage of Scripture is the first major section of Genesis (chapters 1—11), which traces the course of events from the creation of the universe to the calling forth of Abraham and the beginning of the history of Israel.

One of the hymns of Israel, Psalm 136, forms an excellent backdrop against which to see the unfolding of biblical history. It sets the conception of God as Creator in proper relation to man as creature and worshiper.

> Oh, give thanks unto the LORD, for he is good;
> for his mercy endureth forever.
> Oh, give thanks unto the God of gods;
> for his mercy endureth forever.
> Oh, give thanks to the Lord of lords;
> for his mercy endureth forever.
> To him who alone doeth great wonders;
> for his mercy endureth forever. (vv. 1-4)

Psalm 136 thus begins with a three-fold doxology and then lists various reasons why we can praise God and why we are called upon to give thanks for His goodness. It is interesting that after giving a general reason for praise (that He "alone doeth great wonders"), the psalmist directs our attention first to God's creative acts:

> To him who by wisdom made the heavens;
>   for his mercy endureth forever.
> To him who stretched out the earth above the waters;
>   for his mercy endureth forever.
> To him who made great lights;
>   for his mercy endureth forever:
> The sun to rule by day;
>   for his mercy endureth forever:
> The moon and stars to rule by night;
>   for his mercy endureth forever. (vv. 5-9)

But immediately after expressing and developing the fact of God as Creator, the psalmist sweeps on to a second reason for praising God—the way God acted in history when the Jewish nation was captive in Egypt.

> To him who smote Egypt in their first-born;
>   for his mercy endureth forever:
> And brought out Israel from among them;
>   for his mercy endureth forever. (vv. 10, 11)

The psalmist goes on to talk about the exodus, the dividing of the Red Sea, the overthrow of Pharaoh, and the capture of the land of Canaan (vv. 12-21).

Then he turns to praise God for the way God is acting at the particular moment of space-time history in which this psalm was written:

> Even an heritage unto Israel, his servant;
>   for his mercy endureth forever.
> Who remembered us in our low estate;
>   for his mercy endureth forever:
> And hath redeemed us from our enemies;
>   for his mercy endureth forever.
> Who giveth food to all flesh;
>   for his mercy endureth forever. (vv. 22-25)

Finally, in the last verse the psalmist writes in such a way that he speaks even for us at our own point in history and invites us to call upon God and praise Him:

> "Oh, give thanks unto the God of heaven;
> for his mercy endureth forever. (v. 26)

So Psalm 136 brings us face to face with the biblical concept of creation as a fact of space-time history, for we find here a complete parallel between creation and other points of history: the space-timeness of history at the time of the Jewish captivity in Egypt, of the particular time in which the psalm itself was written, and of our own time as we read the psalm today. The mentality of the whole Scripture, not just of this one psalm, is that creation is as historically real as the history of the Jews and our own present moment of time. Both the Old and the New Testaments deliberately root themselves back into the early chapters of Genesis, insisting that they are a record of historical events. What is the hermeneutical principle involved here? Surely the Bible itself gives it: the early chapters of Genesis are to be viewed completely as history—just as much so, let us say, as records concerning Abraham, David, Solomon or Jesus Christ.

In the Beginning

The opening verse of Genesis, "In the beginning God created the heavens and the earth," and the remainder of chapter 1 brings us immediately into a world of space and time. Space and time are like warp and woof. Their interwoven relationship is history. Thus the opening sentence of Genesis and the structure of what follows emphasize that we are dealing here with history just as much as if we talked about ourselves at this moment at a particular point of time in a particular geographic place.

In saying this, of course, we are considering the Jewish concept of truth. Many people today think that the Jewish concept is rather close to the modern one—that truth is irrational. But this is not the case. In fact, when we examine the Greek concept of truth in relationship to the Jewish concept, we find an important difference. Many of the Greek philosophers saw truth as the expression of a nicely-balanced metaphysical system, rather like a mobile. That is, as long as the system balanced, it could be left alone and considered true. The Jewish concept is the opposite of this.

First, the Jewish concept is completely opposite from the modern concept of truth because it is concerned with that which is open to discussion, open to rationality, and is not just an existential leap. Here it is like the Greek notion. And yet it differs from and is deeper than the Greek concept because it is rooted in that which is historical. For example, we find Moses insisting, "You saw! You heard!" In Deuteronomy 4 and 5, just before he died, Moses reminded the Jews who stood before him that when they were young, they themselves had seen and heard what had occurred at Sinai—that is, in space-time history. Their parents had died in the wilderness, but they, the children, had seen and heard in history. Joshua spoke the same way a bit later in Joshua 23:3ff.

As a matter of fact, we have an exact parallel in these and other Old Testament passages to John's explanation of why he wrote the Gospel of John. "And many other space-time proofs [that is what the idea is here] truly did Jesus in the presence of his disciples, which are not written in this book; but these are written, that ye might believe that Jesus is the Christ, the Son of God; and that believing ye might have life through his name" (John 20:30, 31).

As we deal with the Jewish writings in the Bible and with the book of Genesis in particular, we must not understand it solely in Greek terms nor, certainly, in terms of an existential leap. Instead, we have an insistence upon history, truth that is rooted in space and time.

Before the Beginning

Although Genesis begins, "In the beginning," that does not mean that there was not anything before that. In John 17:24, Jesus prays to God the Father, saying, "Thou lovedst me before the foundation of the world." Jesus says that God the Father loved Him prior to the creation of all else. And in John 17:5 Jesus asks the Father to glorify Him, Jesus Himself, "with the glory which I had with thee before the world was."

There is, therefore, something that reaches back into eternity— back before the phrase "in the beginning." Christ existed, and He had glory with the Father, and He was loved by the Father before "in the beginning." In Ephesians 1:4 we read, ". . . he [God] hath chosen us in him [Christ] before the foundation of the world. . . ." Thus, before "in the beginning" something other than a static situation existed. A choice was made, and that choice shows forth thought and will. We were chosen in Him before the creation of the world. The same thing is emphasized in 1 Peter 1:20, where the sacrificial death of Jesus is said to have been "foreordained before the foundation of the world." Likewise Titus 1:2 says that God promised eternal life "before the world began."

This is very striking. How can a promise be made before the world began? To whom could it be made? The Scripture here speaks of a promise made by the Father to the Son or to the Holy Spirit because, after all, at this particular point of sequence there was no one else to make the promise to.

Finally, the same point is made in 2 Timothy 1:9, where we read about God, "who hath saved us, and called us with an holy calling, not according to our works, but according to his own purpose and grace, which was given us in Christ Jesus before the world began."

We are faced, therefore, with a very interesting question: When did history begin? If one is thinking with the modern concept of the space-time continuum, then it is quite obvious that time and history did not exist before "in the beginning." But if we are thinking of history in contrast to an eternal, philosophic other or in contrast to a static eternal, then history began before Genesis 1:1.

We must choose our words carefully here, of course. How shall we talk about the situation before "in the beginning"? To avoid confusion, I have chosen the word *sequence,* in contrast to the word *time* as used in the concept of the space-time continuum. It will remind us that something was there before "in the beginning" and that it was more than a static eternal.

After creation, God worked into time and communicated knowledge to man who was in time. And since he did this, it is quite obvious that it is not the same to God before creation and after creation. The Scripture pictures this before "in the beginning" as something that can be stated. While we cannot exhaust the meaning of what is involved, we can know it truly. It is a reasonable concept, one that we can discuss.

This subject is not merely theoretical. What is involved is the reality of the personal God in all eternity in contrast to the philosophic other or impersonal everything which is frequently the twentieth-century theologian's concept of God. What is involved is the reality of the personal God in contrast to a theoretical unmoved mover, or man's purely subjective thought protection. There is more here than contentless, religious truth achieved through some sort of existential leap. Consequently, when we read, "in the beginning God created the heavens and the earth," we are not left with something hung in a vacuum: something existed before creation and that something was personal and not static; the Father loved the Son; there was a plan; there was communication; and promises were made prior to the creation of the heavens and the earth.

This whole conception is rooted in the reality of the Trinity. Without the Trinity, Christianity would not have the answers that modern man needs. As I have said elsewhere, Jean-Paul Sartre well pointed out the basic philosophic problem that faces us: the fact that something, rather than nothing, is there. This is the incontestable and irreducible minimum for beginning to move as a man. I cannot say nothing is there; it is quite plain that something is there. Furthermore, it is also clear that this something that is there has two parts. I am there, and something in contrast to myself is there.

This leads us, of course, to the modern notion of Being. Being is there. But the question immediately arises: "Has it always been there?"[1] This is modern man's basic mystery.

Man is shut up to relatively few answers. I think we often fail to understand that the deeper we go into study at this point, the simpler the alternatives become. In almost any profound question, the number of final possibilities is very few indeed. Here there are four: (1) Once there was absolutely nothing, and now there is something; (2) everything began with an impersonal something; (3) everything began with a personal something; and (4) there is and always has been a dualism.

The first of these—that once there was absolutely nothing and now there is something—has, as far as I know, never been seriously propounded by anyone, and the reason for this is clear. For this explanation to be true, *nothing* must really be *nothing*—totally nothing—neither mass, nor motion, nor energy, nor personality. Think, for example, of a circle that contains everything there is, and there is nothing in the circle; then remove the circle. This is the concept of absolute nothing. As I say, I know no one who has propounded the concept that all that now is has come out of such absolute nothing.

The fourth notion, that of an eternal dualism, can be dealt with rather quickly because it has never stood under close analysis, for men naturally press on behind the dualism and its particulars toward a unity by which to comprehend the duality. This is true whether it is the dualism of electromagnetism and gravity, or some shadowy Tao behind Yin and Yang. Parallel dualisms (for example, ideas—or ideals—and matter, or brain and mind) either tend to stress one at the expense of the other, or leave the unsatisfied question of how they march on together with no reason for doing so.

In contrast to this, the impersonal beginning, the notion that everything began with an impersonal something, is the consensus of the Western world in the twentieth century. It is also the consensus of almost all Eastern thinking. Eventually, if we go back far enough, we come to an impersonal source. It is the view of scientism, or what I have called elsewhere modern modern science, and is embodied in the notion of the uniformity of natural causes in a closed system. And it is also the concept of much modern theology if one presses it back far enough.

An impersonal beginning, however, raises two overwhelming problems which neither the East nor modern man has come anywhere near solving. First, there is no real explanation for the fact that the external world not only exists, but has a specific form. Despite its frequent attempt to reduce the concept of the personal to the area of chemical or psychological conditioning, scientific study demonstrates that the universe has an express form. One can go from particulars to a greater unity, from the lesser laws to more and more general laws or super-laws. In other words, as I look at the Being which is the external universe, it is obviously not just a handful of pebbles thrown out there. What is there has form. If we assert the existence of the impersonal as the beginning of the universe, we simply have no explanation for this kind of situation.

Second, and more important, if we begin with an impersonal universe, there is no explanation of personality. In a very real sense the question of questions for all generations—but overwhelmingly so for modern man—is, "Who am I?" For when I look at the "I" that is me and then look around to those who face me and are also men, one thing is immediately obvious: Man has a "mannishness." You find it wherever you find man—not only in the men who live today, but in the artifacts of history. The assumption of an impersonal beginning cannot adequately explain the personal beings we see around us; and when men try to explain man on the basis of an original impersonal, man soon disappears.[2]

In short, an impersonal beginning explains neither the form of the universe nor the personality of man. Hence it gives no basis for understanding human relationships, building just societies, or engaging in any kind of cultural effort. It's not just the man in the university who needs to understand these questions. The farmer, the peasant, anyone at all who moves and thinks needs to know. That is, as I look and see that something is there, I need to know what to do with it. The impersonal answer at any level and at any place at any time of history does not explain these two basic factors—the universe and its form, and the "mannishness" of man. And this is so whether it is expressed in the religious terms of pantheism or modern scientific terms.

But the Judeo-Christian tradition begins with the opposite answer. And it is upon this that our whole Western culture has been built. The universe had a personal beginning—a personal beginning on the high order of the Trinity. That is, before "in the beginning" the personal was already there. Love and thought and communication existed prior to the creation of the heavens and the earth.

Modern man is deeply plagued by the question, "Where do love and communication come from?" Many artists who pour themselves out in their paintings, who paint bleak messages on canvas, many singers, many poets and dramatists are expressing the blackness of the fact that while everything hangs upon love and communication, they don't know where these come from and they don't know what they mean.

The biblical answer is quite otherwise: something was there before creation. God was there; love and communication were there; and therefore, prior even to Genesis 1:1, love and communication are intrinsic to what always has been.

The Trinity
If we press on in a slightly different way, we can see even more of the nature of the God who existed prior to creation. In Genesis 1:26 we read: "And God said, Let us make man in our image. . . ." As we have seen in the New Testament, God the Father not only loved the Son, but made a promise to Him. And so we should not be taken by surprise when we read the phrase "Let us" or the phrase in Genesis 3:22, "the man is become as one of us." This same phrase also occurs in Isaiah 6:8: "Also I heard the voice of the Lord, saying, Whom shall I send, and who will go for us?"[3]

The teaching that the Trinity was already there in the beginning is especially emphasized in John 1:1-3. As a matter of fact, the concept has particular force because it picks up the first phrase of Genesis and makes it, it seems to me, into a technical term: *"In the beginning* already was [the Greek imperfect here is better translated *already was* than *was*] the Word, and the Word already was with God, and the Word already was God. The same was in the beginning with God." Then in the third verse the Greek aorist tense[4] is used in contrast to the imperfects that preceded it: "All things were made [*became*] by him. . . ." Thus we find first a statement that the Word already was, but then in sharp contrast to this we find something new was brought into being "in the beginning" when He who already was there made what now is.

Furthermore, we know who the personality called the Word (*Logos*) is; verses 14, 15 make it plain: "And the Word was [*became*] flesh, and dwelt among us . . . , [and] John [John the Baptist] bare witness of him. . . ." Of course, the One John bare witness to is Jesus Christ.

Here too a contrast is carried over between the imperfect and the aorist in the Greek. The One who already was [the imperfect tense] the Word in the beginning (verse 1), and who had a part in creating all things, became [aorist tense] flesh (verse 14). I believe that John, the writer of the Gospel, deliberately made such a distinction. That is, in the "beginning" this Word already was, but subsequent to this and in contrast to it there were two absolute beginnings: The first occurred when all things were made (became), and the second when the Word became flesh. Thus, the absolute beginning of the creation and the absolute beginning of the incarnation stand in contrast to the *always wasness* of the Logos. In John 1:1 this is related to the term, "in the beginning." I think, therefore, that "in the beginning" is a technical term meaning "in the beginning of all that was created," in contrast to the preexistence of the nonstatic, personal-infinite, Triune God who did the creating out of nothing.

The phrase "in the beginning" is repeated in Hebrews 1:10, and, as in John 1:1-3, it emphasizes the fact that Christ was already there before creation and was active in creation. That same idea is repeated, though not the phrase itself, in Colossians 1:16, 17, because there we are told that "by him were all things created." Furthermore, 1 Corinthians 8:6 contains an interesting parallel: "But to us there is but one God, the Father, of whom are all things, and for whom we exist; and one Lord Jesus Christ, by whom are all things, and we exist by him." Paul sets forth a parallel between the Father creating and the Son creating.

Thus we have considerable detail concerning the specific relation of the Trinity to the act of creation. It is true, of course, that the part of the Holy Spirit in creation is not as clear as that of the Father and the Son, but it seems to me that Genesis 1:2 does make His presence known: "And the earth was without form, and void; and darkness was upon the face of the deep. And the Spirit of God moved upon the face of the waters." I realize that there is some question about how the phrase "Spirit of God" should be understood here, but certainly the Bible, the Old and New Testaments together, makes a point of saying that the Trinity was there and that the Father and the Son took part in the process of creating.

I would repeat, therefore, that Genesis 1:1 does not depict an absolute beginning with nothing before it. God was there—and then came creation.

The historic Christian position concerning Genesis 1:1 is the only one which can be substantiated, the only one which is fair and adequate to the whole thrust of Scripture. "In the beginning" is a technical term stating the fact that at this particular point of *sequence* there is a creation *ex nihilo*—a creation out of nothing. All that is, except for God Himself who already has been, now comes into existence. Before this there was a personal existence—love and communication. Prior to the material universe (whether we think of it as mass or energy), prior to the creation of all else, there is love and communication. This means that love and communication are *intrinsic*. And hence, when modern man screams for love and communication (as he so frequently does), Christians have an answer: There is value to love and value to communication because it is rooted into what intrinsically always has been.

The Root of the Biblical Doxology
There is a phrase in the book of Jeremiah that Christians should engrave upon their hearts: "The portion of Jacob is not like them [the idols made by men]: for he is the former of all things" (Jer. 10:16). This is the root of the biblical doxology—"unto him," not it! God is not like those idols made of wood and stone, nor is He like those gods that are merely the extension of men's minds. He is the personal God who was there as the former, the Maker, of all things. He is our portion, and He was before all else.

What a sharp contrast to the new theology! The problem in the new theology is to know whether God is there at all. The new theologians are saying the word *God,* but never knowing whether there is anyone back of the word, and therefore not being able to pray. As Paul Tillich once said in Santa Barbara, "No, I do not pray, but I meditate." The Christian, however, not only says that God is really there, but that He was there, that He always has been there, and that He is my "portion" now.

Revelation 4:11 contains a great doxology to this One. Unfortunately, the King James translation does not give its full force. The first phrase should read: "Worthy art thou, our Lord and our God." This reminds us of Jeremiah's phrase, "He is our portion." He is *our* Lord and *our* God. Then the verse continues: "Worthy art thou, our Lord and our God, to receive the glory and the honor and the power: for thou didst create all things, and because of thy will they were, and were created" (ASV). The *New International Version* correctly translates it in modern terms: "By your will they were created, and have their being!" This is the Christian cosmogony.

Here is an answer for modern man overwhelmed by the problem of being, by knowing that something is there and yet not being able to understand it. Everything which has being, except God Himself, rests upon the fact that God willed and brought it into creation. With this I understand why Being is there and why it has form, and I understand that particular part of being which I myself am and the "mannishness" (personality) that I find in me. Things fall into place, not through a leap in the dark, but through that which makes good sense and can be discussed. Once and for all, God did create the Being of the external world and man's existence. They are not God and they are not an extension of God, but they exist because of an act of the will of that which is personal and which existed prior to their being.

How contrary this is to today's whole drift, both in the theological and in the secular world as they roll and drift and speak of the intrinsically impersonal! And how distinct from any form of intrinsic dualism! Rather, this is the biblical answer to the twentieth-century dilemma.

Often in a discussion someone will say, "Didn't God, then, if He is personal and if He loves, need an object for His love? Didn't He *have* to create? And therefore, isn't the universe just as necessary to Him as He is to the universe?" But the answer is, No. He did not have to create something face-to-face with Himself in order to love, because there already was the Trinity. God could create by a free act of the will because before creation there was the Father who loved the Son and there was also the Holy Spirit to love and be loved. In other words, God had someone face-to-face with Himself in the three Persons of the Trinity. Our forefathers were certainly right when they formulated the Nicene and the Chalcedonian Creeds and insisted on the true Trinity in all its force. This wasn't just some passing Greek philosophic concept. When Greek thinking raised these questions, the Christians saw that in what the Bible taught they had the answer. Everything hangs on this point—and at no time more than today.

Thus, we know why Being in the modern sense is there rather than nothing being there. No wonder that we read in Revelation: "Worthy art thou, our Lord and our God, to receive the glory and the honor and the power." This Christian doxology is rooted not in an irrational, contentless religious experience that cannot be thought of or discussed, not in the thought-forms that surround us and into which, if we are not careful, we so easily drop, but in a true creation. It is rooted in a meaningful existence where "A is A" and "A is not non-A." It is wrong to praise God merely as an upper-story, contentless, religious experience. That is one form of taking His name in vain.

Let us notice too that our praise to God is not first of all in the area of soteriology. If we are being fully scriptural, we do not praise Him first because He saved us, but first because He is there and has always been there. And we praise Him because He willed all other things, including man, into existence.

Therefore, when we read in Genesis 1:1, "In the beginning God created the heavens and the earth," what a tremendous statement this becomes as we speak into the modern world! Upon this hangs any distinctively Christian answer which is going to be strong enough for men in the twentieth century.

Creation by Fiat

How did God create? We read in Hebrews 11:3, "Through faith we understand that the worlds were framed by the word of God."[5] The phrase I am primarily interested in here is "the word of God."

First, we have both a parallel with and a distinction from an artist's creation. As a younger Christian, I never thought it right to use the word *creation* for an artist's work. I reserved it for God's initial work alone. But I have come to realize that this was a mistake, because, while there is indeed a difference, there is also a very important parallel. The artist conceives in his thought world, and then he brings forth into the external world. This is true of an artist painting a canvas, a musician composing a piece of music, an engineer designing a bridge, or a flower arranger making a flower arrangement. First there is the conception in the thought world and then a bringing forth into the external world. And it is the same with God. God who existed before had a plan, and He created and caused these things to become objective. Furthermore, just as one can know something very real about the artist from looking at his creation, so we can know something about God by looking at His creation. The Scripture insists that even after the Fall, we still know something about God on this basis.

And yet the differences between the artist and God are over-whelming, because we, being finite, can only create in the external world out of that which is already there. The artist reaches over and uses his brush and his pigments. The engineer uses steel and pre-stressed concrete for his bridge. Or the flower arranger uses the flowers, the moss and the rocks and the pebbles that were already there. God is quite different. Because He is infinite, He could and did create originally out of nothing—*ex nihilo*. There was no mass, no energy particles, before He created. We work through the manifestation of our fingers. He, in contrast, created merely, as it says in the passage we have just quoted from Hebrews, by His word. Here is power beyond all that we can imagine in the human, finite realm. He was able to create and shape merely by His spoken word.

Some Christians became excited about the big bang theory, thinking that it favored Christianity. But they really missed the point—either the point of Scripture or the big bang theory or both. The simple fact is that what is given in Genesis 1:1 has no relationship to the big bang theory—because from the scriptural viewpoint, the primal creation goes back beyond the basic material or energy. Even if one accepts the big bang theory, Genesis 1:1 would then go beyond it by saying that God created out of nothing the primal stuff present at the big bang. We have a new thing created by God out of nothing by fiat, and this is the distinction.

Suppose you could take back everything in the world and compress it into a heavy molecule only three centimeters in each direction, and suppose that everything came from that. This is still no answer to man's basic problem, because it does not explain how that molecule came to be there or how from that molecule could come the form and complexity of the present universe, or something as personal and as "mannish" as man. For this, the scriptural answer is needed.

Second Peter 3:5 is another expression of that answer: "For this they [the scoffers who say that Christ is not really coming again] willingly are ignorant of, that by the word of God the heavens were of old, and the earth standing out of the water and in the water." God by fiat brought the world into existence.

But we should point out something further: "But the heavens and the earth which are now, by the same word are kept in store, reserved unto fire against the day of judgment and perdition of ungodly men" (2 Pet. 3:7). This passage thus reflects not only creation but the flow of history—both its beginning and its continuation. God not only brought the heavens and the earth into existence by divine fiat; He still works into history. He has not become a slave of His creation. Nor is He a slave of history because He made history as it is now. History is going somewhere—there is a flow to history. And the same "word of God" will come forth when God speaks again with judgment and with fire. Thus, while there is a uniformity of natural causes in the external world that God had made, it is not in a closed system. God can still speak when He will, and Peter says that one day in history He indeed will speak again, with judgment.

This concept of creation by a spoken word is wonderfully expressed in two passages in the Psalms, in which true propositional truth in verbalized form is spoken with total beauty. The first is in Psalm 33:6, 9: "By the word of the LORD were the heavens made. . . ." Notice how this exactly parallels the New Testament passages above—"by the word of the LORD." And then notice in the ninth verse: "For he spoke, and it was"—or, "For he spoke, and it came to be." You should draw a big black line through the word *done* as it appears in the King James translation, for it doesn't appear in the original, and I don't know why the translators ever put it there. It spoils the impact and meaning. Rather: "He spoke, and it was." That which was not, on his spoken fiat, became. This is the beginning of the flow of the space-time continuum, history as we know it.

The second passage is in Psalm 148:5: "Let them praise the name of the LORD; for he commanded, and they were created." This is the Old Testament equivalent of Revelation 4:11, the basis of the doxology: God really is there, and He made to be all things that are.

It is either not knowing or denying the createdness of things that is at the root of the blackness of modern man's difficulties. Give up creation as space-time, historic reality, and all that is left is what Simone Weil called uncreatedness. It is not that something does not exist, but that it just stands there, autonomous to itself, without solutions and without answers. Once one removes the createdness of all things, meaning and categories can only be some sort of leap, with or without drugs, into an irrational world. Modern man's blackness, therefore, rests primarily upon his losing the reality of the createdness of all things (all things except the personal God who always has been).

But because I and all Christians know truly, even though not exhaustively, *why* something is there, why the world has form and men have "mannishness," I can meet a Simone Weil or a modern man in despair and we can talk. There is a discussible answer as to why things are the way they are, and this is the framework for my thankfulness, as it should be for every Christian. Unless we reach back into the things that we have discussed here, even thankfulness for salvation becomes meaningless, because it is suspended in a vacuum. In truth, as Jeremiah says, "The portion of Jacob is not like them: for he is the Maker of all things." I now can be thankful both for the knowledge of what is and for my salvation in Jesus Christ. For both are rooted in the fact that the portion of Jacob is not like the gods old or new. He is different: He is the former, the Maker, of all things.

CHAPTER TWO

Differentiation and the Creation of Man

God the Creator is our portion. He calls us to love and to worship Him for His bringing into being all that is. The Bible is not silent concerning why this should be so.

"Created"

The word *created* (Heb. *bārā'*) is used only a limited number of times in Scripture. This is especially true of the specific form used in Genesis 1:1, 21, 27 and 5:1, 2. In the unfolding creation this is used at three crucial points. The first of these is the point at which God created out of nothing (Gen. 1:1), the second the point at which God created conscious life (Gen. 1:21), and the third the point at which God created man (Gen. 1:27).

The third passage is especially interesting because the word *created* in this special form is repeatedly used: "So God *created* man in his own image, in the image of God *created* he him; male and female *created* he them." It is as though God put exclamation points here to indicate that there is something special about the creation of man. This is strengthened as we turn to the summary in Genesis 5:1, 2: "This is the book of the generations of Adam. In the day that God *created* man, in the likeness of God made he him;

male and female *created* he them; and blessed them, and called their name Adam, in the day when they were *created*." Both passages put a triple emphasis on the word. God is saying that three aspects of creation—creation out of nothing, creation of conscious life, and creation of man—are unique.

Differentiation[1]

Genesis 1:2 reads: "And the earth was without form [this can be translated that the earth was waste], and void; and darkness was upon the face of the deep." At this point in the process of creation, that which has been made up to this time lacks differentiation. In other words, it would seem that we have here the creation of *bare being*. What God has made is without form; there is no differentiation between the parts. Then, as we go on into the third verse and beyond, we find a continuing, unfolding differentiation. There are thus two steps: (1) creation out of nothing, and (2) differentiation.

The second step is not to be confused with the first. For one thing, in almost every case differentiation is introduced with *let*. For example, "And God said, Let there be light: and there was light" (Gen. 1:3), or, "Let there be a firmament in the midst of the waters . . . and it was so" (Gen. 1:6, 7). In short, God says something like, "Let it be this way," a different kind of act than creation itself.

The word *let* has an even more general usage in some verses. For example, in Genesis 1:14, after God says, "Let there be lights in the firmament of the heaven," he goes on to say, "Let them be for signs, and for seasons, and for days, and years." And in the second portion of verse 26 he says, "and let them [men] have dominion." That is, in these places God is not so much making something come into being, or even differentiating it as being, as he is indicating what this sort of being means. Note, however, that in most of the uses of the word *let* in this chapter God is still working by fiat, just as He did in creation. He is saying, "Let this take place," and it takes place.

True Communication and Exhaustive Communication

We are considering here matters which lie far in the past and concern cosmic events. That raises a question: Can we really talk in any meaningful sense at all about them? It is helpful, first, to distinguish between true communication and exhaustive communication. What we claim as Christians is that when all of the facts are taken into consideration, the Bible gives us true knowledge although not exhaustive knowledge. Man as a finite creature is incapable of handling exhaustive knowledge anyway. There is an analogy here with our own communication between men; we communicate to each other truly, but we do not communicate exhaustively. A Christian holding the strongest possible view of inspiration still does not claim exhaustive knowledge at any point.

The Bible is a most efficient book. We must remember its purpose: It is God's message to fallen men. The Old Testament gave men what they needed from the Fall till the first coming of Christ. The Old and New Testaments together give all that men need from the Fall until the second coming of Christ. Many other details which we need are also given, but the main purpose is kept central and uncluttered. For example, angels are touched on many times, but the Bible is not a book on angelology. What is told us about angels is true and propositional, but always in relation to men. Heaven is the same; we are given factual knowledge concerning what we need to know about Heaven, but not a great deal of detail. Cosmic creation is included because we need to know these things which were before the Fall. What the Bible tells us is propositional, factual and true truth, but what is given is in relation to men. It *is* a scientific textbook in the sense that where it touches the cosmos it is true, propositionally true. When we get to Heaven, what we learn further will no more contradict the facts the Bible now gives us than the New Testament contradicts the Old. The Bible is *not* a scientific textbook, if by that one means that its purpose is to give us exhaustive truth or that scientific fact is its central theme and purpose.

Therefore, we must be careful when we say we know the flow of history. We must not claim, on the one hand, that science is unnecessary or meaningless, nor, on the other hand, that the extensions we make from Scripture are absolutely accurate or that these extensions have the same validity as the statements of Scripture itself. But all that does not change the fact that biblical revelation is propositional, to be handled on the basis of reason in relationship to science and coordinated with science. The content of Scripture is not upper-story, and the whole of Scripture is revelational.[2]

As we look at the differentiations that occur when God says "Let it be this way," we can have confidence that this is true history, but that does not mean that the situation is exhaustively revealed or that all our questions are answered. This was the case with our forefathers; it is so for us and will be for everyone who comes after us. Indeed, as we stand before God in time to come, even as we see Him face to face, His communication then—certainly being more than what we now have—will still not be totally exhaustive, because we who are finite can never exhaust the infinite. What we know can be true and normative, and yet not be a completely detailed map containing all of the knowledge which God Himself has.

God Divides

After the initial creation out of nothing, therefore, come the various differentiations. The first differentiation comes in Genesis 1:3, 4: "And God said, Let there be light: and there was light. And God saw the light, that it was good: and God divided the light from the darkness." (The word *divided* or *separated* is the key, for it is repeated over and over throughout this chapter.) The first differentiation is between darkness and light. When I was younger, I was puzzled by the fact that light is referred to at this particular place, and yet today we know that it fits with what science says at this moment. With the splitting of the atom the discussion shifted; light is closely related to energy, and it is not surprising that out of *bare being* light (in contrast to the sun) is spoken of as the first differentiation.

The second differentiation comes in verse 6: "And God said, Let there be a firmament in the midst of the waters, and let it divide the waters from the waters." Some scholars who have tried to minimize the teaching of the Bible have said that the word *firmament* indicates that the Jews had an idea of a brass or iron covering over the world. But this is not the picture at all. *Firmament* simply means "expanse." It is a rather broad word, as we can see from the fact that the *firmament* is where the moon and the sun and the stars are (v. 14). Perhaps for our generation the word *space* would be the best equivalent. But it is also the place where the birds fly (v. 20). In any case, the idea that it is merely a hard covering and reflects a primitive notion of a three-story universe is in error. Rather, what is being referred to is differentiation in the area of being—a differentiation of the openness that is about us.

In verse 9 the differentiation continues and concentrates on earth itself: "And God said, Let the waters under the heavens be gathered together into one place, and let the dry land appear: and it was so." Now we have sea and land. There is a constant refining, as it were, as we come down through these steps.

Verse 11 contains a fourth differentiation: "And God said, Let the earth bring forth grass, vegetation, the plant yielding seed, and the fruit tree yielding fruit after its kind, whose seed is in itself, upon the earth: and it was so." So the earth puts forth vegetation, and we have here a differentiation between nonlife and life of a vegetable sort.

Differentiation continues in verses 14-16 where God makes lights in the firmament and divides the day from the night on the earth. It is verse 16 which gives the most difficulty: "And God made two great lights; the greater light to rule the day, and the lesser light to rule the night: he made the stars also." However, the primary emphasis is that on the earth the day is divided from the night. The primary thrust is a continued differentiation as existence moves from bare being to light (or energy) and on into a differentiated space, areas of water and earth, the nonliving and the living plants, and day and night on the earth.

Verses 20 and 21 take up one of the most crucial differentiations—that between conscious and unconscious life. Let me point out, again, that it is at this particular place that the word *created* in its special form is used: "And God said, Let the waters bring forth abundantly the moving creature that hath life, and fowl that may fly above the earth in the open firmament of heaven. And God *created* great whales [or, the great creatures of the sea], and every living creature that moveth, which the waters brought forth abundantly, after their kind, and every winged fowl after his kind: and God saw that it was good." Thus comes conscious life in the air. In fact, a better translation of the second half of verse 20 is "*Let fowl fly.*" The word *let* is not in the Hebrew, but the form of the word *to fly* requires it. In other words, *let* is used throughout this section—in verses 3, 6, 9, 11, 14 and now twice in 20. But at this point of conscious life, the unique note of *create* is stressed, just as it was previously at the unique original creation out of nothing.

In verse 24, we come to the seventh differentiation: "And God said, Let the earth bring forth the living creatures after their kind, cattle, and creeping things, and beasts of the earth after their kind: and it was so" (ASV). In this division, conscious life on the earth is distinguished from conscious life in the water and conscious life in the air. At this point, everything has been produced and differentiated with the exception of one thing, and that is man. And so we come, finally, to the distinction which is so overwhelmingly important to us.

God sets man apart from bare being, vegetable life, and the conscious life of fish, birds and animals. Genesis 1:26 reads: "And God said, Let us make man in our image, after our likeness." Man stands in marked contrast to everything which has been created before. First, as we have already seen, the word *create* is applied to him, and that means that God made man in a special way: Man was made "in the image of God."

We should see this passage in relation to Genesis 2:7, where additional detail is added: "And the LORD God formed man of the dust of the ground, and breathed into his nostrils the breath of life; and man became a living soul." Lest we make too much of the word *soul,* we should note that this word is also used in relation to other living things with conscious life. So in reality the emphasis here is not on the soul as opposed to the body, but on the fact that by a specific and definite act God created man to be a living thing with conscious life. God made man in His image by a specific act of creation. This is strongly emphasized, as we saw before, by the fact that the special word *create* is used three times over, in both Genesis 1:27 and 5:1, 2.

Genesis 1 and Genesis 2

Some scholars today see Genesis 1 and 2 as two separate accounts, almost as if they were watertight compartments in which nothing from the one relates to anything from the other. But according to Scripture's own exegesis of these chapters, this is not allowable. Actually, the first and second chapters of Genesis form a unit; neither account stands complete in itself. The two passages are complementary, each containing unique material that is important for an understanding of man.

But there is a stronger case for unity than the simple recognition of interplay and overlapping between the two accounts. Jesus Himself ties them together. Hence, in order to set this unity aside, we would have to deny the way Jesus approached the two chapters. In answering the Pharisees' question concerning divorce, Jesus said, "Have ye not read, that he which made them at the beginning made them male and female. . . ." Jesus is alluding here to Genesis 1:27. But he continues: "And [God] said, For this cause shall a man leave father and mother, and shall cleave to his wife:

and they twain shall be one flesh." These latter words in Matthew 19:4, 5 are a quotation from Genesis 2:24. So Jesus puts the passages from Genesis 1 and Genesis 2 together as a unit.

Mark 10:6-8 gives further indication of this unity: "But from the beginning of the creation God made them male and female." This hearkens back to Genesis 1:27. Immediately following it Jesus says, "For this cause shall a man leave his father and mother, and cleave to his wife." This derives from Genesis 2:24, and thus again the two are linked as one. Then Jesus goes on: "And they twain shall be one flesh: so then they are no more twain, but one flesh." These passages tied together are the basis of Jesus' moral standard concerning marriage. Jesus reaches back and puts together the creation of man in Genesis 1 with the creation of man in Genesis 2 to show a unity that forms the basis for his view of marriage.

More light is shed on the relationship between Genesis 1 and Genesis 2 by a consideration of a literary structure that occurs throughout the entire book of Genesis: first, less important things are dealt with rapidly, and then the things more important to the central theme of the Bible are returned to and developed more fully. This is so, for example, in the account of Isaac and his two sons, Jacob and Esau. Esau's story comes first, but it is Jacob's which is most fully developed. Likewise, Genesis 1 first deals briefly with man in his cosmic setting, and then Genesis 2 turns to man and puts him at the center of the theme of the book. The Bible is, as we have said, the book of fallen men. Its purpose is to tell us, on this side of the Fall, who we are and what God wants us to know. Consequently, after God has dealt with man in his cosmic setting in the first chapter of Genesis, He puts man at the center, beginning midway in chapter 2. While the accounts in Genesis 1 and Genesis 2 have a different emphasis in this way, they are not pitted against each other.

The Historicity of Adam and Eve[3]
Jesus' treatment of Genesis 1 and 2 also brings to the fore the issue of the historicity of Adam and Eve. It is difficult to get away from the fact that Jesus was treating Adam and Eve as truly the first human pair in space and time. If we have any questions concerning this, surely they are resolved as we consider other New Testament passages.

Romans 5:12, for example, contains a strong testimony that Adam and Eve were in fact space-time people: "Wherefore, as by one man sin entered into the world, and death by sin. . . ." Thus, there was a first man, one man. Paul continues in verse 14, "Nevertheless death reigned from Adam to Moses, even over them that had not sinned after the similitude of Adam's transgression. . . ." Adam, it is obvious, is viewed as being just as historic as Moses. If this were not the case, Paul's argument would be meaningless. Verse 15 strengthens this: "But not as the offense, so also is the free gift. For if through the offense of the one, the many are dead, much more the grace of God, and the gift by grace, which is by the one man, Jesus Christ, hath abounded unto many." Here, therefore, is a parallel between the historicity of Adam (the first man) and two others—Christ and then ourselves. He is dealing with men in history when he deals with "the many," and so he makes a triple parallelism—the historicity of Adam, the historicity of Christ, and the historicity of me.

The point Paul makes in Romans is strengthened still further in 1 Corinthians 15:21, 22: "For since by man came death, by man came also the resurrection of the dead. For as in Adam all die, even so in Christ shall all be made alive." The emphasis is again on the parallel between the historicity of Jesus Christ (whom you must remember Paul had seen on the Damascus road) and the historicity of the man he here called Adam. Verse 45 continues the same thrust: "And so it is written, The first man Adam was made a living soul; the last Adam was made a quickening spirit." The "so it is written" alludes to Genesis 2:7. If one wishes to dispense with the historicity of Adam, certainly he must wonder at such a strong parallelism between Adam and Christ.

Often it is said that this parallelism is only Pauline, but the Gospel of Luke gives us exactly the same thing. Tracing the descent of Jesus backwards, Luke lists a number of characters of history, including such people as David, Jesse, Jacob and Abraham, and ends as follows: "Which was the son of Enos, which was the son of Seth, which was the son of Adam, which was the son of God" (3:38). Thus we have another triple parallelism—a parallelism between the objective, historic existence of a whole group of people we know to be historic through the Old Testament and New Testament references, the objective, historic existence of Adam, and the objective existence of God Himself. If we take away the historicity of Adam, we are left rather breathless! If we tamper with this ordinary way of understanding what is written in the Bible, the structure of Christianity is reduced to only an existential leap.

But let us go further. In 1 Timothy 2:13, 14 we read: "For Adam was first formed, then Eve. And Adam was not deceived, but the woman being deceived was in the transgression." Here is something additional: Not only is Adam historic, but Eve in the midst of her rebellion is seen to be historic as well. And 2 Corinthians 11:3 further testifies to this: "But I fear, lest by any means, as the serpent beguiled Eve through his subtilty, so your minds should be corrupted from the simplicity that is in Christ." The parallel here is between Eve and myself. Paul appeals to those of us who are objectively real—who are in history—not to fall into a like situation. And without embarrassment, Paul obviously expects his readers to assume with him the historicity of Eve and the historicity of the details set forth in Genesis.

Notice too how clearly this is the case in 1 Corinthians 11:8, 9: "For the man is not of the woman, but the woman of the man. Neither was the man created for the woman; but the woman for the man." Here the fact that Eve was created after Adam is an important part of Paul's argument. One would also have to take into account the way in which Paul quotes the early part of Genesis in 1 Corinthians 6:16 and in Ephesians 5:31. (And finally, in 1 John 3:12, Cain is taken as historic, and in Hebrews 11, Abel, Enoch and Noah are placed as parallel to Abraham and all that followed him in history.)

We have, therefore, a strong testimony to the unity of Genesis 1 and 2 and to the historicity of Adam and Eve. They bear the weight of the authority of Paul and Luke and as well that of Jesus.

The Creation of Eve
In Genesis 2 Adam is created prior to Eve. There is no human being standing before him. He is alone. Adam, being created in a specific, unique fashion in the image of God, differentiated from all that has preceded him, finds that nothing corresponds to him. In the Hebrew one can feel the force of this, especially in verse 20: "But for Adam there was not found an help meet for him [that is, a helper opposite to him]." The emphasis here is on a counterpart to Adam—someone parallel to him, yet someone different. This

counterpart, which we now know so very well in the man-woman relationship in life, simply didn't exist at this time. Something wasn't there.

"And the LORD God said, It is not good that the man should be alone; I will make an help meet for him" (Gen. 2:18). And the biblical statement continues: "And the LORD God caused a deep sleep to fall upon Adam, and he slept: and he took one of his ribs, and closed up the flesh instead thereof; and the rib, which the LORD God had taken from the man, made he a woman, and brought her unto the man. And Adam said, This is now [this can be translated *this one at this time,* which gives it the historical emphasis] bone of my bones, and flesh of my flesh: she shall be called Woman, because she was taken out of Man. Therefore shall a man leave his father and his mother, and shall cleave unto his wife, and they shall be one flesh" (Gen. 2:21-24).

The intriguing thing here is that Jesus, in a passage we have already looked at in the New Testament (Matt. 19:4, 5), calls what is given in verse 24 a direct statement of God. God says this because of the way Eve was made, being taken out of the man. So it is hard to tamper with this straightforward way of speaking of the early portion of Genesis without losing the possibility of real meaning in language or in communication. We are told that God made woman in this particular way.

Certainly the fact of the woman's creation out of the man has a very definite philosophic importance, because it means that mankind is really a unit. Man didn't just come out of nowhere. Nor has he sprung up from numerous starts. There was a real beginning, a beginning in a real unity in one man, one individual, differentiated from all that preceded him, and then differentiated in terms of male and female. It is this picture of man which gives strength to the Christian concept of the unity of mankind. The world today is trying to find a basis for claiming all men are one, but the Christian does not have this problem, for he understands why mankind is really united.

Furthermore, we can begin to understand something about marriage because God Himself ties the marriage bond into the reality of the unity of mankind. Hence, we can understand something of that particular union when the male and female constitute one whole, become one flesh. Man, with a capital M, equals male and female, and the one-man, one-woman union reunites the unity.

As Christians, we should not let this section of Genesis in regard to the creation of Eve be shoved aside as something unimportant. At first it might seem that we would not lose much; yet eventually it brings real destruction. The Bible describes the creation of Eve as a specific differentiation—in its own way as much a differentiation as the creation of Adam himself.

There is special force, therefore, in Genesis 5:1, 2: "This is the book of the generations of mankind. In the day that God created man, in the likeness of God made he him; male and female created he them; and blessed them, and called their name mankind [or man], in the day when they were created."[4] The second time the word *created* is used in this passage, it appears in relationship to both male and female. This is parallel to Genesis 1:27—"Male and female *created* he them." The structure is now complete.

Hence, to summarize where we are in the flow of history, we can say that there is first creation out of nothing, then differentiation in various forms, then differentiation of man from all that preceded, and then, in a very special way, differentiation of Eve from Adam, woman from man. The whole sequence testifies to Adam and Eve standing in space-time history.

The Image of God
What is it that differentiates Adam and Eve from the rest of creation? We find the answer in Genesis 1:26—"And God said, Let us make man in our image. . . ." What differentiates Adam and Eve from the rest of creation is that they were created in the *image of God*. For twentieth-century man this phrase, *the image of God,* is as important as anything in Scripture, because men today can no longer answer that· crucial question, "Who am I?" In his own naturalistic theories, with the uniformity of cause and effect in a closed system, with an evolutionary concept of a mechanical, chance parade from the atom to man, man has lost his unique identity. As he looks out upon the world, as he faces the machine, he cannot tell himself from what he faces. He cannot distinguish himself from other things.

Quite in contrast, a Christian does not have this problem. He knows who he is. If anything is a gift of God, this is it—knowing who you are. As a Christian, I know my differentiation. I can look at the most complicated machine that men have made so far or ever will make and realize that though the machine may do some things that I cannot do, I am different from it. If I see a machine that is stronger than I am, it doesn't matter. If it can lift a house, I am not disturbed. If it can run faster than I can, its speed doesn't threaten me. If I am faced with a giant computer which can never be beaten when it plays checkers—even when I realize that never in history will I or any man be able to beat it—I am not crushed. Others may be overwhelmed intellectually and psychologically by the fact that a man can make a machine that can beat him at his own games, but not the Christian.

The Christian knows that in the flow of history, man comes from a different origin. It is not that God has not made both man and the great machine of the universe, but that He has made man different from the rest of the universe. And that which differentiates man from the machine is that his basic relationship is upward rather than downward or horizontal. He is created to relate to God in a way that none of the other created beings are.

It is on the basis of being made in the image of God that everything is open to man. Suddenly personality does not slip through my fingers. I understand the possibility of fellowship and of personality. I understand that because I am made in the image of God and because God is personal, both a personal relationship with God and the concept of fellowship as fellowship has validity. The primary factor is that my relationship is upward. Of course, I have relationships downward as well, but I am differentiated from all that is below me and I am no longer confused.

This differentiation makes genuine love possible. One cannot picture machines as loving. Though one computer may combine with another computer to bring forth a combined answer to some sort of question, we would not call this a love relationship. Furthermore, if we are made in the image of God, we are not confused as to the possibility of communication; and we are not confused concerning the possibility of revelation, for God can reveal propositional truth to me because I am made in His image. Finally (as theologians have long pointed out), if man is made in the image of God, the incarnation, though it has many mysteries, is not foolishness. The incarnation is not irrational, as it surely is if man sees himself as only the finite in face-to-face relationship with a philosophic other.

Consequently, I should be thankful for the comprehension given here in Genesis—that in the flow of history man has been made in the image of God, for it gives an intellectual, emotional and psychological basis to my understanding of who I am.

The Dominion of Man

It is on the basis of being created in the image of God that man has dominion over the other things in the world about him. It isn't that man is simply stronger; as a matter of fact, he isn't always stronger. Dominion itself is an aspect of the image of God in the sense that man, being created in the image of God, stands between God and all which God chose to put under man. As that which was created, man is no higher than all that has been created; but as created in the image of God, he has the responsibility to consciously care for all that which God put in his care.

Furthermore, being created in the image of God frees us from the burden of thinking that whatever *is* therefore must be *right*. We have been given a dominion which puts a moral responsibility on us. We don't need to succumb therefore to the ethics of the Marquis de Sade, where might, or whatever is, is right.

But let us go further. We read in Genesis 1:26: ". . . and let them have dominion over the fish of the sea, and over the fowl of the air, and over the cattle, and over all the earth, and over every creeping thing that creepeth upon the earth." These words are soon repeated: "And God blessed them, and God said unto them, Be fruitful, and multiply, and fill [the King James' *replenish* is inaccurate] the earth, and subdue it; and have dominion over the fish of the sea, and over the fowl of the air, and over every living thing that moveth upon the earth. And God said, Behold I have given you every herb bearing seed, which is upon the face of the earth, and every tree, in which is the fruit of a tree yielding seed; to you it shall be for meat" (Gen. 1:28, 29). We should clarify this translation, for the word *herb* is not meant to be a contrast with other plants, but rather indicates the total plant life, and the phrase *bearing seed* is, in the Hebrew, "seeding seeds." Furthermore, the word *meat* simply means "food," and not meat as opposed to vegetables. So perhaps one could more clearly translate verse 29 this way: "I have given you every plant seeding seeds, which is upon the face of the earth, and every tree which is the fruit of a tree seeding seeds; to you it shall be for food." Thus, man in his dominion is to have the plants for his use.

A further implication of his dominion is brought out in Genesis 2:19, 20: "And out of the ground the LORD God formed every beast of the field, and every fowl of the air; and brought them unto Adam to see what he would call them: and whatsoever Adam called every living creature, that was the name thereof. And Adam gave names to all cattle and to the fowl of the air, and to every beast of the field." Thus the implications of his dominion extended beyond the plant kingdom all the way to that which has conscious life.

Perhaps one of the most striking expressions of the concept of man's dominion is found in Psalm 8:5-8:

> For thou hast made him a little lower than the angels, and hast crowned him with glory and honor. Thou madest him to have dominion over the works of thy hands; thou hast put all things under his feet: all sheep and oxen, yea, and beasts of the field, the fowl of the air, and the fish of the sea, and whatsoever passeth through the paths of the seas.

This passage does, of course, have a prophetic reference to Jesus Christ, but it is also applicable to mankind in general. All of these elements of reality—animals, birds and marine life—are under the dominion of man, and man has a responsibility for them as well as the right to properly use them.

Psalm 115:16 further testifies to the fact, but adds a qualification: "The heaven, even the heavens, are the LORD's: but the earth hath he given the children of men." Not all of creation, therefore, but a certain area is spoken of as being specifically put under man's reign.

By the way, this does not mean that man as he was originally created had no work to do: "And the LORD God took the man, and put him into the garden of Eden to dress it and to keep it" (Gen. 2:15). As we shall see later, the work he was then to perform was not work as we now know it, but man's life was not just one long period of indolence. Man had work to do before the Fall. He was given dominion, and even though he has administered it very badly since the Fall, he still has that dominion.

The Image of God and Fallen Man

It is important to note that fallen man still retains something of the image of God. The Fall separates man from God, but it does not remove his original differentiation from other things. Fallen man is not less than man. Thus we read in Genesis 9:6: "Whoso sheddeth man's blood, by man shall his blood be shed: for in the image of God made he man." Man is such a special creation that to take his life in a wanton, murderous way deserves a particular punishment. I feel that often the hue and cry against capital punishment today does not so much rest upon humanitarian interest or even an interest in justice, but rather in a failure to understand that man is unique. The simple fact is that Genesis 9:6 is a sociological statement. The reason that the punishment for murder can be so severe is that man, being created in the image of God, has a particular value—not just a theoretical value at some time before the Fall, but such a value yet today.

We find a parallel in James 3:9—"Therewith [speaking of our tongues] bless we the Lord and Father; and therewith curse we men, who are made after the likeness of God" (ASV). This likeness is parallel to the term, *the image of God.*

The Christian, therefore, has a sociological base which is extremely strong. As humanists are fighting today against prejudice, they have little philosophical base for their battle. But as a Christian I do: no matter who I look at, no matter where he is, every man is created in the image of God as much as I am.

So the Bible tells me who I am. It tells me how I am differentiated from all other things. I do not need to be confused, therefore, between myself and animal life or between myself and the complicated machines of the second half of the twentieth century.

Suddenly I have value, and I understand how it is that I am different. I understand how it is that God can have fellowship with me and give me revelation of a propositional nature. Furthermore, I can see that all men are so differentiated from non-man, and I must look upon them as having great value. Coming back to Genesis 9:6, anyone who murders a man is not just killing one who happens to be of a common species with me, but one of overwhelming value, one made in the image of God. As James says, any man, no matter who he is, stranger or friend, a Christian or someone who is still in rebellion against God, is made after the likeness of God. A man is of great value, not for some less basic reason, but because of his origin.

Thus the flow of history has tremendous implications for every aspect of our lives. I stand in the flow of history. I know *my* origin. My lineage is longer than the Queen of England's. It does not start at the Battle of Hastings. It does not start with the beginnings of good families, wherever or whenever they lived. As I look at myself in the flow of space-time reality, I see my origin in Adam and in God's creating man in His own image.

CHAPTER THREE

God and His Universe

As the Creator, God shapes and fashions and brings bare being into form—a form which is truly reflective of the One who fashions it. And when God is finished with this process, what He has made speaks of the God who made it.

The Goodness of Creation

Genesis 1 tells us over and over again an important thing about this creation. In verse 4 we read, "And God saw the light, that it was good." The phrase *that it was good* is repeated in verses 10, 12, 18, 21 and 25. And verse 31 sums up the whole of God's judgment: "And God saw everything that he had made, and, behold, it was very good." This is not a relative judgment, but a judgment of the holy God who has a character and whose character is the law of the universe. His conclusion: "Every step and every sphere of creation, and the whole thing put together—man himself and his total environment, the heavens and the earth—conforms to Myself."

Everything at each of the various levels of creation fulfills the purpose of its creation. The machine part of the universe acts with perfect machineness. The animals and the plants act with their animalness and their plantness in perfection. Man stands at his particular level of creation as being in the image of God, and having a reference upward rather than downward; and God is able to say that man, too, in his "mannishness" at this particular point in space-time history, is equally good: "Man conforms to Myself on his level of creation."

Thus we find a doxology of all creation—everything glorifying God on its own level: the machine as machine praising and glorifying God, the man as a man, and everything in between doing likewise. Even though many of these beings are not at all conscious of what they are doing, they are speaking for God in all His wonder and glorifying Him in fulfilling the purpose for which they were made. There is no sin. Each thing stands in a proper relationship to God and speaks of what God is. And because each thing is functioning in the total context of what God is (God's being there as the Creator), and because each is functioning perfectly on the level for which it was made, all things are fulfilled on their own level—the machine, the animal, and man himself.

Tillich would tell us that man equals fallen man. But in Genesis the "mannishness" of man is to be found not in his fallenness, but in the circle in which he was created; it is to be found in his being in the image of God and in relationship to the God who is there. The infinite, triune God Himself can look over all that he has created and say, "This is perfect, man is good—body and soul, male and female. The entire man is good. The unity of the individual man is good." Thus we find here a complete rejection of the common notion that the Fall was sexual in nature, that taking the fruit was actually a reference to the first sexual act. God looks upon man and woman together and says, "All of this is good," and in Genesis 1:28 He tells them to have children.

As we come to the end of the account of creation, we stand in the place of wonder. Creation is past. And yet that does not mean that God ceases to be able to work into the world that He has made. God is not a prisoner of His own universe. By divine fiat God can change the universe that He has created, just as by divine fiat He brought it into existence in the first place. There was, for example, a fiat changing the universe after the Fall of man. That God can work by fiat into the universe He has made is an important thing for twentieth-century men to comprehend. We will take it up in detail later.

Day
Before we move on there is a point we need to consider. This is
the concept of *day* as related to creation. What does *day* mean in
the "days" of creation? The answer must be held with some openness. In Genesis 5:2 we read: "Male and female created he them;
and blessed them, and called their name Adam, in the *day* when
they were created." As it is clear that Adam and Eve were not
created simultaneously, *day* in Genesis 5:2 does not mean a period
of twenty-four hours. It is unfortunate that the *New International
Version* does not use the word "day" in Genesis 5:2. The word
they translate "time" is the same word in Hebrew as "day" in
Genesis 1.

In other places in the Old Testament, the Hebrew word *day*
refers to an era, just as it often does in English. See, for example,
Isaiah 2:11, 12, 17 for such a usage. The simple fact is that *day* in
Hebrew (just as in English) is used in three separate senses, to
mean: (1) twenty-four hours, (2) the period of light during the
twenty-four hours, and (3) an indeterminate period of time.
Therefore, we must leave open the exact length of time indicated
by *day* in Genesis. From the study of the word in Hebrew, it is not
clear which way it is to be taken; it could be either way. In the
light of the word as used in the Bible and the lack of finality of
science concerning the problem of dating, in a sense there is no
debate, because there are no clearly defined terms upon which to
debate.

Creation and the Existence and Character of God
In contrast to all Eastern and most modern theological thinking,
Genesis makes plain that the world as we have it is not an extension of the essence of God. The fact of creation prevents this
conception. And the whole of the Judeo-Christian tradition rooted
in this portion of the Bible and the whole of the Bible itself constantly bears testimony to that idea. The world is not just a dream
of God but is really there, separated from God and possessed
with an objective reality. But it does speak of what God is. In fact,
it speaks loudly and clearly of what God is in four different areas.

First, the external world, even as it stands now since the Fall,
speaks of existence itself. As I have pointed out before in reference
to Jean-Paul Sartre, the basic philosophic problem is that something is there, rather than nothing being there. Being exists.

Therefore, the first thing that the external, objective world speaks of is the existence of God as truly being. That is, the universe is there, existence is there, God is there.

Second, the universe has order. It is not chaos. One is able to proceed from the particulars of being to some understanding of its unity. One is able to move ever deeper into the universe and not come upon a precipice of incoherence. We find this emphasized in Genesis 1, which points out that God made all these things to produce after their own kind. Here is order. And so it is with the God of Scripture. He is not the philosophic other, nor the impersonal everything, nor that which is chaotic or random. He is a God who is (and I use this word carefully and worshipfully) a *reasonable* God.

Third, the universe speaks of God's character. God not only is and is a God of order and of reason, but God is good. He created a universe that was totally good, and, as it originally came from God by fiat, this too speaks of Him.

Fourth, the universe speaks of God as a Person. When God made man in His own image, he stated something more fully about Himself than He has in any other part of the whole scope of the universe. Angels would also speak of this, but the Bible's emphasis is on man, and it is man that we all know. In the midst of that which is, there is something personal—man. And this gives evidence of the personality of the great Creator of the whole. If God had stopped his creation with the machine or the plant or the animal, there would have been no such testimony. But by making man in His own image, the triune God who communicates and who loves prior to the creation of all else has created something that reflects His personality, His communication, and His love. Man can be communicated to by God because, unlike non-man, man has been made in the image of God. Man is a verbalizing being, and God can communicate to man in verbalization. Man thinks in propositions, and God can communicate to man propositionally in verbalized form.

For example, in Genesis 2:16 we read, "And the LORD God commanded the man, saying, Of every tree of the garden thou mayest freely eat: But of the tree of the knowledge of good and evil, thou shalt not eat of it: for in the day that thou eatest thereof thou shalt surely die." Here we learn that God was in communication with man prior to the time of man's fall. God was in fellowship, a relationship of love, with man. Notice that this communication is not just a first-order, contentless, existential experience, but rather true, propositional communication.

Immediately following Adam and Eve's decision to eat the fruit, there is a further indication of God's propositional communication: "And they heard the voice of the LORD God walking in the garden in the cool of the day: and Adam and his wife hid themselves from the presence of the LORD God among the trees of the garden. And the LORD God called unto Adam, and said unto him, Where art thou?" (Gen. 3:8, 9). Then, after Adam and Eve answered God's questions, God spoke to them in a series of great propositional statements. Man stood in communication with God both before and after the Fall.

It is likewise true that men communicate among themselves. Each time one man communicates with another, whether he knows it or not, even if he is the greatest blasphemer that ever lived or the atheist swearing at God, even when he swears, even when he says, "There is no God"—he bears testimony to what God is. God has left Himself a witness that cannot be removed.

The universe, therefore, speaks of Being existing. It speaks of order and reason. It speaks of a good and reasonable God, and it speaks of a personal God.

The end of man is to stand as a finite, personal being in personal relationship with the infinite-personal God who is there. When we hear the first command of Christ to love God with all our heart and soul and mind, we are not faced with just an abstract duty, a devotional exercise separated from all that is reasonable. Rather we have an infinite reference point that gives meaning to all of our finite reference points. This infinite reference point not only exists, but is personal and can communicate with us and we with Him, an infinite reference point whom we may love.

This is the purpose of man: to love God on a personal, not a machine level. Other things in the universe are properly on a machine level: the hydrogen atom is a machine, the star system is a machine. Their relationship to God is mechanical. But any time we come to a service and sing the doxology mechanically, we have made a mistake. We are not praising God on the level of who we are.

Of course, man is called upon not just to love God, but also to love other men. And suddenly, in this setting, this kind of love becomes a sensible statement. Even the unbelieving man or the blasphemer who falls in love testifies, whether he knows it or not, to the fact of what God is. As bare being exhibits the existence of God, as an originally good universe exhibits the moral goodness of God, so the communication of man to man, and one man's loving another (whether in a man-woman sexual relationship or in the relationship of friendship), testify to what is.

God can say, "Do you want to know something of what I am like? Look at creation as I made it." The universe is not an extension of the essence of God, but in all its parts it does speak of Him.

The man-woman relationship is no longer a mockery, or a curse, as it often is for modern man. We know that God did not make man as an individual to stand alone for very long, only being able to love God. For while loving God was the purpose of his creation, God quickly gave him a counterpart—like himself, yet different—that immediately opened up love and communication on man's own level. Therefore, each time we see a truly loving man-woman relationship or a truly loving friend relationship, while these things have great value in themselves, yet we see something more than just "mannishness" loving "mannishness." Each of these at the same time stands as a testimony of who God is.

This is a testimony even after the Fall, as we read in Romans 1:19, 20: "Because that which may be known of God is manifest in them; for God hath shown it unto them. For the invisible things of him from the creation of the world are clearly seen, being understood by things that are made, even his eternal power and Godhead." The point here is that "from the creation" (since the moment of creation) the things that God has made are a testimony to His being, to His goodness, and to His personality.

Creation at Peace with Itself

When God made creation, creation was at peace with itself. Genesis 1:29, 30 might indicate that the food of both men and beasts included only vegetable life. This is not explicitly stated here, but it might be implied. A change in man's relationship to the rest of creation may be indicated when God spoke to Noah, instituting another set of covenants and bringing about a change in the flow of history: "Every moving thing that liveth shall be food for you; even as the green herb have I given you all things" (Gen. 9:3). God may be saying something like this: "Previously I gave you all the green plants for food, but now every living thing is yours to eat as well." God does say, "And the fear of you and the dread of you shall be upon every beast of the earth, and upon every fowl of the air, upon all that moveth upon the earth, and upon all the fishes of the sea; into your hand they are delivered" (Gen. 9:2). The full implications are not clear, but considering what the Bible teaches concerning the restoration of creation when Christ returns, it *is* clear that at creation, creation was at peace with itself.

History Is Going Someplace

History is not just static, as some existentialists or Eastern thinkers would tell us. History is really going someplace. Just as there is a beginning (from a creation *ex nihilo*), history flows and goes on into the future. Scripture also indicates that a time will come when creation is returned to peace with itself. Romans 8:21-23 says, ". . . the creation itself also shall be delivered from the bondage of corruption into the glorious liberty of the glory of the children of God. For we know that the whole creation groaneth and travaileth in pain together until now. And not only they, but ourselves also, who have the first fruits of the Spirit, even we ourselves groan within ourselves, waiting for our adoption, the redemption of our body" (ASV). Verse 20 has already indicated that the creation was not always this way. And there is coming a day when the creation will be restored. It is the same time when the bodies of the Christians will be resurrected.

The phrase in verse 23 indicating that we are yet today waiting for the adoption is interesting. In one sense, a Christian is already adopted (this is considered in the first part of Romans 8), for the Christian having accepted Christ as his Savior has already had his guilt removed, has been justified, and is now the child of God. Nevertheless, we wait for an adoption that does not come until the second coming of Christ and the resurrection of our bodies. This full adoption, which involves the change in the external world of ourselves (the redemption of our bodies), is associated in verse 23 with the redemption of the whole of creation. Notice too that everyone and everything is in this: "The whole creation groaneth and travaileth in pain *together*." We are all caught. Things are not what they were, but they will be at the time when Christ comes back and our bodies are raised.

We have, I believe, a description of this period in Isaiah 11:6-9: "The wolf also shall dwell with the lamb, and the leopard shall lie down with the kid; and the calf and the young lion and the fatling together; and a little child shall lead them. And the cow and the bear shall feed; their young ones shall lie down together: and the lion shall eat straw like the ox. And the sucking child shall play on the hole of the asp, and the weaned child shall put his hand on the adder's den." This passage does not speak of a psychological change in man's view of nature, but an objective change in the external world.

There is, of course, some difference among Christians as to just what period of time this refers to. There are two possibilities. One is that there is a millennium in which Christ reigns on earth for a thousand years before eternity. This is the opinion that I hold. Some Christians think that these passages refer to eternity. Nonetheless, whether they refer to eternity or to a millennial reign of Christ, it makes no difference to our point here: the creation which God made was at peace with itself and will eventually be restored to peace with itself. In other words, there will come a time when all creation once more speaks, not only of the existence of God and His personality, but also of the goodness of God as the original creation exhibited that goodness.

There is, therefore, in Judeo-Christian thinking, in contrast to modern thinking, a flow of history—an absolute beginning and an end of the present era of history.

Just as the world was "subjected to vanity" when man fell, so when man is fully restored in the future on the basis of the work of Jesus Christ, the Lamb of God, creation will be restored on the same basis. Every restoration rests upon the finished work of Christ. This includes (1) the restoration that opens the way for the sinner to come back to God, be justified, be counted a child of God, be given purpose in the present life and put into communication with God now; (2) the future restoration in which the Christian's body will be changed at the second coming of Christ; and (3) the restoration of all things to the character of the original creation.

Therefore, we read in Revelation 4:11—"Worthy art thou, our Lord and our God, to receive the glory and the honor and the power: for thou didst create all things, and because of thy will they were [existed], and were created" (ASV). So, as we have pointed out, we first praise God because He is the Creator of all things. But surely there is something wrong with the world we are confronted with now. Whether we look at ordinary modern man or the tortured works of modern artists or the world around us, there seems to be a flaw. And indeed the flaw is in man, but it is also in the world around us which is not at peace with itself. The testimony of creation as to the existence and personality of God still stands in the objective universe and in man as man. But as we look out over things and see the sin of man and the creation itself at war with itself, we are left with a problem. As the world now is, its testimony to the goodness of God is not clear. The fifth chapter of Revelation points out what is needed and stands in unity with the statement concerning the original creation in Revelation 4:11. Redemption is the key. It is the Lamb of God who is able, when nothing else in heaven above or earth beneath or under the earth— in other words, nothing in creation itself—is able to bring the needed change. The solution was Christ's redemptive work in history, in space and in time, as the Lamb of God.

We are therefore told in Revelation 5:9-11 that man sings to the Lamb of God because man is redeemed: "Thou art worthy to take the book, and to open its seals; for thou wast slain, and hast redeemed us to God by thy blood out of every kindred, and tongue, and people, and nation." The same structure is evident in verses 12-14: "Worthy is the Lamb that was slain [notice this is the past tense because it is past history] to receive power, and riches, and wisdom, and strength, and honor, and glory, and blessing." Following this verse comes something that is surely related to what we have seen in Romans 8 as to what will happen in the future: "And every created thing which is in the heaven, and on the earth, and under the earth, and on the sea, and all things that are in them, heard I saying unto him that sitteth on the throne, and unto the Lamb, be the blessing, and the honor, and the glory, and the dominion, forever and ever. And the four living creatures said, Amen. And the elders fell down and worshipped" (Rev. 5:13, 14, ASV). They worship. They adore. Because at that time in the future, all will have come to rest and will be in its place on the basis of Christ's redemptive work as He died on the cross.

Other portions of Scripture implicitly (not explicitly) support this. The ark, for example, not only carried Noah, but also the animals. The covenant with Noah in Genesis 9:12, 13, 16 includes not only men, but also every living creature and "the earth." The blood of the Passover in Israel covered not only the firstborn of the Jews, but the firstborn of their beasts.

There is to be one great paean of praise to redemption—a redemption that will include not just man but the whole of creation, a time when creation will again speak of the great facts of which it spoke originally. Its existence shows the existence of the God who is. The "mannishness" of man says God is personal. And all creation will say, "God is good."

CHAPTER FOUR

The Point of Decision

Let us go back to the beginning. Creation is finished. Each created thing is operating in the circle of its own creation, standing in its proper place, and all things are at rest and in balance. Man, as made in the image of God, has a unique place because he has been made different from the machines, the plants and the animals.

To Love God

Jesus once stated exactly that peculiar place man has in the various circles of creation. One of the Pharisees had asked him, "Master, which is the great commandment in the law?" And Jesus replied, "Thou shalt love the Lord, thy God, with all thy heart, and with all thy soul, and with all thy mind. This is the first and great commandment" (Matt. 22:36-38). Some 1,500 years before this, in Deuteronomy 6:4-6, we find this same concept: "Hear, O Israel: The LORD our God is one LORD: and thou shalt love the LORD thy God with all thine heart, and with all thy soul, and with all thy might. And these words, which I command thee this day, shall be in thine heart." Thus at the time of Moses, the central issue is not merely an outward keeping of the commandments, but something far more profound. Man is to *love* God.

47

But it is equally important—and this is brought out in both Matthew and Deuteronomy—for man to remember *whom* he is to love. Loving a superior is different from loving an equal. Take, for example, the love of a child for a parent. If a child constantly says, "I love you," and yet at the same time is constantly and openly disobedient, the parent can say, "Your actions do not indicate your love." The reason for this is that there is a hierarchy inherent in the relationship between the parent and child. The two people do not stand on a horizontal plane in every regard. Parenthood involves an *office*. As Israel is brought face to face with the loving Creator who is there, Israel is not merely to say, "I love you," rooting their reaction only in emotions. The kind of love proper here is also rooted into obedience, simply because of the nature of the relationship between the two parties. Love of the creature toward the Creator must include obedience or it is meaningless. Jesus' teaching in Matthew is the same.

With this principle in mind, then, we can begin to understand Adam and Eve's relationship to God in the early chapters of Genesis. Genesis 2:16, 17 reads: "And the LORD God commanded the man, saying, Of every tree of the garden thou mayest freely eat: But of the tree of the knowledge of good and evil, thou shalt not eat of it; for in the day that thou eatest thereof thou shalt surely die." Basically, this command is no different from the commandments in Deuteronomy 6:4-6 and Matthew 22:36-38. The first law for man is to love God with all his heart and all his soul and all his mind. If one is a creature in the presence of the Creator, to love includes to obey.

But something else is involved, for here is the idea that obedience to this law is the purpose of man, the only way that man can be fully man.

Today people constantly ask, "Does man have a purpose?" In some areas of the world man is told that he has meaning only in reference to the state. In other places he is told that he has meaning only in his sexual life. Elsewhere he is told he has meaning only through affluence. But all of these turn to sawdust in his hands. The Bible gives us a quite different answer: The purpose of man—the meaning of man—is to stand in love as a creature before the Creator.

But the man who stands before God stands there in God's image as a true personality, and the love which he is to give is not mechanical. The machine can obey God mechanically; when it does, it is doing all that God meant it to do. The far-flung system of the universe operates, much of it, as a great machine; and as such it fulfills its purpose. That is all it was meant to do. But man is a different being, made in a different circle of creation. He is to love God, not mechanically, but by the wonder of choice. Here stands an unprogrammed part of creation—unprogrammed chemically or psychologically—real man in a real history, a wonder in the midst of a world of uniformity of cause and effect. In the flow of history, man is brought face to face with that for which he has been made—face to face in a loving relationship to the God who is there.

One Tree

Love and obedience in Genesis 3 are placed in the context of a commandment concerning a tree—the tree of the knowledge of good and evil. It is important to note that the test Adam faces does not involve a choice between an evil tree that God has made and a good tree that God has made, for God has made no evil things. If He had, or if God had programmed man so that man must disobey Him, then we would have here a concept like the Hindu idea that eventually both good and evil, cruelty and noncruelty, spring from God and thus are finally equal.

But God has not made a bad tree. He has simply made a tree. And there is nothing intrinsic about this tree that is different in any way from the other trees. Rather, God has simply confronted man with a choice. He could just as well have said, "Don't cross this stream; don't climb this mountain." He is saying, "Believe Me and stand in your place as a creature, not as one who is autonomous. Believe Me and love Me as a creature to his Creator, and all will be well. This is the place for which I have made you."

It is perfectly true that in making man as he did, God made the possibility of evil. But the bare possibility of evil is not the actualizing of it. And in making that possibility, God validated choice and validated man as man—a being significant in history. If He had left him without choice, you could speak forever of man being man, man being significant, but it would be only meaningless words.

All love—man to woman and woman to man, or friend to friend—is bound up with choice. Without choice, the word *love* is meaningless. And, incidentally, as modern man has lost the concept of choice in the midst of determinism, the word *love* has increasingly become meaningless.

God has indeed made the possibility of man's choosing, including the possibility of choosing wrongly. But God has not made evil. There is not an evil tree and a good tree. There is simply choice. When God finished creating, there was nothing made which was contrary to His character.

Let us look more closely at the specific kind of tree. It is not simply the tree of *knowledge,* but of a specific kind of knowledge— the knowledge of good and evil. It was not an evil thing to have knowledge. Such a concept would contradict the giving of dominion to man and be in conflict with Genesis 2:19, 20, where man as man had knowledge to give proper names to the creatures.

Adam and Eve already knew good; everything around them was good, and their relationship to God and to each other was good. And in knowledge from God they knew the possibility of evil and its result: "Thou shalt not eat of it: for in the day thou eatest thereof thou shalt surely die" (Gen. 2:17). What was involved was the experiential knowledge of evil in contrast to God's telling them about evil. They are, of course, finite in contrast to God being infinite. God can know all possibilities—even what could be but will not be, as well as all that will be. The Bible makes plain that God, as infinite, knows all possibilities, even if they never will be actualized. In 1 Samuel 23:9-29 we are told that God knew (and told David) what would happen in case a certain circumstance occurred, even though the situation changed and thus the circumstance never did occur and the possible result never was actualized.

In the case of Adam and Eve, as finite, they had received from God true knowledge concerning the result of eating and revolt; but when they did revolt they then had experiential knowledge of evil and all the flow of resulting cruelty and sorrow. It was not knowledge as knowledge that was wrong, but *the choice* made against God's loving warning and command.

Notice too that God's command to them was not an unmotivated command, not a bare, unexplained command. Adam and Eve were warned about the result, a loss that involved their own best interests. The command was a rational, propositional command and a loving warning.

So let us look again at Genesis 2:17: "But of the tree of knowledge of good and evil, thou shalt not eat of it: for in the day that thou eatest thereof thou shalt surely die." The last phrase is extremely strong in the Hebrew and could very well be rendered, "dying, thou shalt die." Reformed theology speaks of this commandment as a covenant of works. That is, first there are two parties. In one way they are equal (both of them have personalities, the one being in the image of the other), and in another way they are not (one is infinite and the other finite; one is Creator, the other the created). And, second, there is a condition in the midst of the covenant, a condition of love couched in the terms of obedience insofar as it involves a creature before the Creator. Third, there is a promise involved—life. Surely, what is promised here is not just a continuing physical life, but rather all of those things which we later know to be life indeed in Jesus Christ our Lord. Of course, man does not need a Savior at this point, because he has not sinned. Thus there is no place here for soteriology, no place for the Lamb of God—not yet. Soteriology is related to fallen man. The promise of life is "fullness of life," just as the penalty is "fullness of death."

Note that in the day, the twenty-four hours, when Adam sinned, he did not physically die. He died in a way that the New Testament labels a "present death." Before a man now accepts Christ as his Savior, it is not just that he will die, but that he is already dead. He is separated from God; he has no purpose and no final meaning.

Therefore, in the day that Adam ate, he died. There are three steps in this death. First comes separation from God, the infinite-personal reference point, and immediately thereafter meaninglessness in the present life. Even though man continues to breathe, and with his wife brings forth children, he is dead. And to this extent our voices as Christians are joined with the voices from the opposite end of the spectrum—the existentialists and the modern men—who say with us, "Amen. Man is dead." And thus perhaps it is easier to say this and be, in some sense at least, understood than it was fifty or a hundred years ago.

Second, there is physical death. A few short years, though Adam's life was longer than ours, and Adam's body will rot in the grave.

Third, there is eternal death in the penalty that is meted out. Those separated from God will ultimately "be punished with everlasting destruction from the presence of the Lord, and from the glory of his power" (2 Thess. 1:9). The end of the eating is not just the present situation, as horrible and abnormal as it is, not just physical death, not just a blank, a vacuum. There is a horizontal extension—eternal death and eternal separation from the God who is really there, from His glory and His grace.

We must be careful to notice the loving provisions that God gave. Man was made in the image of God. God had told him that evil was possible, but man was good because he had not yet chosen evil. Man was in constant fellowship with God: "And they heard the voice of the LORD God walking in the garden" (Gen. 3:8). He was surrounded by a perfect environment, God Himself having selected a special place for man within this creation: "And the LORD God planted a garden eastward in Eden; and there he put the man whom he had formed" (Gen. 2:8). Adam knew something of his place in history, and he knew who Eve was: "And Adam called his wife's name Eve; because she was the mother of all living" (Gen. 3:20). The word *Eve* really means "living." Adam chose her name, and in doing so showed that he knew who he was. Furthermore, man had a truly free choice with power to obey or to transgress. He was not (either materially or psychologically) deterministically conditioned. He was not programmed. Finally, it was a simple test and everything involved in it was made absolutely plain.

Enter the Serpent
We will begin to look now at a new stage in the flow of biblical history: "Now the serpent was more subtil than any beast of the field which the LORD God had made" (Gen. 3:1).

Immediately questions arise. We want to know more than we are actually given. So it is necessary for us to remind ourselves again just what kind of book the Bible is. As I have already indicated, the Bible is a book for fallen men. Wherever it touches upon anything, it does so with true truth, but not with exhaustive truth. That is, where it speaks of the cosmos, science, what it says is true. Likewise, where it touches history, it speaks with what I call true truth—that is, propositional, objective truth.

When the Bible talks about the supernatural world and tells us of Heaven and things beyond this earth, it presents corollaries to the theme of the book—the propositional communication in verbalized form from God to fallen man. The corollaries given are those we need to know to get the major thrust, the central purpose of the Bible. But it does not answer every question that we might ask about any of these matters. If everything concerning which we have a proper curiosity was given, the book would be larger than the great libraries of the world and no one could read through it all. John seems to have this thought in mind in the last verse of the Gospel of John: "And there are also many other things which Jesus did, which, if they should be written every one, I suppose that even the world itself could not contain the books that should be written."

It is in this context that data concerning the supernatural world is given. We might well enjoy a book about the supernatural world. That half of the universe intrigues us and it stands, not somewhere far off, but immediately before us, almost as a fourth dimension, so that there is indeed a cause and effect relationship between it and our own visible world at every existential moment. It really is not less natural and no less real than the seen part of the universe, and we cannot understand the seen half if we write off the existence of the unseen portion. But while we would be interested to find out some of these things in more detail, we are given adequate knowledge. Information about the supernatural world is brought in to help us understand who we are as man— lost man looking for meaning, and saved man looking toward the second coming of Christ. When the serpent enters, we are introduced to this other half of the universe.

One of the lies of Satan, by the way, is his attempt to convince us to follow modern liberal thought in breaking the Bible into pieces and destroying its unity. We recognize, of course, that while the Scripture is a whole, it records an increasing revelation as time passes. But it all forms a unit, and while we have increasing revelation we do not have contradictory revelation.

Interestingly enough, it is often toward the end of the Bible that clear explanations of earlier parts are given. By the time we study through the full circle of the whole book, we have what explanations we need, for now, of all the parts. Thus in Revelation we read this: "And the great dragon was cast out, that old serpent, called the Devil, and Satan, who deceiveth the whole world; he was cast out into the earth, and his angels were cast out with him" (Rev. 12:9). It is unfortunate that the King James translation leaves out the definite article applied to Satan. One cannot translate *Satan* as a general adversary. Rather, he is *the* adversary, *the* Satan. He is the one who has deceived the whole world. But he is not alone; he has angels who are cast out with him.

One is reminded of the flaming poetry of Milton, who described Satan and his hosts so well. Along with Satan there were those who chose his way, those who joined his cortege, that leads not only to rebellion but to condemnation. Later in Revelation we are given further information: "And he [an angel] laid hold on the dragon, the old serpent, which is the Devil, and Satan, and bound him for a thousand years" (Rev. 20:2, ASV). Notice that this serpent is a special serpent. A definite article is used here again. You can call him the old serpent, or the Devil, or the Satan. In any case, with this information before us, who we are dealing with in Genesis 3:1 is clearly identified. The definite article that is applied to Satan in Revelation 12:9 and to the serpent in Revelation 20:2 and Genesis 3:1 is important. It has, in fact, been suggested that with the addition of the Hebrew definite article in Genesis 3:1, we have something called in Hebrew grammar an article of eminence. And if this is the case, the serpent actually is, even here, made a proper name—The Serpent.

Jesus tells us something significant about the Devil when He challenges those who rejected Him while claiming to have God as their Father: "Ye are of your father the devil, and the lusts of your father ye will do. He was a murderer from the beginning, and abode not in the truth, because there is no truth in him. When he speaketh a lie, he speaketh of his own: for he is a liar, and the father of it" (John 8:44). The point is that the Devil does not abide, does not stand, in the truth. Rather, he is the liar behind all liars and stands in the lie back of all lies—that the creature can be equal with God. This was his own point of rebellion against his Creator, God. Every other lie is only an extension of this one. And this is who the devil is —the originator of The Lie.

This is the context, then, in which we should understand what I call the theology of the Fall. In Genesis we have a free man with an unprogrammed choice. And coming to this free man from the outside is the temptation of Satan. But we must go back even before this, and bind together Satan's fall and Adam's fall. Satan, without an outside temptation, had already chosen to revolt. He revolted from himself outward. Adam and Eve, on the other hand, were tempted by the father of The Lie, someone outside themselves. Although there is some debate over this, and without wishing to be dogmatic about it, I think that Isaiah 14:12-15 gives us the fall of Satan: "How art thou fallen from heaven, O Lucifer [that is, Daystar], son of the morning! How art thou cut down to the ground, which didst weaken the nations! For thou hast said in thine heart, I will ascend into heaven, I will exalt my throne above the stars of God; I will sit also upon the mount of the congregation, in the sides of the north; I will ascend above the heights of the clouds, I will be like the Most High. Yet thou shalt be brought down to hell, to the sides of the pit."

Assuming that the word *stars* refers to the other angels, he was saying, in short, "I will be greater than all the rest." But he goes further, specifically adding, "I will *make myself* like the Most High." Satan, the liar, the originator of The Great Lie, in his heart (that is, within himself, from himself outward) says, "I will be greater than the rest, and I will be equal with God."

The story of Satan in Isaiah is paralleled almost exactly in Genesis in regard to man's revolt. Satan wants to be equal with God, but the end of this is that he will be brought down into the abyss. In Genesis 3 the woman would be equal with God, but she ends in death. As we consider the entrance of the serpent into the garden, we see the revolt about to spread across the world of mankind which God has made. There is no revolt among the machines, nor the plants, nor the animals. But in the circle of that which can rebel, angels and men, we see rebellion.

I think it is clear that the Devil used the animal, the serpent, as his first try to challenge and defeat God in the world of mankind. In other words, The Serpent used a serpent. This is not the only time he employed Devil-possession. In contrast to demon-possession, there are at least two other cases where the Devil himself used Devil-possession.

Luke 22:3 tells us that at a crucial moment in the life of the Messiah (who had come to bruise The Serpent's head), Satan possessed Judas: "Then entered Satan into Judas surnamed Iscariot." Satan did not delegate this job to a second, but took it on himself. He entered into Judas.

The third place where there is a special effort on the part of Satan is yet to take place—at the time of the Antichrist, when an antilaw personality will revolt against God. Revelation 13:4 portrays a tremendous picture of that future day when the forces of humanism—the united economic, religious and governmental forces—draw together in revolt, casting down the gauntlet before the God who is. Proud humanism is no longer naturalistic; it is joined to the acme of the occult. Under the reign of the Antichrist, we read, "they worshipped the dragon (identified in Rev. 12:9 and 20:2 as Satan, The Serpent) which gave his authority unto the beast [Antichrist]: and they worshipped the beast, saying, Who is like unto the beast? who is able to make war with him?" So Satan is here in the battle again, completely committed to the struggle.

Returning to the third chapter of Genesis, we are not taken by surprise. Satan's use of something else, whether it be a Judas or an Antichrist or a serpent, is not in any one of these cases unique.

The Temptation

With revolt already in the universe, with the angelic host split and a hierarchy of evil, the leader himself tempts Eve: "Yea, hath God said, Ye shall not eat of every tree of the garden?" (Gen. 3:1). The woman stands in her glory—the glory of being created in the image of God with no necessity upon her to choose evil. Standing in a perfect environment, having heard the voice of God, she is at a place where she can choose. What a wonder is man! Not mechanical man, not merely biological man, but man who can choose in a situation, as in the image of God, with no necessity upon him.

Satan comes to her and says, "Yea, hath God said, Ye shall not eat of every tree of the garden?" What will she reply? "And the woman said unto the serpent, We may eat of the fruit of the trees of the garden: But of the fruit of the tree which is in the midst of the garden, God hath said, Ye shall not eat of it, neither shall ye touch it, lest ye die" (vv. 2, 3). It has been pointed out that Eve added something here. God apparently had not said, "Don't touch it," but rather, "Don't eat it." I am not sure we should make much of this, but it should be noted. The serpent replies in a direct contradiction: "Ye shall not surely die" (v. 4). And the issue is joined.

But Satan offers something further: "For God doth know that in the day ye eat thereof, then your eyes shall be opened and ye shall be as God, knowing good and evil" (v. 5). It is unfortunate that in the King James *God* is translated as plural, for it is not that they will be like some primitive gods, but that each of them will be like God Himself. Notice the direct contradiction. God said in the day you eat, you shall die; Satan said in the day you eat, you will be like God.

In a way, there is a half-truth here. Satan's approach has often taken that form ever since. It is true that Eve is indeed going to learn something. If she chooses to disobey and to rebel, she will have what she could not have otherwise—an experiential knowledge of evil and its results. So in a way Satan is telling her the truth. But what a useless, horrible knowledge! It is the knowledge of the child whose mother says, "Don't go near that fire, because if you do you will get hurt. You will catch fire and be burned." But the little child goes on in disobedience, falls into the fire, and spends the next three days dying in agony. The child has learned something that it wouldn't have known experientially if it had listened to the knowledge given by its mother. But what a knowledge!

Eve's fall is not a fall upward, but a fall downward in every conceivable way. She already knows from the voice of God that "in the day you eat you will die." She can have experiential knowledge, but that knowledge is no truer knowledge than the knowledge from God, and the result is that the whole human race will be in agony.

It is a lie, of course, that she is going to be like God, because experiential knowledge of evil is not what makes God God. God is God because He is infinite, the nondependent one. No created being will ever be able to be like Him in this. Even in the area of knowledge, what Satan has said is a lie because God is infinite; He knows all the possibilities, and is not bound by limitedness. We, however, with all our knowledge are still bound by limitedness and always will be. So what Satan has said is a half-truth, but a total lie.

Eve's response is, first, to consider the situation: ". . . the woman saw that the tree was good for food, and that it was pleasant [a delight] to the eyes, and a tree to be desired to make one wise . . ." (v. 6). Three steps are involved: She looked at the tree and saw that it was good for physical food and that it was delightful to look at, and she desired the knowledge which would make her equal to God. Eve, with these things in her mind, is actually standing in the situation of the last commandment of the Ten Commandments: "Thou shalt not covet" (Ex. 20:17). After all the external commandments comes the commandment on which all the others rest. Coveting, wanting that which is not properly mine as I stand as a creature before the law of God, is really the basis of all sin, for it is the internal attitude which leads to the external breaking of the other nine commandments. This is what Paul had reference to in Romans 7:7 when he pointed out that the center of his own sin was coveting. Jesus also made it explicit in Matthew 5:21, 22. He said that it isn't murder itself but the hatred that was in your heart first, ultimately leading to the murder, that stands at the heart of the issue. Likewise, he indicated in verses 27 and 28 that adultery is already there when it's only in one's mind. The internal later flows out into the external.

Eve stands exactly there—in the area of the internal where choices are always made. Paul in 2 Corinthians 11:3 hearkens back to her situation at the point of space-time history as he advises the church of his own day, "But I fear, lest by any means, as the serpent beguiled Eve through his subtilty, so your minds should be corrupted from the simplicity that is in Christ." We live in our thought-life. This is who I am. And for Eve the choice was this: whether to remain as a creature or to try in rebellion to have what the finite creature can never have and to be what the finite creature can never be. And we hold our breath to see what Eve will choose in the inner man.

CHAPTER FIVE

The Space-Time Fall and Its Results

Eve was faced with a choice. She pondered the situation, and then she put her hand into the history of man and changed the course of human events.

The Fruit Is Eaten

The Genesis account is short and to the point: "And when the woman saw that the tree was good for food, and that it was pleasant to the eyes, and a tree to be desired to make one wise, she took of the fruit thereof, and did eat, and gave also unto her husband with her; and he did eat" (Gen. 3:6). The flow is from the internal to the external; the sin began in the thought world and flowed outward. The sin was, therefore, committed in that moment she believed Satan instead of God. Nonetheless, a history is involved, for first she believed Satan, then she ate, and then she gave the fruit to Adam.

Genesis 3:17 refers to this historical flow, for God in speaking to Adam says that he "hearkened unto the voice of thy wife, and hast eaten of the tree." And we are reminded, as we have seen in 2 Corinthians 11:3, that as the serpent beguiled Eve through his subtlety (at her point of history), so our own minds (at our point of history) may also be corrupted from the simplicity that is in Christ.

Paul in 1 Timothy 2:14 points out something further: "And Adam was not deceived, but the woman being deceived was in the transgression." Temptation is extremely hard to resist when it is bound up with the man-woman relationship. For example, in Exodus 34:16 we are warned not to let the man-woman relationship lead us into idolatry (spoken of as going "a whoring after their gods").

Two great drives are built into man. The first is his need for a relationship to God, and the second his need for a relationship to the opposite sex. A special temptation is bound up with this sexual drive. How many young women are faithful as Christians until they come to a certain age and feel with their whole being, without ever analyzing it, the need for marriage and are then swept over into marrying a non-Christian man. And how many men are faithful until they feel the masculine drive and give up their faithfulness to God by marrying a woman who carries them into spiritual problems for the rest of their life. I look upon such young men and young women as I see them going through this, and I cry for them, because in a way there is no greater agony than suddenly to fall in love and then to realize that one must say no to this natural drive because it leads in that particular case to a severing of our greater relationship—our relationship to God. While what happened in the Garden of Eden was a space-time historic event, the man-woman relationship and force of temptation it must have presented to Adam is universal.

The Results of the Fall for the Human Race

The results of Adam and Eve's action are recorded in many places in Scripture, but nowhere more clearly than in Romans 5:12-19 where Paul emphasizes that Adam and Eve's action marked the entrance of sin into the human race. I will quote here part of this passage:

> Therefore, as through one man sin entered into the world, and death through sin; and so death passed [spread] unto all men, for that all sinned: for until the law sin was in the world; but sin is not imputed when there is no law. Nevertheless death reigned from Adam unto Moses, even over them that had not sinned after the likeness of Adam's transgression, who is a figure of him that was to come. . . . For if by the trespass of the one the many died . . . For if, by the

trespass of the one, death reigned through the one . . . So then as through one trespass the judgment came unto all men to condemnation. . . . For as through the one man's disobedience the many were made sinners . . . (ASV).

The repetition makes the point obvious: By the action of one man in a historic, space-time situation, sin entered into the world of men. But this is not just a theoretical statement that gives us a reasonable and sufficient answer to man's present dilemma, explaining how the world can be so evil and God still be good. It is that in reality, from this time on, man *was* and *is* a sinner. Though some men do not like the teaching, the Bible continues like a sledgehammer, driving home the fact that evil has entered into the world of man, all men are now sinners, all men now sin. Listen to God's declaration concerning the human race in Jeremiah 17:9— "The heart is deceitful above all things, and desperately wicked; who can know it?"

Incidentally, in one way it is easier today than it was a few years ago to proclaim the sinfulness of man. On every side artists, novelists and protest singers are saying, "What's wrong with man? Something's wrong with man." The Bible agrees and gives us a realistic view of life: "The heart is deceitfully wicked."

I think the strongest words were spoken by Jesus Himself in John 8:44, where he turns on those who are claiming the Fatherhood of God and says: "Ye are of your father the devil, and the lusts of your father it is your will to do" (ASV). In other words, Jesus is saying, "You choose to be in Satan's parade."

Isaiah writes, "All we like sheep have gone astray; we have turned every one to his own way" (Isa. 53:6). It is obvious that if "all we like sheep have gone astray," I can no longer merely say *they* have gone astray, but I must say *I* have gone astray. I, too, sin. Paul picks this up in the letter to the Romans as he summarizes the status of all the races, first the Gentiles and then the Jews: "As it is written, There is none righteous, no, not one: There is none that understandeth, there is none that seeketh after God. They are all gone out of the way, they are together become unprofitable; there is none that doeth good, no, not one" (Rom. 3:10–12). If there is none that is righteous, no, not one, then I am included. I have written the word *me* in the margin of my Bible at this place. Galatians 3:10 carries this on with force: "For as many as are of the works of the law are under the curse; for it is written, Cursed is everyone that continueth not in all things which are written in the book of the law, to do them." All mankind stands in this place. Not only the revealed law of God, but also every moral motion of every man who has ever lived condemns men, because men keep neither the revealed law of God, nor even live consistently according to their own moral motions. This is the point of Romans 2:1, 2: "Therefore, thou art inexcusable, O man, whosoever thou art that judgest; for wherein thou judgest another, thou condemnest thyself; for thou that judgest doest the same things. But we are sure that the judgment of God is according to truth against them which commit such things."

What Paul says involves the whole man as he comes to Scripture. The Bible never leaves this as a generalization or as an abstraction. Paul writes, "Therefore, thou art inexcusable, O man." Perhaps the most important part of this is that it is in the singular, for it speaks to every individual who hears or reads: ". . . whosoever thou art that judgest; for wherein thou judgest another, thou condemnest thyself; for thou that judgest doest the same things." The simple fact is that it is not only the man who has the written law of God, the Bible, who stands under the judgment of law, but every man who ever lived. I have pointed out elsewhere that wherever anthropologists and sociologists have been, they have found that men have moral motions. The specific standards may be different, but all men operate under moral categories. So Paul says here that a man stands condemned on the basis of his own moral motions, for every time he condemns another man he has put himself under the same condemnation. Every man makes moral judgments concerning other men and then does not keep them himself. The results? All men are sinners, and all men sin.

This indictment includes those who are now Christians as well as non-Christians. Men are not born Christians—a sort of special race. Every single man who is now a child of God was at one time a rebel. We are all hewn from the same rock, whether we come from a church background or a nonchurch background. No sacerdotalism can help man.

Am I a Christian today? Never forget, then, that yesterday I was as much a rebel as anyone who walks on the face of the earth. As Ephesians 2:2, 3 says in burning words: "In times past ye walked according to the course of this world, according to the prince of the power of the air, the spirit that now worketh in the children of disobedience." He is talking here to the church at Ephesus. But he continues and adds himself to the list, he steps over and joins us, for it is not just "ye" but "we": "Among whom also we all had our conversation [meaning here our total way of life, our "life-form"] in times past in the lusts of our flesh, fulfilling the desires of the flesh and of the mind, and were by nature the children of wrath, even as others." This is who we are. If we are Christians today, this is who we have been. We had a different king—the father of lies. We must not be proud, for as Ephesians 5:8 says, "For ye were sometimes darkness, but now are ye light in the Lord." Remember, we were also marked by Adam's sin, and we were sinners: "And you, that were sometime alienated and enemies in your mind by wicked works, yet now hath he reconciled" (Col. 1:21).

Don't be proud. As you look out across the world of sinners, weep for them. Be glad indeed if you are redeemed, but never forget as you look at others that you have been one of them, and in a real sense we are still one with them, for we still sin. Christians are not a special group of people who can be proud; Christians are those who are redeemed—and that is all!

Everywhere we turn we find the same thing: "For we ourselves [notice the "we" again] also were sometimes foolish, disobedient, deceived, serving divers lusts and pleasures, living in malice and envy, hateful, and hating one another" (Tit. 3:3). Paul never allowed those who followed his teaching to forget that they were not a special kind just because they may have been Jews at the beginning and circumcised, or just because they were now baptized Christians. Each one must say, "I have been the rebel, I have been the sinner." The force of this is perhaps brought most fully in the statement in 1 John 1:10: "If we say that we have not sinned, we make him [God] a liar, and his word is not in us." To forget in our emotional reactions as well as in our words that we indeed have been sinners, not just involved in the results of Adam's sin, but deliberately sinning ourselves over and over and over again—to forget this is to call God a liar.

Thus, all men are under the judgment of God. Even the marvelous chapter that speaks so clearly of hope, the third chapter of the Gospel of John, twice emphasizes that men are under God's judgment. We read, for example, these words in John 3:18: "He that believeth on him is not condemned; but he that believeth not is condemned already, because he hath not believed in the name of the only begotten Son of God." The testimony of John the Baptist in the last verse of this chapter is even more emphatic: "He that believeth on the Son has everlasting life; and he that believeth not the Son shall not see life, but the wrath of God abideth on him" (v. 36). In a world that loves synthesis, the Bible stands with a message of total antithesis: he who believes has life, *but* he who does not is subject to the wrath, the judgment, of God. Here, then, is the basic result of the space-time Fall that we are considering in the flow of history—men are rebels and under the judgment of God.

Guilt Before God

Other results of sin were immediately evident in the Garden of Eden: "And the eyes of them both were opened, and they knew that they were naked; and they sewed fig leaves together, and made themselves aprons" (Gen. 3:7). The word *aprons* in the Hebrew is interesting. Actually, it simply means to "gird yourself about," so people have translated the word in various ways. One Bible, the Breeches Bible of 1608, got its name from the way it translated this word. But whatever an *apron* is, it is something one puts around himself.

The significance is that Adam and Eve were brought to a realization of what they had done. They began to feel afraid and to feel guilt—and well they might, for their guilt-feelings were rooted in true guilt. When a man has sinned against God, he not only has guilt-feelings, he has true guilt (and he has true guilt even if he does not have feelings of guilt).

"And they heard the voice of the LORD God walking in the garden in the cool of the day: and Adam and his wife hid themselves from the presence of the LORD God among the trees of the garden" (v. 8). This is the verse we have used in our previous studies to indicate the wonder of the open communication which God had with man. In the garden, in the cool (or the wind) of the day, there was open fellowship, open communion—open propositional communication between God and man before the Fall. But now that which was his wonder and his joy, the fulfillment of his need, an infinite-personal reference point with whom he could have communion and communication, became the reason for his fear. He was going to meet God face to face! Once man had shaken his fist in the face of God, what had been so wonderful became a just reason for fear, because God was really there.

So we read: "And the LORD God called unto Adam, and said unto him, Where art thou? And he said, I heard thy voice in the garden, and I was afraid, because I was naked; and I hid myself.

And he said, Who told thee that thou wast naked? Hast thou eaten of the tree, whereof I commanded thee that thou shouldest not eat? And the man said, The woman whom thou gavest to be with me, she gave me of the tree, and I did eat. And the LORD God said unto the woman, What is this that thou hast done? And the woman said, The serpent beguiled me, and I did eat" (vv. 9-13).

The first thing we notice here is that Adam and Eve immediately begin to try to pass the guilt from themselves to another; and we have, therefore, the division which is at the very heart of man's relationship with man from this point on. The human race is divided—man against man. We do not have to wait for modern psychologists to talk about alienation. Here it is. The man is alienated from his wife, the wife from her husband, as they turn against each other, especially at the points of blame and guilt. All the alienation that any poet will ever write about is here already.

In a way, both Adam and Eve were right. Eve had given the fruit to Adam, and Satan had tempted Eve. But that does not shift the responsibility. Eve was responsible and Adam was responsible, and they stood in their responsibility before God.

God's Judgment on Man and Nature

As God speaks to the parties involved at this moment of history, we find four steps in his judgment of their action. First, he speaks to the serpent who has been used by Satan: "And the LORD God said unto the serpent, Because thou hast done this, thou art cursed above [*from among*] all cattle, and above every beast of the field; upon thy belly shalt thou go, and dust shalt thou eat all the days of thy life" (v. 14). As we shall see, all nature becomes abnormal; yet the serpent is singled out in a special way "from among all cattle."

Second, in verse 15 he speaks to Satan; we will return to that.

Third, he speaks to the woman: "Unto the woman he said, I will greatly multiply thy pain [this is more accurate than the King James word *sorrow*] and thy conception; in pain thou shalt bring forth children; and thy desire shall be to thy husband, and he shall rule over thee." There are two parts here: the first relates to the womanness of the woman—the bearing of children—and the second to her relationship to her husband. In regard to the relationship to her husband, he says, "And thy desire shall be to thy husband, and he shall rule over thee." This one sentence puts an end to any unstructured democracy. In a fallen world, unstructured democracy is not possible. Rather, God brings structure into the primary relationship of man—the man-woman relationship. In a fallen world (in every kind of society—big and small—and in every relationship) structure is needed for order. God Himself here imposes it on the basic human relationship. Form is given, and without such form freedom would only be chaos.

It is not simply because man is stronger that he is to have dominion (that's the argument of the Marquis de Sade). But rather he is to have dominion because God gives this as structure in the midst of a fallen world. The Bible makes plain that this relationship is not to be without love. As the New Testament puts it, the husband is to love his wife as Christ loved the Church (Eph. 5:23). In a fallen world, it is not surprising to find that men have turned this structure into a kind of slavery. It is not meant to be a slavery. In fact, it is in cultures where the Bible has been influential that the balance has been substantially restored. The Bible balances the structure and the love.

Nevertheless, it is still true: since the Fall, what God says in verse 16 is to be the structure of the form of the basic human relationship—the man-woman relationship. It is right that a woman should feel a need for freedom, a feeling of being a "human being" in the world. But when she tries to smash the structure of this basic relationship, finally what she does is to hurt herself. It is like unraveling the knot that holds the string of human relationships together. All other things flow from it—the loss of her own children's obedience and the crumbling of all society about her. In a fallen world, we need structure in every social relationship.

The Abnormal Universe

Fourth, God speaks to the man: "And unto Adam he said, Because thou hast hearkened unto the voice of thy wife, and hast eaten of the tree, of which I commanded thee, saying, Thou shalt not eat of it: cursed is the ground for thy sake; in toil [the word *sorrow* in the King James is inaccurate] shalt thou eat of it all the days of thy life" (v. 17). In other words, at this point the external world is changed.

It is interesting that almost all of the results of God's judgment because of man's rebellion relate in some way to the external world. They are not just bound up in man's thought-life; they are not merely psychological. Profound changes make the external, objective world abnormal. In the phrase "for thy sake," God is relating these external abnormalities to what Adam has done in the Fall.

All of these changes came about by fiat. Creation, as we have already seen, came by fiat. And though we have come to the conclusion of creation with the creation of Eve, yet fiat has not ceased. The abnormality of the external world was brought about by fiat. Putting it into twentieth-century terminology, we can say this: the universe does not display a uniformity of cause and effect in a closed system; God speaks and something changes. We are reminded here of the long arguments that date back to the time of Lyell and Darwin concerning whether there could be such a thing as catastrophe—something that cut across the uniformity of cause and effect. Scripture answers this plainly: yes, God spoke, and that which He had created was changed.

So now the earth itself is abnormal. We read, for example, in Genesis 5:29, which speaks of the world before the flood: "And he [Noah's father] called his name Noah, saying, This same shall comfort us concerning our work and toil of our hands, because of the ground which the LORD hath cursed." The name *Noah* itself simply means *rest* or *comfort*. The Scripture says that at this point in the flow of biblical history, men knew very well that the toil of their hands was a result of God's having changed the earth.

Why is it like this? Because, one might say, you, O unprogrammed and significant Adam, have revolted. Nature has been under your dominion (in a sense it is, as an extension of himself, as a king's empire is an extension of himself). Therefore, when you changed, God changed the objective, external world. It as well as you is now abnormal.

It is interesting that in each of the steps of God's judgment, toil is involved: the serpent goes upon his belly; the woman has pain in childbirth; the man has toil in his work.

Verse 18 continues, "Thorns also and thistles shall it bring forth to thee." The word *thistles* here means luxuriously growing but useless plants. The phrase "shall it bring forth to thee" has in the Hebrew the sense of "it shall be caused to bud." This phrase, therefore, suggests that here, too, the change was wrought by fiat. Furthermore, the phrase suggests the modern biological term *mutation,* a nonsterile sport. That is, the plants had been one kind of thing and were reproducing likewise, and then God spoke and the plants began to bring forth something else and continue to reproduce in that new and different form.

The introduction of toil does not mean the introduction of work, because in Genesis 2:15, as we have seen, God took man and put him in the Garden of Eden "to dress it and to keep it."

There was work before the Fall, but certainly we can see the force of the distinction before and after the Fall in the language of Genesis 5:29, where labor is called the "toil of our hands, because of the ground which the LORD hath cursed." Since the whole structure of the external world has changed, the meaning of work has changed. Thus Genesis 3:19 says: "In the sweat of thy face shalt thou eat bread, till [the concept of "until" is important here] thou return unto the ground; for out of it wast thou taken: for dust thou art, and unto dust shalt thou return."

The results are twofold. First, man shall have his food (and all else) by the sweat of his brow. Second, there is an end to this—an end that is not a release. The end is the greatest abnormality in the external world—the dissolution of the total man. A time will come at the end of each man's life when he physically dies, and the unity of man—the unity of body and soul—is torn asunder. Christianity is not Platonic; the soul is not considered all-important. Rather, at physical death that unity which man is meant to be is fractured. This is the second kind of death brought about by the Fall, the first being immediate separation from fellowship with God and the third being eternal death as men are judged in their rebellion and separated from God forever.

Christianity as a system does not begin with Christ as Savior, but with the infinite-personal God who created the world in the beginning and who made man significant in the flow of history. And man's significant act in revolt has made the world abnormal. Thus there is not a total unbroken continuity back to the way the world originally was. Non-Christian philosophers almost universally agree in seeing everything as normal, assuming things are as they have always been. The Christian sees things now as not the way they have always been. And, of course, this is very important to the explanation of evil in the world. But it is not only that. It is one way to understand the distinction between the naturalistic, non-Christian answers (whether spoken in philosophic, scientific or even religious language) and the Christian answer. The distinction is that as I look about me, I know I live in an abnormal world.

Among contemporary philosophers Martin Heidegger in his later writings suggested a sort of space-time fall. He said that prior to Aristotle, the pre-Socratic Greeks thought in a different way. Then when Aristotle introduced the concept of rationality and logic, there was an epistemological fall. His notion, of course, had no moral overtones at all, but it is intriguing to me that Heidegger came to realize that philosophy cannot explain reality if it begins with the notion that the world is normal. This the Bible has taught, but the Bible's explanation for the present abnormal world is in a *moral* Fall by a significant man, a fall which has changed the external flow of history as no epistemological fall could do. Heidegger's problem was that while he well saw the need of a fall, he would not bow before the existence of the God who is there and the knowledge that God has given us. Hence he ends up with an insufficient fall and an insufficient answer.

Separations
Another way to look at the results of the Fall is to notice the separations that are caused by sin. First is the great separation, the separation between God and man. It underlies all other separations, not only in eternity but right now. Man no longer has the communion with God he was meant to have. Therefore, he cannot fulfill the purpose of his existence—to love God with all his heart, soul and mind—to stand as a finite personal point before an infinite-personal reference point and be in relationship with God Himself. When man sinned, the purpose of his existence was smashed. And modern man is right when he says that man is dead. It is not that man is nothing, but that he is no longer able to fulfill his "mannishness." Genesis 3:23, 24 shows this separation between man and God in a real, historic, graphic sense.

As evangelicals, we sometimes emphasize the first separation and fail to properly emphasize all the others that now exist. The second great separation is separation of man from himself. Man has fear. Man has psychological problems. How does a Christian understand these? Primarily as the abnormal separation of man from himself. Man's basic psychosis is his separation from God carried into his own personality as a separation from himself. Thus we have self-deception. All men are liars, but, most importantly, each man lies to himself. The greatest falsehood is not lying to other men, but to ourselves. A related aspect is the loss of ability to acquire true knowledge. All his knowledge is now out of shape because the perspective is wrong, the framework is wrong. That is, man does not lose all his knowledge, but he loses "true knowledge," especially as he makes extensions from the bits and pieces of knowledge he does have.

Furthermore, man has separated his sexual life from its original high purpose as a vehicle of communication of person to person.

Sexuality loses its personal dimension; men and women treat each other as things to be exploited. Finally, at physical death comes the separation of the soul from the body, the great separation of a man from himself.

The third of the great separations is man from man. This is the sociological separation. We have seen already how Adam was separated from Eve. Both of them immediately tried to pass off the blame for the Fall. This signals the loss of the possibility of their walking truly side by side in true democracy. Not only was man separated from his wife, but soon brother became separated from brother, Cain killing Abel. And, as we will see in the following chapter, there is a separation between the godly and the ungodly line of men. The godly line (those men who have returned to God) and the ungodly line (the unsaved humanity going on in rebellion) constitute two humanities. In one sense, of course, there is one humanity because we all come from one source. We are one blood, one flesh. But in the midst of one humanity, there are two humanities—the humanity that still stands in rebellion and the humanity that is redeemed.

Soon in the flow of history we come to the tower of Babel, and with it we have the division of languages. Modern linguistics has helped us to understand how great the issues are here. So much is involved with language. Then after the time of Abraham comes the division between Jew and Gentile. These separations (and others related to them) are like titanic sonic booms in the sociological upheavals coming down to, and perhaps especially in, our day.

The fourth separation is a separation of man from nature and nature from nature. Man has lost his full dominion, and now nature itself is often a means of judgment. There is, for example, the flood at the time of Noah and, of course, nature pitted against Job. The separation of man from nature and nature from nature seems also to have reached a climax in our day.

Man's sin causes all these separations between man and God, man and himself, man and man, and man and nature. The simple fact is that in wanting to be what man as a creature could not be, man lost what he could be. In every area and relationship men have lost what finite man could be in his proper place.

But there is one thing which he did not lose, and that is his "mannishness," his being a human being. Man still stands in the image of God—twisted, broken, abnormal, but still the image-bearer of God. Man did not stop being human. As we have seen in Genesis 9:6 and in James 3:9, even after the Fall men are still in the image of God. Modern man does not see man as fallen, but he can find no significance for man. In the Bible's teaching man is fallen but significant.

Let us not be misled: man is still man. The unsaved painter can still paint. The unsaved lover can still love. He still has moral motions. And the unsaved thinker can still think. And furthermore, he lives on after his own death. He doesn't just come to the end of his life and suddenly the clock stops. Man has meaning and significance. He may think that his history is just trash and junk, but it is not so.

Watch a man as he dies. Five minutes later he still exists. There is no such thing as stopping the existence of man. He still goes on. By the Fall man has not lost his being as a human being. He has not lost those things which he intrinsically is as a man. He has not become an animal or a machine. And as I look out over the human race and see the lost—separated from God, separated from themselves, separated from other people, separated from nature—they are still people. Man still has tremendous value.

CHAPTER SIX

The Two Humanities

Division, separations—they rend the fabric of society. The history of man is the record of splits and schisms, every one of which has its origin in the primal separation of man from God. We turn now to some of the early forms which these separations took in the flow of biblical history.

Thy Seed and Her Seed

In Genesis 3:15 we have a rather different aspect of the curse that comes from Adam's rebellion. God here speaks to Satan who used the serpent: "And I will put enmity between thee and the woman, and between thy seed and her seed; he shall bruise thy head, and thou shalt bruise his heel" (ASV). It is important to emphasize that the seed here is considered personal, "he." The one who is promised here is a person. A person will bruise Satan's head, and in doing so will be wounded.

Let us reflect further on "thy seed and her seed"—the seed of the serpent and the seed of the woman. The reference to "her seed" is unusual in Semitic languages because, as in our own thinking, the male is considered the one who has the seed. Descent is indicated in men as in animals as the descent or offspring of the male. Why is it different here? Is it possible that this way of speaking already cast a shadow of the virgin birth? Does it suggest that when the Messiah was born, he would be the seed of the woman and that in his conception there would be no male seed?

Another implication of Genesis 3:15 is indicated in Hebrews 2:14. Speaking of Jesus, the writer of Hebrews says, "Forasmuch, then, as the children are partakers of flesh and blood, he [Jesus] also himself likewise took part of the same, that through death he might destroy him that had the power of death, that is, the devil." Here is an indication that Jesus fulfilled the promise in Genesis 3:15, for it is the Messiah who is to be bruised and yet, in the bruising, destroy the power of death and the Devil. By this death, He would "deliver them who, through fear of death, were all their lifetime subject to bondage" (Hebrews 2:15). That is, there would be a substitutionary note to His death face to face with the adversary, Satan, and by this death the results of the Fall would be overcome.

There is also a tie between Genesis 3:15 and Hebrews 2:13 that I think is not just coincidental—the phrase, "I and the children whom God hath given me." The chief thrust is undoubtedly on the substitutionary aspect of Jesus' death. Yet it also reminds us of that magnificent passage in Isaiah 53:10—"Yet it pleased the LORD to bruise him; he hath put him to grief. When thou shalt make his soul an offering for sin, he shall see his seed, he shall prolong his days, and the pleasure of the LORD shall prosper in his hand." Note again: "He shall see his seed." It is in this sense, therefore, that God has given Jesus children. Romans 16:20 also ties in with Genesis 3:15. Speaking to the Christians in Rome, Paul writes, "And the God of peace shall bruise Satan under your feet shortly." The reference is to the second coming of the Lord Jesus Christ, when God Himself shall bruise Satan under the feet of the Christians.

Therefore, we find that indeed Christ *is the seed* of the woman in Genesis 3:15. And yet from His unique redemptive work he *has a seed* which shall stand against the seed of Satan. And when we bring these together, I think we can feel the force of what is gradually developed through Scripture beginning from this phrase in Genesis 3:15. Christ is to be the second Adam and the second founder of the race.

We remember that in theological terms Adam lived under the covenant of works. That is, he could approach God without any mediator. He did not need a Savior. Soteriology would not have existed in Christian theology if there had been no Fall. Adam stood before God under the covenant of works. Then, when Jesus came, Jesus worked. He continued and finished the work under the covenant of works. Because of the Fall and our own sinning, we can no longer come to God under this covenant. But Christ finished the work needed for us in His substitutionary death, and in doing so He became the second Adam—the second founder of the human race.

Two Suits of Clothes
In Genesis 3:7 we learn that Adam and Eve found out that they were "naked" and so they "sewed fig leaves together and made themselves aprons." That is, immediately after their rebellion as they came face to face with what had previously been their great joy and their great fulfillment—themselves in open communion with God—they were now afraid and tried to cover themselves. But in verse 21 God took this covering away and gave them a coat of skins: "For Adam also and for his wife did the LORD God make coats of skins, and clothed them." Probably these were the first animals to die. This indicates, I believe, that man could not stand before God in his own covering. Rather, he needed a covering from God—a covering of a specific nature—a covering that required sacrifice and death, a covering not provided by man but by God. One would want to be careful not to press this into a dogma, but it is my opinion that this was the beginning of the Old Testament sacrificial system looking forward to the coming of the One who would crush Satan's head. If this is so, God Himself provided this picture. In the same way, in the reality which this pictures, the Father in His love sent the Son.

We might note at this point that the death of Jesus Christ was not an afterthought in history. It isn't that sometime, say, around 100 B.C. God said, "What shall we do about this?" and then suddenly the idea of the death of Christ dawned on Him. Rather, 1 Peter 1:19, 20 and other passages indicate that the death of Christ, "the precious blood of Christ, as of a lamb without blemish and without spot," was "foreordained before the foundation of the world." Thus the death of Christ in space and time, planned before history began, the solution of man's rebellion in the light of God's character of holiness and love, stood in the natural flow of all that had been.

The Ultimate Separation

We recall that numerous separations came about because of the Fall. There were alienations between God and man, man and himself, man and other men, man and nature, and nature and nature. The last separation is the separation between the Father and the Son when Jesus died on the cross. The separations that resulted from man's Fall were brought to their climax as Jesus, the second person of the Trinity, being bruised and bearing our sins in substitution, cried aloud, "My God, my God, why hast thou forsaken me?" (Matt. 27:46).

In such a setting as this, we are ready to grasp the full impact of the verses in Romans which we considered only partially in the previous chapter. I will quote the whole section this time (Rom. 5:12-21) and from the American Standard Version (1901) in order to make the passage clearer.

> Therefore, as through one man sin entered into the world, and death through sin; and so death passed unto all men, for that all sinned: for until the law sin was in the world; but sin is not imputed when there is no law. Nevertheless death reigned from Adam until Moses, even over them that had not sinned after the likeness of Adam's transgression, who is a figure of him that was to come. But not as the trespass, so also is the free gift. For if by the trespass of the one the many died, much more did the grace of the one man, Jesus Christ, abound unto the many. And not as through one that sinned, so is the gift: for the judgment came of one unto condemnation, but the free gift came of many trespasses unto justification. For if, by the trespass of the one, death reigned through the one; much more shall they that receive the abundance of grace and of the gift of righteousness reign in life through the one, even Jesus Christ. So then, as through one trespass the judgment came unto all men to condemnation; even so through one act of righteousness the free gift came unto all men to justification of life. For as through the one man's disobedience the many were made sinners, even so through the obedience of the one shall the many be made righteous. And the law came in besides, that the trespass might abound; but where sin abounded, grace did abound more exceedingly: that, as sin reigned in death, even so might grace reign through righteousness unto eternal life through Jesus Christ our Lord.

It is clear that Christ is the second Adam, the second founder of the human race. He picks up the covenant of works at the place where Adam forfeited it. As Lazarus Spengler wrote so long ago in 1524:

> As by one man all mankind fell
> And, prone to sin, then faced hell,
> So by one Man, who took our place,
> We now are sure of God's grace.
> We thank thee, Christ; new life is ours. . . .

This is exactly what was promised in Genesis 3:15: "And I will put enmity between thee and the woman, and between thy seed and her seed; he shall bruise thy head, and thou shalt bruise his heel" (ASV). Already we have the death of Christ in promise—the first promise—made immediately after the rebellion and the Fall. The death of Christ, therefore, is presented as the solution to all the separations of which we spoke.

By the sufficiency of the death of Christ, these separations will be perfectly healed at His second coming. And yet the Bible says that in the present life, on the basis of the shed blood of the Lord Jesus Christ, through faith and in the power of the Holy Spirit, there is now to be substantial healing in regard to all these separations. Sir Francis Bacon (1561-1626) pointed this out in *Novum Organum Scientiarum*. I've quoted this in some of my other books, but it fits here as well: "Man by the Fall fell at the same time from his state of innocence and from his dominion over nature. Both of these losses, however, can even in this life be in some part repaired; the former by religion and faith, the latter by the arts and sciences." This is to be the Christian view of life. A Christian, understanding the abnormality of nature, can see the arts and the sciences substantially delivered under God. And he can see even in this life a substantial reparation of the division between man and nature which one day, at the second coming of Jesus, will be perfect and complete.

Therefore, in the flow of history as we come to Genesis 3:15 we see that (except for Christ's work) the covenant of works is past. From this time on the covenant of grace applies. From here to the last man who will ever pass from death to life, man no longer can come in his own works. It is well to put it in the first person singular: I cannot come by my own works. I can come only through Christ's finished work. I can come only on the basis of the covenant of grace, the benefits of which I now receive as a free gift.

We can say this in a different way. Prior to the Fall, Adam in coming to God only had to bow once—as a creature before the

Creator. But now, after the Fall of Adam, we must bow twice—as a creature before the Creator and as a sinner coming to a holy God through Jesus' work.

Acceptable and Unacceptable Worship
So far in our study of the flow of history, we have covered two major steps: the situation in the beginning when all was good, and the introduction of the abnormality brought about by the Fall. Our third major subject is acceptable and unacceptable worship after the Fall.

In Genesis 4:1 we read: "And Adam knew Eve his wife; and she conceived, and bore Cain, and said, I have gotten a man from the LORD." Here is the first baby to be born. What a wonder it must have been for Eve suddenly to have in her hands a little baby from her own body. Imagine her amazement as she looked at it: "Why, yes, it's just like Adam! I have gotten a man from the Lord!"

We wonder if she could possibly have had in mind the promise in Genesis 3:15. There is no way to be sure, of course. But do you suppose she said to herself, "Maybe this is the one who will bring the solution to the problem we introduced"? As Christians living on this side of the New Testament, we think of the contrast to Mary to whom the seed of the woman was really born in the virgin birth. In Hebrews 12:24 the writer is speaking to men living after the time of Jesus, reminding them that they have come "to Jesus the mediator of the new covenant, and to the blood of sprinkling, that speaketh better things than that of Abel." In Genesis 4:10 God said that Abel's blood was calling out concerning the fact that Cain had killed him. It was the cry of the first murder, brother killing brother, a part of the separation because of the Fall. Christ's blood is the solution.

But in Genesis 4:1 Eve has just given birth to Cain! So if she had in mind that this was the one who was to solve the problems of the Fall, how wrong she was! Born naturally, he brings forth the results of the fallen human race. A savior? No, he is going to kill his brother. What a contrast between the firstborn child and Christ!

In Genesis 4:2 we have the birth of the second child: "And she again bore his brother Abel." As the two grow up, we are brought to the question of acceptable and unacceptable worship this side of the Fall: "And in process of time it came to pass, that Cain brought of the fruit of the ground an offering unto the LORD.

And Abel, he also brought of the firstlings of his flock and of the fat thereof. And the LORD had respect unto Abel and his offering; but unto Cain and to his offering he had not respect. And Cain was very wroth, and his countenance fell" (vv. 3, 4).

Hebrews 11:4 tells us what was involved: "By faith Abel offered unto God a more excellent sacrifice than Cain." The distinction is that Abel's act of sacrifice was *by faith*.

The whole process is related to Romans 4 which gives the clearest possible description of such faith: "Abraham believed God, and it was counted unto him for righteousness" (Rom. 4:3). This is God's description of faith, the very opposite of a Kierkegaardian leap into the void. God gave for Abraham a specific, propositional promise and Abraham believed God. This belief was reckoned unto him for righteousness. In other words, Abraham's faith involved content.

How much content Abel had we do not know, but then we should be conscious of the fact that the Bible does not tell us how he knew to bring an offering at all. And this is not unusual; in the book of Genesis information has often been given that we do not know has been given until someone acts on it—for example, the clean and unclean beasts of the time of Noah (Gen. 7:2) or Abraham and the tithe (Gen. 14:20). So here it is clear that Abel did have knowledge about offerings, even though the Bible has not told us when this knowledge was given. We could wonder if Abel's parents had told him of the promise of Genesis 3:15 and the skins. And while this would be only speculation, one thing is not speculation: from this time onward, sacrifice was known and practiced, and the New Testament ties this up with the sacrifice of Christ.

We can hardly forget the words of John the Baptist, who (while he is recorded in the New Testament) is the last Old Testament prophet. When Jesus was just appearing on the public scene, one of the Gospel writers recorded this: "The next day John seeth Jesus coming unto him, and saith, Behold the Lamb of God, who taketh away the sin of the world" (John 1:29). You will notice that John the Baptist gives no explanation. He doesn't need to, because the Jews understood the Old Testament emphasis at this particular point.

In 1 Corinthians 5:7 Paul calls Christ our Passover in the same way, expecting understanding without explanation. The book of Hebrews repeatedly draws the parallel of the death of Christ and the Old Testament sacrifices. For example, Hebrews 7:26, 27: "For such an high priest became us, who is holy, harmless, undefiled, separate from sinners, and higher than the heavens; who needeth not daily, as those high priests to offer up sacrifice, first for his own sins, and then for the people's: for this he did once, when he offered up himself." And, as we have already seen, Revelation 5:11, 12 refers to Jesus as the Lamb of God who has been slain and is therefore worthy to receive the power and the glory.

The Historicity of Cain and Abel

Just as in the case of Adam and Eve, the New Testament considers Cain and Abel as characters in history. We read in 1 John 3:12— "Not as Cain, who was of that wicked one, and slew his brother. And wherefore slew he him? Because his own works were evil, and his brother's righteous." Jude 11 repeats this: "Woe unto them! for they have gone in the way of Cain. . . ." But notice that while in both cases the historicity of Cain is assumed, more than a historic fact is involved. In the flow of history, there is a *line of Cain* in which we should not walk. In contrast, in Hebrews 11:4 Abel is put in a line of historic characters, the line of faith, and we are commanded to walk in this line. More than this, Abel is the first one named in this line, and so in a real way this could be called the *line of Abel*.

The way of Cain is contrasted with the way of Abel, and that contrast is introduced in Genesis 4:6, 7. "And the LORD said unto Cain, Why art thou wroth? and why is thy countenance fallen? If thou doest well, shalt thou not be accepted? And if thou doest not well, sin lieth at the door. And unto thee shall be his desire, and thou shalt rule over him." Some take the possible reading of "sin offering" rather than "sin" to be the proper reading here. But while the detail of the translation of these verses may be discussed, the central thought is definite. God is saying, "Why is your countenance fallen, Cain? You can still be accepted. You've made a mistake, but there is a way out." It seems to me that God is telling Cain to go back and do what he should have done in the first place. By picking up the thread of acceptable worship, he could stop the rebellion (as far as he himself was concerned) right there. Instead he did something else: "And Cain talked with Abel his brother: and it came to pass, when they were in the field, that Cain rose up against Abel, his brother, and slew him" (v. 8). Instead of going back and doing what would have been right, he did something overwhelmingly wrong.

From here on two lines spread out before us—the way of Cain and the way of Abel. As we have pointed out, a separation between man and man had come as soon as Adam and Eve each tried to shift the blame from himself or herself. But the separation is now accentuated with the contrast between acceptable and unacceptable worship. From here on there are two humanities—the humanity that comes to God, bowing twice, and the humanity that follows in the way of Cain. The separation between man and man now extends to the separation between brothers. The love which should have existed between them as fellow-beings created by God in the image of God has now become hatred and murder.

It is interesting that this murder sprang up, as we are told in the New Testament, exactly at the point of not believing God. One believed God, one didn't.

"And the LORD said unto Cain, Where is Abel, thy brother? And he said, I know not: am I my brother's keeper? And he said, What hast thou done? The voice of thy brother's blood crieth unto me from the ground" (Gen. 4:9, 10). The blood of Abel speaks and cries for judgment and justice, and this cry echoes right down into the book of Revelation where we find the martyrs saying, "How long, O Lord, holy and true, dost thou not judge and avenge our blood on them that dwell on the earth?" (Rev. 6:10).

Abel's blood cries out, "Judgment! Judgment!" And God must and will judge because he is a holy God. If He shrugged his shoulders and walked away, there would be no moral absolute in the universe. Hebrews, fortunately, gives us a further dimension. There is another way, one rooted in the blood of Jesus shed in history. This blood "speaketh better things than that of Abel" (Heb. 12:24). The blood of Jesus goes beyond justice and offers mercy. It cries "Salvation!" on the basis of Jesus' death to all who will hear.

The Culture of the Ungodly Line

Genesis 4:11-24 tells of the gradually developing culture of the ungodly line. For man is still really man, and he can bring forth a culture. But it is a culture with a mark upon it, a culture without the true God.

We need to note here, in passing, that verses 11-24 do not constitute a chronology any more than do the genealogies of the godly line which begin at verse 25. Rather, these passages exactly fit the literary form found in all parts of Genesis: the unimportant aspects (in this case the ungodly line) are quickly gotten out of the way so that the more central aspects (the godly line) might be dealt with in detail. We do not, therefore, know how much time elapses before we come to Genesis 4:24. It is not necessary that verse 24 contain history that precedes that in verse 25, for verse 24 brings to a close the consideration of the ungodly line, and verse 25 picks up the godly line.

Verses 23 and 24 are a perfect description of the ungodly, humanistic culture of all generations: "And Lamech said unto his wives, Adah and Zillah, Hear my voice; ye wives of Lamech, hearken unto my speech; for I have slain a man who wounded me, and a young man hurting me." Or to paraphrase this: "Because a man wounded me, I paid him back. I just killed him." Look at what Lamech did! Isn't that terrific? "O you wives, listen to me, both of you: This fellow hit me. I fixed him. I killed him." "If Cain shall be avenged sevenfold, truly Lamech seventy and sevenfold." Here is humanistic culture without God. It is egoism and pride centered in man; this culture has lost the concept not only of God, but of man as one who loves his brother.

The Culture of the Godly Line
Genesis 4:25 takes up the godly line: "And Adam knew his wife again; and she bore a son, and called his name Seth: For God, said she, hath appointed me another seed instead of Abel, whom Cain slew." Seth, therefore, takes the place of Abel, as the vehicle of the godly line. "And to Seth, to him also there was born a son; and he called his name Enos: then began men to call on the name of the LORD." Or possibly, "Men began to call themselves *by the name of the Lord.*" In other words, at this particular place the godly line marks itself with the name of God in exactly the same way as Christians later were marked by the name of Christ. Both marked themselves by the name of the One they followed.

We learn, by the way, from Genesis 5:3 that when Seth was born, Adam was 130 years old. Therefore, there was not a great deal of time between the creation of man and the Fall, because all the way up to the time of the birth of Seth only 130 years had passed.

In conclusion, I would make three points. First, Adam and Eve had thrown away the opportunity to come to God on the basis of the covenant of works. From then on, the only way men could come to God was on the basis of the covenant of grace. It was not that there was no work involved in this covenant, but that the work was Christ's, not man's. This is true whether, as in the Old Testament, men looked forward to the work of Christ to come in history (the promise becoming known in increasing detail as time passed), or whether, as in our case, we look back to the death of Christ as the Savior in history.

Therefore, since Cain everyone in the world stands either in the place of Cain or the place of Abel. From this time on in the flow of history, there are two humanities. The one humanity says there is no God, or it makes gods in its own imagination, or it tries to come to the true God in its own way. The other humanity comes to the true God in God's way. There is no neutral ground.

Second, as far as the promise in Genesis 3:15 is concerned, the Messiah could have come from anywhere in the human race. But Seth brings the first narrowing of the promise. From this time on, the Messiah will come from his line.

Third, when we look at Cain killing Abel, we can see a horrible lack of the love which should have existed between men as equal creatures—not just because they were fleshly brothers, though this makes the matter sharper, but simply because they were equally created by God. They were of the same flesh, the same blood, of one kind, of one race. In contrast to Cain, we who are Christians and therefore stand as the seed given to Christ in His substitutionary work are to show in the present life the restored brotherhood in restored love. This is the Christian's calling. We are to show the opposite of what Cain, that murderer, showed. If we have become the second humanity, if we have come indeed under the blood of the second founder of the race, the second Adam, men should look at us as we stand surrounded by the seed of the line of Cain and they should see a reversal of Cain's attitude. This should be true not just in our simple acts, but in our whole culture.

The Bible makes plain who stands among this brotherhood. In Matthew 12:47-50 Jesus' natural mother and His natural brothers came as he was talking to the people. "Then one said unto him [Jesus], Behold, thy mother and thy brethren stand without, desiring to speak with thee." But Jesus points out that the merely physical relationship is not central: "Who is my mother? And who are my brethren? And he stretched forth his hand toward his disciples, and said, Behold my mother and my brethren! For whosoever shall do the will of my Father, who is in heaven, the same is my brother, and sister, and mother." Here then is the brotherhood. The same thing is made evident in Matthew 23:8 where Jesus instructs his disciples, "But be not ye called Rabbi; for one is your Master, even Christ, and all ye are brethren." Thus a new humanity has been established on the basis of the work of Christ, and this new humanity is to love the brotherhood as brothers, and all men as neighbors.

We have long known that men were to live in a loving relationship with each other. As 1 John 3:11, 12 says, "This is the message [or commandment] that ye heard from the beginning, that we should love one another." John is saying that this commandment dates not just from Moses, but from the time when God created men to be men: "Not as Cain, who was of that wicked one, and slew his brother." Here is the contrast. We are called as Christians to step out from the line of Cain and to reverse that line. The world should be able to look upon us and see a love that stands, first of all, among the brotherhood, but also extends (as commanded in the story of the good Samaritan) to all men.

Evangelism is a calling, but not the first calling. Building congregations is a calling, but not the first calling. A Christian's first call is to step from the line of Cain into the line of Abel, upon the basis of the shed blood of the Lamb of God—to return to the first commandment to love God, to love the brotherhood, and then to love one's neighbor as himself.

Abraham was a man of faith, a man of God, who in a specific way is a perfect example of standing in the line of Abel in contrast to the line of Cain. Facing Lot, his nephew, at a crucial time in a difficult relationship which had developed between them, Abraham said, "Let there be no strife, I pray thee, between me and thee, and between my herdsmen and thy herdsmen; for we are brethren" (Gen. 13:8). Abraham stood in precisely the place where all those who have become children of God should stand. And notice that there was a cost to doing so. Abraham said to Lot, "Is not the whole land before thee? Separate thyself, I pray thee, from me: if thou wilt take the left hand, then I will go to the right; or if thou depart to the right hand, then I will go to the left." Abraham paid a tremendous price. He stood in complete contrast to Cain. He gave the first choice of grazing land to a younger man. Abraham in costly love stood in the spirit of the godly line. In every age and every situation, this is the Christian's place.

CHAPTER SEVEN

Noah and the Flood

History flows on, the course having been set by Adam and Eve and humanity divided by Cain and Abel. The history of divided humanity develops from the two lines delineated in Genesis 4:16-24 (the line of Cain) and Genesis 4:25—5:32 (the line of Seth). In the account which follows these genealogies, we are introduced to a world in which moral decay comes to so permeate society that only one man is left in the godly line. But this puts us ahead of our story.

"And He Died"
Throughout Genesis 5, which begins by recapitulating the heritage of the line of Seth, emphasis is placed on the conclusion of each man's life. Verse 5, in reference to Adam, ends, "and he died." Verses 8, 11, 14, 17, 20, 27 and 31, in reference to Seth, Enos, Cainan, Mahalaleel, Jared, Methuselah and Lamech, also end, "and he died." Thus, as we run through this genealogy, we are reminded over and over that we live in an abnormal world; since man has revolted, things are not the way God made them originally. But there is a curious exception to the phrase *and he died.* Verse 24 comments, "And Enoch walked with God, and he

was not; for God took him." Both verses 22 and 24 contain that first phrase "and Enoch walked with God," indicating that Enoch was indeed a man of God. The same phrase is used with reference to Noah in Genesis 6:9. But with Enoch something else is special: "He was not; for God took him."

Hebrews 11:5 gives us further information: "By faith Enoch was translated [*taken up*] that he should not see death, and was not found, because God had translated him; for before his translation he had this testimony, that he pleased God." A similar *translation*, Elijah's, is explained in more detail in 2 Kings 2. Enoch and Elijah stand out as unique, being taken to God without dying.

Genealogy and Chronology

Genesis 5 raises a very interesting question. What is the connection between this Old Testament genealogy and chronology? Before the turn of the century, Professor William Greene at Princeton Theological Seminary and Professor Benjamin B. Warfield following him maintained that the genealogies in Genesis should not be taken as a chronology. While much of their scholarship had to be a response to liberal theology's attack on biblical history, I think that the understanding that these genealogies are not a chronology is obvious from Scripture itself.

First, the relationship between the sequence of names and chronology is not always a straight line. In Genesis 5:32 we read, "And Noah was five hundred years old; and Noah begat Shem, Ham, and Japheth." It would appear from this passage that Shem is older than Ham who is older than Japheth. But in Genesis 9:24 we are told that "Noah awoke from his wine, and knew what his *youngest* son had done unto him" (ASV). The reference is to Ham. Likewise, anyone reading Exodus 2 would certainly feel that Moses was the oldest son. Nevertheless, we learn in Exodus 7:7 that his brother Aaron was actually three years older. Consequently, the content of these various passages are accurate, but chronology was not what the authors had in mind. Undoubtedly Shem was named first because he was the most important in the flow of biblical history. What they were recording *was* the flow of history—the thing we are talking of in this book—the flow of origins, especially of the Jews, for whom such things were of great importance, as we shall see in a moment. The Bible does not mislead us. It indicates that the genealogies are not chronological.

A second reason why we must not take genealogy for chronology is that several passages make it obvious that the writers knew the chronology, but that they still deliberately omitted several steps in the genealogy. For example, if we compare 1 Chronicles 6:3-14 with Ezra 7:2, we find that Ezra, despite the fact that he was a scribe and surely would have known all of the steps, omitted names in the genealogical tree. Not only this, but he seems to have added two names omitted in the 1 Chronicles genealogy. Of course, some of these men may have been known by more than one name as was common in Old Testament history, and there is a possibility of a later scribe's error. Nonetheless, it does seem that some names were consciously omitted by Ezra.

An even more startling case which shows what the Jewish people were doing with their genealogies occurs in 1 Chronicles 26:24. Here we read, "And Shebuel the son of Gershom, the son of Moses, was ruler of the treasures." The time is that of David, roughly 1,000 B.C., and the issue is that Shebuel had an official position on the basis of his genealogical line. The intriguing thing is that Gershom is the first-generation son of Moses, and yet between him and the next man, Shebuel, stand at least 400 years. There is no doubt that we have here a tremendous gap in years and in intervening generations. Thus we are reminded that the purpose of all this is to indicate the flow of official, historic lines. It is important to say, "This man comes from such and such an origin."

Another clear case is found in Matthew's genealogy of Christ. In Matthew 1:8 we read, "And Asa begat Jehoshaphat; and Jehoshaphat begat Joram; and Joram begat Uzziah" (ASV). Yet if we go back into the Old Testament we will find that Uzziah's father, grandfather and great-grandfather are omitted in Matthew's genealogy. (See 1 Chronicles 3:11, 12; in this list Uzziah is called Azariah.) The important point is that Jesus is to be seen in the right genealogical line, and after that has been accomplished, chronology is of little or no interest.

Prior to the time of Abraham, there is no possible way to date the history of what we find in Scripture. After Abraham, we can date the biblical history and correlate it with secular history. When the Bible itself reaches back and picks up events and genealogies in the time before Abraham, it never uses these early genealogies as a chronology. It never adds up these numbers for dating.

There is a third reason why it should be quite obvious that these genealogies are not meant to be a chronology. If they were, it would mean that Adam, Enoch and Methuselah were contemporaries, and that just doesn't seem to fit at all. If this were the case, the silence of the Bible in regard to these interrelationships would seem curious. But the situation is even more striking after the flood, because in this postdiluvian era if genealogy were chronology, all of the postdiluvians, including Noah, would have still been living when Abraham was fifty years of age. That would seem to be impossible. Furthermore, Shem, Salah and Eber would all have outlived Abraham, and Eber would still have been living when Jacob was with Laban. The simple fact is that this does not fit into the rest of biblical history. We will consider this matter further when we take up Genesis 10—11 (in Chapter Eight, pages 106-111), but at this particular place we can say very clearly that the Bible does not invite us to use the genealogies in Scripture as a chronology.

The Sons of God and the Daughters of Men

Genesis 6:1, 2 raises a question which men have discussed for many years: "And it came to pass, when men began to multiply on the face of the earth, and daughters were born unto them, that the sons of God saw the daughters of men that they were fair; and they took them wives of all whom they chose." The difficulty is with the phrase "the sons of God," because this phrase can mean either of two things: (1) the godly line, those who were calling themselves by the name of the Lord (as in Genesis 4:26); or (2) the angels (as in Job 1:6). What has stirred men's curiosity is that the book of Jude seems to refer to this. Verses 6, 7 read, "And angels that kept not their own principality, but left their proper habitation, he hath kept in everlasting bonds under darkness unto the judgment of the great day. Even as Sodom and Gomorrah, and the cities about them, having in like manner given themselves over to fornication and gone after strange flesh [the Greek says *other flesh*], are set forth as an example, suffering the punishment of eternal fire" (ASV). This passage seems to say that there are angels who left their own proper place and are specifically under judgment because they acted like the people of Sodom and Gomorrah. That is, as the people of Sodom and Gomorrah sought "other flesh" in homosexuality, these angels sought flesh that was "other flesh"; they involved themselves with human women in what could be called fornication.

There is further interest concerning this if one understands it as a commingling of the angelic and the human, for then it is possible that it was the original historic source of an element common in mythology. More and more we are finding that mythology in general, though greatly contorted, very often has some historic base. And the interesting thing is that one myth that one finds over and over again in many parts of the world is that somewhere a long time ago supernatural beings had sexual intercourse with natural women and produced a special breed of people.

Such a notion is strengthened by Genesis 6:4: "There were giants [*Nephilim*] in the earth in those days; and also after that, when the sons of God came in unto the daughters of men, and they bore children to them, the same became mighty men who were of old, men of renown." One can speculate, therefore, that the mighty men which were of old, men of renown, might be the historic reality behind these myths.

The other reading—that verse 2 denotes that there were those in the godly line who intermarried with others in the ungodly line to the destruction of the godly line—fits into the whole of Scripture, for there is a constant prohibition throughout the Old and New Testaments against the people of God marrying those who are not of the people of God. The Old Testament says repeatedly: if you marry those who are not God's people, and if you give your sons and daughters to them, the godly line will be destroyed. The New Testament contains the same command: "Be ye not unequally yoked together with unbelievers: for what fellowship hath righteousness with unrighteousness? and what communion hath light with darkness?" (2 Cor. 6:14). This passage has to do with those links which are central to men's lives, and no link is more central than marriage. This point is made explicit in the great marriage passage in 1 Corinthians 7:39. Paul instructs the church that "the wife is bound by the law as long as her husband liveth; but if her husband be dead, she is at liberty to be married to whom she will; *only in the Lord.*" The principle is clear: God's people are to marry God's people.

It is, therefore, possible to interpret Genesis 6:2 as indicating the intermarriage between the godly line and the ungodly line.

One Man Left in the Godly Line
Genesis 6:5-12 brings us to a point in history where there is only one man left in the godly line.

And God saw that the wickedness of man was great in the earth, and that every imagination of the thoughts of his heart was only evil continually [the Hebrew reads, *every day*]. And it repented the LORD that he had made man on the earth, and it grieved him at his heart. And the LORD said, I will destroy man [blot out man] whom I have created [note again this word created] from the face of the earth; both man, and beast, and the creeping thing, and the fowls of the air [not the fishes, because in the form of destruction, the flood, of course, fish can live]; for it repenteth me that I have made them. But Noah found grace in the eyes of the LORD. These are the generations of Noah: Noah was a just man and perfect in his generations, and Noah walked with God. And Noah begat three sons, Shem, Ham, and Japheth. The earth also was corrupt before God, and the earth was filled with violence. And God looked upon the earth, and behold, it was corrupt; for all flesh had corrupted his way upon the earth.

We might ask, "Isn't it strange that only one man is left in the godly line?" But surely Scripture points out that this is the general course of every era. Man's heart is in rebellion against God, and the rebellious heart must be taken into account in balance with the factor of a sufficient knowledge of God. In each era the case is similar. For example, by the time of Abraham, the world had thrown away almost all of its knowledge of the true God. Likewise, by the time of Christ, the Jews had so turned from God that only a minority accepted their Old-Testament-prophesied Messiah. And we are amply warned that the end of our own era will be exactly the same. Because of the rebellion of man's heart the course is not upward. Therefore, speaking of the end of our age, Jesus could say, "When the Son of man cometh, shall he find faith on the earth?" (Luke 18:8). As we shall see shortly, Jesus expressly connects the time of Noah with the time of His second coming.

"These Are the Generations"
Genesis 6:9 uses a phrase which is one of the striking literary forms of Genesis: "These are the generations of . . ." In verse 9 the reference is to Noah, but the phrase has already been used in Genesis 2:4 and 5:1. It is, in fact, used eleven times in Genesis.

In 1936 Wiseman suggested that the phrase *these are the generations of* is not the beginning but the end of a section. The phrase means "this is (has been) the story of . . ." As he pointed out, the tablets of that time put such a title at the bottom rather than at the top. Thus, for example (if Wiseman was correct in applying this to Genesis), in Genesis 2:4, "These are the generations of the heavens and of the earth" would summarize that which had already been given. This would be likewise true of Genesis 5:1: "This is the book of the generations of Adam." Wiseman suggested that Moses had other materials in front of him when he wrote the book of Genesis and that he incorporated them. This is only speculation, but it is interesting; for if this were so, then the inspiration would be in the choice of the material used. It would be parallel to Hezekiah's men copying out the proverbs of Solomon (Prov. 25:1).

In any case, the important thing is that Genesis is without question broken into sections signaled by these phrases. There is, first, the cosmic creation ("these are the generations of the heavens and of the earth," Gen. 2:4); second, the period of Adam ("this is the book of the generations of Adam," Gen. 5:1); third, the period of Noah ("these are the generations of Noah," Gen. 6:9); and fourth, the era of Noah's sons ("these are the generations of the sons of Noah, Shem, Ham, and Japheth," Gen. 10:1). This phrase also occurs in Genesis 11:10, 27; 25:12, 19; 36:1, 9; 37:2. This phrase is a literary form that gives unity to the whole book of Genesis. In *No Final Conflict,* Chapter Two, I deal at length with the unity of the book of Genesis.

The Building of the Ark

The generation we are concerned with now, however, is Noah's. In Genesis 6:13-15 we find God warning Noah, telling him to escape the coming judgment: "And God said unto Noah, The end of all flesh is come before me; for the earth is filled with violence through them; and, behold, I will destroy them with [*from* or *with respect to*] the earth. Make thee an ark of gopher wood; rooms [it should be translated more like *a place to rest* or *nest*] shalt thou make in the ark, and shalt pitch it within and without with pitch. And this is the fashion which thou shalt make it of: the length of the ark shall be three hundred cubits, the breadth of it fifty cubits, and the height of it thirty cubits."

There are two things to notice in this section. First, the plan of the ark was not dreamed up by Noah. He was not a boat engineer. Rather, the plan of the ark derived from God Himself. It was a specific, propositional revelation that dealt with detail. At another great moment, when the tabernacle was to be built, God also gave the specific plans and dimensions of all that concerned it (Ex. 25:9-40).

God says to Noah, "A tremendous judgment is coming and here is the way to escape. Build a huge boat." It's interesting that among the common myths in the world's history, no other one is so widespread as the story of the flood. From China to the American Indians and even the pre-Colombian Indians, one finds in strange forms the myth of the great flood. Most of these myths have weird elements, foolish elements—for example, the descriptions of the boat that was used. In the Bible these strange and foolish elements are not there. We would say, then, that the Bible gives us the history of the flood; the myths all over the world are contorted, but show that men everywhere have a memory of it. Here in the Bible is the one flood story whose details, including the construction of the vessel, are reasonable.

If we assume that the cubit mentioned is 18 inches (one cannot be absolutely sure), we can calculate that the ark would contain 1,518,750 cubic feet. Quite a boat! The deck area of the three stories would total 101,250 square feet. Furthermore, a boat with the dimensions given is floatable. It just so happens, in fact, that the size of this ark is almost exactly the size of the *Great Eastern* which laid the first North Atlantic cable. Hence, compared to the various myths and other stories of the flood throughout the world, this one bears the mark of history.

The New Testament, of course, insists that the flood and the Noah account are history. Hebrews 11:7 reads: "By faith Noah, being warned of God of things not seen as yet, moved with fear, prepared an ark to the saving of his house, by which he condemned the world, and became heir of the righteousness which is by faith." Notice again, just as with Abel in Hebrews 11:4 and Abraham in Romans 4:3, faith is related to a propositional promise from God. Noah could not yet see the flood, but he had a propositional statement that judgment was to come, and he was told in a most propositional statement the dimensions of the boat he was to build. And he was asked to build a boat somewhere with no adequate water in sight: This was his act of faith—believing a propositional promise of God.

More striking yet is the parallel which Jesus drew between His own future space-time coming and the flood in the past. Jesus emphasizes that His future second coming is a historic event: "But of that day and hour knoweth no man, no, not the angels of heaven, but my Father only. But as the days of Noah were, so shall also the coming of the Son of man be" (Matt. 24:36, 37). The word translated "coming" used throughout the New Testament in relation to Christ's second coming means *presence*. It is "a being alongside of"; that is, there is coming a future time when Jesus will be present on the earth—historically, space-time present in the same way as He was on earth when He spoke these words. Jesus continues, "For as in the days that were before the flood they were eating and drinking, marrying and giving in marriage, until the day that Noah entered into the ark, and knew not until the flood came, and took them all away, so shall also the coming [here again *presence*] of the Son of man be. Then shall two be in the field; the one shall be taken, and the other left. Two women shall be grinding at the mill; the one shall be taken, and the other left" (vv. 38–41).

The parallel is interesting even in detail, for it takes up the normality of life upon the earth before the flood came and parallels it with the normality of life just before Jesus comes. Just as life was going along in an unbroken line and the flood came, so life will be going on in an unbroken line and the first step in the second coming of Christ will occur.

Many other passages speak clearly of the historicity of the flood. Isaiah 54:9 records God as saying, "For this is like the waters of Noah unto me; for as I have sworn that the waters of Noah should no more go over the earth, so have I sworn that I would not be wroth with thee, nor rebuke thee." That is, God is saying that His promise is as sure as the events concerning the historic fact of the flood. Likewise, 1 Peter 3:20 says in a parenthetical way, ". . . the longsuffering of God waited in the days of Noah, while the ark was a preparing, wherein few, that is, eight souls were saved through water" (ASV). The specificity of the number, eight, underscores the fact that the event was considered historical. Furthermore, 2 Peter 2:5 speaks about God who "spared not the old world, but saved Noah, the eighth person [that is, eight people, Noah and seven others], a preacher of righteousness, bringing in the flood upon the world of the ungodly." Notice another historic detail: Noah was a preacher of righteousness. This, by the way, is the text which some Christians have used to picture Noah preaching as he built the ark; that's really an extension of the text, but seems warranted. Noah didn't just build a boat in faith resting on the warning of God; he also preached righteousness.

In 2 Peter 3:3-7 the flood is again paralleled to the second coming of Christ. Prior to the time when Jesus is to come, there will be scoffers who will say, "Where is the promise of his coming? For since the fathers fell asleep, all things continue as they were from the beginning of the creation." To paraphrase this in twentieth-century language: "Where is the promise of His coming? There has been an absolute uniformity of natural causes in a closed system. Why are you talking about something catastrophic? It's always been like this, and we say it's going to keep on being like this." Peter explains this reaction: "For this they willingly are ignorant of, that by the word of God the heavens were of old, and the earth standing out of the water and in the water, by which the world that then was, being overflowed with water, perished. But the heavens and the earth which are now, by the same word are kept in store, reserved unto fire against the day of judgment and perdition of ungodly men." Thus past historical events in the time of Noah are paralleled with coming historical events.

But there is a further note here—a note of universality. If the judgment at the second coming of Christ is taken to be universal, isn't the judgment by water at the time of Noah also universal? Christians who love the Scripture have discussed at length whether the flood was universal or not. I believe it was, but I do not think by any means that we should make it a "test of orthodoxy." We cannot base a case on the word "earth" in Genesis 7:4 ("every living substance [thing] that I have made will I destroy off the face of the *earth*"), because the word can be translated "ground." Rather, the argument for universality rests on other factors, including the parallel between the second coming of Christ and the flood as it is given in the New Testament passages we have just considered. The tone of the language that is used in Genesis suggests this as well. It seems to have a totality about it, the same kind of thrust as Genesis 1—a thrust conveying universality. For instance, in Genesis 7:23 we read, "And every living thing was destroyed [*blotted out*] that was upon the face of the ground, both man, and cattle, and the creeping things, and birds of the heavens; and they were destroyed [*blotted out*] from the earth: and Noah only was left, and they that were with him in the ark" (ASV). That sounds universal. Furthermore, the word "ground" (as it appears in both the American Standard Version and the King James translation of this verse) and the word "earth" in this verse are two different words in Hebrew. Admittedly, both can be more limited; but the fact that two different words are used may add some weight to the argument in favor of universality with regard to the flood. Also, in Genesis 7:23 the other living things are closely paralleled to men, and Genesis 9:19 and 10:32 make it absolutely certain that Noah and his family were the only people left. That the flood was universal as far as people are concerned is made totally final in the Scripture.

Another difficulty arises if the flood is not universal, and I don't see how anyone can quite get around this factor. If a flood occurs in a limited area, a lot of animals can be drowned, but not all of them. There's no way you can eliminate them all unless they are all in a sealed canyon. When a forest fire or flood comes, the animals take off.

One further indication that the flood was universal is found in God's statement after the flood is over: "And I will remember my covenant, which is between me and you and every living creature of all flesh: and the waters shall no more become a flood to destroy all flesh [or, all life]" (Gen. 9:15). Unless the flood were universal and did in fact destroy all animals on the earth, I don't understand how to interpret the phrase "the waters shall no more become a flood to destroy all flesh [or all life]." Of course, this does not include the fish. The promise does not preclude smaller floods, nor does it preclude the possibility that the world could be destroyed by fire. The covenant is, however, specific: no flood will again destroy all flesh.

The Date of the Flood
We have already pointed out that since the genealogies do not constitute a chronology, we cannot date the flood. There are reasons to think that if the dating systems used in present anthropological studies are correct, the flood should be dated *considerably before* 20,000 B.C. Let me say that I think these dating systems are still open to question, but *if* they are correct, then this date is to be considered. If all men but Noah and his family were destroyed (Scripture clearly states this), then the flood would have had to occur before this date. Most anthropologists estimate that the American Indians entered America from the Orient in about 20,000 B.C. across either an ice bridge or a land bridge over the Bering Strait. Thus, because the Indians were descendants of Noah and his sons, the flood would have had to be prior to this

time. It is interesting that both the North American Indians and the pre-Colombian Indians of South America had flood myths.

Noah Enters the Ark

If we take the various New Testament passages and put them together with the Old Testament material, we see that while Noah was building the ark he was preaching and that there was the normal flow of life just like that on any day today. We hear cars on the road, people are in the village, people are in the city, others are farming, some people are making their dinners, there is a couple making love, a baby being born, and life is moving on in its general stream. This is exactly the picture that the Bible gives of the situation immediately before the flood.

Then, when the ark was built, God said to Noah, "Of every clean beast thou shalt take to thee by sevens, the male and his female; and of beasts that are not clean by two, the male and his female. Of fowls also of the air by sevens, the male and the female; to keep seed alive upon the face of all the earth" (Gen. 7:2, 3). It is apparent that Noah already had a knowledge from the past, a knowledge which the Bible does not record as being given at a specific point, because Noah needed no explanation of the difference between "clean" and "unclean." Such a knowledge with regard to clean and unclean is also assumed in Genesis 8:20. This fact is interesting because it means that these men may very well have known considerably more than we think.

Finally, it comes time for Noah and his retinue to go into the ark, for God says, "For yet seven days, and I will cause it to rain upon the earth forty days and forty nights; and every living substance [thing] that I have made will I destroy from off the face of the earth" (Gen. 7:4). Genesis 7:10 says, "And it came to pass after seven days, that the waters of the flood were [came] upon the earth." God is saying to them, "Now the ark is finished; you've been preaching here, but that is over. You're to go into the ark and stay there for seven days." I believe that to follow this command called for very strong faith on Noah's part.

Remember, the boat is out on dry land. We don't know the altitude at which it was built, but it would be something like having an ocean liner in Huemoz. What a strange sight! People are people, and psychology is psychology. You can imagine them coming up and poking at the boat and, to put it mildly, being skeptical. The black preachers in America used to weave tremendous stories of Noah preaching as he built and people coming by, standing before the boat and laughing. Of course, it is a stretch of the imagination, and yet it must have been strange to get into this boat and then just sit there for seven days.

What a picture of Christian faith this is! It is not that there are no propositional promises; it is not that there are no good and sufficient reasons to know that the things are true. But faith is standing against what is seen at the moment and being willing to be out on the end of a limb in believing God. It is not a leap; it is not a denial of rationality. But it is sitting in this boat out in the middle of Huemoz when most people say it just doesn't make sense. If any generation has ever been in this situation, it is ours. We are surrounded by a total, monolithic consensus that says to us, "It doesn't make sense; it is against the uniformity of cause and effect in a closed system!"

Genesis 7:7 expressly says that there were eight people: "And Noah went in, and his sons, and his wife, and his sons' wives with him, into the ark, because of the waters of the flood." There is an interesting parallel here to the destruction of Sodom and Gomorrah (Christ Himself draws it), in that a whole family was involved in one man's faithfulness. Thus we find that not only Lot was brought out, but those daughters who would listen to his warning in Sodom. Likewise, there is a parallel with the Passover, because when the Jews killed their Passover beast in Egypt, and put the blood on the door, both the firstborn in the family and the firstborn of the animals in the Jewish house were protected from death.

Verses 11 and 12 are a parenthesis covering the whole forty-day period. Verse 11 says, "In the six hundredth year of Noah's life, in the second month, the seventeenth day of the month, the same day were all the fountains of the great deep broken up, and the windows of heaven were opened." Surely this is an insistence on history. The genealogies are not meant to be a chronology, but the Bible dates this event in detail in regard to the central character of the event.

Verse 11 also tells us there were two sources of water which opened up—"the fountains of the great deep" and "the windows [floodgates] of heaven." The water involved was something more than forty days of rain. Verse 11 could cover a wide field of possibilities.

The flood is thus presented as catastrophic, not necessarily in the flow of the uniformity of cause and effect we know now.

Furthermore, 2 Peter 3:3-7 parallels the catastrophic flood to the future catastrophic destruction by fire.

Modern man believes in a uniformity of natural causes in a closed system, and therefore such a thing as a catastrophe in the sense of an abrupt change is not considered possible. John Woodward (d. 1772), the father of the study of fossils, made plain that he held the concept of orderly procedure *and* catastrophe—that is, that there could be great breaks. Just a little over a century ago, Charles Lyell began to insist on uniformity as opposed to catastrophe. The concept of catastrophe in general was thrown away, especially in geology. And with it the creation account and the flood account were rejected.

Today, interestingly enough, geologists are finding it necessary to bring catastrophe (though they usually do not use this term) back into the story, for they have not been able to demonstrate that everything (in the order of events we know today) flows in a simple cause-and-effect line.

We must remember that the Christian position does not deny cause and effect. Rather, as I have stressed in my other books, it was the Christian base that gave a reason to expect cause and effect, orderly procedure. It is the concept of cause and effect in a closed system which is at issue. God has not made Himself a prisoner to the machine of the universe. He can act into it. And consequently, a Christian, whether he is considering a great catastrophe such as the flood or something less dramatic, does not have to choose between a random universe without cause and effect and a universe of cause and effect in a closed system. God is a living God and can work into the machine at any time he wants to.

There are many problems for those who reject the catastrophic. Any events which do not fit the order of events we know today give difficulty. For example, science wrestled with a great mystery involving a curious event that happened about 10,000 B.C. in what is now the Arctic. I am referring here, of course, to the frozen mammoths and other animals. As far as we can tell, for the past 12,000 years this area has been uniformly cold. But, as is obvious from the study of these great mammoths and the other animals that have been found there, up to that time it had been warm. It seems that when the animals froze, they died so quickly that plants of a warmer climate were still in their mouths, neither spit out nor swallowed.

This is a matter of science that has nothing to do with the Bible, and I am not trying to relate it to the flood. I think it probably occurred after the flood. Nevertheless one cannot say that the idea of a great catastrophe is stupid. These great beasts were frozen with such rapidity that the meat was still good to eat when it was found. Scientists who are familiar with deep-freezing have figured out that on the basis of the mass of these huge animals, the temperature would have had to drop within a few hours to -150°F.

The point is that we can discuss such things as the flood and still be giving honest answers to honest questions. There is no reason for a Christian to be defensive just because he is surrounded by men whose framework is the uniformity of natural causes in a closed system and who have arbitrarily given up the notion of catastrophe.

God Shuts the Door

Genesis 7:16 is a striking verse: "And they that went in, went in male and female of all flesh, as God had commanded him: and the LORD shut him in." This is a hard verse, and I am thankful that Noah did not have to shut the door. Knowing that men would soon be drowning all around him, I don't see how Noah could have done it. But he wasn't asked to. He was asked to be faithful— a preacher of righteousness. He was asked to believe God and God's propositional promise. He was asked to build a boat. But after he built the boat, the time came when God shut the door. That was the end of the time of salvation. It was closed because God had closed it at a point in the flow of history.

In the rest of the seventh chapter, then, the destruction comes. God's judgment falls against sin; for God is holy, and there are moral absolutes, and we live in a moral universe. If God does not hate and judge sin, then He is not a holy God, there are no moral absolutes, and we do not live in a moral universe. But the whole Bible resounds with emphasis: God does hate sin and God will judge sin. There comes a day when God shuts the door.

We have already seen the parallel between the judgment that God brought upon the men of Noah's day and the judgment which is to come at the second coming of Christ. Genesis 6:5 and Matthew 24:37, 38 are in many ways parallel passages. Both times are times when man stands in total revolt, times of great wickedness. Men in both days are unaware until destruction overtakes them: "For as in the days that were before the flood they were eating and drinking, marrying and giving in marriage, until the day that Noah entered into the ark, and knew not until the flood came, and took them all away, so shall also the coming of the Son of man be. Then shall two be in the field; the one shall be taken, and the other left. Two women shall be grinding at the mill; the one shall be taken, and the other left" (Matt. 24:38-41). Jesus draws a conclusion from this: "Watch, therefore; for ye know not what day [this is the correct translation] your Lord doth come" (v. 42). And lest we miss the point, Jesus repeats it: "Therefore be ye also ready; for in such an hour as ye think not the Son of man cometh" (v. 44). Jesus is saying you do not know what day (v. 42) and you do not know what hour (v. 44).

This judgment does not come only to the open pagans. One parable indicates that some even within the Church are really not God's people. Jesus concludes, "Watch, therefore; for ye know neither the day nor the hour in which the Son of man cometh" (Matt. 25:13). A time of judgment does arrive. This is the flow of history.

CHAPTER EIGHT

From Noah to Babel to Abraham

As the ark comes to rest, a new era in the history of man begins. Again from a unified beginning (in the family of Noah), the course of man's history runs to divisions—for example, the divisions of Babel.

The Ark Comes to Rest

In Genesis 8:2 we read, "The fountains also of the deep and the windows of heaven were stopped, and the rain from heaven was restrained." That is, both sources of the flood water were shut off. "The ark rested in the seventh month, on the seventeenth day of the month, upon the mountains of Ararat" (v. 4). Ararat, as mentioned in 2 Kings 19:37, Isaiah 37:38 and Jeremiah 51:27, is the land of Armenia. Assyrian documents likewise speak of the kingdom of Ararat. It is not a mythical land by any means, but one that is well known in both past and present history.

Throughout chapters 7 and 8 a very careful chronology is recorded: "This happened on such a day, and that happened on such another day." The warp and woof of space-time history continued to be woven. Thus, there was a time when the ark came to rest and a geographical point at which it happened in the land of Armenia.

Another sort of corroboration for the historical nature of this event occurs in Genesis 8:7-9: "And he sent forth a raven, which went forth to and fro, until the waters were dried up from off the earth. Also he sent forth a dove from him, to see if the waters were abated from off the face of the ground; but the dove found no rest for the sole of her foot, and she returned unto him into the ark, for the waters were on the face of the whole earth: then he put forth his hand, and took her, and pulled her in unto him into the ark." The form of the narrative gives the impression that something really occurred. It doesn't sound like a myth or a story.

There is, for example, a notable difference between the account here and the epics of Homer. In Homer, the characters have little psychological depth. Erich Auerbach in *Mimesis* stresses the contrast between the Bible's presentation and that of Homer. He says that the heroes in Homer's epics arise each morning as if it were the first day that the world began, while the biblical account has a valid, psychological depth which emphasizes historicity. In reading the Bible we do not feel that we are dealing with cardboard situations, and this passage in Genesis 8:7-9 is a good example of this.

We read that Noah put out his hand and "caused the dove to come in unto him in the ark" (this is more accurate than the King James rendering). Then the dove is sent out again: "And he stayed yet other seven days; and again he sent forth the dove out of the ark; and the dove came in to him in the evening; and, lo, in her mouth was an olive leaf plucked off: so Noah knew the waters were abated from off the earth" (vv. 10, 11). This is one of those biblical events that men keep as a symbol even after they quite openly say they no longer believe the Scripture. The dove with an olive branch in its mouth is universally used to signify peace. Incidentally, it is another indication that people are ignorant if they do not know the facts of the Bible, for so many of these symbols assume a comprehension that derives from the Scripture itself.

When Noah had learned that the waters had abated, he "removed the covering of the ark" (v. 13). This is a sharp contrast to Genesis 7:16 where we read that when Noah had entered the ark, "the LORD shut him in." God shut the door, sealed it, and closed the possibility for further entrance. But Noah himself was able to open it when the right moment came. Then God specifically commanded that Noah go out from the ark, and he did so (vv. 15-19).

Noah's Sacrifice

When Noah had come forth from the ark, he made a sacrifice: "And Noah builded an altar unto the LORD; and took of every clean beast, and of every clean fowl, and offered burnt offerings on the altar" (Gen. 8:20). As we have pointed out, we constantly come to situations in the Old Testament, especially in Genesis, where men have knowledge that we would not expect them to have. In other words, God has taught them things that are not recorded in Scripture. We cannot assume, just because a certain knowledge is not recorded in Scripture, that we can make an absolute negative that they did not have such knowledge.

The Life Is in the Blood

It is in chapter 9 that we first find God specifically giving the animals to man for food: "And God blessed Noah and his sons, and said unto them, Be fruitful, and multiply, and replenish the earth. And the fear of you and the dread of you shall be upon every beast of the earth, and upon every fowl of the air, upon all that moveth upon the earth, and upon all the fish of the sea; into your hand are they delivered. Every moving thing that liveth shall be food for you; even as the green herb have I given you all things" (Gen. 9:1-3). At the time of Noah, therefore, God expressly said that meat was open to them for food. It was all right for them to eat the flesh of animals.

But there is a limit: "But flesh with the life thereof, which is the blood thereof, shall ye not eat" (v. 4). Blood, as is shown in the later writings of Moses, specifically in Leviticus, is tied up with the life of the animal and is reserved for atonement. They were commanded to be careful at that point.

Likewise, we see why God commands capital punishment: "And surely your blood of your lives will I require; at the hand of every beast will I require it, and at the hand of man; at the hand of every man's brother will I require the life of man. Whoso sheddeth man's blood, by man shall his blood be shed; for in the image of God made he man" (Gen. 9:5, 6). God commands capital punishment simply because of the unique value of that which the murderer has killed. When a man is murdered, an image-bearer of God is killed. Man continues after the Fall to be in the image of

God, and that makes murder heinous indeed. Modern man who relates himself to the machine and to the animal does not really understand the tremendous stature of man, and therefore he sees no reason why murder is inherently different from any other crime.

Capital punishment was, however, not to be administered carelessly. For example, we could consider God's commands concerning the cities of refuge as the Jews came into a new land and became a state there (Num. 39:9-34; Josh. 20:1-9). A careful distinction was made between premeditated murder and a mistake or an accident. In the case of a clearly demonstrated premeditated murder, a man commits a serious crime because he has personally taken it in his own power to destroy a unique and tremendous being—one that stands as qualitatively and not just quantitatively different from all else.

A New Step in the Covenant Relationship
So far in our study we have covered two steps in the covenant relationship, the covenant promises of God to fallen man. The first, in Genesis 3:15, though not explicitly referred to as a covenant, is certainly a promise. It was a promise made to man concerning the coming solution of the problems which derive from man's rebellion against God. The second step occurs in Genesis 6:18, 19 as God is talking to Noah: "But with thee will I establish my covenant; and thou shalt come into the ark, thou, and thy sons, and thy wife, and thy sons' wives with thee. And of every living thing of all flesh . . ." That is, God is saying, "With you and with every living thing I will establish My covenant." It is worth noting that this is the covenant which God in Isaiah 54:9 refers to as parallel to a further covenant He is making with the Jews. That is, God points back to the covenant with Noah that He made in history in order to stress the certainty of further promises to the Jews that He is making in history at a later time.

Let us examine the Noahic covenant in some detail. First, it is an everlasting covenant. "And the bow shall be in the cloud; and I will look upon it, that I may remember the everlasting covenant between God and every living creature of all flesh that is upon the earth" (Gen. 9:16).

Second, it is established both with Noah and his descendants (vv. 9, 11, 12) and with "every living creature" (vv. 10-12, 16). God is making a covenant not only with man who can understand it, but with the beasts who cannot understand it. Verse 13 general-izes it even further: "I do set my bow in the cloud, and it shall be for a token of a covenant between me and the *earth*."

If we remember what we saw in Romans 8:19-23 concerning God's promises with regard to all creation at the time of the second coming of Christ, God's care of all creation in His covenant here in Genesis will not take us by surprise. It is a part of the total scriptur-al framework.

The sign that marks the covenant with Noah is the rainbow (v. 13). Sometimes it is assumed that the Bible suggests that rainbows had never existed before. There is no reason why this needs to be the case. For one thing, later on there are two other signs given to mark covenant promises—circumcision in the case of Abraham and baptism in the case of Christians. But neither of these two tokens was new. They had been used by many people before and were simply given a Jewish or a Christian meaning—a definite meaning from God Himself. This may, therefore, be true for the rainbow as well. God may simply have given it a new meaning. It is possible, however, that completely new physical conditions ex-isted after the time of the flood and that the rainbow was a new thing. The Bible does not tell us, and either way would fit what these verses say.

Each of the covenant signs is appropriate, the rainbow specifi-cally contrasting with circumcision, the covenant sign given to Abraham. The latter was a sign in man's body and was totally appropriate because man alone was involved; it marked an indi-vidual as one of the covenant people. Here, however, more than man is involved, and so the sign is not given in the body of Noah but in the sky, that which "covers" the whole of that to which the covenant applies—man and the rest of creation as well. Consider the aptness of the sign of baptism in the New Testament. In the Old Testament the father in a special way worshiped for the whole family, and thus the covenant sign of circumcision was appropri-ate. In the New Testament the wall of partition was broken down, and women as well as men now come directly to God, worshiping equally and immediately before him. Hence, the covenant sign of baptism is appropriate.

Often at L'Abri we have long discussions about the fact that man, if he is only rationalistic, cannot really be sure that the sun is going to rise tomorrow morning; all he has is statistics and aver-ages. The Christian can be sure. His certainty is not only based upon the observation of ten million sunrises, but on the total structure that gives a sufficient answer and, in that structure, the promise of God. As long as the earth goes on in the era in which we are, we can be sure of this: the sun will rise and the sun will set and the seasons will come in their natural and proper place. For this is the promise of God: "While the earth remaineth, seedtime and harvest, and cold and heat, and summer and winter, and day and night shall not cease" (Gen. 8:22).

A New Step in the Messianic Prophecy

The first Messianic prophecy is Genesis 3:15, that the seed of the woman shall bruise the serpent's head. A specific woman will be involved, but the promise, as far as its application is concerned, is as wide as the whole human race. Later it becomes clear that this one who will fulfill Genesis 3:15 will come through the line of Seth and not through the line of Cain. And in the present passage, Genesis 9:26, 27, we see a further detailing: "And he said, Blessed be Jehovah, the God of Shem; and let Canaan be his servant. God enlarge Japheth, and let him dwell in the tents of Shem" (ASV). In other words, the promise that was first given to all men is now narrowed to the Semitic peoples. The Semitic peoples are a large group, related by language, living in what we now call the Near East. Yet, these verses in Genesis make plain that though the promise will be fulfilled through the Semitic people, it is actually open to the whole human race. It is simply that the Semitic people will be the channel—the cradle, as it were—the conduit out of which the whole of mankind will have a blessing.

Genealogy, Not Chronology

Chapter 10 again brings us to the genealogies, and as we have said before (in Chapter Seven, pages 86-88), the genealogies themselves make it evident that their purpose is not chronology. For example, Genesis 10:2 speaks of a man bringing forth *countries*: "The sons of Japheth: Gomer, and Magog, and Madai, and Javan, and Tubal, and Meshech, and Tiras." Gomer, Magog, Tubal—these are countries. Verse 4 depicts a man as bringing forth *peoples*. This is clearer in the Hebrew, where the *im* endings indicate the plural. God is saying, "Do you want to know the flow of history? It's the flow of history that is important, and this is it." In verse 7 a man brings forth *places*, because Cush, Seba and Havilah are places, not people. And verse 13 has *im* endings again; peoples are bringing forth peoples, rather than individuals bringing forth individuals. Verse 15 indicates a man bringing forth a place. Finally, in verses 16-18 we are told that sites, etc. came from one man— Canaan. Even though some individuals are named here, and not all are tribes, it certainly seems to me that to take these genealogies as chronology misses the mark. We will continue this study of genealogies in relation to chronology on page 109.

The Generations of the Sons of Noah

In Genesis 10:1 we turn again to the literary form "these are the generations of," this time in relationship to the sons of Noah: "Now these are the generations of the sons of Noah: Shem, Ham, and Japheth: and unto them were sons born after the flood." Beginning with verse 2, again the unimportant is dealt with first and quickly—with sufficient, true propositional truth, but quickly. Then the record turns to the more important line, Shem's, that flows on throughout the rest of the Bible.

We have seen that the literary form "these are the generations of" runs through the entire book of Genesis and makes it a complete unit. Therefore, to treat the book of Genesis as less than a literary unit, to divide Genesis into two halves and read the two halves differently, is totally arbitrary. The only way to escape this is to say that the phrases "these are the generations of" were added by a final redactor (editor), as some of the documentarian higher critics do. But this argument rests on subjective decisions based on naturalistic presuppositions; it demands a final redactor who puts things in an order which fits their theories, their naturalistic position. Here the theory generates the data. The redactor would not be necessary if the weakness of their theory did not require him.

We have just spoken of the second literary form that emphasizes this same thing; namely, that throughout the whole book of Genesis, the factors not central to the main purpose of the book are dealt with first and quickly, and then the record returns to the central theme and treats it at length. These two literary forms together mean that we should approach the whole of Genesis with the expectation that the whole is to be read in the same way, from the first chapter to the last, before and after the time of Abraham. It could properly be said that these two factors make Genesis one of the most unified books in the Bible. In the light of this, anyone desiring to read parts of Genesis with a different form must give a clear reason why he does so. The witness of the New

Testament makes this doubly certain: In every one of its references to any part of Genesis, it takes the material to be normal space-time history, down to the small data. It always deals with the events in normal, straightforward, literary form.

We come in Genesis 10:21 and 11:10 to the line of Shem, because his is the important line. At 10:25 we read: "And unto Eber were born two sons: the name of the one was Peleg; for in his days was the earth divided." This may locate for us in the line of Shem the time when the division at the tower of Babel took place. Verse 32 sums up the flow lines from the three sons of Noah: "These are the families of the sons of Noah, after their generations, in their nations: and by these were the nations divided in the earth after the flood." This verse and Genesis 9:19 indicate that the entire human race as it now stands came specifically from the three sons of Noah.

Babel

The next stage in the flow of history is an interesting and important event. It occurs in a place that is clearly delineated—the land of Shinar, which is Babylonia in its widest sense. Genesis 11:1 reads: "And the whole earth was of one language, and of one speech." In the flow of history, language was one. There was a common language among the descendants of Noah.

This isn't surprising, considering the tenacity with which men hold onto language. In Switzerland, for example, there are four languages and there is a language group clinging firmly to each one. Within one of them, the Romansh, there are about 60,000 people speaking two dialects, and this situation could continue practically forever. Therefore, that men with a common origin are speaking one language is to be expected.

Verse 4 makes what might be called the first public declaration of humanism: "And they said, Go to, let us build us a city and a tower, whose top may reach unto heaven; and let us make us a name, lest we be scattered abroad upon the face of the whole earth." We have already found this sort of humanism in the family of Cain, but what a strong humanistic statement this is! *Let's make a name for ourselves,* so that *we* can maintain a human unity as *we* achieve social stability.

In verse 7 God acts into this situation: "Come, let us [note the communication among members of the Trinity] go down, and there confound their language, that they may not understand one another's speech" (ASV). The basic confusion among people is expressly stated to be language—not the color of skin, not race, not nation. Language is the key to the divisions of the peoples of the world.

The Bible indicates here, as it does constantly in the early chapters of Genesis, that all the divisions of the whole world are a result of sin and the righteous judgment of God. Men said, Let us make a name for ourselves lest we be scattered. This was an attempt to make a unity on their own basis. But "the LORD scattered them abroad from there upon the face of all the earth" (v. 8). And this He did on the basis of their own speech.

Thus another division has emerged—not just one between man and God, man and himself, man and man, man and nature, and nature and nature, but also between the men of the earth in their nations with implications that reach out into racial and cultural divisions, linked to linguistic differences. And all of them are rooted in the same source—the sin of man. Here at the tower, and always, man seeks to be autonomous.

The word *Babel* is interesting because it is given two different meanings. Genesis 11:9 says: "Therefore is the name of it called Babel, because the LORD did there confound the language of all the earth." In Hebrew the word *Babel* means "confusion." The Babylonians themselves used the word to mean "the gate of God." So the Babylonians said, "We are the gate of God," and God said, "No, you are confusion." Throughout Scripture, right up to the book of Revelation, the concept of Babylon stands crucial, Babylon saying, "We are the gate of God," and the Bible answering, "No, this is the place where the basic confusion of language occurred. You are confusion." Our own word *Babylon* is simply the word *Babel* with a Greek ending.

The Generations of Shem

Genesis 11:10 takes up the generations of Shem as the Bible carries us still further along in the general flow of history. Here again we need to deal with the problem of genealogy and chronology. There are a number of things to notice.

First, in the Septuagint (the Greek translation of the Old Testament dating before the time of Christ) an extra name (Kainan) is recorded in verse 12. Kainan is stated to have lived 130 years, the phraseology fitting into exactly the same form as the other names. The intriguing thing (this is purely speculative) is that if this name does belong here, then this genealogy contains ten steps, the same number as the genealogy of the prediluvians in Genesis 5. One wonders, therefore, if this is a parallel to the genealogy of Christ in Matthew 1, where names are left out and then it is stated that there are fourteen generations from Abraham to David, and fourteen generations from David to Babylonian captivity, and fourteen generations from the Babylonian captivity to Christ (Matt. 1:17).

People often ask how Genesis 11:10ff. could not be a chronology with all the detail it contains, for example, in verses 12, 13: "And Arphaxad lived five and thirty years, and begat Salah: And Arphaxed lived after he begat Salah four hundred and three years, and begat sons and daughters."

In Matthew 1:8, as I have pointed out, there is a tremendous jump in the genealogy. There could have been no mistake involved in making this jump, because the people who recorded these things knew the genealogies very well. Matthew 1:8 reads: "And Asa begat Jehoshaphat; and Jehoshaphat begat Joram; and Joram begat Uzziah" (ASV). But we saw, by comparing this to 1 Chronicles 3:11, 12, that Uzziah's father, grandfather, and great-grandfather are omitted in Matthew's genealogy. So there is a lengthy break here. Therefore, what this passage in Matthew is really saying is: When Joram was a certain unnamed number of years old, he begat *someone who led to* Uzziah. And then, after Joram begat that unnamed individual, Joram lived a certain number of years and died.

But for the sake of the illustration let's be a little more imaginative and read it like this: "When Joram was thirty years old, he begat *someone who led to* Uzziah, and then Joram lived a certain number of years, had other children, and died." That is what this portion of Matthew 1:8 means. It does not state the number of years, but it does give us the form. And this is precisely the form we find throughout Genesis 11. In other words, the word "begat" in Genesis 11 does not require a first-generation father-son relationship. It can mean, *fathered someone who led to*. Adding this phrase to the genealogy in Genesis 11 would not change the situation at all. For example, if you added such a phrase to Genesis 11:14, 15, then you would have exactly the same situation as in Matthew 1:8, because it would simply say that Salah begat *someone who led to* Eber. That is precisely what Matthew 1:8 says about Joram and Uzziah. Consequently there is no reason to let Genesis

11 change our conclusion that the genealogies do not constitute a chronology.

People have asked why the details are added. The best answer that has been given, I think, is simply that they form a parallel with the prediluvians where the ending of the form was *and he died.* The present passage doesn't say *and he died,* but it seems to involve the same mentality. The details are given, *and he lived so many years,* and then of course he died. The important names were the ones that were given, for they show the line.

When we realize that these genealogies give no guidance as to dating, we can understand why Professor B. B. Warfield said, "It is to theology, as such, a matter of entire indifference how long man has existed on earth."

In the flow of history in Genesis 1—11, therefore, I feel there really is no final discussion possible concerning dating. On the Bible's side there are the questions we have just considered, and on modern science's side there are certainly many questions as to whether science's dating systems are accurate. As I said in regard to the use of the Hebrew word "day" in Genesis 1, it is not that we have to accept the concept of the long periods of time modern science postulates, but rather that there are really no clearly defined terms upon which at this time to base a final conclusion.

The First Correlation with Secular History

In Genesis 11:26 we come to an entirely new situation, because here there is a reference to the man Abraham to whom we can assign a specific date. We move from biblical history that is not open to correlation with secular history to biblical history that is open to such correlation. This does not imply that what has preceded is any less historic than what is recorded from this point on. But with Abraham we can assign an approximate date—2,000 B.C.

In Genesis 11:28 we are told that Abraham came from Ur of the Chaldees. We know a good deal about Ur of the Chaldees at the time when Abraham lived there and before because of the excavation that was done by Sir Charles Leonard Woolley in 1922 and 1934. We know, for example, that these people worshiped the moon goddess, but that they were far advanced in civilization and culture. Abraham was not just some strange wanderer, a Bedouin from the back side of the desert who didn't know anything. The excavations show us that the houses were made of brick and were whitewashed for aesthetic purposes. They stood two stories high.

In the larger houses there were up to ten to twenty rooms. They had wonderfully equipped kitchens, a good plumbing system and sanitation. From the evidence that has been found, some people have thought that perhaps they taught cube root in their schools. The University of Pennsylvania has a cup dating two centuries before the time of Abraham that shows the magnificent workmanship these men were capable of. This cup is so marvelously made that no one today can surpass it, and it indicates the luxury of that place. Woolley's excavation volumes covering the Royal Tomb shows pictures of the same marvelous work in gold and in alabaster as well.

In Genesis 12:1-3 we read: "Now the LORD had said unto Abram, Get thee out of thy country [that is, from this highly cultured place], and from thy kindred, and from thy father's house, unto a land that I will show thee. And I will make of thee a great nation, and I will bless thee, and make thy name great; and thou shalt be a blessing: . . . and in thee shall all families of the earth be blessed." The Apostle Paul, in his letter to the Galatians, quotes from this section of Genesis and carefully ties what he is saying into the promise given there: "Even as Abraham believed God, and it was accounted to him for righteousness. Know ye, therefore, that they who are of faith, the same are the children of Abraham. And the scripture, foreseeing that God would justify the heathen through faith, preached before the gospel unto Abraham, saying, In thee shall all nations be blessed. So then, they who are of faith are blessed with faithful Abraham" (Gal. 3:6-9).

The promises of God, reaching back to Genesis 3:15, are coming by the time of Abraham into an even more clearly delineated area. The solution, which will be appropriate to the real dilemma of man and will take care of the consequence of guilt before a holy God who exists, will come through Abraham. After Abraham the flow of history goes on, and the promise through the Old Testament continues to become clearer. We come finally to that last prophet of the Old Testament line, John the Baptist, who, when Jesus came and the moment of fulfillment was at hand, said, "Behold the Lamb of God, who taketh away the sin of the world" (John 1:29).

The Flow of History: The Significance of Man
Thus the flow of history continues. History comes from someplace. History is going someplace. We are not born without a

background. And there is a solution to the dilemma of man in the midst of history. What a contrast to modern man who has come to the awful conclusion that history isn't headed anywhere simply because he doesn't know that the history in Genesis 1—11 is true! But that goes for all of us. We too must listen, if we are to understand.

Many events happened before we were born, and many others that we cannot remember occurred in our early life. If we are to know about them, our parents or others must tell us. A multitude of things which occurred before my time and which are personally important to me, I must learn from others. History is involved— things which really happened, but which I must be told by another. It is exactly the same with the whole human race.

Historical knowledge is extending back further and further as we find older writing and as our excavations and our understanding of the artifacts increases. Secular history can tell us much about our past as a human race, and therefore our own place in it. But no matter how much writing we turn up and translate, no matter how many excavations we make and how many artifacts we study, secular history has not unearthed a clue to help explain the final *why* of what we find.

All the way back to the dawn of our studies we find man still being man. Wherever we turn—to the caves in the Pyrenees, to the Sumerians, and further back to the Neanderthal man burying his dead in flower petals—it makes no difference: everywhere men show by their art and their acts that they observed themselves to be unique. And they were unique, unique as men in the midst of non-men. And yet they were as flawed with the dilemma of man, divisions of all kinds, as we are today.

So, just as a child needs to be told something of his personal history, mankind needs to be told of its history. Unless we are told about our beginnings, which secular study cannot trace, we cannot make sense of our present history. Twentieth-century man is looking at something—himself and the facts of history. He knows that something is really there, but he doesn't know what. This is exactly what Genesis 1—11 tells him. These chapters give the history which comes before anything secular historians have been able to ascertain, and it is that presecular history which gives meaning to man's present history. Imagine a little child who hasn't yet been told that he is indeed the legitimate heir to the throne. He lives in pauper's rags. Then somebody comes and tells him his previous history, and he takes his rightful place. It is exactly this that we need. And it is exactly this that the history of Genesis 1—11 gives. It sets in perspective all the history we now have in our secular study.

Some people assume that one can spiritualize the history of the first eleven chapters of Genesis and it will make no difference. They assume that they can weaken the propositional nature of these chapters where they speak of history and the cosmos, and that nothing will change.[1] But everything changes. These chapters tell us the *why* of all history man knows through his studies, including the why of each man's personal history. For this, Genesis 1—11 is more important than anything else one could have.

In these chapters we learn of the historic, space-time creation out of nothing; the creation of man in God's image; a real, historic, space-time, moral Fall; and the understanding of the present abnormality in the divisions that exist between God and man, man and himself, man and man, man and nature, and nature and nature. These chapters also tell us the flow of the promise God made from the beginning concerning the solution to these divisions. This is what Genesis 1—11 gives us, and it is climatic. Naturalistic, rationalistic history only sees the results. If I am to understand the world as it is and myself as I am, I must know the flow of history given in these chapters. Take this away, and the flow of the rest of history collapses.

If a man attributes a wrong cause to the dilemma and divisions of men, he will never come up with the right answer, no matter how good a will he has. Man as he stands since the Fall is not normal, and consequently the solution must be appropriate to what we know to be the cause of his problems and his dilemma. A mere physical solution is inadequate, because man's dilemma is not physical. Nor can it be metaphysical, because the problem of man, as we know it in Genesis 1—11, is not primarily metaphysical. The problem of man is moral, for by choice he stands in rebellion against God. And any appropriate solution must fill this moral need.

He who is the seed of the woman has bruised the serpent's head. But what good is that to us if we will not listen? If we won't listen, we won't understand.

NO FINAL CONFLICT

Introduction

It is my conviction that the crucial area of discussion for evangelicalism in the next years will be the Scripture. At stake is whether evangelicalism will remain evangelical.

The issue is whether the Bible is God's verbalized communication to men giving propositional truth where it touches the cosmos and history, or whether it is *only* in some sense "revelational" where it touches matters of religion. The early chapters of Genesis relate to this discussion, but ultimately the question is not (and cannot be) confined to them: the whole Bible is involved.

The attack is coming from two sides: (1) from certain theologians who say that the only material in the Bible that is revelational is that which does not touch upon areas open to empirical research (e.g., history or the cosmos); (2) from scientists who are Christians, but who say that the Bible teaches us little or nothing where it touches on that in which science has an interest. In both cases we are left with the Bible as an authority only in religious matters.

Philosophically and theologically these two are really the same, but because they use different conceptual frameworks and different language systems (that is, theological or scientific ones), both must be understood. However, both are the same in that both involve the victory of the existential methodology. That is, both attempt to hold on to the value system and the meaning system of the Bible while, at the same time, separating the value and meaning systems, as "upper stories," from that which is open to verification and reason and from any need of correlation with the theories of modern science.

I am convinced the result of this discussion will determine the value of the heritage we leave to our children and grandchildren.

To deal with these crucial questions, I bring four things together:

1. The section dealing with the Bible from the speech I gave at the International Congress on World Evangelization, Lausanne, Switzerland, in July 1974.

2. A lecture entitled, "The Freedom and Limitation in Cosmogony as Set by the Bible." (This lecture is a unity, but to make convenient chapter lengths I have divided it into two portions—Chapters 2 and 3.) I have worked on this material for many years and gave it for the first time at the L'Abri Ashburnham Conference in England in September 1974. It deals with the *possibilities* open to us where the Bible touches science in the first chapters of Genesis—that is, the possibilities that exist if we hold to the historic Christian view that both the Old and New Testaments in their entirety are the written Word of God without error in all that they affirm about history and science as well as about religious matters.

This lecture does *not* set forth final conclusions. Instead, it deals with the circle within which we have freedom to work as we hold what evangelicalism has historically held about the Bible. In passing, I would also say I am convinced that what evangelicalism has held about the Bible is what the Bible teaches about itself and what the Church through the ages has understood and taught about the Bible.

In the original volume, *No Final Conflict,* there was a chapter restating the studies in *Genesis in Space and Time* regarding the genealogies in the book of Genesis. This is omitted here as it is contained in Chapters 7 and 8 of *Genesis in Space and Time.*

Genesis in Space and Time and *No Final Conflict* should be read, and studied, as a unity.

3. Two long and important footnotes in the original volume, *Genesis in Space and Time.* I fear these were largely lost because they were used as footnotes rather than included in the text.

4. A portion of a talk I gave in Washington, D.C., on February 25, 1976 to the Joint Convention of the National Association of Evangelicals and the National Religious Broadcasters.

Bringing these four studies together in one volume, where they may be considered as a unit, has, I am convinced, considerable importance for present, and ongoing, crucial discussion.

CHAPTER ONE

The Issue at Stake

We must say that if evangelicals are to be evangelicals, we must not compromise our view of Scripture. There is no use in evangelicalism seeming to get larger and larger, if at the same time appreciable parts of evangelicalism are getting soft at that which is the central core—namely, the Scriptures.

We must say with sadness that in some places, seminaries, institutions and individuals who are known as evangelical no longer hold to a full view of Scripture. The issue is clear: is the Bible truth and without error wherever it speaks, including where it touches history and the cosmos, or is it only in some sense revelational where it touches religious subjects? That is the issue.

The heart of neo-orthodox existential theology is that the Bible gives us a quarry out of which to have religious experience, but that the Bible contains mistakes where it touches that which is verifiable—namely, history and science. But unhappily we must say that in some circles this concept now has come into some of that which is called evangelicalism. In short, in these circles the neo-orthodox existential theology is being taught under the name of evangelicalism.

The issue is whether the Bible gives propositional truth (that is, truth that may be stated in propositions) where it touches history and the cosmos, and this all the way back to pre-Abrahamic history, all the way back to the first eleven chapters of Genesis, or whether instead of that it is only meaningful where it touches that which is considered religious. T. H. Huxley, the biologist, the friend of Darwin, the grandfather of Aldous and Julian Huxley, wrote in 1890 that he visualized the day not far hence in which faith would be separated from all fact, and especially all pre-Abrahamic history, and that faith would then go on triumphant forever. This is an amazing quote for 1890, before the birth of existential philosophy or existential theology. He indeed foresaw something clearly. I am sure that he and his friends considered this some kind of a joke, because they would have understood well that if faith is separated from fact and specifically pre-Abrahamic, space-time history, it's only another form of what we today call a trip.

But unhappily, it is not only the avowedly neo-orthodox existential theologians who now hold that which T. H. Huxley foresaw, but some who call themselves evangelicals as well. This may come from the theological side in saying that not all the Bible is revelational, or it may come from the scientific side in saying that the Bible teaches little or nothing when it speaks of the cosmos.

Martin Luther said, "If I profess with the loudest voice and clearest exposition every portion of the truth of God except precisely that little point which the world and the Devil are at that moment attacking, I am not confessing Christ, however boldly I may be professing Christ. Where the battle rages, there the loyalty of the soldier is proved, and to be steady on all the battle front besides, is merely flight and disgrace if he flinches at that point."

In our day that point is the question of Scripture. Holding to a strong view of Scripture or not holding to it is the watershed of the evangelical world.

We must say most lovingly but clearly: evangelicalism is not consistently evangelical unless there is a line drawn between those who take a full view of Scripture and those who do not.

CHAPTER TWO

The Unity of the Book of Genesis

If we try to separate the religious passages in the book of Genesis from those which touch on history and the cosmos, the religious passages are relegated to an upper-story situation. They have been removed from any connection to space-time verification, and that means no historical or scientific study can refute them. But it also follows that no studies can verify them. In short, there is no reason to accept the upper-story religious things either. The upper-story religious things only become a quarry out of which to have our own personal subjective, existential, religious experience. There is no reason, then, to think of the religious things as being other than in one's own head.

It should be noted in studying the book of Genesis that there is no literary distinction between the sections dealing with history and the sections dealing with the cosmos, on the one hand, and religious subjects, on the other hand. Further, as we shall see later, the New Testament takes the Old Testament as history at the most crucial point of affirming that Adam and Eve are historic characters.

What I quoted in Chapter 1 from T. H. Huxley applies at specifically this place. J. S. Bezzant, an old-fashioned liberal at Cambridge University, in *Objections to Christian Belief* also puts his finger on the problem of those who separate the portions in Genesis and in the Bible as a whole that speak of history and the cosmos from those that speak of religious matters. In general, Bezzant speaks against historic Christianity itself, but here he suddenly swings around and speaks to neo-orthodoxy. And he says this: "When I am told that it is precisely its immunity from proof which secures the Christian proclamation from the charge of being mythological, I reply that immunity from proof can 'secure' nothing whatever except immunity from proof, and call nonsense by its name." The neo-orthodox position is that the Bible contains mistakes in the areas of history and science, but we are to believe it anyway in the religious areas, that somehow a "religious word" breaks forth from it. The result is that religious things become "truth" inside of one's head—just as the drug experience or the Eastern religious experience is "truth" inside of one's head.

Further, it means that the next generation of Christians will have the ground completely swept from under them. It is my observation that those who are taught a weakened view of the book of Genesis by their professors almost always carry it further into the whole Bible and are left really shaken as far as any real basis for their Christianity is concerned. And there is a reason for being shaken, for there is no reason to keep what the Bible says religiously if we have put it in an upper story and thrown away that of which the Bible speaks when it touches history and the cosmos.

God could have given us the religious truths which He sets forth in the Bible in a theological outline the way some theologians have set forth theological outlines. But instead of this, he gave us religious truths in a book of history and a book that touches on the cosmos as well. What sense does it make for God to give us true religious truths and at the same time place them in a book that is wrong when it touches history and the cosmos?

As we consider the way *the Bible itself sets forth these matters,* our thesis is that the Bible, including the first eleven chapters of Genesis, sets forth propositional truth, both where it touches history and the cosmos and where it touches religious matters.

Because almost everyone accepts that the second half of Genesis—namely, from Abraham on—is historic, it is important to consider the indications that the whole book of Genesis is a unit.

The Internal Argument

The argument for the unity of the book of Genesis falls into two parts, the internal and the external. The former, the internal, itself falls into two parts. The first of these is the literary unity in the entire book of Genesis exhibited by the *toledoths*, or what is translated in the King James Version as "these are the generations of." P. J. Wiseman in 1936 pointed out (and he may be correct in this) that this phrase falls at the end of the section preceding it rather than at the beginning of the section which follows. The important thing is that this phrase continues uniformly throughout the whole book of Genesis, thus indicating unity.

In Genesis 2:4 we read, "These are the generations of the heavens and of the earth. . . ." If we take Wiseman's position, we would consider this the summing up of what occurs from Genesis 1:1 through 2:3. In 5:1 we read, "This is the book of the generations of Adam." In 6:9, "These are the generations of Noah. . . ." In 10:1, "Now these are the generations of the sons of Noah: Shem, Ham, and Japheth. . . ." In 11:10, "These are the generations of Shem. . . ." In 11:27, "Now these are the generations of Terah. . . ." In 25:12, "Now these are the generations of Ishmael. . . ." In 25:19, "And these are the generations of Isaac. . . ." In 36:1, "Now these are the generations of Esau. . . ." In 36:9, "And these are the generations of Esau. . . ." In 37:2, "These are the generations of Jacob. . . ." In the first eleven chapters of Genesis this phrase is repeated six times, and after chapter eleven, it is repeated five times—almost an equal division.

The second internal indication of unity in the book of Genesis is a rather unique literary form that is used throughout: namely, the unimportant subjects are always dealt with first, then the important subjects carry on. The unimportant subjects are given tersely, and then the central matter flows on at length. This literary form is uniform throughout the whole book of Genesis. We can consider, as an example, those places where an unimportant son is dealt with quickly and then an important son is dealt with in detail. And the subsequent movement of biblical history flows on from the important son.

Considering these two factors together, we have a strong internal indication of the unity of the entire book of Genesis. And since the second half is accepted as history, there is no reason to approach the first half on any other basis.

The External Argument
The second reason for taking the entire book of Genesis as historic is the external argument. The case may be put simply and concisely: Absolutely every place where the New Testament refers to the first half of Genesis, the New Testament assumes (and many times affirms) that Genesis is history and that it is to be read in normal fashion, with the common use of the words and syntax.

To the best of my knowledge, the following passages are exhaustive, in the sense that they are all those in the New Testament which refer to the first half of Genesis.

We read in Matthew 19:4, 5—"(Jesus) answered and said unto them, Have ye not read that he who made them at the beginning, made them male and female; and said, For this cause shall a man leave father and mother, and shall cleave to his wife, and they twain shall be one flesh?" Here Jesus clearly gives a normal reading to the text and treats it as an historic statement. It is interesting that he ties together Genesis 1 and Genesis 2 by quoting from Genesis 1 in Matthew 19:4 and from Genesis 2 in 19:5.

In Luke 3:38 the genealogy of Christ includes, "who was the son of Enos, who was the son of Seth, who was the son of Adam, who was the son of God." This genealogy begins in 3:23 with those characters who are unquestionably historic: "And Jesus himself began to be about thirty years of age, being (as was supposed) the son of Joseph, who was the son of Heli . . ." and so on, and so on, and so on. After reciting a list of Old Testament characters, including David and Abraham, this genealogy concludes with the mention of Enos, Seth and Adam who, like the other characters, are clearly taken to be historic.

In Romans 5:12 we read, "Wherefore, as by one man sin entered into the world, and death by sin, and so death passed upon all men, for all have sinned." In this verse is the affirmation that Adam was a real man. Verse 14 teaches, "Nevertheless, death reigned from Adam to Moses. . . ." So here the historicity of Adam is affirmed to be equal to the historicity of Moses. And verse 15 says, "But not as the offense, so also is the free gift. For if through the offense of one many are dead, much more the grace of God, and the gift by grace, which is by one man, Jesus Christ, hath abounded unto many." Here the historicity of Adam is affirmed to be equal to the historicity of Christ.

In 1 Corinthians 6:16 Paul asks, "What? Know ye not that he

who is joined to an harlot is one body? For two, saith he, shall be one flesh." Paul, referring back to Genesis 2:24, links the historic reality of a man being joined to a prostitute to the historic reality to which the Old Testament refers—namely, the relationship of Adam and Eve.

1 Corinthians 11:8 says, "For the man is not of the woman, but the woman of the man." This statement is crucial because it affirms as a historic statement the fact that Adam came first and Eve came from Adam.

1 Corinthians 11:9 continues, "Neither was the man created for the woman, but the woman for the man." Paul again refers to the historic fact that after Adam was created, God created Eve for Adam.

1 Corinthians 11:12 adds, "For as the woman is of the man, even so is the man also by the woman; but all things of God." This strikes me as an intriguing statement, for the historicity of the birth of every one of us is affirmed to be parallel to the historicity of Eve coming from Adam, as told in the book of Genesis.

1 Corinthians 15:21 states, "For since by man came death, by man came also the resurrection of the dead." Paul affirms a parallel between the historicity of Christ, specifically at the time of Christ's resurrection, and the historicity of Adam's rebellion.

1 Corinthians 15:22 continues, "For as in Adam all die, even so in Christ shall all be made alive."

1 Corinthians 15:45 tells us, "And so it is written, The first man, Adam, was made a living soul." Here the didactic statement that Adam was the first man is affirmed.

2 Corinthians 11:3 says, "But I fear, lest by any means, as the serpent beguiled Eve through his subtilty, so your minds should be corrupted from the simplicity that is in Christ." The historicity of Eve's temptation by the serpent is paralleled to our temptations in space-time history.

Ephesians 5:31 states, "For this cause shall a man leave his father and mother, and shall be joined unto his wife, and they two shall be one flesh." This parallels what Jesus says in Matthew.

We read in 1 Timothy 2:13, 14, "For Adam was first formed, then Eve. And Adam was not deceived, but the woman, being deceived, was in the transgression." These are further affirmations of the historic fact that Eve was taken from Adam and the historic fact that Eve was the one who first sinned.

The Bible also affirms the historicity of Cain and Abel. First John 3:12 says, "Not as Cain, who was of that wicked one, and slew his brother." And Jude 11 says, "Woe unto them! For they have gone in the way of Cain, and ran greedily after the error of Balaam for reward, and perished in the gainsaying of Korah." Here it is affirmed that Cain is equally historic as these other men.

It is important for us, having looked at the New Testament references to the first half of Genesis, to notice that Genesis itself emphasizes strongly that Adam was a historic character. We read in Genesis 4:1, "And Adam knew Eve his wife; and she conceived, and bore Cain, and said, I have gotten a man from the LORD." This verse is meaningless unless both Adam and Eve, as well as the birth of the child, are taken to be historic.

Genesis 4:25, 26 has similar content: "And Adam knew his wife again; and she bore a son, and called his name Seth. For God, said she, hath appointed me another seed instead of Abel, whom Cain slew. And to Seth, to him also there was born a son; and he called his name Enos: then began men to call upon the name of the LORD." Again it is impossible to take this in any way except emphasizing a historic space-time event.

Genesis 5:5 is striking in this regard: "And all the days that Adam lived were nine hundred and thirty years: and he died." The phrase "and he died" is meaningless except in the context of space-time history. And of course the phrase "and he died" declares Adam to be as historic as those other men whose deaths are named one after another in this chapter.

It is clear that the Israelites took these early passages of Genesis to be historic. Jeremiah 27:5 reads, "I have made the earth, the man and the beast that are upon the ground, by my great power and by my outstretched arm, and have given it unto whom it seemed meet unto me." In 27:6 this statement about creation is made parallel to the historicity of Nebuchadnezzar.

Psalm 136 describes in detail the creation as it is portrayed in Genesis, and then parallels this description to the historic events in Egypt and the events on the east bank of the Jordan as the Jews marched toward Palestine.

In the light of both the internal and external evidence, it seems absolute that both the Old and New Testaments assume that we will read the book of Genesis as a total unity.

And both the Old and New Testaments affirm that the first half of Genesis is space-time history.

"The Bible Is Not a Scientific Textbook"

There is no reason, therefore, to consider science free from the propositions set forth in the Scripture. We often hear the statement, "The Bible is not a scientific textbook." Should we say this or not? It depends on what we mean.

Years ago, before I heard anyone else use this phrase, I used it, but I meant by it that we must remember what the central purpose of the Bible is. The central purpose of the Bible is to give us what fallen man needs to know between the Fall and the second coming of Christ. This is the theme of the book and is dealt with with great intensity and great uniformity throughout the Bible. It seems to me that everything else is secondary to this and is to be seen in reference to this central theme.

For example, the Bible is not a book of angelology. So there is a lot we do not know about angels. This does not mean that we do not know a good deal about angels from the Bible, but we do not have a comprehensive statement about them. The Bible teaches about angels in reference to the central theme.

I would say the same thing about scientific matters. The Bible is not a scientific textbook—in the sense that science is not its central theme, and we do not have a comprehensive statement about the cosmos. But the Bible tells us much about the cosmos in reference to the central theme. In Genesis 1 we have the statement of the creation of the cosmos, and thus as we come to Genesis 2 and the central focus is placed upon man, we can understand man's setting.

"The Bible is not a scientific textbook" is true in the sense in which we have just spoken. But many people today use the statement in a different way—that is, to say that the Bible does not affirm anything about that in which science has an interest. When the statement is used to mean this, it must be totally rejected. The Bible does give affirmations about that in which science has an interest.

God has given four revelations to man. The first two are general revelation, the second two special revelation. The general revelations are, first, the universe and its form, and second, man and his "mannishness." It should be noted that Paul stresses both of these in Romans 1. The two special revelations are the verbalized communication from God to man in the Bible, and second the revelation of God in Christ. Rightly understood, these four revelations will always compose one revelation.

When we face apparent problems between present scientific theories and the teaching of the Bible, the first rule is not to panic, as though scientific theory is always right. The history of science, including science in our own day, has often seen great dogmatism about theories which later have been discarded. Thus there is no inherent reason why a current scientific theory should immediately be accepted. And there is no inherent reason why a Christian should be put in a panic because the current scientific theory is opposite to what is taught in the Bible.

When we come to a problem, we should take time as educated people to reconsider both the special and general revelations; that is, we should take time to think through the question. There is a tendency among many today to consider that the scientific truth will always be more true. This we must reject. We must take ample time, and sometimes this will mean a long time, to consider whether the apparent clash between science and revelation means that the theory set forth by science is wrong or whether we must reconsider what we thought the Bible says.

The Bible does not give us exhaustive truth about the things of the cosmos, and therefore science has a real function. Also, science, as a study of general revelation, has shown us things that have caused us to understand the Bible better. The outstanding illustration of this is in the various archaeological discoveries in the Near East.

CHAPTER THREE

The Freedom and Limitation in Cosmogony as Set by the Bible

We come now to the possible freedoms which the Bible gives us as we consider the cosmos. I will name seven. I am not saying that any of these points will ultimately prove to be the case. I simply want to point out what freedoms the Scripture gives us as we consider what the general revelation is saying about cosmogony.

In *Genesis in Space and Time,* Chapters 7 and 8, I consider the question of the genealogies in Genesis. The fact that the genealogies are not chronologies gives us a definite freedom in regard to dating; but this is different from the *possible* freedoms I speak of in the present chapter. In the present chapter I am speaking of freedoms which *may* be possible, and nothing beyond that.

1. There is a possibility that *God created a "grown-up" universe.* For example, Adam, the first night he existed, might have seen the light of the furthest stars without waiting for long light years to pass before they could be seen.

To this possibility, we must quickly add one note. This does not mean that God is capricious. And surely it does not imply, and I would totally reject, the concept Bishop Samuel Wilberforce suggested at Oxford in Darwin's time: that God created the fossils in the earth in order to fool fools. This is totally out of character with the God of the Bible.

However, just because it was stated so horribly in the days of Darwin is no reason not to suggest that God may have in some sense and in some areas created a grown-up universe. One could ask, for example, whether the trees when they were created had rings.

It should be noted that if God created a grown-up universe, this would throw off those who extend the cause-and-effect universe as it is now backwards to the beginning, as though the beginning must be uniform with that which is the case now.

2. There is a possibility that there is a break between verses 1 and 2, or verses 2 and 3, of Genesis 1, and that from that point on *the Bible is speaking of a reforming of a partially disordered creation rather than the original creation.* This has often been related to Satan's fall. If this were so, it would give more time, although it seems to me that since the genealogies were not meant to be chronologies there is no problem of needing time.

The weakness of this idea as it is sometimes presented as a dogma is that there are no supporting verses for it in the rest of the Bible. It seems to me that the verses often cited really do not refer to it. Therefore, this must be seen as being only a hypothesis. Nevertheless, it does remain a theoretical possibility, and that is all I am setting forth in this list.

2a. I label this point 2a because, though it is not necessarily related to the way possibility 2 is usually presented, yet there is a relationship between it and possibility 2. This idea relates to the writing of C. S. Lewis, especially in his books *Out of the Silent Planet* and *Perelandra.* Lewis sets forth the concept that Satan ruled the earth before the creation of man. Then Satan revolted against God and this caused the earth to be abnormal, to become, as Lewis expressed it, "the silent planet."

Notice what this presents as a possibility. Satan ruled the earth, and, by his revolt, he caused the death of the animals. In other words, the abnormality of the world and specifically the death of the animals came before the fall of Adam. This would, of course, bear on such a subject as dinosaur bones. (I must say in passing that I am not at all convinced it has been proven that the dinosaurs became extinct prior to the advent of man. As one thinks of, for example, the fossilized footsteps of man *in situ* along with the dinosaur tracks in Paluxy, Texas, one can ask whether scientists would not have used this as evidence that man lived at the same time as the dinosaurs, were it not for the fact that it contradicts their own theory.)

While there are no verses to support this view of Lewis', one does find in Isaiah 14:16, 17 something that may bear upon it: "They that see thee shall narrowly look upon thee, and consider thee, saying, Is this the man who made the earth to tremble, who did shake kingdoms, who made the world as a wilderness?" If one takes Isaiah 14 as referring to the fall of Satan as well as to Nebuchadnezzar, then the phrases "who made the earth to tremble" and "who made the world as a wilderness" could possibly refer to Lewis' suggestion. I do not think that tying this into Lewis' position is at all strong, but remember we are only talking about possibilities.

If Lewis' position is the case, then man was put in a prepared garden in a spoiled universe and the statement "have dominion" (Gen. 1:28) takes on added depth. The phrase "and ye shall die" also appears in a different light because it would mean that death already existed. Adam's failure then would have caused an added curse in the areas specifically stated in the Bible itself. The book of Revelation in 16:18 does say, "And there were voices, and thunders, and lightnings; and there was a great earthquake, such as was not since men were upon the earth." This could indicate that there were tremendous actions on the earth prior to the advent of man, which someone might conceivably stretch to apply to Lewis' position.

3. There is a possibility of a *"long day" in Genesis 1*. The only way to determine what the word *day* means in Genesis is to study the way the word is used elsewhere in the Hebrew. If one takes the position that the word *day* refers to a "long day," that is very different from saying that one can make Genesis mean anything one wants it to mean or that Genesis 1 is saying nothing. It is simply a question of what the Hebrew word *day* means.

In studying such questions, it is a rule that one looks for another use of the word by the same author and one as close as possible to the passage being considered. It is therefore significant that in Genesis 2:4 the word *day* covers the entire span of the creation of the heavens and the earth. And in Genesis 5:2 the word *day* is also used as a period of time rather than as a twenty-four-hour span. That text says, "Male and female created he them; and blessed them, and called their name Adam, in the day when they were created." From the first two chapters of Genesis, it seems quite clear that Adam and Eve were not created in the same twenty-four-hour period. It is unfortunate that the *New International Version* does not use the word *day* in these passages. The word used in the Hebrew is the same word used for "day" in Genesis 1.

Of course we can also think of 2 Peter 3:8—"But, beloved, be not ignorant of this one thing, that one day is with the Lord as a thousand years, and a thousand years as one day." This verse perhaps bears on the possibility of a long day, but we cannot in any way base a dogmatic statement on it. A much more important verse is Psalm 90:4—"For a thousand years in thy sight are but as yesterday when it is past, and as a watch in the night." The reason this passage is important is that this psalm is attributed to Moses, and therefore it would have special bearing upon the Genesis passages. Isaiah 2:11 and 17 should also be added here: "The lofty looks of man shall be humbled, and the haughtiness of men shall be bowed down, and the LORD alone shall be exalted in that day." (Verse 17 repeats, "and the LORD alone shall be exalted in that day.") It is apparent that *day* is not a span of twenty-four hours, but a period of time.

To these biblical considerations has to be added the problem which arises from the scientific side, the problem of radiological dating. Scientists accept the uniformity of the emission of radiological material; but they accept this, I think, by faith, in that they have taken what we know about regularity of emission for a very, very short time and have extended it back for billions of years. This is a tremendous projection, especially when one can theoretically imagine things that could change the rate through the years.

Remember we are only speaking of possibilities regarding the length of *day*. But if one did accept the concept of a long day, this would not imply that he would automatically subscribe to the modern scientific concept of an extremely old earth.

If anyone wonders what my own position is, I really am not sure whether the days in Genesis 1 should be taken as twenty-four hours or as periods. It seems to me that from a study of the Bible itself, one could hold either position.

4. There is a possibility that *the flood affected the geological data*. One does not have to go as far as to say that all the geological strata were caused by the flood in order to say that if the flood is what the Bible seems to indicate it was, it would very possibly have caused extensive geological disruption. In this case, there-

fore, certain things about the strata would be the result of the flood, and this would have to be taken into consideration.

5. The fifth possibility turns upon *the use of the word* kinds *in Genesis 1*. For example, Genesis 1:11 says, "And God said, Let the earth bring forth grass, the herb yielding seed, and the fruit tree yielding fruit after its kind. . . ." One must notice that this is the simple Hebrew word for *kind,* and it is not necessarily to be equated with the modern scientific word *species.* It is conceivable, therefore, that there could have been changes beyond little horses becoming big horses. Specifically, it is conceivable that changes could have occurred in the range of the species themselves without conflicting with this word *kind.*

6. The sixth possibility concerns the question of *the death of animals before the Fall.* I am *not* now linking this with C. S. Lewis' exposition. Rather, from the Bible's own presentation one can raise the possibility of the natural death of animals before the Fall. In other words, one can suggest that there is a distinction to be made between animals dying in what I would call the *chase,* killed by others, and animals merely dying. This, of course, would bear upon the fact that there then would be fossils from before the time of the Fall.

If we watch a dog die in a warm chimney corner, there is no struggle. It is like a leaf falling from a tree. The depth psychologists are right, I think, in stressing that animals show no fear of nonbeing, no fear of death. One could think of there being natural cycles for the animals, up to all that does not include man, with death not by the chase and not in agony or fear.

No one is troubled by the thought of a tree dying naturally. Possibility 6 would mean that plants were eaten before the Fall, but that conscious life was not, and there was no cruelty. Nature would not be "red in tooth and claw" prior to the Fall of man.

Isaiah 65:25 bears interestingly upon this. Speaking of the return of Christ, it describes the earth after His coming like this: "The wolf and the lamb shall feed together, and the lion shall eat straw like the bullock, and dust shall be the serpent's meat. *They shall not hurt nor destroy* in all my holy mountain, saith the LORD." Looking over this entire section in Isaiah, one finds no reason to say that there will be no death in that time of Christ's reign upon the earth. But the Bible does say that there will be no cruelty, no death because of the chase.

We should note that 1 Corinthians 15:21 does *not* bear on this discussion. It reads, "For since by man came death, by man came also the resurrection of the dead." It seems to me that this clearly is talking about the death of man and the future resurrection of men from the dead. There is no note in the Bible that animals will be raised from the dead.

Remember, all we are speaking of is that which are bare possibilities.

7. *Only the word* bara *must mean an absolute new beginning.*

There are three places in Genesis 1 where *bara* is used in contrast to two other formulations. The first of these other formulations is the word *made (asah)*. The second formulation is *let (yehi)* such and such come forth—for example, in Genesis 1:3, "And God said, Let there be light." The word *bara* is used in only three places: (1) for the original creation out of nothing, (2) for the creation of conscious life—that is, in contrast to plants, and (3) for the creation of man. As a matter of fact, in Genesis 1:27 the word is repeated three times as though for emphasis: "So God created man in his own image, in the image of God created he him; male and female created he them." It seems possible to consider that there is a distinction between the places where *bara* is used and the places where the more general words *make* and *let* are used.

I list this matter of *bara* as a freedom because in the other places where *bara* is not used, there is a theoretical possibility of a sequence rather than an absolute new beginning.

To conclude this section, I urge you again to remember that I am not saying that any of these positions are my own or that they will prove to be the case. I am simply stating theoretical possibilities as we consider the correlation between what the Bible sets forth about cosmogony and what we can study from general revelation.

Two Limits

Having delineated these seven freedoms, I will now mention two limits that seem to me to be absolute. The first is that the use of the word *bara* insists that at the original creation, at the creation of conscious life, and at the creation of man there was specific discontinuity with what preceded.

One other limitation is that Adam was historic and was the first man, and that Eve was made from Adam. It could not be: male-female-male-female-male-female, and then suddenly Zip!—male-female of man. It would be worthwhile here to read again all the

New Testament references to the early chapters of Genesis found on pages 12-14. Among these it is most important to recognize that 1 Corinthians 11:8 affirms that Eve came from Adam: "For the man is not of the woman, but the woman of the man." First Corinthians 11:12 and 1 Timothy 2:13 also relate to Eve's coming from Adam.

Consequently, what is involved here (as in this whole discussion) is not just the first chapters of Genesis, but the authoritativeness of the New Testament as well, and especially the writings of Paul. If Paul is wrong in this factual statement about Eve's coming from Adam, there is no reason to have certainty in the authority of any New Testament factual statement, including the factual statement that Christ rose physically from the dead. If we say this factual statement about Eve was culturally oriented, then every factual statement of the New Testament can be said to be culturally oriented; and any or all of the factual statements of the New Testament can be dealt with arbitrarily and subjectively. The Bible gives a specific limitation: Adam was created by God, and then Eve was made from Adam by God.

In passing it should be noted that it is not inconsequential that Eve came from Adam; rather, this gives the basis for the absolute unity of the whole human race.

Having set forth these two limitations, I must now say I have never heard anyone holding any form of theistic evolution who follows these two limitations. I think the reason for this is that holding these limitations in any system of theistic evolution would separate the one who holds such an evolutionary theory from the usual evolutionists as completely as holding a totally nonevolutionary theory would. To put that another way, someone affirming these limitations would be as completely separated from those who hold the evolutionary position in its normal form as would someone who did not hold any form of evolution. And this is the reason, I think, it has not been put forward, at least never to the best of my knowledge.

In conclusion, I would make two points. First, even if I were still an agnostic, as once I was, I would not accept the concept of evolution from the molecule to man in an unbroken line. My rejection of this does not turn upon my being a Christian, but comes rather because I think this concept is weak and certainly has not been proven (in any sense of the word *proven*). It is a theory with many unproofs. It has not been demonstrated either theoretically or empirically that time and chance can explain either the universe with its high complexity or man as man. Statistically, Murray Eden of MIT has insisted that it is impossible that the universe and its complexity were produced by pure chance out of chaos in any amount of time that has so far been suggested (see "Heresy in the Halls of Ivy—Mathematicians Question Darwin," in *Scientific Research,* November 1967, pp. 59-66). And equally, no one has demonstrated that man as man could have been brought forth from non-man merely on the basis of time and chance. When this has been tried, it ends by reducing man to non-man and man's aspirations to illusions.

Both Darwinism as it was first presented as the survival of the fittest and neo-Darwinism have been shown to have not only philosophical, but methodological and statistical problems. And trying to make final explanations on the basis of reductionism has now largely been set aside. The concept of an unbroken line from the molecule to man on the basis of time and chance is, it seems to me, very clearly a faith position held by modern rationalistic man. He holds it tenaciously because it is the only thing which he has to give unity to the particulars of knowledge which he has in his hand; and it is all he has to give an illusion of meaning for man in a meaningless universe.

If modern rationalistic man were to give up his theory of evolution in an unbroken line from the molecule to man on the basis of time and chance (and with it the unnecessary but usually held corollary of sociological evolution), he would be left with his bits of knowledge like loose beads scattered on the floor. To put it another way, the evolutionary theory of an unbroken line from the molecule to man on the basis of time and chance is the only frame of reference that modern rationalistic man has; therefore, he holds it in faith.

Second, I do not hold to a concept of theistic evolution, but it must be said that there is a certain possible range of freedom for discussion in the area of cosmogony while bowing to what God has affirmed.

CHAPTER FOUR

No Final Conflict

There may be a difference between the methodology by which we gain knowledge from what God tells us in the Bible and the methodology by which we gain it from scientific study, but this does not lead to a dichotomy as to the facts. In practice, it may not always be possible to correlate the two studies because of the special situation involved; yet if both studies can be adequately pursued, there will be no final conflict.

For example, the tower of Babel: Whether we come at it from biblical knowledge given by God or by scientific study, either way when we are done with our study, the tower of Babel was either there or it was not there. The same thing is true of Adam. Whether we begin with the conceptual apparatus of archaeology and anthropology or whether we begin with the knowledge given us in the Bible, if it were within the realm of science's knowledge to do so, in both cases we would end with knowledge about Adam's bones. Science by its natural limitations cannot know all we know from God in the Bible; but in those cases where science can know, both sources of knowledge arrive at the same point, even if the knowledge is expressed in different terms. And it is important to keep in mind that there is a great difference between

139

saying the same thing in two different symbol systems and actually saying two different exclusive and even incompatible things, but hiding the difference with the two symbol systems. What the Bible teaches where it touches history and the cosmos, and what science teaches where it touches the same areas do not stand in a discontinuity. There indeed must be a place for the study of general revelation (the universe and its form, and man with his "mannishness")—that is, a place for true science. But on the other side, it must be understood that there is no automatic need to accommodate the Bible to the statements of science. There is a tendency for some who are Christians and scientists to always place special revelation (the teaching of the Bible) under the control of general revelation and science, and never or rarely to place general revelation and what science teaches under the control of the Bible's teaching. That is, though they think of that which the Bible teaches as true and that which science teaches as true, in reality they tend to end with the truth of science as more true than the truth of the Bible.

Facts and Brute Facts

Words have become so devalued today that we often have to use cumbersome terms to make what we mean understood. The word *fact* does not necessarily mean anything anymore. *Fact* can just mean upper-story religious truth, and therefore we have to use an awkward term like *brute fact*. In this particular case, we are fortunate because the liberal theologians themselves have at times used the term *brute fact* for what they *do not mean* by facts.

By *brute facts* we do not mean some Cartesian concept of "eternal facts." There are no facts back of God, any more than there are morals or values back of God. There are no autonomous facts which exist regardless of God. But once God created, that which he created had objective reality. And as God created history with space-time significance, that which happens in history also has objective reality.

The historicity of the Fall is a perfect example. The historic Fall is not an interpretation: it is a *brute fact*. There is no room for hermeneutics here, if by hermeneutics we mean explaining away the *brute factness* of the Fall. That there was a Fall is not an upper-story statement—that is, it is not *in this sense* a "theological" or "religious" statement. Rather, it is a historic, space-time, *brute-*

fact, propositional statement. There was time, space-time history, before the Fall, and then man turned from his proper integration point by choice, and in so doing there was *moral* discontinuity; man became abnormal.

In speaking of *facts* and *brute facts,* we are speaking of facts in the space-time sense, that which is open to the normal means of verification and falsification.

This does *not* mean they are then to be taken as sterile facts. These biblical facts are facts in past history, but they have, and should have, meaning in our present existential, moment-by-moment lives.

Furthermore, in speaking of the Bible's statements as propositional truth, we are *not* saying that all communication is on the level of mathematical formula. There can be other levels (for example, figures of speech or the special force of poetry); but there is a *continuity*—a unity, not a *discontinuity*—between these "other levels" and a flow of propositions given in normal syntax and using words in their normal definition, and this is a continuity which reason can deal with.

Take an example outside of the Bible: Shakespeare's communication with his figures of speech is a much richer human communication than is mere mathematical formula. The "other levels" (for example, his figures of speech) add enrichment. Yet, if, as in far-out modern prose and poetry, there are only, or almost only, figures of speech, with no adequate running continuity that can be stated in propositional form using normal syntax and words with normal meanings, no one knows what is being said. As a matter of fact, some modern writers and artists deliberately work this way so that this will be the case. Their work becomes only a quarry for subjective experiences and interpretations inside of the head of the reader or viewer.

The early chapters of Genesis quickly come to this place if they are read other than as in propositional form using normal syntax and words in their normal meaning. As an example, Paramhansa Yogananda did this in his book *Autobiography of Yogi* and most easily turned these chapters into a powerful Hindu tract.

There is a danger of evangelicalism becoming less than evangelical, of its not really holding to the Bible as being without error in all that it affirms. The Bible does affirm certain things in regard to history and the cosmos, just as definitely as it affirms certain religious truths. When there is a separation made between these affirmations, we are then left with the victory of the existential methodology under the name of evangelicalism. Holding to a strong view of Scripture or not holding to it is the watershed of the evangelical world.

CHAPTER FIVE

The Watershed of the Evangelical World

There are two reasons in our day for holding a strong, uncompromising view of Scripture. First, and foremost, this is the only way to be faithful to what the Bible teaches about itself and what Christ teaches about Scripture. This should be reason enough in itself. But today there is a second reason why we should hold a strong uncompromising view of Scripture. There may be hard days ahead of us—for ourselves and for our spiritual and our physical children. And without a strong view of Scripture as a foundation, we will not be ready for the hard days to come.

Christianity is no longer providing the consensus for our society. And Christianity is no longer providing the consensus upon which our law is based. We are in a time when humanism is coming to its natural conclusions in morals, in values, and in law. All that society has today are relative values based upon statistical averages.

Soft days for evangelical Christians are past, and only a strong view of Scripture is sufficient to withstand the pressure of an all-pervasive culture built upon relativistic thinking. We must remember that it was a strong view of the absolutes which the infinite-personal God had given in the Old Testament, the revelation in Christ, and the then growing New Testament which enabled the early Church to withstand the pressure of the Roman Empire.

But evangelicalism today, although growing in numbers as far as the name is concerned, throughout the world and the United States, is not unitedly standing for a strong view of Scripture.

The *existential methodology* has infiltrated that which is called evangelicalism. The existential methodology dominates philosophy, art, music, and general culture such as the novel, poetry and the cinema. It is also the current dominant form of *liberal theology*. What is this? This position is that in the area of reason, the Bible has many mistakes in it. In the area of history and where the Bible touches the cosmos—that is, those places where the Bible touches that which is of interest to science—the Bible has many mistakes. But nevertheless, we can hope for some sort of upper-story religious experience in spite of the fact that the Bible contains mistakes. That is the present dominant form of *liberal theology*.

But unhappily this form of theology is now functioning in many places under the name of evangelicalism. It began a few years ago like this in certain evangelical circles: Where the Bible touches history and the cosmos, there are mistakes. But, nevertheless, it was stressed, we can still continue to hold on to the meaning system, the value system, and the religious things which the Bible teaches. Here are two quotations from men widely separated geographically across the world to show what I mean by the acceptance of the fact that in the area where the reason operates, the Bible contains mistakes. These are men in evangelical circles.

> But there are some today who regard the Bible's plenary and verbal inspiration as insuring its inerrancy not only in its declared intention to recount and interpret God's mighty redemptive acts, but also in any and in all of its incidental statements or aspects of statements that have to do with such nonrevelational matters as geology, meteorology, cosmology, botany, astronomy, geography, etc.

In other words the Bible is divided into two halves. To someone like myself this is all very familiar—in the writings of Jean-Paul Sartre, of Albert Camus, of Martin Heidegger, of Karl Jaspers, and in the case of thousands of modern people who have accepted the existential methodology. This quotation is saying the same thing they would say, but specifically relating this existential methodology to the Bible.

Another quote. This is a translation from another language and a country far off from the United States.

> More problematic in my estimation is the fundamentalist extension of the principle of noncontradictory Scripture to include the historic, geographic, statistical and other biblical statements, which do not touch in every case on the questions of salvation and which belong to the human element of Scripture.

Both of these statements do the same thing. They make a dichotomy. They make a division. They say that there are mistakes in the Bible, but nevertheless we are to keep hold of the religious things. This is the way the existential methodology has come into evangelical circles.

Now look with me at what the Lausanne Covenant says about Scripture.

> We affirm the divine inspiration, truthfulness and authority of both Old and New Testament Scriptures in their entirety as the only written Word of God, without error in all that it affirms, and the only infallible rule of faith and practice.

I ought to say that the little phrase, "without error in all that it affirms" was not a part of my own contribution to the Lausanne Congress. I didn't know that phrase was going to be included in the Covenant until I saw it in its final printed form. But let me speak about why historically it is a proper statement, if the words are dealt with fairly. We are not saying the Bible is without error in the things it does not affirm. And one of the clearest examples, of course, is where the Bible says, "The fool hath said in his heart, there is no God." The Bible does not teach there is no God. The Bible does not affirm that. Furthermore, we are not saying the Bible is without error in all *the projections* which people have made on the basis of the Bible. So that statement, as it appeared in the Lausanne Covenant, is a perfectly proper statement in itself. However, as soon as I saw it in its printed form I knew it was going to be abused. In August 1975, Dr. Billy Graham wrote me as follows: "I was thinking of writing a brief booklet on 'in all that it affirms' which I took to mean the entire Bible. Unfortunately, this statement is being made a loophole by many."

Unhappily, this statement, "in all that it affirms," has indeed been made a loophole by many. How has it been made a loophole? It has been made a loophole through the existential methodology which would say that the Bible affirms the value system and certain religious things set forth in the Bible. But on the basis of the existential methodology these men say in the back of their minds, even as they sign the Covenant, "But the Bible does not affirm without error that which it teaches in the area of history and the cosmos."

Because of the widely accepted existential methodology in certain parts of the evangelical community, the old words *infallibility, inerrancy* and *without error* are meaningless today unless some phrase is added such as: the Bible is without error not only when it speaks of values, the meaning system and religious things, but it is also without error when it speaks of history and the cosmos. If some such phrase is not added, these words today are meaningless. *Infallibility* is used today by men who do not apply it to the whole of Scripture, but only to the meaning system, to the value system and certain religious things, leaving out any place where the Bible speaks of history and the things which would interest science.

Those weakening the Bible in the area of history and where it touches the cosmos do so by saying these things in the Bible are *culturally oriented*. That is, in places where the Bible speaks of history and the cosmos, it only shows forth views held by the culture in the day in which that portion of the Bible was written. For example, when Genesis and Paul affirm, as they clearly do, that Eve came from Adam, this is said to be only borrowed from the general cultural views of the day in which these books were written. Thus not just the first eleven chapters of Genesis, but the New Testament is seen to be relative instead of absolute.

But let us realize that one cannot begin such a process without going still further. These things have gone further among some who still call themselves evangelicals. They have been still trying to hold on to the value system, the meaning system and the religious things given in the Bible, but for them the Bible is only culturally oriented where it speaks of history and the cosmos. Now in the last few years an extension has come to this. Now certain moral absolutes in the area of personal relationships given in the Bible are *also* said to be culturally oriented. I will give you two examples. There could be others.

First, easy divorce and remarriage. What the Bible clearly teaches about the limitations placed upon divorce and remarriage is now put by some evangelicals in the area of cultural orientation.

They say these were just the ideas of that moment when the New Testament was written. What the Bible teaches on these matters is to them only one more culturally oriented thing, and that is all. There are members, elders and ministers in churches known as evangelical who no longer feel bound by what the Scripture affirms concerning this matter. They say that what the Bible teaches in this area is culturally oriented and is not to be taken as an absolute.

The same is true in the area of the clear biblical teaching regarding order in the home and the church. The commands in regard to this order are now also considered culturally oriented by some speakers and writers under the name of evangelical.

In other words, in the last few years the situation has moved from hanging on to the value system, the meaning system and the religious things while saying that what the Bible affirms in regard to history and the cosmos is culturally oriented to the further step of still trying to hold on to the value system, the meaning system and religious things, but now lumping these moral commands along with the things of history and the cosmos as culturally oriented. There is no end to this. The Bible is made to say only that which echoes the surrounding culture at *our* moment of history. *The Bible is bent to the culture instead of the Bible judging our society and culture.*

Once men and women begin to go down the path of the existential methodology under the name of evangelicalism, the Bible is no longer the Word of God without error—each part may be eaten away step by step. When men and women come to this place, what then has the Bible become? It has become what the liberal theologians said it was back in the days of the twenties and the thirties. We are back in the days of a scholar like J. Gresham Machen, who pointed out that the foundation upon which Christianity rests was being destroyed. What is that foundation? It is that the infinite-personal God who exists has not been silent, but has spoken propositional truth in *all* that the Bible teaches—including what it teaches concerning history, concerning the cosmos and in moral absolutes as well as what it teaches concerning religious subjects.

What is the use of evangelicalism seeming to get larger and larger if significant numbers of those under the name of evangelical no longer hold to that which makes evangelicalism evangelical? If this continues, we are not faithful to what the Bible claims for itself and we are not faithful to what Jesus Christ claims for the Scriptures. But also—let us not ever forget—if this continues, we and our children will not be ready for difficult days ahead.

Furthermore, if we acquiesce we will no longer be the redeeming salt for our culture—a culture which is committed to the concept that both morals and laws are only a matter of cultural orientation, of statistical averages. That is the hallmark—the mark of our age. And if we are marked with the same mark, how can we be the redeeming salt to this broken, fragmented generation in which we live?

I would like to state again the last line which dealt with the Scripture in my Lausanne speech. We must say most lovingly but clearly: evangelicalism is not consistently evangelical unless there is a line drawn between those who take a full view of Scripture and those who do not.

We who bear the name evangelical need to be unitedly those who have the same view of Scripture as William Cowper had when he wrote the hymn, "The Spirit Breathes Upon the Word." In contrast to any concept of the Bible being borrowed through cultural orientation, the second verse of that hymn reads:

> A glory gilds the sacred page,
> Majestic, like the sun:
> It gives a light to every age;
> It gives, but borrows none.

Volume Two ● *Book Three*

JOSHUA AND THE FLOW
OF BIBLICAL HISTORY

CHAPTER ONE

Joshua's Preparation

Joshua is an important book for many reasons—for the history it records and for its internal teaching. But what makes the book of Joshua overwhelmingly important is that it stands as a bridge, a link between the Pentateuch (the writings of Moses) and the rest of Scripture. It is crucial for understanding the unity the Pentateuch has with all that follows it, including the New Testament.

The story of the man Joshua begins not in the book of Joshua, but in the book of Exodus. After the Israelites had crossed the Red Sea in their flight from Egypt, they came just a few days later to Rephidim (Ex. 17). There they began to murmur against God; Moses, by God's direction, smote the rock, and God provided water in a miraculous way. Almost immediately after this, the Amalekites came against the Israelites to make war with them, the first battle the Israelites had to fight during their days of march.

At this point Joshua is named for the first time: "And Moses said unto Joshua, Choose us out men, and go out, fight with Amalek" (Ex. 17:9). So we first meet Joshua as the general of the forces of the Lord, a role that would immediately in this setting teach him a lesson—namely, that God will not tolerate the rebellion of men against Himself.

The Amalekites, of course, were not a part of the promise made to Abraham. They were non-Jews—Semitic, but non-Jews. The Amalekites were rebelling against the living God. This action is clearly portrayed as rebellion in Exodus 17:16—"Because the hand of Amalek is against the throne of the LORD [or, Because there is a hand against the throne of Jehovah], therefore hath the LORD sworn, the LORD will have war with Amalek from generation to generation." In other words, the war of Amalek and the Amalekites against the Israelites was not just the surrounding world making war with God's people; the war was a blow against the throne of God. The Amalekites were challenging with the sword God's rule, God's throne, God's rightful place over all the world.

Exodus 17:16 indicates that the Amalekites understood something of the fact that they were fighting not only against the Israelites, but also against the God who stood behind the Israelites. One can question how much knowledge they had, but their actions remind me of twentieth-century men who understand that what they are really fighting against is at least the concept of the Judeo-Christian religion and the culture which was based upon it.

So Joshua is introduced to us as a general in the midst of a warfare which impressed upon him that God will not tolerate the rebellion of men against Himself.

Joshua also learned another important lesson through the conflict with the Amalekites: power is not merely the power of the general and the sword, but power is the power of God. Moses sent Joshua out to fight, while he himself climbed to the top of a hill with the rod of God in his hand—the same rod that he had stretched over the Red Sea until it had rolled back, the same rod that God had used in many of the miracles. The rod had originally been the rod of Moses, but had become the rod of God, a representation of God's power. As the rod was raised, the Israelites prevailed; as it sank, the Amalekites prevailed (Ex. 17:11). This is not to be thought of as magic. God was teaching these people a serious lesson in their first warfare, and no one was to learn it better than Joshua the general. In the midst of battle, is one to fight? Yes. To be a good general? Yes. But when everything is done, the power is to be understood as God's, not man's.

In Exodus 17:14 another note is added: "And the LORD said unto Moses, Write this for a memorial in *the* book. . . ." It seems clear that a definite article is used here. There was a book of God which continued to grow, and this was the Pentateuch itself. What was written in it was what God said should be put there. Early in Joshua's life, therefore, he was in a definite way wrapped up with the *book*. As we shall see, this becomes exceedingly important in the book of Joshua itself.

On Mount Sinai

The next time we see Joshua is in Exodus 24:13: "And Moses rose up, and his minister Joshua; and Moses went up into the mount of God." Immediately before this, these two men had been joined by some others for a very special event: "Then up went Moses, and Aaron, Nadab, and Abihu, and seventy of the elders of Israel; and they saw the God of Israel: and there was under his feet as it were a paved work of a sapphire stone, and as it were the body of heaven in its clearness. And upon the nobles of the children of Israel he laid not his hand; also they saw God, and did eat and drink" (Ex. 24:9-11).

The leaders went partway up the mount, and they ate. Then Joshua apparently went up still further with Moses. In this event were two strong emphases: the first upon *the reality of God,* and the second on *the glory of God.* All the leaders would have perceived this as they ate before him.

The eating before God was not unique. In fact, one of the great things in Scripture is that we eat before God. This is beautiful, because eating is such a lowly activity. It is connected with our body and our bodily functions in a way that hardly anything else is, for what we eat becomes our body. Yet constantly in the Scriptures God's people are brought together to eat in his presence. For instance, the Passover, which was established in Egypt and then at Mount Sinai, was really an eating in the presence of God. So is the Lord's Supper, which took place in the New Testament and continues today. Finally, we are expressly told that at the second coming the marriage supper of the Lamb will take place, and all the redeemed, with resurrection bodies, will eat in the presence of God. Among the many things which are marvelous about this is the very reality of it—the solidness of it. It highlights the fact that the whole man was made by God and is accepted by God.

Another thing is clearly seen in God's preparation of Joshua: Joshua was reminded of the interplay between the seen and the unseen worlds. There is no vast chasm between them; the unseen world is right here. The unseen world is always immediately present, not far-off. Above everything and overshadowing everything is the reality of God in His glory. It undoubtedly stood Joshua in good stead many times in the future for him to understand that God was close at hand, that He is the God who exists and who is "here."

In Exodus 24:17 we read, "And the sight of the glory of the LORD was like devouring fire on the top of the mount in the eyes of the children of Israel." All the children of Israel saw space-time, historic manifestations on the top of Mount Sinai, so that later, after this generation had died, Moses could stand on the plain of Moab and say to those who had been little children when these manifestations occurred, "You saw! You heard!" This is the very opposite of the modern concept of the existential religious leap, for it is woven into a strong space-time fabric.

At the Golden Calf

Joshua is mentioned next at a very sober time, the time of the golden calf (Ex. 32). God said to Moses, "Go down quickly because even while you've been up here on the mount, the people have revolted against Me!" So down came Moses and Joshua from the mountain.

As he came down, "Joshua heard the noise of the people as they shouted, [and] he said unto Moses, There is a noise of war in the camp" (Ex. 32:17). Maybe he heard this with his general's ears, with his mind attuned to battle. But Moses responded, "It has nothing to do with war." It would have been much better if it had been war, for it was something much more serious. "It is not the voice of them who shout for mastery," Moses said. "Neither is it the voice of them who cry for being overcome; but the noise of them that sing do I hear" (v. 18). "Singing," you say. "Well, that's better than war." In this case, though, it was worse. War is not the greatest evil to come upon a people. "And it came to pass, as soon as he came nigh unto the camp, that he saw the calf, and the dancing; and Moses' anger waxed hot, and he cast the tables out of his hands, and brake them beneath [at the foot of] the mount" (v. 19).

Let us visualize Moses' response. He came down from the mountain and into the foothills—the slope at the bottom. He and Joshua saw the golden calf, and Moses immediately smashed the

tablets of stone upon which God had written the Ten Commandments. These were the very tablets upon which God Himself had
written with His finger. God had communicated in verbalized
form and brought His words onto the tablets in the language of
the people. Now Moses had destroyed them.

Imagine how the young man Joshua felt. Moses had left him
and gone beyond. There had been thunder and lightning. Moses
came down and had stone tablets in his hands, and on these tablets
were words which could be read, words which had been placed
there by God Himself. Imagine the emotion! Yet, when the two
men came back into the camp, the people were in total rebellion.
Here Joshua learned another truth: the terribleness of sin, especially among the people of God. This was sobering, and Joshua never
forgot it.

The people made a god that was no god. And as soon as they
had done this, there was a complete moral breakdown. The people
took off their clothes and threw themselves into the same kind of
sexual rite that was practiced by the cultures which surrounded
them. We can think here of the orgy in Schoenberg's opera, *Moses
and Aaron*. Though most of the rest of the opera is not true to the
Scriptures, this part is. There was an orgy at the golden calf. In
this case the moral breakdown was not separated from their
worship, but was properly connected with it, because they were
worshiping a god that was no god. As Paul points out in Romans
1, turning away from the living God always leads to moral breakdown. It has in our day. The last few generations have turned
away from the living God, and now we are surrounded by a moral
breakdown, including an all-prevailing sexual orgy.

In addition to having this terribleness impressed upon him,
Joshua also saw that merely using the name of God is not sufficient. After Aaron had made the calf, he said, "These are thy gods,
O Israel, which brought thee up out of the land of Egypt" (Ex.
32:4). According to tradition, the children of Israel actually placed
the most holy name of God—the Tetragrammaton—on the
golden calf. But merely to use the name was nothing. This was
worse, much worse, than not using the name of God at all. So
Joshua would have understood that merely using the name of God
is not enough.

Joshua would also have seen that there is a place for godly
anger. Moses broke the tables and God never scolded him for this,
not even a little. There was good reason for Moses' anger. After

he had broken the tables of stone, Moses ground up the golden calf, put the powder upon the water, and said to Israel, "All right! This is your drinking water. Go and drink it!"—a tremendous statement of godly anger against that which is sinful. We must say that the exercise of godly anger is dangerous to us because we so often mix it with egoism. But let us not forget that there *is* a place for godly anger. There were times when Christ, too, was angry. We can think, for example, of Christ driving out the money-changers (John 2:15) and His being angry at the abnormality of death before the tomb of Lazarus (John 11:33).

In the Tabernacle

The fourth time we see Joshua is in Exodus 33: "And it came to pass, as Moses entered into the tabernacle, the cloudy pillar descended and stood at the door of the tabernacle, and the LORD talked with Moses. . . . And the LORD spoke unto Moses face to face, as a man speaketh unto his friend. And he turned again into the camp; but his servant Joshua, the son of Nun, a young man, departed not out of the tabernacle" (vv. 9, 11). Moses was unique. The Lord spoke with him face to face, as one speaks to his friend; and in the midst of this unusual situation, the young man Joshua was being taught. Joshua was going to school; Joshua was being prepared for his future leadership. It was imperative that he learn, since the great man Moses would die and Joshua would be left to carry on. Here, as in Exodus 24, he learned the reality of God in His glory, but with an additional note: God could and would guide. God not only exists, but He guides His people as they live in, and walk through, the world of time and space.

Prophesying in the Camp

Joshua is next mentioned in an intriguing passage in Numbers:

> And Moses went out, and told the people the words of the Lord, and gathered the seventy men of the elders of the people, and set them round about the tabernacle. And the LORD came down in a cloud, and spoke unto him, and took of the Spirit that was upon him, and gave it unto the seventy elders: and it came to pass that, when the Spirit rested upon them, they prophesied, and did not cease. But there remained two of the men in the camp, the name of the one was Eldad, and the name of the other Medad; and the Spirit rested upon them; and they were of them that were written, but went not out unto the tabernacle; and they prophesied in the camp. And there ran a young man, and told Moses, and said, Eldad and Medad do prophesy in the

camp. And Joshua, the son of Nun, the servant of Moses, one of his young men, answered and said, My lord Moses, forbid them. And Moses said unto him, Enviest thou for my sake? Would God that all the LORD's people were prophets, and that the LORD would put his Spirit upon them! (Num. 11:24-29).

Joshua had another lesson to learn, and a very serious one: God's glory is to come first. There is a great difference between leadership and self-aggrandizement. There is to be leadership among the people of God, according to the gifts He bestows, but there is not to be glorification of oneself or other men. Joshua asked that Eldad and Medad be forbidden to prophesy because they had not come before Moses in the tabernacle; but Moses answered magnificently, "Don't envy for my sake." Maybe Moses' response is one of the reasons the Bible says that Moses was a meek man. Though Moses was such a tremendous leader, he would not tolerate Joshua's glorifying him.

The young man Joshua was learning a lesson that anybody who is ever going to be worth anything in leadership must learn. None of us learns it completely, of course, and yet we must master it if we are going to be of any use in the Church of God. A leader must never confuse himself with God. When a person begins to exercise certain gifts and God brings him to a place of leadership in the Church of Christ, how easy it is to do this. Yet this is the destruction of all true spiritual leadership.

Joshua also had to learn that a person cannot bind God with man-made rules. Joshua had a man-made rule: God really should not have placed His Spirit on the two men in the camp. This did not fit into Joshua's concept of what was good and proper. God has bound Himself with rules based on his own character, which He will never break; but men (including God's leaders) must never try to bind Him with their own rules. He will not keep these rules.

Spying Out the Land
In Numbers 13 we see more of Joshua's preparation. He was one of the twelve men God sent to spy out the promised land. The sixth verse says that from the tribe of Judah Caleb was sent, and the eighth verse mentions: "of the tribe of Ephraim: Hoshea, the son of Nun." In the sixteenth verse, we find that "Moses called Hoshea, the son of Nun, Joshua." So this was Joshua. *Hoshea* means, "he saves"; but Moses changed his name to *Joshua*, "Jehovah saves," so that Joshua would even in his name remember that

it is not man who saves, but God who must save. *Jesus*, of course, is the Greek form for the Hebrew name *Joshua*.

When the spies returned, they gave contrasting opinions. The majority advised, "No. Trying to conquer the land is too dangerous. The people are too great." But two of the spies, Caleb and Joshua, remembered who God is and reported in line with the greatness of God and His covenant promises: "And Caleb stilled the people before Moses, and said, Let us go up at once, and possess it; for we are well able to overcome it" (Num. 13:30). Here Caleb was affirming, "It's a great land, and we will be able to conquer it because we have a great God."

The people, however, followed the ten spies. "All the congregation lifted up their voice, and cried; and the people wept that night" (Num. 14:1). We can see the fiber of these two men as they spoke out and rebuked those who were following the majority report:

> And Joshua, the son of Nun, and Caleb, the son of Jephunneh, who were of them that searched the land, rent their clothes; and they spoke unto all the company of the children of Israel, saying, The land, which we passed through to search it, is an exceeding good land. If the LORD delight in us, then he will bring us into this land, and give it us; a land which floweth with milk and honey. Only rebel not ye against the LORD, neither fear ye the people of the land; for they are bread for us; their defense is departed from them, and the LORD is with us: fear them not. (Num. 14:6-9)

Despite this rebuke, the people still acted upon the *majority report*. I emphasize this phrase for a purpose. We cannot go by majority reports. A democracy works on the basis of the majority, but this does not imply, by any means, that the majority opinion is always right. In this case, the majority was desperately wrong. Two against ten—nevertheless, the minority was right! When the people acted upon the majority report, they were indeed doing what Joshua and Caleb warned them against—they were rebelling against God.

So the young man Joshua learned another lesson. He learned that even when the majority was totally against him, he had to be willing to stand with God. He had to resist his own people when they were wrong, even if it led to physical danger. In this case it did: "But all the congregation bade stone them with stones" (Num. 14:10). "Kill these two! Get them out of the way!" the majority cried out. The people did not kill Joshua and Caleb; nevertheless, Joshua learned to exhibit courage even in the midst of physical danger and even though the majority in error were the people of God.

Joshua also learned once more the terribleness of rebellion against God among God's own people, for God decreed that none of these rebels would enter the promised land. We must understand that this moment was a watershed. Back around 2,000 B.C. God had given a promise to Abraham, and the Jewish *race* had begun. Before that, there were Semitic people, but no Jews. In the time of Moses (about 500 years later), that which had been a race was constituted a *nation* when the people came out of Egypt, crossed over the Red Sea, came to Sinai, and received their laws from God. The Bible was not only their religious law; it was also their civil law as a nation. All that remained, therefore, was to possess the land.

For the Jews, the land was the cord which bound together the other blessings. The Abrahamic covenant included a national promise to the Jews which was related to the land. The first promise God had given to Abraham was, "Get thee out of thy country, and from thy kindred, and from thy father's house, unto a land that I will show thee" (Gen. 12:1). When God next spoke to Abraham, he emphasized the same thing: "For all the land which thou seest, to thee will I give it, and to thy seed forever. . . . Arise, walk through the land in the length of it and in the breadth of it; for I will give it unto thee" (Gen. 13:15, 17). Later, God said to Abraham, "I am the LORD that brought thee out of Ur of the Chaldeans, to give thee this land to inherit it" (Gen. 15:7).

But God also told Abraham he would not have the land at once: "Know of a surety that thy seed shall be a stranger in a land that is not their's, and shall serve them; and they shall afflict them four hundred years; . . . But in the fourth generation they shall come hither again; for the iniquity of the Amorites is not yet full" (Gen. 15:13, 16). God told Abraham that his descendants were not going to have the land immediately and that there was a reason for this: the iniquity of the Amorites was not yet full.

At the time the spies went out, the iniquity of the Amorites had become full; so it was time to go into the land. The third piece was now to be put into place: the race, the nation and the land were to be brought together.

The Israelites had traveled from Egypt to Sinai in only two

months. God kept them at Sinai for one year, to consolidate them, no doubt, and especially to give them the Ten Commandments, the entire civil law, and all the other great things that are revealed in the books of Moses. This means that by the time the spies went out, only one year and two months had elapsed from the people's being slaves in Egypt to the unity of the promises of the race, the nation and the land standing ready to be fulfilled. Suddenly came the rebellion of the people, and God stretched out a year and two months into forty years. For thirty-eight years after this, the Israelites wandered in the wilderness until everybody over the age of twenty, except Joshua and Caleb, had died.

So Joshua learned a lesson of the terribleness of God's people rebelling against Him. Surely, he never forgot—thirty-eight years lost because of rebellion! Rebellion against God is no light thing. It always brings its results in the present life. At this time it postponed the completion of the complex of race, nation and land.

God told the people, "Doubtless ye shall not come into the land, concerning which I swore to make you dwell therein, except Caleb, the son of Jephunneh and Joshua, the son of Nun" (Num. 14:30). Only two people who were adults at this time would live to go in. Here Joshua learned something else: God keeps his promises. Just imagine the Israelites as they walked for thirty-eight years through the wilderness. One person would die, and then another; one set of bones would be laid aside, and then another, until every single person was dead. Moses went into the plain of Moab with only two men from that generation behind him— Joshua and Caleb. Joshua saw in dramatic fashion that God keeps His promises and distinguishes among men in the structure of history.

Joshua's Ordination

On the plain of Moab, when "there was not left a man of them, save Caleb, the son of Jephunneh, and Joshua, the son of Nun" (Num. 26:65), the time came for Joshua's ordination. This is what we read:

> And the LORD said unto Moses, Take thee Joshua, the son of Nun, a man in whom is the Spirit, and lay thine hand upon him; and set him before Eleazar, the priest, and before all the congregation, and give him a charge in their sight. And thou shalt put some of thine honor upon him, that all the congregation of the children of Israel may be obedient. And he shall stand before Eleazar, the priest, who shall ask

counsel for him after the judgment of Urim before the LORD; at his word shall they go out, and at his word they shall come in, both he, and all the children of Israel with him, even all the congregation. And Moses did as the LORD commanded him: and he took Joshua, and set him before Eleazar the priest and before all the congregation, and he laid his hands upon him, and gave him a charge, as the LORD commanded by the hand of Moses. (Num. 27:18-23)

After all the years of preparation, Joshua was now marked, in the presence of God's people, as the man of God's choice. Thus he would have learned that leadership, if it is real, is not from men. It was not even from Moses, but only from God. Men can ordain, but leadership does not derive from them. Men, even Christian men, can generate leadership, but leadership generated only by men is only on the level of any human leadership and will bring no more true spiritual results than any human charisma.

Moses' Final Address
In the book of Deuteronomy, we are close to the end of the time of Moses and close to the beginning of the book of Joshua. Moses addressed the people several times before his death, and among his words were these:

I am an hundred and twenty years old this day; I can no more go out and come in. Also the LORD hath said unto me, Thou shalt not go over this Jordan. The LORD thy God, he will go over before thee, and he will destroy these nations from before thee, and thou shalt possess them; and Joshua, he shall go over before thee, as the LORD hath said. And the LORD shall do unto them as he did to Sihon and to Og, kings of the Amorites, and unto the land of them, whom he destroyed. And the LORD shall give them up before your face, that ye may do unto them according unto all the commandments which I have commanded you. Be strong and of good courage, fear not, nor be afraid of them; for the LORD thy God, he it is who doth go with thee; he will not fail thee, nor forsake thee. And Moses called unto Joshua, and said unto him in the sight of all Israel, Be strong and of good courage; for thou must go with this people unto the land which the LORD hath sworn unto their fathers to give them; and thou shalt cause them to inherit it. And the LORD, he it is who doth go before thee; he will be with thee, he will not fail thee, neither forsake thee; fear not, neither be dismayed. (Deut. 31:2-8)

"I am going to die," Moses said, "but don't be afraid. God is going to go over before you." Notice the order, which must not get reversed. God goes before; therefore, His people can go without fear. The human leader, Joshua, went before too, but the reason Joshua could go without fear was not that his natural abilities and his faithfulness were so great (though these were evident by this time), but that God would go before him. This order must always be carefully maintained.

Undoubtedly Moses was thinking back to the time thirty-eight years before when the parents of these people were afraid, and God condemned them to die in the wilderness; so he warned, "Don't do it again!" But there was something else. Moses was pointing out that as God had acted in the past, He would act in the future. The promises were not "pie in the sky."

Those who are the people of God should reflect often on the continuity of the promises of God. The people of God should look back through the Scripture. They should also be able to look back through the history of their own lives. Seeing that God has cared for them in the past, they should not be afraid of tomorrow, because God is going to go before them then as well. Moses' tremendous emphasis was that the reason the people did not need to be afraid was not that they had Joshua (though wasn't it wonderful that they did have Joshua?), but that God would go before both them and Joshua.

So we see here three steps: The Lord goes before His people, the Lord goes before the human leader, and then the people can go without fear. The line is laid down. And as it has been in the past, it will be in the future.

Shortly after Moses spoke these words, a touching thing occurred—touching because it hearkened back to a memory from Joshua's youth. Now, when Joshua was much older, "The LORD said unto Moses, Behold, thy days approach that thou must die. Call Joshua, and present yourselves in the tabernacle of the congregation, that I may give him a charge. And Moses and Joshua went, and presented themselves in the tabernacle of the congregation. And the LORD appeared in the tabernacle in a pillar of a cloud; and the pillar of the cloud stood over the door of the tabernacle" (Deut. 31:14, 15). We do not know if this had happened many times in the intervening years, but we do know that when Joshua was a young man he had gone into the tabernacle with Moses, and the cloud of the glory of God had come down upon them. I think God means for us to see a link. As a young man, Joshua had learned something. As the time came for Joshua to step out into leadership, this lesson was repeated. The two men were again in the tabernacle, directly under the shekinah-glory of God.

In Deuteronomy 31 is another point of extreme importance. "Moses went and spoke these words unto all Israel," verse 1 tells us. This was a verbalized communication from God through Moses. But in verses 9-12 the importance of this is brought to its peak:

> And Moses wrote this law, and delivered it unto the priests, the sons of Levi, who bore the ark of the covenant of the LORD, and unto all the elders of Israel. And Moses commanded them, saying, At the end of every seven years, in the solemnity of the year of release, in the feast of tabernacles, when all Israel is come to appear before the LORD thy God in the place which he shall choose, thou shalt read this law before all Israel in their hearing. Gather the people together, men, and women, and children, and the stranger that is within thy gates, that they may hear, and that they may learn, and fear the LORD your God, and observe to do all the words of this law.

The commands of God were carried through Moses to the people in a written, propositional form. We are watching here the Scripture growing before our eyes. The text has already said that Moses wrote; now he writes again. And what is he writing? The Pentateuch—Genesis, Exodus, Leviticus, Numbers and Deuteronomy.

In verses 24-26 the mention of the Pentateuch continues:

> And it came to pass, when Moses had made an end of writing the words of this law in a book, until they were finished, that Moses commanded the Levites, who bore the ark of the covenant of the LORD, saying, Take this book of the law, and put it in the side of the ark of the covenant of the LORD your God, that it may be there for a witness against thee.

The book was placed in the ark or by the ark to remind the people that it was connected with God. It was the Word of God in written form. The first five books of the Bible were now complete. God had given in written propositional form the great religious truths He wanted men to have up until that point of history, and He had told them (and us) facts of the cosmos and history as well.

Deuteronomy 34:7, 8 describes the death of Moses: "And Moses was an hundred and twenty years old when he died; his eye

was not dim, nor his natural force abated. And the children of
Israel wept for Moses in the plains of Moab thirty days. So the
days of weeping and mourning for Moses were ended." Joshua, I
think, now learned his final lesson in preparation: no man is indispensable. I do not like that statement if it is left alone, simply
because I think the Bible says more than that. We must say, "No
man is indispensable," but we must not forget Deuteronomy
34:10: "And there arose not a prophet since in Israel like unto
Moses, whom the LORD knew face to face." Here Moses'
uniqueness is emphasized. So we can say at the same time, without being contradictory, no man is indispensable, but every man is
unique. Men are dispensable; but this does not mean that one man
fills another man's place in the same way as a person would remove one concrete block and put another concrete block in its
place. In the final analysis, nobody takes the place of anybody else.
This is the wonder of personality and the wonder of God using
personality in leadership.

Joshua Is Ready

Now, after all these years of preparation, Joshua was ready to
enter the land: "And Joshua, the son of Nun, was full of the Spirit
of wisdom; for Moses had laid his hands upon him. And the
children of Israel hearkened unto him, and did as the LORD commanded Moses" (Deut. 34:9). This was not a mechanical readi-
ness. An act of the will was involved. If we do not stress this, we
will be giving an inaccurate picture of Joshua's preparation. It is
not that you feed preparation into a mill and a leader comes out the
other end. It is not that way, any more than that you feed facts
into a mill and a Christian comes out the other end. There must be
an act of the will in becoming a Christian, and there must be an act
of the will for any man, no matter what his preparation, to become a leader in God's work.

At the end of his own life, Joshua said to the people, "And if it
seem evil unto you to serve the LORD, choose you this day
whom ye will serve, whether the gods which your fathers served
that were on the other side of the flood, or the gods of the Amorites, in whose land ye dwell; but as for me and my house, we will
serve the LORD" (Josh. 24:15). This was not a choice Joshua
made only at the end of his life. All through his preparation we see
a series of acts of his will.

There is no leader who does not have to choose. You can take two men with equal preparation, and one serves the Lord while the other does not. We must realize that whether we are young or old, God does not deal with us as sticks and stones. He has made us as people, and He expects us to respond as people. Even when God has prepared a person, if there is to be real spiritual leadership, the leadership will require a constant, existential, moment-by-moment act of the will: "If the rest of you wish to go the way of the majority, go! As for me and my house, we will serve the Lord."

Is there always a long time of preparation for spiritual leadership? Not always, but usually. We can think of those in the Scripture, including Christ, who for years were prepared for the crucial leadership they would exercise. We must be careful; we cannot make this a rule, because Paul did say to Timothy, "Let no man despise thy youth" (1 Tim. 4:12). We must not insist that no man can be given important leadership until he has gray hair—or no hair at all! At the same time we must understand that if we are young and want to be used in the Lord's work, we must be ready for a time of preparation. Usually there is preparation before leadership. Both Moses and Joshua had many, many years of preparation.

Let us review what Joshua learned in his preparation:

God will not tolerate the rebellion of men against Himself.

Power is not merely the power of the general and the sword. It is not to be the power of man, but true power is the power of God.

God is not far-off; God is always immediately present.

Sin is terrible, especially among the people of God.

Merely using the name of God is not sufficient.

God can and will guide.

God's glory is to come first. There is a real difference between leadership and self-aggrandizement.

A person cannot bind God with man-made rules.

A man of God must stand and trust God—even against his own people, even if in the minority, even in the midst of physical danger.

Even in His judgment, God keeps His promises and distinguishes among men. He does not treat men like a series of numbers.

True spiritual leadership does not come from the hands of men, but from God.

No man is indispensable; yet each man is important and unique. Usually there is preparation before leadership.

God taught Joshua all these things as Joshua followed Moses in the wilderness. Then, with these lessons learned, Joshua was ready to lead the people into the promised land.

CHAPTER TWO

The Three Changeless Factors

After Joshua acted as the general against the Amalekites, "the LORD said unto Moses, Write this for a memorial in a book" (Ex. 17:14). This book became the center of the life of the people of Israel from this point on. Over and over the Pentateuch tells how it came to be composed. In Numbers, for example, we find, "And Moses wrote their goings out according to their journeys by the commandment of the LORD" (Num. 33:2). Just as Exodus 17 specifically refers to the writing of the book of Exodus, Numbers 33 specifically refers to the writing of the book of Numbers.

In the plain of Moab, with the forty-year wandering over, the writing still continued under the command of God. Deuteronomy 31 portrays the growth of the Pentateuch, emphasizing that Moses wrote in the book. Of course, one of the liberal theories is that the Pentateuch was carried down through the spoken word for a long period prior to the writing. But this theory directly contradicts what the Pentateuch itself claims, because in Deuteronomy 31:9 we read, "And Moses wrote this law, and delivered it unto the priests, the sons of Levi." So Moses not only spoke; he also wrote. He gave propositional, verbalized communication from God to man in written as well as spoken form. We are told about the production of Exodus, Numbers, and Deuteronomy. Something was *written*.

Deuteronomy 31 also makes clear that what was written was not to be a priestly book hidden away from the people, as if they could not understand it. Quite the contrary—from time to time it was to be read not only before the priests, but also before the common people:

> And Moses wrote this law, and delivered it unto the priests, the sons of Levi, who bore the ark of the covenant of the LORD, and unto all the elders of Israel. And Moses commanded them, saying, At the end of every seven years, in the solemnity of the year of release, in the feast of tabernacles, when all Israel is come to appear before the LORD thy God in the place which he shall choose, thou shalt read this law before all Israel in their hearing. Gather the people together, men, and women, and children, and thy stranger who is within thy gates, that they may hear, and that they may learn, and fear the LORD your God, and observe to do all the words of this law; and that their children, who have not known anything, may hear, and learn to fear the LORD your God, as long as ye live in the land to which ye go over Jordan to possess it. (Deut. 31:9-13).

The people, of course, could not have their own Bibles. This would not be possible until after Gutenberg. But this does not mean that the Pentateuch was an exotic book, a mere symbol. It was not like the ark of the Lord, never to be seen. While the ark of the Lord was hidden away from the common eyes and covered when the people traveled, the book was brought out periodically and read. This was a reminder, therefore, that it was not a book too holy for common use. It was important because it was from God, but it was common because it was to be understood by all the people. The people were to know the content which God had given through Moses in the book.

In Deuteronomy 31:19 Moses speaks of "this song." One of the liberal theories is that the Pentateuch was passed down by song and only written down much later, but again the book of Deuteronomy contradicts this. While it is true that the people were to learn the song and pass it on to their children, the text also says, "Write this song."

We see, then, a sequential structure: God commanded something to be written in a book, and Moses wrote it over a period of forty years. As we get to the end of the book of Deuteronomy, the writing of Moses is finished. When Moses completed the Pentateuch, he commanded that it be kept in a sacred place, "in the side of the ark of the covenant" (Deut. 31:26). It was to be preserved and read regularly to all the people.

The First Changeless Factor: The Written Book
This brings us finally to Joshua 1:

> Now after the death of Moses the servant of the LORD, it came to pass that the LORD spoke unto Joshua, the son of Nun, Moses' minister, saying, Moses, my servant, is dead; now therefore arise, go over this Jordan, thou, and all this people, unto the land which I give to them, even to the children of Israel. Every place that the sole of your foot shall tread upon, that have I given unto you, as I said unto Moses. From the wilderness and this Lebanon even unto the great river, the river Euphrates, all the land of the Hittites, and unto the Great Sea toward the going down of the sun, shall be your coast. There shall not any man be able to stand before thee all the days of thy life. As I was with Moses, so I will be with thee; I will not fail thee, nor forsake thee. Be strong and of good courage; for unto this people shalt thou divide for an inheritance the land which I swore unto their fathers to give them. Only be thou strong and very courageous, that thou mayest observe to do according to all the law, which Moses, my servant, commanded thee; turn not from it to the right hand or to the left, that thou mayest prosper whithersoever thou goest. This book of the law shall not depart out of thy mouth, but thou shalt meditate therein day and night, that thou mayest observe to do according to all that is written therein; for then thou shalt make thy way prosperous, and then thou shalt have good success (or, do wisely). (Joshua 1:1-8).

As the Israelites stood ready to enter the land, God's main emphasis was upon *the book.*

Joshua was to have special revelations from God through the priest: "And he (Joshua) shall stand before Eleazar, the priest, who shall ask counsel for him after the judgment of Urim before the LORD" (Num. 27:21). We are not sure exactly what the Urim was, the way it functioned, or how God used it to reveal Himself, but we do know it was one way God through the priest revealed propositional content to His people. But though Joshua was going to have this special leading from the Lord, this was not to detract from the central reference point and chief control: the written book. The Word of God written in the book set the limitations. Thus, Joshua was already functioning in the way Bible-believing Christians function. Sometimes God does lead in other ways, but such leading must always be within the circle of His external, propositional commands in Scripture. Even if a person had an Urim and a Thummim as well as a priest to guide him, this would not change his basic authority. The primary leading would come from the written, propositional revelation of God, from the Bible.

So we see that the written book was the first of the three changeless factors that stood with Joshua as he assumed leadership. "Only be thou strong and very courageous," God commanded him, "that thou mayest observe to do according to all the law, which Moses, my servant, commanded thee; turn not from it to the right hand or to the left, that thou mayest prosper whithersoever thou goest. This book of the law shall not depart out of thy mouth, but thou shalt meditate therein day and night, that thou mayest observe to do according to all that is written therein; for then thou shalt make thy way prosperous, and then thou shalt have good success [or, do wisely]." Joshua had been walking beside Moses (the young man beside the older) for forty years; yet God's command to Joshua was not just general. It was not, "Try to remember what Moses told you and follow it." Rather, Joshua was to search out and constantly study the sharp and definite commands in the written book.

The Lord especially emphasized three things. First, the law was not to depart out of Joshua's mouth; he was to talk about it. Second, he was to meditate on it day and night. Meditation is a cognitive activity; it takes place in the area of reason. God's law is not something that should be mechanically reproduced, nor is it contentless (to express it in contemporary terms). Third, he was to practice the commands in his historic, space-time situation. Talk about it; think about it; do it! Jesus' teaching had the same emphasis, "Here are My words. Do them!"

Throughout his life, Joshua was obedient. Of all the factors which gave him such success, the most important was that he heeded God's admonition about the book. For example, at Ebal and Gerizim Joshua carried out exactly Moses' instruction to read the law before all the people. (See Joshua 8; we will study this in more detail in Chapter 7.) Joshua lived out his life in a practical way within the circle of the written revelation.

This faithfulness continued to the end of his life. Joshua's charge to the people when he was ready to die was simple and final: "Be ye therefore very courageous to keep and to do all that is written in the book of the law of Moses, that ye turn not aside therefrom to the right hand or to the left" (Josh. 23:6). Joshua kept the command of God all the days of his life, and before he died he urged the people that followed him to do the same: "Live your life within the circle of the propositions given in the written book."

The Growth and Acceptance of the Canon

Joshua's relation to the book teaches us an important lesson about how the canon grew and was accepted. Joshua knew Moses, the writer of the Pentateuch, personally. Joshua knew his strengths and weaknesses as a man; he knew that Moses was a sinner, that Moses made mistakes, that Moses was just a man. Nonetheless, immediately after Moses' death Joshua accepted the Pentateuch as more than the writing of Moses. He accepted it as the writing of God. Two or three hundred years were not required for the book to become sacred. As far as Joshua was concerned the Pentateuch was the canon, and the canon was the Word of God. The biblical view of the growth and acceptance of the canon is as simple as this: when it was given, God's people understood what it was. Right away it had authority.

This is why I think the book of Joshua is so crucial. It stands as the bridge between the Pentateuch and the post-Pentateuchal period and provides the key for understanding some important relationships between various parts of the whole Scripture.

The fact that Joshua's generation accepted the Pentateuch as authoritative is more than a mere breath of fresh air in the heavy smog which surrounds present liberal scholarly discussion. To the Israelites, the canon was not just academic, not merely theological, but practical. Joshua and the people had a continuity of authority as they moved through history. The book was to be their environment, their mentality.

At the time of Moses, they had the authority of both Moses and the law God had commanded Moses to write. When they woke up the morning after Moses died, and when they entered the promised land, they were not left in a vacuum. To use another image, because of the continuity provided by the book, there was no fracture in the authority. In the practical problems of life, they had an objective standard of judgment which stood in an unbroken flow.

One practical problem, for instance, was how to judge prophecies. Moses had written that if a man made a prophecy and it did not come to pass, it was not from God (Deut. 18:22). But this, of

course, left an even more acute problem: what happens when
people make strange prophecies that do come to pass? Then where
do the prophecies come from? How can you tell? Moses had laid
down these guidelines:

> Whatsoever thing I command you, observe to do it; thou shalt not
> add thereto, nor diminish from it. If there arise among you a prophet,
> or a dreamer of dreams, and giveth thee a sign or a wonder, and the
> sign or the wonder come to pass, whereof he spake unto thee, saying,
> Let us go after other gods, which thou hast not known, and let us
> serve them, thou shalt not hearken unto the words of that prophet, or
> that dreamer of dreams; for the LORD your God proveth you, to
> know whether ye love the LORD your God with all your heart and
> with all your soul. Ye shall walk after the LORD your God, and fear
> him, and keep his commandments, and obey his voice, and ye shall
> serve him, and cleave unto him. And that prophet, or that dreamer of
> dreams, shall be put to death, because he hath spoken to turn you
> away from the LORD your God, which brought you out of the land
> of Egypt, and redeemed you out of the house of bondage, to thrust
> thee out of the way which the LORD thy God commanded thee to
> walk in. So shalt thou put the evil away from the midst of thee. (Deut.
> 12:32—13:5)

This passage from Deuteronomy reveals the standard that God
himself gave: judge the prophet whose prophecy comes to pass by
comparing what he says with the objective written standard.
Whether a prophecy comes to pass or not is not the final test. The
final test is whether a prophet's teaching stands in continuity with
what is written in the book.

Because of the book, the first of the great changeless factors,
God's people had a way to make objective, not merely experiential, judgments. The whole man, with his reason, could consider
what Moses' writings said. In this time of change from the great
lawgiver (Moses) to the post-Pentateuchal period, the Israelites
had a standard, a very practical guide.

In the book of Joshua, we watch the canon grow even more.
Joshua 5:1 contains the phrase "until we were passed over." The
person who wrote the narrative was there! (This reminds us of the
"we" passages in Acts.) Joshua 5:6 has the words "which the
LORD swore unto their fathers that he would give us, a land that
floweth with milk and honey." Again, the writer was present at
these events. When the Pentateuch was finished, the book of

Joshua, a continuation of the canon, flowed on; and it was a first-person situation.

Joshua 24:26 tells us who this person was: "And Joshua wrote these words in the book of the law." How did the canon grow? Moses wrote, and Moses died. Joshua continued to write, and the canon continued to grow. Incidentally, as a quick parenthesis, it is quite clear that the Bible always accepts Joshua as a historic character. Nehemiah 8:17 illustrates this when it says that the children of Israel had not kept the feasts of booths since the days of Joshua, the son of Nun.

As Joshua faced his task, then, he had with him this first great changeless factor: the written book. It provided a continuity of authority, but it was growing and would continue to grow. It grew, but it was not discontinuous. Joshua, as he led the people, had an objective standard by which to judge everything else, and the standard was so clear that God expected the ordinary people to understand it when it was periodically read to them.

The Second Changeless Factor: The Power of God

When the people were ready to enter the land, they left Shittim, an area near the east bank of the Jordan where they had been lodging, and moved up to the east bank of the Jordan River. Three days later occurred an incident which revealed the second changeless factor: the power of God.

> And the LORD said unto Joshua, This day will I begin to magnify thee in the sight of all Israel, that they may know that, as I was with Moses, so I will be with thee. And thou shalt command the priests that bear the ark of the covenant, saying, When ye are come to the brink of the water of Jordan, ye shall stand still in Jordan. And Joshua said unto the children of Israel, Come hither, and hear the words of the LORD your God. And Joshua said, Hereby ye shall know that the living God is among you, and that he will without fail drive out from before you the Canaanites, and the Hittites, and the Hivites, and the Perizzites, and the Girgashites, and the Amorites, and the Jebusites. Behold, the ark of the covenant of the LORD of all the earth passeth over before you into Jordan. Now, therefore, take you twelve men out of the tribes of Israel, out of every tribe a man. And it shall come to pass, as soon as the soles of the feet of the priests who bear the ark of the LORD, the Lord of all the earth, shall rest in the waters of Jordan, that the waters of Jordan shall be cut off from the waters that come down from above, and they shall stand upon an heap.

And it came to pass, when the people removed from their tents to pass over Jordan, and the priests bearing the ark of the covenant before the people, and, as they who bore the ark were come unto Jordan and the feet of the priests who bore the ark were dipped in the brim of the water (for Jordan overfloweth all its banks all the time of harvest), that the waters which came down from above stood and rose up upon an heap very far from the city of Adam, that is beside Zarethan; and those that came down toward the sea of the plain, even the Salt Sea, failed, and were cut off; and the people passed over right against Jericho. And the priests who bore the ark of the covenant of the LORD stood firm on dry ground in the midst of Jordan, and all the Israelites passed over on dry ground, until all the people were passed clean over Jordan. . . .

And it came to pass, when the priests who bore the ark of the covenant of the LORD, were come up out of the midst of Jordan, and the soles of the priests' feet were lifted up unto the dry land, that the waters of Jordan returned unto their place, and flowed over all its banks, as they did before. (Josh. 3:7-17; 4:18)

The priests carried the ark into the Jordan, and, while they stood in the water, God rolled back the Jordan. How God did this we are not told. Whether it was by direct command or through some material means, as when the east wind blew back the Red Sea, does not matter. What matters is that the waters were stopped, even though it was the time of flood, and all the people passed over on dry land. Then the priests walked out, and the waters returned.

God did a remarkable thing here, and the text expressly says that he did it for a purpose: "On that day the LORD magnified Joshua in the sight of all Israel; and they feared him, as they feared Moses, all the days of his life" (Josh. 4:14). God rolled back the waters for Joshua just as He had done for Moses forty years earlier. The exact sign He had given at the exodus from Egypt, He now gave at their entrance into the promised land. The sign which had most conclusively shown the power of God upon Moses was now associated with Joshua. "As I was with Moses, so I will be with thee," God had told Joshua (Josh. 3:7). Now He dramatically demonstrated that this was so.

The accounts of the two miracles even share some words in common. Joshua 3:13 and 16 speak of the waters standing "upon an heap." The song of Moses, in Exodus 15, states in poetic form that "the floods stood upright as an heap" (v. 8). God told Joshua to command the priests, "Ye shall stand still in Jordan" (Josh. 3:8).

On the edge of the Red Sea, Moses said to the people, "Fear not, stand still, and see the salvation of the LORD" (Ex. 14:13). These repetitions imply the parallel which the book of Joshua identifies explicitly: "For the LORD your God dried up the waters of Jordan from before you, until ye were passed over, as the LORD your God did to the Red Sea" (Josh. 4:23).

To us, the parting of the Red Sea is ancient history, but to the people who watched the Jordan roll back, it was not. Joshua, Caleb and all the older people had been at the Red Sea, because those who were under twenty when the Red Sea was rolled back were still living. Therefore, they were recalling something in their own personal history. We can picture these Israelites coming up to the River Jordan, the older ones remembering the Red Sea, and the younger ones recalling the accounts of their parents who over and over again had described to them the wonder of that event. Joshua and Caleb especially would have remembered. Then to have God suddenly give the same sign as they were entering the promised land—a symbol of the continuity of the authority and the power of God—must have given them a tremendous sense of wonder, awe and certainty.

Even at the end of his life, Joshua reminded the people that some of them could remember all that had happened in the days of Moses: "He put darkness between you and the Egyptians, and brought the sea upon them, and covered them, and your eyes have seen what I have done in Egypt. . . . [God] did those great signs in our sight" (Josh. 24:7, 17). He was calling upon the older men and women to remember a history which was not just a history of the past (as it is to us), but a personal experience.

Joshua himself had also seen this power manifested in the battle against the Amalekites. When Moses had stood with his hands upheld, the Israelites had won; when his hands went down, the Amalekites had won. God certainly taught Joshua something to remember all the days of his life: "The power is Mine! The power is Mine!" As the people crossed over the Jordan, Joshua would have known again that the power was there and that it was a changeless power, not a power just for one period in history. The power was there, and the power was the Lord's. The power is not in anything or anybody independent of God. It is the same power through the whole Bible, and God's power is not diminished in our period of history. It is the same power: past, present, and future.

The Third Changeless Factor: The Supernatural Leader
The third changeless factor is the continuity of a Person:

> And it came to pass, when Joshua was by Jericho, that he lifted up his eyes and looked and, behold, there stood a man over against him with his sword drawn in his hand; and Joshua went unto him, and said unto him, Art thou for us, or for our adversaries? And he said, Nay, but as captain of the host of the LORD am I now come. And Joshua fell on his face to the earth, and did worship, and said unto him, What saith my lord unto his servant? And the captain of the LORD's host said unto Joshua, Loose thy shoe from off thy foot; for the place whereon thou standest is holy. And Joshua did so. . . . And the LORD said unto Joshua, See, I have given into thine hand Jericho, and its king, and the mighty men of valor. (Josh. 5:13-17; 6:2)

The power which continued in Joshua's time was neither impersonal nor magical. The power was related to a Person—a Person who also has continuity in history.

The continuity of the supernatural leader was made explicit in the incident near Jericho. Here the One who confronted Joshua said, "As captain of the host of the LORD am I now come," thus implying that He had been present before in a different capacity. Joshua had seen and known this Person in the past, but now He was coming in a specific capacity, as the captain of the host of the Lord.

This, too, paralleled Moses' experience. Moses was in the desert when he received his special call at the burning bush. Suddenly he was confronted with a Person—the great "I AM"—who said to him, "Draw not nigh hither: put off thy shoes from off thy feet, for the place whereon thou standest is holy ground" (Ex. 3:5). The captain of the Lord's host gave Joshua the same instructions (Josh. 5:15). Joshua, filled with emotion, would have quickly undone his sandals and kicked them off, realizing he was now in Moses' place.

When God spoke to Moses from the burning bush, He constantly mentioned the past. In light of the insistence of the text, I can never understand how liberal theologians can try to maintain that this was a God new to the Israelites. This idea would seem impossible, because in Exodus 3:6 we read, "I am the God of thy father, the God of Abraham, the God of Isaac, and the God of Jacob. And Moses hid his face. . . ." He was hiding his face before the same God who had appeared to Abraham 500 years before. In Exodus 3:15 God reiterates, "Thus shalt thou say unto the children of Israel, The LORD God of your fathers, the God of Abraham, the God of Isaac, and the God of Jacob, hath sent me unto you." So there was this strong emphasis: "I am not a new God; there is a continuity in who I am and in My leadership." Verse 16 also speaks of "the LORD God of your fathers."

When God turned Moses' rod into a snake, it was a sign to Pharaoh. It was also a sign to the people of God that God would accomplish a purpose among them. What was this purpose? "That they [the children of Israel] may believe that the LORD God of their fathers, the God of Abraham, the God of Isaac, and the God of Jacob, hath appeared unto thee" (Ex. 4:5). The sign was to be a proof to the people that there was a continuity of supernatural leadership, back to the time of Abraham and before.

At the end of his life, on the plain of Moab, Moses spoke about this continuity:

> I am an hundred and twenty years old this day; I can no more go out and come in. Also the LORD hath said unto me, Thou shalt not go over this Jordan. The LORD thy God, he will go over before thee; and he will destroy these nations from before thee, and thou shalt possess them; and Joshua, he shall go over before thee, as the Lord hath said. And the LORD shall do unto them as he did to Sihon and to Og, kings of the Amorites, and unto the land of them, whom he destroyed. And the LORD shall give them up before your face, that ye may do unto them according unto all the commandments which I have commanded you. Be strong and of good courage, fear not, nor be afraid of them; for the LORD thy God, he it is that doth go with thee; he will not fail thee, nor forsake thee. And Moses called unto Joshua, and said unto him in the sight of all Israel, Be strong and of good courage; for thou must go with this people unto the land which the LORD hath sworn unto their fathers to give them, and thou shalt cause them to inherit it. And the LORD, he it is that doth go before thee; he will be with thee, he will not fail thee, neither forsake thee; fear not, neither be dismayed. (Deut. 31:2-8).

We find here a double continuity. Moses said to the people, "Don't be afraid. The same God who dealt with Sihon and Og will deal with the men across the river." Then, turning to Joshua, he exclaimed, "The same God who has been with me will go before you, Joshua. Don't be afraid!" Joshua had seen the leading of the Lord in the cloud and the fire. He had been in the tabernacle when God had spoken to Moses. So he already knew this One who met him near Jericho. So Joshua, looking back across Jordan, would have remembered all the wonders he had seen under the leadership of this same supernatural leader.

When Joshua first saw the captain of the host of the Lord, he reacted as a real man. Sword in hand, Joshua rushed up and challenged him. When the Person spoke to Joshua, Joshua suddenly understood who this was, and back into his memory flowed all I have just mentioned plus much more, surely, that is not recorded. It must have been an overwhelming moment for Joshua as he was picking up the reins of the leadership of God's people. This was now much more than a memory; it was a historical reality in the here and now. Here and now was the same supernatural leader, the same Person. Moses was dead, but the true leader would go on. Because this One said to Joshua, "I have given into thine hand Jericho" (Josh. 6:2), and because he knew this One kept His promises, Joshua was able to turn to his people before the walls of Jericho and say without any fear, "Shout; for the LORD hath given you the city" (Josh. 6:16). Why? Because the power was personal, and the Person was there.

The Three Changeless Factors Today
As he passed from the Pentateuchal period into the post-Pentateuchal period, Joshua knew the book, the supernatural power, and the supernatural leader, who was the living God. We are not living in the time of Joshua, but the New Testament says that these three great changeless factors are true for us as the children of God today. These continuities flow from the Pentateuch through the rest of the Old Testament into the New Testament and down through history to us.

Listen to Paul: "If any man think himself to be a prophet, or spiritual, let him acknowledge that the things that I write unto you are the commandments of the LORD" (1 Cor. 14:37). Does that sound familiar? Of course! It is exactly what Moses said. If somebody comes to us, how are we to judge what he says? Judge, says Paul, on the basis of what God has written in the Book. There is no difference whatsoever in the objective standard. We have the same high possibility of objectivity, but now in a book that is enlarged. The continuity that Joshua had in his time of need, we have in our own needy generation.

Paul wrote something similar to the Thessalonians: "Therefore, brethren, stand fast, and hold the traditions which ye have been taught, whether by word or our epistle" (2 Thess. 2:15). Here again is a parallel to Moses.

Perhaps the clearest New Testament statement of the continuity of authority was made by Peter. He reminded his readers that he had stood on the Mount of Transfiguration. What a great certainty—to have heard the voice from Heaven and seen Jesus glorified! Nevertheless, Peter said, "Yes, but that was mine; and you won't have that because you weren't there. But there's something greater that we share in common." To quote directly from his letter, "We have also a more sure word of prophecy, unto which ye do well that ye take heed, as unto a light that shineth in a dark place, until the day dawn, and the day star arise in your hearts; knowing this first, that no prophecy of the scripture is of any private interpretation. For the prophecy came not in old time by the will of man, but holy men of God spoke as they were moved by the Holy Ghost" (2 Pet. 1:19-21). Peter was saying the same things as Paul. We have a written revelation; we can judge by it, and its authority is final.

Peter also brought the Old Testament and New Testament together: "that ye may be mindful of the words which were spoken before by the holy prophets, and of the commandment of us, the apostles of the Lord and Savior" (2 Pet. 3:2). He specifically included the writings of Paul in the continuity of authority: "And account that the longsuffering of our Lord is salvation, even as our beloved brother, Paul, also according to the wisdom given unto him hath written unto you; as also in all his epistles, speaking in them of these things, in which are some things hard to be understood, which they that are unlearned and unstable wrest, as they do also the other scriptures, unto their own destruction" (2 Pet. 3:15, 16).

We today have the first of the three changeless factors—a written, objective, propositional authority. As God said to Israel, "Whatsoever thing I command you, observe to do it; thou shalt not add thereto, nor diminish from it" (Deut. 12:32), John affirmed at the end of the Bible, in the book of Revelation, "For I testify unto every man that heareth the words of the prophecy of this book, If any man shall add unto these things, God shall add unto him the plagues that are written in this book; and if any man shall take away from the words of the book of this prophecy, God shall take away his part out of the book of life, and out of the holy city, and from the things which are written in this book" (Rev. 22:18, 19). It is as though God is saying, "How can you miss this? There is continuity of written objective authority all the way from the Pentateuch through the New Testament."

Concerning the second changeless factor, consider a statement of the resurrected Jesus: "All power is given unto me in heaven and in earth" (Matt. 28:18). The same power which was exhibited at the time of Moses and Joshua, Jesus claimed was now given to Him. Jesus connected this statement to the coming of the Holy Spirit: "Ye shall receive power, after the Holy Spirit is come upon you; and ye shall be witnesses unto me both in Jerusalem, and in all Judea, and in Samaria, and unto the uttermost part of the earth" (Acts 1:8). As God said to Joshua, "Remember the power? The Red Sea and Jordan rolled back!" Jesus declared to His disciples, "Don't be afraid, for this entire age will receive power from the indwelling Holy Spirit."

The power which parted the Red Sea and the Jordan flows on constantly. Facing a lost world—Jerusalem, Samaria, the ends of the earth—until Jesus comes, the Church of God has that power. The same power is available to the people of God—in the past, present and future.

The continuity of the third changeless factor, the supernatural, divine leader, comes to us with special force. In 1 Corinthians 10:4, Paul discusses the time when Moses struck the rock: "And [our fathers] did all drink the same spiritual drink; for they drank of that spiritual Rock that followed them, and that Rock was Christ." The One who was in the wilderness and the One who stood before Joshua and said, "As captain of the host of the LORD am I now come," is the same Person we know after the incarnation as Jesus Christ.

This Person spoke about the continuity of His leadership. He told His followers, "Lo, I am with you always, even unto the end of the world" (Matt. 28:20). The One who was with Moses at the rock and with Joshua at the beginning of the campaign against Jericho has promised, "Till I come again, I will be with you."

It is wonderful that the same leader is with us. Was the captain who went before Joshua in his battles some human leader? No. Must we struggle today in our own wisdom and puny strength? No; the power is there. The same leader is present, and the same leader will lead.

When Joshua saw this leader, he "fell on his face to the earth, and did worship, and said unto him, What sayeth my lord unto his servant? And the captain of the LORD's hosts said unto Joshua, Loose thy shoe from off thy foot; for the place whereon thou standest is holy." Are we to know the power of the leader who is there? Well, then let us get our shoes off! Let us never forget the words of Paul: "I am the slave of Jesus Christ." If our shoes are not off before this leader, we will not know His power. But when we take off our shoes, then, circled by the objective, written authority of the book, we will experience the continuity of both the power of God and the leadership of the great One. For the Person at the burning bush, the God of Abraham, Isaac and Jacob, the captain of the Lord's host, Jesus Christ—this One is still with us.

Each of the three great changeless factors that stood at such a crucial time as Joshua's, at the change from the Pentateuchal to the post-Pentateuchal period, continues unbroken. There are changes in history, but these three things go on without changing. We in our battles in the twentieth century have the same book, the same power, and the same leader.

CHAPTER THREE

The Continuity of the Covenant

Another historic continuity was exhibited especially clearly at the time of Joshua—the continuity of the Abrahamic covenant. God Himself reminded Joshua of the promise God had made to the patriarchs: "Be strong and of good courage; for unto this people shalt thou divide for an inheritance the land, which I swore unto their fathers to give them" (Josh. 1:6). The promise had been made, and now it was going to be fulfilled.

At the golden calf, when God had said, "This people has revolted against Me and deserves My judgment in a total way," Moses pleaded the people's cause: "Remember Abraham, Isaac, and Israel, thy servants, to whom thou didst swear by thine own self, and saidst unto them, I will multiply your seed as the stars of heaven, and all this land that I have spoken of will I give unto your seed, and they shall inherit it forever" (Ex. 32:13). Now as the people enter the land, Joshua, too, looks back to a covenant promise God made to Abraham, Isaac and Jacob: the land was to belong to the Israelites.

The Abrahamic Covenant
Let us study in some detail the Abrahamic covenant, which contained the promise of the land. This was its beginning:

> Now the LORD had said unto Abram, Get thee out of thy country, and from thy kindred, and from thy father's house, unto a land that I will show thee; and I will make of thee a great nation, and I will bless thee, and make thy name great; and thou shalt be a blessing: And I will bless them that bless thee, and curse him that curseth thee: and in thee shall all families of the earth be blessed. (Gen. 12:1-3)

Abraham was in Ur of the Chaldees when God spoke to him. First, God ordered him to leave one geographic location and travel to another geographic location, a place that was going to belong to him. Linked to this was a national blessing: a great nation would descend from him. Second, God told him that he would be a blessing beyond his own race to all the world. These were the terms of this special covenant God made with Abraham around the year 2,000 B.C.

In order to understand this covenant, however, we have to go back further still, all the way to an event we cannot date but which nevertheless occurred in history, in space and in time. God first spoke to man about a covenant of grace as soon as man had revolted against him. This revolt meant that man could no longer come to God on the basis of works. We may speak, therefore, of *the covenant of works* prior to the Fall and *the covenant of grace* after the Fall. That is, God introduced the covenant of grace because man the rebel could no longer come to him on the basis of his own works.

God first stated the covenant of grace when he cursed the serpent: "And I will put enmity between thee and the woman, and between thy seed and her seed; he shall bruise thy head, and thou shalt bruise his heel" (Gen. 3:15). At this point the person who would fulfill this statement—the "seed" who would come—is not specified beyond the fact that he would be a human being.

Soon, though, this covenant was limited in a special way: "And Adam knew his wife again; and she bore a son, and called his name Seth. For God, said she, hath appointed me another seed instead of Abel, whom Cain slew. And to Seth, to him also there was born a son; and he called his name Enos: then began men to call upon the name of the LORD [or better, to call themselves by the name of the Lord]" (Gen. 4:25, 26). A division of the human race occurred. The first son, Cain, killed his brother Abel, and another son, Seth, was born to take Abel's place. The human race is united—it comes from one ancestor; yet it is divided into two human races, one having turned back to God and the other standing in the flow of the rebellion. The promised one would come from the former strand.

Later, God limited the covenant of grace further, narrowing the lineage of the promised one from the whole human race down to the Semitic people. This occurred in the time of Noah (again, an event of history, though one we cannot date). Noah prophesied to his three sons, "Blessed be the LORD God of Shem; and Canaan shall be his servant. God shall enlarge Japheth, and he shall dwell in the tents of Shem; and Canaan shall be his servant" (Gen. 9:26, 27). Usually it is considered, and probably quite correctly, that Shem is the ancestor of the Semitic people.

Finally, around 2,000 B.C. (the first time we can bring the biblical narrative into a clear relationship with recorded secular history), the covenant of grace was brought down to a specific man, Abraham, and to a specific nation, Israel. Abraham came from the high Sumerian culture. He was called into a different land and became the first Jew.

As we have seen, the covenant God made with Abraham had two aspects. The more important was a spiritual promise: all the world would be blessed through Abraham. This related to the promise that somebody was coming who would crush the serpent's head. Christ, of course, eventually came from Abraham to the whole human race.

The second aspect of the Abrahamic covenant was the national blessing. In addition to the spiritual blessing to the whole world, God promised Abraham, "I will make of thee a great nation" (Gen. 12:2). In relation to the national blessing came a corollary blessing—the promise of the land. If I were making an outline, I would put spiritual blessing as point 1, national blessing as point 2, and the land as point 2a.

In all its parts, this covenant was *unconditional*. Later, God added conditional portions. If the Israelites as a nation were obedient, certain good things would happen (see, for example, Deuteronomy 27—28). If they were disobedient, they would be taken into captivity. We see the same interplay, by the way, in God's dealings with David and Solomon. David was given an unconditional portion—from him would come the Messiah. But Solomon had a conditional portion—if Solomon and his descendants continued with God, the Messianic line would come through them. Since they did not fulfill the condition, the Messianic line through Mary did not descend through Solomon. Christ was born of David, but not Solomon. Mary came through another son of David and Bathsheba, Nathan (Luke 3:31). The Messiah had to be born of David and of Abraham, because this was God's unconditional promise. So, while God later added conditional portions, the Abrahamic covenant as a whole could be called *an eternal covenant*.

Let us now study the two aspects of this covenant in more detail.

The Spiritual Portion

Shortly after Christ had died, Peter stood in the temple area and preached to the Jews:

> For Moses truly said unto the fathers, A prophet shall the Lord, your God, raise up unto you of your brethren, like unto me; him shall ye hear in all things, whatsoever he shall say unto you. . . . Yea, and all the prophets from Samuel and those who follow after, as many as have spoken, have likewise foretold of these days. Ye are the children of the prophets, and of the covenant which God made with our fathers, saying unto Abraham, And in thy seed shall all the kindreds of the earth be blessed. Unto you first God, having raised up his Son, Jesus, sent him to bless you, in turning away every one of you from his iniquities. (Acts 3:22, 24-26)

Peter was teaching that Moses had given a Messianic prophecy: the Christ would come as a prophet parallel to Moses. That is, Peter first turned the people's minds toward Moses. The Jews, of course, were well instructed in all this; so Peter only had to say a few words and they understood the flow. Peter then related Moses' prophecy to the Abrahamic covenant. Peter's sermon has meaning only in relation to this covenant. Right away on Pentecost, Peter said that the Gentiles were going to have a part in the spiritual blessing, though he seems not to have understood its full import until his experience with Cornelius (Acts 10) and his confrontation with Paul (Gal. 2:14).

Then he addressed the people as Jews and said to them, in effect, "You have an opportunity now, individually, to enter into the spiritual part of the Abrahamic covenant." This was a clear indication that not every Jew is under the spiritual portion of the covenant merely because he is part of the nation. Each individual must make a personal decision with regard to the Messiah.

Paul emphasized to the Romans that non-Jews, too, can come under the spiritual portion of the Abrahamic covenant: "Therefore, it is of faith, that it might be by grace, to the end the promise might be sure to all the seed; not to that only which is of the law [that is, to those who are Jews], but to that also which is of the faith of Abraham, who is the father of us all" (Rom. 4:16). Paul was encompassing both the Jewish and Gentile believers of his day under the Abrahamic covenant. He tied this up by quoting one of God's statements to Abraham: "As it is written, I have made thee a father of many nations" (Rom. 4:17).

Paul wrote to the Galatians, "Abraham believed God, and it was accounted to him for righteousness. Know ye, therefore, that they who are of faith, the same are the children of Abraham. And the scripture, foreseeing that God would justify the heathen through faith, preached before the gospel unto Abraham, saying, In thee shall all nations be blessed" (Gal. 3:6-8). This is the New Testament's exegesis of what Genesis means when it says that the whole world is blessed in Abraham: the blessing is one of forgiveness of sins on the basis of the work of Christ. With it comes the corollary that when we accept Christ as our Savior we become spiritual Jews, Abraham's children in faith. If we are Gentiles, we do not become national Jews. But whether we are Jew or Gentile, we have the blessing of being spiritual children of Abraham when we follow Abraham's example—that is, when we stop calling God a liar and believe Him. The first step in believing in Christ (the Messiah) as Savior is believing God.

Two other verses in Galatians reinforce this exegesis: "That the blessing of Abraham might come on the Gentiles through Jesus Christ, that we might receive the promise of the Spirit through faith" (Gal. 3:14); and "If ye be Christ's, then are ye Abraham's seed, and heirs according to the promise" (Gal. 3:29). What promise? The spiritual portion of the Abrahamic covenant.

One major way Abraham showed his faith was his willingness to sacrifice his son. In this we have a forecast of the death of Christ and an indication of Abraham's knowledge that more was involved here than the immediate situation, to such an extent that after Abraham had taken his long journey to the place where God had ordered him to go, "Abraham called the name of that place Jehovah-jireh"—that is, "The Lord will see or provide" (Gen. 22:14). The phrase definitely indicates the future: "As it is said to this day, In the mount of the LORD it shall be seen" (Gen. 22:14).

It is intriguing that the place, Moriah, to which Abraham was taken over these many weary miles was exactly the site that later was to be Jerusalem (2 Chron. 3:1). We have to be careful about saying how much Abraham himself understood in all the details, but there was no blind "leap of faith." Abraham had had much contact with God before this, and much knowledge from God before this event. Here was a forecast that something was coming, a forecast that the Lord would especially provide in this place. The whole setting is a picture of the great sacrifice, when God the Father sent the Son, and the Son was willing to go.

In addition to the fact that when we believe the promises of God as Abraham did we become Abraham's spiritual children, Paul emphasized the personal act of faith through which Abraham entered into a relationship with God:

> For what saith the scripture? Abraham believed God, and it was counted unto him for righteousness. . . . And he received the sign of circumcision, a seal of the righteousness of the faith which he had yet being uncircumcised, that he might be the father of all them that believe, though they be not circumcised, that righteousness might be imputed unto them also; and the father of circumcision to them who are not of the circumcision only, but who also walk in the steps of that faith of our father, Abraham, which he had being yet uncircumcised. . . . Therefore, it is of faith, that it might be by grace, to the end the promise might be sure to all the seed; not to that only which is of the law, but to that also which is of the faith of Abraham, who is the father of us all. (Rom. 4:3, 11, 12, 16).

That people were not spiritual Jews just because they were natural Jews was true before Christ as well as after. There were two Israels: those who were born into the national line only, and those who believed God and His promises. In talking about the Old Testament Jews, Paul said it is "not as though the word of God hath taken no effect. For they are not all Israel, who are of Israel; neither, because they are the seed of Abraham, are they all children" (Rom. 9:6, 7). A person did not automatically fall under the spiritual promises to Abraham because he was a member of national Israel.

This will also be true in the future. Speaking of the Jews' destiny as a nation, Paul wrote, "For if the casting away of them be the reconciling of the world, what shall the receiving of them be, but life from the dead?" (Rom. 11:15). I will not exegete this entire verse, but I do want to point out that a time is coming when the nation will be a spiritual, believing Israel. Romans 11:25 adds, "Blindness in part is happened to Israel, until the fullness of the

Gentiles be come in." The phrase "in part" is a happy one, for multitudes of individual Jews from the book of Acts onward have believed and become spiritual Jews, as well as being natural Jews by birth. Looking to the future of the Jews as a nation, Romans 11:26 says, "And so all Israel shall be saved." And it is in this setting that Romans 11:29 says, "For the gifts and calling of God are without repentance." As there is a continuity of the book, the power and the divine leader, so there is a continuity of spiritual blessings—in the past, present and future—under the spiritual portion of the Abrahamic covenant.

The National Portion
The national portion of the Abrahamic covenant had a strong relationship to the land. In his first promises to Abraham God used the phrases, "unto a land that I will show thee" and "unto thy seed will I give this land." And this promise is referred to constantly throughout the Scriptures. David composed a song about it in approximately the year 1,000 B.C.: "Be ye mindful always of his covenant; the word which he commanded to a thousand generations, even of the covenant which he made with Abraham, and of his oath unto Isaac, and hath confirmed the same to Jacob for a law, and to Israel for an everlasting covenant, saying, Unto thee will I give the land of Canaan, the lot of your inheritance" (1 Chron. 16:15-18). David used the term "everlasting covenant" in relation to the Jews as a nation and then quoted immediately the promise about the land. "The lot of your inheritance" could be translated, "the cord of your inheritance." The picture is that the people of Israel have various blessings, like individual beads, but the string which ties the separate beads together is the land of Canaan.

Psalm 105 contains an exact parallel: "He hath remembered his covenant forever, the word which he commanded to a thousand generations. Which covenant he made with Abraham, and his oath unto Isaac, and confirmed the same unto Jacob for a law, and to Israel for an everlasting covenant, saying, Unto thee will I give the land of Canaan, the lot of your inheritance" (Ps. 105:8-11). Again, the terms "everlasting covenant" and "the lot (the cord) of your inheritance" are used. Again, the land ties the promises together.

After Abraham had gone into Egypt and returned to Shechem, God repeated his promise to Abraham: "For all the land which thou seest, to thee will I give it, and to thy seed forever. And I will make thy seed as the dust of the earth, so that if a man can number the dust of the earth, then shall thy seed also be numbered. Arise, walk through the land in the length of it and in the breadth of it; for I will give it unto thee" (Gen. 13:15-17). God began by mentioning the land, for this was the heart of His promise. To whom was He going to give it? To the nation forever. I think his seed being "as the dust of the earth" refers to both the national and spiritual seed; so Christians, too, fall in that number.

Later, God repeated the promise, this time in a startling way:

> And he brought him forth abroad, and said, Look now toward heaven, and tell the stars, if thou be able to number them: and he said unto him, So shall thy seed be. And he believed in the LORD; and he counted it to him for righteousness. And he said unto him, I am the LORD that brought thee out of Ur of the Chaldeans to give thee this land to inherit it. And he said, Lord GOD, whereby shall I know that I shall inherit it? And he said unto him, Take me an heifer of three years old, and a she-goat of three years old, and a ram of three years old, and a turtledove, and a young pigeon. And he took unto him all these, and divided them in the midst, and laid each piece one against another: but the birds divided he not. And when the fowls came down upon the carcasses, Abram drove them away. And when the sun was going down, a deep sleep fell upon Abram; and, lo, an horror of great darkness fell upon him. And he said unto Abram, Know of a surety that thy seed shall be a stranger in a land that is not theirs, and shall serve them; and they shall afflict them four hundred years; and also that nation, whom they shall serve, will I judge: and afterward shall they come out with great substance. And thou shalt go to thy fathers in peace; thou shalt be buried in a good old age. But in the fourth generation they shall come here again; for the iniquity of the Amorites is not yet full. And it came to pass that, when the sun went down, and it was dark, behold a smoking furnace, and a burning lamp that passed between those pieces. In the same day the LORD made a covenant with Abram, saying, Unto thy seed have I given this land, from the river of Egypt unto the great river, the river Euphrates. (Gen. 15:5-18)

This incident turned upon God's response to Abraham's question, "Whereby shall I know that I shall inherit it?" In an important moment, God gave a tremendous answer. I would call this *the cutting of the friendship covenant* between God and Abraham.

The cutting of a friendship covenant was well-known in almost every land of the ancient East. To cut a friendship covenant, one took a prescribed kind of animal and cut it in half. The two halves were placed a distance apart, and the two parties walked together between them. This action bound generations of families together forever. Because it was so binding, it was rarely done.

Cutting a friendship covenant was practiced in China as recently as the last century. There a cock was used. Either before walking between the pieces or afterwards, the parties would also take a beautiful piece of tapestry with a cock woven into it and tear it in two. Each family would keep a half. Generations later, when somebody brought to a member of a family a half of a tapestry which matched a half he had, he was bound to provide friendship at any cost. This was both beautiful and profound.

God cut an everlasting covenant of friendship with Abraham. They did not walk between the pieces together, because God is God and Abraham was only Abraham. But God represented Himself with a burning lamp of fire, which went between the two pieces and thereby eternally established the covenant. Though I have no way to prove it, I am convinced that when the Bible speaks of Abraham being God's friend (see 2 Chron. 20:7; Isa. 41:8; Jas. 2:23), it is referring to the cutting of the friendship covenant.

God reminded Abraham of this covenant when Abraham was ninety-nine years old:

> And I will make my covenant between me and thee, and will multiply thee exceedingly. And Abram fell on his face: and God talked with him, saying, As for me, behold, my covenant is with thee, and thou shalt be a father of many nations. Neither shall thy name any more be called Abram, but thy name shall be Abraham; for a father of many nations have I made thee. And I will make thee exceedingly fruitful, and I will make nations out of thee, and kings shall come out of thee. And I will establish my covenant between me and thee and thy seed after thee in their generations for an everlasting covenant, to be a God unto thee, and to thy seed after thee. And I will give unto thee, and to thy seed after thee, the land wherein thou art a stranger, all the land of Canaan, for an everlasting possession; and I will be their God. (Gen. 17:2-8)

First God mentioned the national promise, then the spiritual one. God again called the covenant "an everlasting covenant," and the promise of the land to the Jews as the Jews once more had a part. Paul interpreted one of the statements to mean that others besides the Jews would fall under *the spiritual blessing:* "As for me, behold, my covenant is with thee, and thou shalt be a father of many nations." (See Rom. 4:17.)

So over many years God made it abundantly clear to Abraham that a great nation would come from him and that He would give this nation the land of Canaan.

The Promises Repeated

After Abraham died, God reassured Abraham's son, Isaac, that He would fulfill His promises. Not surprisingly, God began with the land: "Sojourn in this land, and I will be with thee, and will bless thee; for unto thee, and unto thy seed, I will give all these countries, and I will perform the oath which I swore unto Abraham thy father" (Gen. 26:3). He then went on to repeat the spiritual portion: "In thy seed shall all the nations of the earth be blessed" (Gen. 26:4). God spoke the promise to Isaac a second time, though this time the land was not mentioned (Gen. 26:23, 24).

The covenant was also made twice with Jacob. Having come into conflict with his brother Esau, Jacob fled the land. At a certain place he stopped for the night. He dreamed that he saw a ladder reaching to Heaven, and in the dream God spoke to him. As in his dealings with Abraham and Isaac, God began with the promise of the land: "And, behold, the LORD stood above it, and said, I am the LORD God of Abraham, thy father, and the God of Isaac: the land whereon thou liest, to thee will I give it, and to thy seed" (Gen. 28:13). And he also spoke of the spiritual promise: "In thy seed shall all the families of the earth be blessed" (Gen. 28:14).

God repeated the covenant to Jacob when he was coming back to the land after his years abroad. Though Jacob's name was changed, the covenant retained the same elements: the national blessing and the land.

> And God appeared unto Jacob again, when he came out of Padan-aram, and blessed him. And God said unto him, Thy name is Jacob: thy name shall not be called any more Jacob, but Israel shall be thy name: and he called his name Israel. And God said unto him, I am God Almighty: be fruitful and multiply; a nation and a company of nations shall be of thee, and kings shall come out of thy loins; and the land which I gave Abraham and Isaac, to thee I will give it, and to thy seed after thee will I give the land. (Gen. 35:9-12)

Years later in Egypt, as Joseph, one of Jacob's sons, lay dying, the promise about the land was on his mind: "And Joseph said unto his brethren, I die; and God will surely visit you, and bring you out of this land unto the land which he swore to Abraham, to Isaac, and to Jacob. And Joseph took an oath of the children of Israel, saying, God will surely visit you, and ye shall carry up my bones from here" (Gen. 50:24, 25). Because these were the covenant promises of God and because God is not a liar, Joseph said to his people, "Don't worry. The promise will be fulfilled. God will take you back in due time. I don't want my bones left here in Egypt. Take them with you when you go." This, incidentally, they did.

When the Passover, a new order of worship, was established, the promise of the land was again involved: "And it shall come to pass, when ye be come to the land which the LORD will give you, according as he hath promised, that ye shall keep this service" (Ex. 12:25). To whom did God make the promise that is mentioned? To Abraham, Isaac and Jacob. When the people entered the land, however, their order of worship was to be the Passover celebration and all that God commanded Moses on Sinai concerning worship, rather than patriarchal worship.

At Mount Sinai, as we have seen, the race finally became a nation. For the first time the word *nation* could be used to describe an immediate historic reality: "Now therefore, if ye will obey my voice indeed, and keep my covenant, then ye shall be a peculiar treasure unto me above all people; for all the earth is mine; and ye shall be unto me a kingdom of priests, and an holy nation" (Ex. 19:5, 6). At Sinai the people were given the law, and the nation was to be a holy nation.

As the people left Sinai, all but one piece was in place. They were now a nation, they had the law, they had been given the new order of worship, they had the book (Ex. 17:14). The last of the pieces, the promise of the land, was ready to be put in place. In only a year and two months after being slaves in Egypt, the people were ready to complete the full complex of the promise of God! Then the spies were sent out, and they came back with the majority report that led the people into real rebellion. There was no need to stay in the wilderness a further thirty-eight years. The people had only to believe the promises which had been given; instead, they rebelled.

At the end of the wilderness wandering, this unnecessary parenthesis in Jewish history, the Lord said to Moses, "This is the land which I swore unto Abraham, unto Isaac, and unto Jacob, saying, I will give it unto thy seed. I have caused thee to see it with thine eyes, but thou shalt not go over there" (Deut. 34:4). Moses was able to look at the land, but he was not able to go into it.

As Joshua waited to enter Canaan, the promise concerning the nation and the land that had been repeated over and over again for all these years was a tremendous factor emotionally, theologically and practically.

We can now more fully understand all that was involved as God spoke to Joshua, particularly as we pay attention to the matter of the land.

> Now after the death of Moses, the servant of the LORD, it came to pass that the LORD spoke unto Joshua, the son of Nun, Moses' minister, saying, Moses, my servant, is dead; now therefore arise, go over this Jordan, thou and all this people, unto the land which I do give to them, even to the children of Israel. Every place that the sole of your foot shall tread upon, that have I given unto you, as I said unto Moses. From the wilderness and this Lebanon even unto the great river, the river Euphrates, all the land of the Hittites, and unto the great sea toward the going down of the sun, shall be your coast. . . . Be strong and of good courage; for unto this people shalt thou divide for an inheritance the land which I swore unto their fathers to give them. . . . Then Joshua commanded the officers of the people, saying, Pass through the host and command the people, saying, Prepare victuals; for within three days ye shall pass over this Jordan, to go in to possess the land, which the LORD your God giveth you to possess it. (Josh. 1:1-4, 6, 10, 11)

Can you imagine the impact Joshua's words had upon the people as they stood looking across the Jordan? Within three days the great promises were going to be fulfilled!

The Gifts of God Are Without Repentance

The continuity of the national portion of the covenant did not end with Joshua, or with Jews today, any more than the continuity of the spiritual portion ended with him. We have seen that the spiritual side of the covenant has something to say to the Jews in the Old Testament, to the Jews in the early church, to the Jews of today and the Jews of the future, and to the Gentiles also. The land, too, was tied with the everlastingness of the covenant: "And I will establish my covenant between me and thee and thy seed after thee in their generations for an everlasting covenant, to be a

God unto thee, and to thy seed after thee. And I will give unto thee, and to thy seed after thee, the land wherein thou art a stranger, all the land of Canaan, for an everlasting possession; and I will be their God" (Gen. 17:7, 8).

As we have seen, Paul, speaking about the future of the Jews, said that "the gifts and calling of God are without repentance [literally, are not repented of]" (Rom. 11:29). In other words, God is not done with the Jews. He has made promises which He Himself has said are everlasting.

Jeremiah, one of the Old Testament prophets, dealt with the everlastingness of the covenant in relation to the land:

> Thus saith the LORD, who giveth the sun for a light by day, and the ordinances of the moon and of the stars for a light by night, who divideth the sea when its waves roar; the LORD of hosts is his name: If those ordinances depart from before me, saith the LORD, then the seed of Israel also shall cease from being a nation before me forever. Thus saith the LORD, If heaven above can be measured, and the foundations of the earth searched out beneath, I will also cast off all the seed of Israel for all that they have done, saith the LORD. (Jer. 31:35-37)

Just as God made an everlasting covenant with nature at the time of Noah—that the order of nature will not be ended throughout this era—He made a covenant with the nation Israel with as great a finality. If one cannot change, the other cannot change.

At a time when because of the Babylonian and Assyrian captivities people were saying, "God has cast off the Jews," Jeremiah wrote,

> Considerest thou not what this people have spoken, saying, The two families which the LORD hath chosen, he hath even cast them off? Thus they have despised my people, that they should be no more a nation before them. Thus saith the LORD, If my covenant be not with day and night, and if I have not appointed the ordinances of heaven and earth, then will I cast away the seed of Jacob . . . for I will cause their captivity to return, and have mercy on them. (Jer. 33:24-26)

This prophecy should ram into our thinking that God's promise regarding the nation is indeed without change.

In this Jeremiah passage the captivity mentioned cannot be just the Babylonian captivity because it is related to the covenant with nature, which continues throughout the whole era. Ezekiel, in a prophecy written at approximately the same time, related the covenant to that future day of which Paul spoke, a future in which Israel as Israel will be saved and will come into the same kind of situation as the individual Jews who believed at Pentecost and since: "A new heart also will I give you, and a new spirit will I put within you; and I will take away the stony heart out of your flesh, and I will give you an heart of flesh. And I will put my spirit within you, and cause you to walk in my statutes, and ye shall keep mine judgments, and do them" (Ezek. 36:26, 27). This relates to the promise of Joel (Joel 2:28—3:1), which was partially fulfilled at Pentecost and which partially remains to be fulfilled.

Clearly, the gifts and calling of God are without repentance in both halves of the Abrahamic covenant—the spiritual and the national.

Was God Unjust?

We are left with one final question—for our century one that is gigantic. Was it unjust for Joshua to drive out the people who were in the land? It is quite clear, as we have seen, that God promised His people the land, but wasn't this unjust to those who were living there already?

During the cutting of the friendship covenant, God said to Abraham, "But in the fourth generation they [Abraham's descendants] shall come here again" (Gen. 15:16). There was a reason they had nothing to do with: "The iniquity of the Amorites [was] not yet full" (Gen. 15:16). At the same time that God swore He would give the Jews the land, He informed Abraham that the Amorites' iniquity had not yet come to that level of revolt which made it the proper time to deal with it.

Immediately before the time of Joshua, however, Moses said to the people,

Speak not thou in thine heart, after the LORD thy God hath cast them out from before thee, saying, For my righteousness the LORD hath brought me in to possess this land; but for the wickedness of these nations the LORD doth drive them out from before thee. Not for thy righteousness, nor for the uprightness of thine heart, dost thou go to possess their land, but for the wickedness of these nations the LORD thy God doth drive them out from before thee, and that he may perform the word which the LORD swore unto thy fathers, Abraham, Isaac, and Jacob. (Deut. 9:4, 5)

Moses was telling the people, "Don't think you are getting the

land because you are so good. Rather, it is because the iniquity of
the people in the land has come to such a climax. The covenant
promise is there, but God has waited hundreds of years for the
Amorites' cup of iniquity to flow over."

I think of the cup of iniquity in a visual way. I imagine myself
holding a cup which has water dripping into it. The water does
not come quickly, but I keep holding the cup up. Gradually the
water rises, and at a certain point it flows over the brim. This is
the principle of the judgment of God: man is in revolt against
God, and God waits in longsuffering until every possibility of
man's turning back is exhausted. When the iniquity is full, when
the cup overflows, God's judgment comes.

This was true at the time of the flood: "And GOD saw that the
wickedness of man was great in the earth, and that every imagination of the thoughts of his heart was only evil continually" (Gen.
6:5). Men were in total rebellion against God. Genesis 6:11, 12
indicates that "the earth also was corrupt before God, and the
earth was filled with violence. And God looked upon the earth,
and, behold, it was corrupt; for all flesh had corrupted his way
upon the earth." God waited, we do not know how long. Then
came the judgment of the flood. When did it take place? When the
cup was full.

In the story of Sodom the same principle is reiterated (Gen.
18:20-33). Because Abraham bargained with God on behalf of the
city, it almost seems as though Abraham understood this principle
with exactitude.

We might paraphrase the biblical account like this. God said to
Abraham, "Sodom is utterly wicked! It is time to destroy this
rotten city!"

Abraham responded, "Lord, if there are fifty righteous people
there, will You refrain from destroying it?"

"Yes," God replied. "If there are fifty righteous people there,
the iniquity is not yet full."

"What if there are forty-five?"

"All right, if there are forty-five, the iniquity is not yet full."

"What about forty?"

"All right."

"Thirty?"

"All right."

"Twenty?"

"All right."

"Ten?"

"Yes, even ten!"

But since not even ten righteous people could be found, Sodom was destroyed. The Sodomites' cup had been filling, filling, filling; and when the iniquity at Sodom reached a certain level, judgment came.

When the Israelites stood on the east bank of the Jordan, the iniquity of the Amorites was full. The sword of Joshua was the sword of God in judgment—an exact parallel to the flood and to the destruction of Sodom.

Many of the Canaanite cities have been dug up, and one can see that the statuettes which were worshipped by the Canaanites at this period were overwhelmingly perverse. The worship was wrapped up not only with complete rebellion against God, but with all kinds of sexual sin. The statuettes were as pornographic as some of today's worst pictures! And in its violence, their culture became equal to ours. So in Moses' time God said, "All right, it is time for the judgment." This reminds us that there is "death in the city" in our own culture.

We have here another continuity: the principle that when iniquity and rebellion come to the full, then God judges. The principle still is in operation. Jesus said, "When the Son of man cometh, shall he find faith on the earth?" (Luke 18:8). Though the Gentile world has had the advantages of the Christian age, wickedness will come to the full before the coming of Christ. The book of Revelation indicates the same thing. Then the principle will be applied again, and the judgment related to the second coming of Christ will fall.

At that time "all Israel shall be saved; as it is written, There shall come out of Zion the Deliverer, and shall turn away ungodliness from Jacob; for this is my covenant unto them, when I shall take away their sins" (Rom. 11:26, 27). God has made a covenant, and all the Jews—all Israel—are going to come to this place of spiritual blessing when the Gentiles' iniquity is full.

Jesus said the same thing: "And they shall fall by the edge of the sword, and shall be led away captive into all nations; and Jerusalem shall be trodden down of the Gentiles, until the times of the Gentiles be fulfilled" (Luke 21:24). When the iniquity is full, the course of events will be reversed, and a blessing will come to Israel as Israel. When the disciples asked Him, "What's it going to be like when You come back and judge?" Jesus replied, "It's going to be like two periods, like the days of Noah and the days of Sodom. When it is like those days, I will come back and judge" (Luke 17:26-30).

The Scripture insists that in a time still future to the present ticking of the clock, when the iniquity of the Gentiles is full, a greater Joshua will come and function once more in judgment:

> And I saw heaven opened and, behold, a white horse; and he that sat upon him was called Faithful and True, and in righteousness he doth judge and make war. His eyes were as a flame of fire, and on his head were many crowns; and he had a name written, that no man knew, but he himself. And he was clothed with a vesture dipped in blood; and his name is called The Word of God. And the armies that were in heaven followed him upon white horses, clothed in fine linen, white and clean. And out of his mouth goeth a sharp sword, that with it he should smite the nations, and he shall rule them with a rod of iron; and he treadeth the winepress of the fierceness and wrath of Almighty God. And he hath on his vesture and on his thigh a name written, KING OF KINGS, AND LORD OF LORDS. (Rev. 19:11-16)

This is the greater Joshua, Jesus Christ. The One who died so that men can escape judgment will be the One who will be the Judge. And it is this Christ who stood before Joshua as the captain of the host of the Lord.

A cup filled with iniquity followed by God's judgment—this is the negative side of the covenant of grace. Why did there have to be a covenant of grace? Because man rebelled and could not come to God in his own goodness. Man was under the judgment of God with true moral guilt before God. So God had to give the covenant of grace at the terrible cost of Christ's death because men were justly under God's condemnation and judgment without it.

We have come now to the last of the continuities I wanted to look at before we examine the book of Joshua in detail. Out of the Pentateuch, through the book of Joshua, to the rest of the Bible and to a time future to ourselves, there is a continuity of the patience of God and the judgment which comes when iniquity is full. The books are not balanced in this life. If we live only between birth and death, we must acknowledge that we live not in a moral universe, but in an amoral universe. But if a holy God exists, we live in a moral universe, and that is wonderful. But again, this carries with it that insofar as the books are not balanced in this life, there will be the judgment of God in the future.

This brings us back to Joshua at Jericho. There he met the

Christ of the cross, the Christ of the book of Revelation, who is the Judge, who told him that Jericho would fall. As we comprehend the continuities of the book, the supernatural power, the supernatural leader and the covenant (including the principle of judgment), we are ready to understand the taking of the land.

CHAPTER FOUR

Rahab

In the last chapter we focused on the continuity of the national portion of the Abrahamic covenant as it flowed down to the time of Joshua and beyond. Is there anything in the crucial moment of history in which Joshua lived which can show us the continuity of the spiritual blessing? Indeed there is: Rahab the harlot.

The Spies' Perspective
While the Israelites were camped at Shittim, Joshua sent two spies across the Jordan. "And they went, and came into an harlot's house, named Rahab, and lodged there" (Josh. 2:1). Why did the two spies go to a harlot's house? The answer is simple: they went where they could easily "get lost," where they could find shelter with some degree of freedom. There is no place like a harlot's house for people coming and going. There is no indication whatever that they went there for any immoral purpose; this simply does not exist in the story.

Rahab gave the spies two things. First, she gave them shelter. They were filled with thankfulness that she had hid them and saved their lives, not only because they escaped personally, but because her help made possible the success of their venture.

Second, she spoke the words which provided the key to the spies' report to Joshua:

> And she said unto the men, I know that the LORD hath given you the land, and that your terror is fallen upon us, and that all the inhabitants of the land faint [literally, melt] because of you. For we have heard how the LORD dried up the water of the Red Sea for you, when ye came out of Egypt; and what ye did unto the two kings of the Amorites, who were on the other side Jordan, Sihon and Og, whom ye utterly destroyed. And as soon as we had heard these things, our hearts did melt, neither did there remain any more courage in any man, because of you; for the LORD your God, he is God in heaven above, and in earth beneath. (Josh. 2:9-11)

In this remarkable set of words Rahab verbalized the truth to these two spies. The spies came to a most unlikely place, and the words of this woman told them exactly what the situation was.

There was a parallel event in the life of Gideon. God told Gideon that Gideon would save Israel from the hand of the Midianites, and Gideon asked for two different signs to confirm this. After responding to Gideon's request, God gave him one more sign that he did not ask for. God told him to go down at night to the camp of the Midianites. So Gideon went down with his servant. Standing on the periphery of the camp, they heard two Midianites talking:

> And when Gideon was come, behold, there was a man that told a dream unto his fellow, and said, Behold, I dreamed a dream, and, lo, a cake of barley bread tumbled into the host of Midian, and came unto a tent, and smote it that it fell, and overturned it, that the tent lay along. And his fellow answered and said, This is nothing else save the sword of Gideon, the son of Joash, a man of Israel; for into his hand hath God delivered Midian, and all the host. And it was so, when Gideon heard the telling of the dream, and the interpretation thereof, that he worshiped, and returned into the host of Israel, and said, Arise; for the LORD hath delivered into your hand the host of Midian. (Judg. 7:13-15)

As with the two spies and Rahab, what Gideon heard was giving encouragement through the words of an enemy. This convinced him of the final outcome, thus enabling him to say with courage, "There is no question that we are going to be victorious." From the mouth of somebody on "the other side" came a verbalization that completely settled the situation.

The spies had real faith. For when they responded to Rahab's request, they told her that her life would be saved "*when* the Lord hath given us the land" (Josh. 2:14). Not *if* but *when*. These men understood that God's promises were going to stand sure. This was a complete contrast to the ten spies at the time of Moses.

Also a great contrast to the failure of thirty-eight years before was the reply the two men gave to Joshua: "Truly the LORD hath delivered into our hands all the land; for even all the inhabitants of the country do faint because of us" (Josh. 2:24). This sounds almost exactly like what Joshua and Caleb had said. The two spies sent to Jericho were faithful, not just in the sense of having good eyes, but in the sense of believing the promises of God.

Rahab's Perspective

Rahab was a harlot in a heathen land. Some people have been embarrassed by this and have tried to tone it down, but it is impossible to do so. That is really what she was. It is the only thing the Hebrew word in Joshua 2:1 can mean.

When she had the men in her house, Rahab besought them in this way:

> Now therefore, I pray you, swear unto me by the LORD, since I have shown you kindness, that ye will also show kindness unto my father's house, and give me a true token; and that ye will save alive my father, and my mother, and my brethren, and my sisters, and all that they have, and deliver our lives from death. And the men answered her, Our life for yours if ye utter not this our business. And it shall be, when the LORD hath given us the land, that we will deal kindly and truly with thee. Then she let them down by a cord through the window; for her house was upon the town wall, and she dwelt upon the wall. And she said unto them, Get you to the mountain, lest the pursuers meet you; and hide yourselves there three days, until the pursuers be returned; and afterward may ye go your way. And the men said unto her, We will be blameless of this thine oath which thou hast made us swear. Behold, when we come into the land, thou shalt bind this line of scarlet thread in the window by which thou didst let us down; and thou shalt bring thy father, and thy mother, and thy brethren, and all thy father's household, home unto thee. And it shall be, that whosoever shall go out of the doors of thy house into the street, his blood shall be upon his head, and we will be guiltless: and whosoever shall be with thee in the house, his blood shall be on our head, if any hand be upon him. And if thou utter this our business, then we will be quit of thine oath which thou hast made us to swear. And she said, According unto your words, so be it. And she sent them

away, and they departed; and she bound the scarlet line in the window. (Josh. 2:12-21).

There is no mention here of husband or children. Those designated to be saved are of her "father's household." Verse 18 shows that none of her family lived with her. This is consistent with the word Scripture uses to describe her. Later, when Jericho was taken, who did the spies bring out? "Rahab, and her father, and her mother, and her brethren . . . all her kindred . . . Joshua saved Rahab, the harlot, alive, and her father's household" (Josh. 6:23, 25). We miss the whole point of the story, therefore, if we become embarrassed and soften it: Rahab was a harlot in a heathen land.

But Rahab had two things going for her. First, she had heard something *propositional*. She had heard what had happened in space-time history when the Hebrews came out of Egypt and when they had fought against Sihon and Og, two nearby powers.

Second, in her presence were two spies who represented to her the whole Israelite nation. This is one reason why it was important that the two men did not go to her because she was a harlot. To her they were representatives of God's people. And they did not waver in their faith before this woman (Josh. 2:14). What she had was the message and the tangible contact with two spies.

Surrounding Rahab, however, was a hostile and awesome environment: Jericho, the mighty fortress, with its great walls. Jericho had stood for hundreds of years; it was impregnable, or so its inhabitants thought. So, though Rahab had heard a propositional message and though she had the two spies standing before her, she was still surrounded by a monolithic mentality, an entire world-view. She was pressured by a powerful city and an ancient culture continuing on in its normal life—eating, drinking, marrying and so forth. At that moment she could see nothing with her eyes which indicated it would fall.

What did Rahab do? In the midst of this tension, Rahab believed. This is the crux of the story. "I know that the LORD has given you the land," she said. "The LORD your God, he is God in heaven above, and in earth beneath" (Josh. 2:9, 11). Her statement about God was universal and total.

How did she know that? We are not told. Often in Scripture we find that people knew things, though we are not told *how* they came to know them. But Rahab knew! And what she knew was totally against her culture. She believed in a new God, a God totally and diametrically opposed to the gods of Jericho, but a God above all other gods, a universal God. In the midst of the Canaanites, the Ammonites, the Amorites—in the midst of their horrible, polluted worship, laden with sex symbols and sex practices—Rahab affirmed a true theological proposition about who God really is.

Abraham in his day believed God, and it was counted to him for righteousness. Joshua also made a personal choice: "And if it seem evil unto you to serve the LORD, choose you this day whom ye will serve, whether the gods which your fathers served that were on the other side of the flood [that is, on the other side of the Euphrates], or the gods of the Amorites, in whose land ye dwell; but as for me and my house, we will serve the LORD" (Josh. 24:15). Rahab stood in exactly the same position. Surrounded by those who worshiped the Canaanite and Amorite gods, she made her decision: "By an act of the will, on the basis of the knowledge that I have, I declare in faith that God is the God of Heaven above and the earth beneath. He is the universal God."

Peter preached to the Jews on Pentecost that the covenant was fulfilled in the coming of Christ, but that each person had to believe individually. As Paul preached throughout the Roman Empire, non-Jews began to believe. At the time of Joshua, Rahab stood in the stream of the spiritual portion of the covenant as a believing non-Jew. She stood where the Gentiles stood in the New Testament when they first believed the gospel in Antioch. She stood exactly where most Christians stand today, for most of us are non-Jewish believers.

This non-Jew believed and passed from the kingdom of the Amorites to the kingdom of the Jews. But she did something much more profound than exchanging one human citizenship for another. She also passed from the kingdom of darkness to the kingdom of God's dear Son. The book of Hebrews makes a tremendous statement about Rahab, paralleling her to other heroes of the faith: "By faith the harlot, Rahab, perished not with them that believed not, when she had received the spies with peace" (Heb. 11:31). There were those who did not believe, but she did believe; so she did not perish. More than this, she became something that not all the Jews were, because, as we have seen, not all the Jews were spiritual Jews. Many who stood in the natural line of the covenant never partook of the spiritual blessings because they did not make Rahab's choice. So curiously enough, she who had been a non-Jewish heathen suddenly became not only a part of the nation of Israel, but also a part of the true Israel. With one act of faith, she stepped into the nation and beyond many of the Jews themselves to become a member of spiritual Israel.

The Scarlet Cord

In Joshua 2 we also find the interesting story of the scarlet cord. This cord, on which Rahab let the spies escape from her house, was also to be the mark upon her house to show that she was different from all the rest. Chapter 2, verse 21 says that the spies departed, and she hung the scarlet line in her window. It seems to me that this indicates that she did not want time to pass without that mark upon her house. So we can imagine her, after she let the spies down, pulling up the rope and tying it to her window.

In the preaching of the Christian Church, all the way back to Clement of Rome (perhaps earlier, but we do not know), this has been taken as a sign of the blood of Christ, the Lamb. One should not be dogmatic about it because the Bible does not explicitly make this connection; nevertheless, many in the Church have emphasized over the centuries that the scarlet cord was a mark of something beyond itself.

Because she placed this mark upon her house, she dwelt in safety. This clearly paralleled the Passover lamb. The Israelites killed the Passover lamb, put its blood on their houses, and then were perfectly safe as the angel of death passed over Egypt. The mark of the blood covered them and their households. The Passover lamb, of course, was looking forward to the coming Messiah. So there is, after all, a parallel between the cord and the blood of the Lamb.

We can imagine Rahab rushing out and gathering all her family into her house upon the city wall. We can imagine her going through the city and calling out, "Hurry! Hurry! Hurry! Come under the mark of the scarlet cord!" Lot did the same thing in Sodom, you remember, but without success. He went throughout the city trying to gather in his family, including his sons-in-law. But they refused and laughed at him; so they died in the city's destruction. In the days of Noah, those who were gathered into the ark were safe. In Jericho, Rahab's family, gathered in the house marked by the scarlet cord, were safe.

We see the spiritual element of the covenant blessing flowing on. When the children of Israel were about to leave Egypt, they were given the blood of the Passover lamb under which to be safe.

When the people were about to enter the land, they were met by a different, but parallel, sign—a red cord hanging from the window of a believer.

Faith in Action

The Bible expressly says that Rahab demonstrated her faith by her works. The spies did not take her away with them. She had to remain in the kingdom of the Amorites between the time when she declared her allegiance to the living God and the time when judgment fell. In Joshua 2 we are reminded forcefully that there was a king in Jericho; and if he had known what had occurred, undoubtedly he would have killed Rahab in the cruelest fashion he could have thought of: "And the king of Jericho sent unto Rahab, saying, Bring forth the men that are come to thee, which are entered into thine house" (Josh. 2:3). Here was war—war between the king of Jericho and the king of the Jews; that is, between the king of Jericho and God.

In the book of James, Rahab is the only person paralleled to Abraham: "Was not Abraham, our father, justified by works, when he had offered Isaac, his son, upon the altar? . . . In like manner also was not Rahab, the harlot, justified by works, when she had received the messengers, and had sent them out another way?" (Jas. 2:21, 25). To properly exegete the book of James, we need to understand that Abraham had faith, but it was a faith open to demonstration. In fact, it was demonstrated at a tremendous cost: he was willing to trust God and to offer his son. Rahab, too, had a faith that had teeth in it, structure to it, strength in it. She was willing to suffer loss to demonstrate that her faith was valid.

This woman Rahab stood alone in faith against the *total* culture which surrounded her—something none of us today in the Western world has ever yet had to do. For a period of time she stood for the unseen against the seen, standing in acute danger until Jericho fell. If the king had ever found out what she had done, he would have become her chief enemy and would have executed her.

Just before the Israelites came out of Egypt, they sacrificed the Passover lamb. They did it "with loins girded, your shoes on your feet, and your staff in your hand" (Ex. 12:11), and they became pilgrims. One cannot partake of the Passover lamb without being ready to see the world as a place of pilgrimage and war. Rahab is an even greater illustration of our position in regard to this, because until Jericho fell she lived as a pilgrim surrounded by her old alien culture.

This is exactly how the Christian lives, and Rahab is a tremendous example for us. Though you and I have stepped from the kingdom of darkness into the kingdom of God's dear Son, we are still surrounded by a culture controlled by God's great enemy, Satan. We must live in it from the moment we accept Christ as our Savior until judgment falls. We, too, are encompassed by one who was once our king, but is now our enemy. It is just plain stupid for a Christian not to expect spiritual warfare while he lives in enemy territory.

Rahab: Ancestor of Christ

But there is even more to Rahab's story of the spiritual continuity of the covenant. Joshua 6:25 says of Rahab: "She dwelleth in Israel even unto this day." She lived the rest of her life as a citizen among God's people. Not only that, she married among these people and became an ancestor of Jesus Christ!

Study the genealogy of Jesus as Matthew records it: "And Nahshon begot Salmon; and Salmon begot Boaz of Rahab; and Boaz begot Obed of Ruth; and Obed begot Jesse; and Jesse begot David, the king" (Matt. 1:4-6). David, of course, was a forebear of Christ.

Rahab's position is mentioned by implication in the book of Ruth: "Now these are the generations of Perez: Perez begot Hezron, and Hezron begot Ram, and Ram begot Amminadab, and Amminadab begot Nahshon, and Nahshon begot Salmon, and Salmon begot Boaz [of Rahab, as Matthew says], and Boaz begot Obed, and Obed begot Jesse, and Jesse begot David" (Ruth 4:18-22). (See also the parallel in 1 Chronicles 2, especially verses 11-12.)

The book of Numbers provides a key to Nahshon's identity. When the tabernacle was raised in the days of Moses (about thirty-nine years before the events involving Rahab), twelve princes came, one from each tribe, and made a special offering. The first one who came was of the tribe of Judah: "And he that offered his offering the first day was Nahshon, the son of Amminadab, of the tribe of Judah" (Num. 7:12). So Nahshon was a great prince of the tribe of Judah, and his son, Salmon, married Rahab. Chronologically, it fits; the timing is just right. Isn't that tremendous? The harlot who became a believer became the wife of a prince of Judah!

Unhappily, some people ask, "But is it fitting that this woman should become a princess and an ancestor of Christ?" I would reply with all the strength that is in me: it is most fitting! In having been unfaithful to the Creator, is not the whole human race a harlot? Indeed, it is most fitting that Rahab should stand in the ancestral line of Christ. Matthew mentions five women in the genealogy he records, and moral charges were brought against every one of them. Jesus Christ did not come from a sinless human line. All, including Mary, needed the Savior. Even she said, "My spirit hath rejoiced in God my Savior" (Luke 1:47). *All* the men and *all* the women in the ancestral line of Christ needed Christ as their Savior.

After all, Rahab did not stand with the people of God as an unclean harlot. She had come under the blood of the coming Christ; she was the harlot cleansed. Is Rahab any worse than we? If it is not fitting that she should be the ancestress of Christ, is it fitting that we should be the bride of Christ? Woe to anybody who has such a mentality as to be upset by Rahab! Such a person does not understand sin, the horribleness of the whole race turning into a prostitute against the living Creator.

We all stand in Rahab's place in the sight of the holy God. Probably we are even worse, for she had little knowledge. There is probably no one reading this book who has as little knowledge as Rahab had when she made her step of faith. We are all sinners. Each one of us is like this woman living up there on the wall. Each of us deserves only one thing—the flaming judgment of God. If it were not for the spiritual portion of the covenant of grace and Christ's death on Calvary's cross, we would all be lost.

If we do not cast ourselves upon Christ, and His finished work, then we are not as wise as that harlot in a heathen land. We are under the judgment of God and will stay under it until we do what Rahab did. She believed. She came under the work of the real Passover Lamb, Jesus Christ. And she passed from the midst of unredeemed humanity to redeemed humanity on the basis of His blood.

So it always is. Jesus Christ stands before all men in one of two capacities (there is no third): either he is Savior or he is Judge. When he stood as captain of the Lord's host, for one woman and her household he was Savior; for the rest of Jericho, he was Judge.

Let those of us who have believed in Christ ask God to help us so that our works will prove our faith, even if this means a threat to us, even if this places us in as much danger as it did Rahab. By God's grace, may our faith have such a structure that even if it is at great cost, even if we are facing danger, we stand fast. Many thousands of our brothers and sisters in Christ are this day facing danger. The great persecutions did not just occur in the past in the land of Caesar. In North Korea, Africa, Vietnam, Laos and other places, Christians are being killed for being Christians. And many more are not always physically killed, but "killed" by being alienated from their own families.

It is hazardous to be a Christian in an age like ours, in a culture that is increasingly alienated from God. But if we have believed, even if we are surrounded and threatened by the kingdom of our previous king, the evil one, may our faith be like Rahab's, observable by courage and by works. Rahab blazes abroad as a tremendous example for all of us.

CHAPTER FIVE

Two Kinds of Memorials

What was happening as Rahab waited in that place of danger with her scarlet cord in the window? What occurred between the time the spies left her and the time Jericho fell?

Soon after the spies had returned to the east side of Jordan and reported to Joshua, Joshua sent officers among the people to prepare them for the great moment of crossing. The ark of the covenant of the Lord was to lead the procession. Because the ark represented the presence of God, there was to be between it and the people a space of 2,000 cubits (about 3,000 feet, or well over half a mile). Finally, Joshua himself told the people, "Sanctify yourselves; for tomorrow the LORD will do wonders among you" (Josh. 3:5).

God said to Joshua, "This day I will begin to magnify thee in the sight of all Israel, that they may know that, as I was with Moses, so I will be with thee" (Josh. 3:7). After this encouragement, God told him how to instruct the priests who would bear the ark. When they came to the brink of the Jordan, they were to stand still in the water. Then the people would know that God was really with them because as the priests' feet touched the river, the river would be rolled back. Why? Because "the ark of the covenant of the Lord of all the earth passeth over before you into Jordan" (Josh. 3:11). Joshua promised the people that "as soon as the soles of the feet of the priests who bear the ark of the LORD, the Lord of all the earth, shall rest in the waters of Jordan, that the waters of Jordan shall be cut off from the waters that come down from above, and they shall stand upon an heap" (Josh. 3:13). Though it was the time of flood, the water would stop.

This was, of course, a continuity with what they had experienced when they came out of Egypt, and Joshua, Caleb and those who were children then would have remembered that event well. Now they were going to see a sign which paralleled the parting of the Red Sea. Though God gave the same sign as he had with Moses, in order to establish Joshua's authority with the people, there was obviously something much more important at work than either Moses or Joshua. There is a continuity of the power of the Lord. In both cases, the power of the Lord was there.

The First Kind of Memorial: Two Piles of Stones
When all the people had passed over the Jordan, Joshua obeyed some important instructions from God.

> The LORD spoke unto Joshua, saying, Take you twelve men out of the people, out of every tribe a man, and command ye them, saying, Take here out of the midst of Jordan, out of the place where the priests' feet stood firm, twelve stones, and ye shall carry them over with you, and leave them in the lodging place, where ye shall lodge this night. Then Joshua called the twelve men, whom he had prepared of the children of Israel, out of every tribe a man; and Joshua said unto them, Pass over before the ark of the LORD your God into the midst of Jordan, and take ye up every man of you a stone upon his shoulder, according unto the number of the tribes of the children of Israel; that this may be a sign among you, that when your children ask their fathers in time to come, saying, What mean ye by these stones? Then ye shall answer them, That the waters of Jordan were cut off before the ark of the covenant of the LORD; when it passed over Jordan, the waters of Jordan were cut off. And these stones shall be for a memorial unto the children of Israel forever. And the children of Israel did so, as Joshua commanded, and took up twelve stones out of the midst of Jordan, as the LORD spoke unto Joshua, according to the number of the tribes of the children of Israel, and carried them over with them unto the place where they lodged, and laid them down there. And Joshua set up twelve stones in the midst of Jordan, in the place where the feet of the priests who bore the ark of the covenant stood; and they are

there unto this day. For the priests who bore the ark stood in the midst of Jordan until everything was finished that the LORD commanded Joshua to speak unto the people, according to all that Moses commanded Joshua; and the people hastened and passed over. And it came to pass, when all the people were clean passed over, that the ark of the LORD passed over, and the priests, in the presence of the people. (Josh. 4:1-11)

These verses describe the first of the two kinds of memorials I want to discuss in this chapter. The Israelites set up two piles of twelve stones so that the people could look back to what God had done in the past as a reminder that He had promised to care for them in the future. Christians through the years have often spoken of "stones in the midst of the Jordan." In the beginning of L'Abri Fellowship, we were going through a great number of difficulties, a real spiritual battle. At that time we sent out our first family prayer letter, pointing out where we were being attacked, but also mentioning the "stones in the midst of Jordan," God's acts for us in the preceding weeks. It was then—July 30, 1955—that we first held our yearly day of prayer, a practice we have carried out from that day to this.

The first pile of twelve stones, one for each of the tribes, was set up in the bed of the Jordan. Inscribed on a stone in the lake near Geneva is the message, "When you read this, weep." Someone carved this because when the water gets that low, the territory is in drought. When you can read the words, then cry, because the country is in trouble. The memorial in Jordan was exactly the opposite. Someone could have written upon it, "When you see this, rejoice and remember." Occasionally, the Jordan gets very low, and the Israelites were able from time to time to see these twelve stones and to recall the great things God had done for them.

The second pile of stones was, in a way, even more exciting. Twelve men each took a stone out of the place where the priests' feet stood firm, put it on his shoulder, and carried it out of the river. These stones which bore the marks of the waters of the Jordan stood on the dry land as a perpetual testimony of God's interest in the Jewish people.

During the first night on the west side, the people camped close to the river, at Gilgal. As they looked up at the mountains which rose steeply to the west, their minds must have been filled with questions. But at the same time, they were in the land, they had taken the twelve stones, and the water had rushed back. That night they would have looked at those twelve stones stacked into a pillar (Josh. 4:20) and realized, "God has done something great. We can have tremendous confidence for the future." These stones were a memorial to God's faithfulness, and therefore a reminder of His trustworthiness in the days which lay ahead.

The Jews had been waiting to enter the land since the time of Abraham. These particular people had been wandering in the wilderness for many years, waiting. Now, though the Jordan in flood had stood in their way, they were in the land. They were where Moses himself had not been allowed to go. And they established the first kind of memorial for all generations.

These stone memorials were set up for two purposes. Joshua told the children of Israel at Gilgal:

> When your children shall ask their fathers in time to come, saying, What mean these stones? then ye shall let your children know, saying, Israel came over this Jordan on dry land. For the LORD your God dried up the waters of Jordan from before you, until ye were passed over, as the LORD your God did to the Red Sea, which he dried up from before us, until we were gone over; that all the people of the earth might know the hand of the LORD, that it is mighty, that ye might fear the LORD your God forever. (Josh. 4:21-24)

First, the stones were to instruct future generations. We can imagine a godly Jew in years to come taking his children to the twelve stones in Gilgal and saying, "Look! These stones were taken up out of the Jordan. I was there. I saw it happen." Then the grandfather would tell the grandchild; and though the people died off, the story would go on.

Second, the stones were to tell the other nations roundabout that this God is different. He really exists; He is a living God, a God of real power who is immanent in the world.

God today gives us, especially at the beginning of our Christian lives or at the start of a Christian work, things that we can remember. This way, when the waves get high, we can look back and see that God has worked, and that helps to give us a faith in the future. It is this work of God in our lives which should be open to observation and should give a testimony to the world roundabout us that God is mighty and God is different, that God is neither a projection of man's thinking, nor a God who cannot move in history. The power of God should also be manifested through the Christian community as a testimony to the world and to the Christians themselves.

The Ark: The Character and Promises of God

In preceding chapters, we have studied a number of continuities: the written book, the supernatural power, the supernatural leader, the spiritual blessings of the Abrahamic covenant, the national blessings of the Abrahamic covenant, and the reverse side of the covenant of grace—judgment. Now we will study two more continuities that were flowing along, both represented by the ark.

"The ark of the covenant of the LORD your God" stood at the center of the narrative we have just discussed. What was the ark? It was a representation of the character of God. The people had no image to worship; in fact, they were commanded not to make an image. One cannot make an image of God, for God is spirit. But God has a character, and the ark was a statement of that character. Basically, the ark was a box with a lid. It contained the law, expressing the fact that God is holy, and on top of it was the atonement cover, the propitiatory, the mercy-seat (to use the beautiful translation that Luther gave us), representing the love of God. God's love covers God's holiness when we come to God in His own way.

The ark was more, however, than a representation of God's character. It was the ark of the *covenant* of the Lord, the ark of the oath and promises of God. Because of His character as shown in the Ten Commandments—He is a holy God and He will not lie—people need not be afraid that He will renege on His promises. Because this is the kind of God He is, He will not turn away; He will not become a liar. As the people watched the ark being carried more than half a mile ahead of them, it represented not only the existence of God and character of God, but also the fact that He had made promises which He meant to keep.

In Joshua 3:11 the ark is called "the ark of the covenant of the Lord of all the earth." God isn't a localized God, but the universal God. His power did not stop when the Israelites crossed the Jordan, any more than it ceased when they left Egypt. He is a God who is universal and not localized—in contrast to the heathens' thought of their gods.

In Joshua 4, the words "the ark of the covenant of the Lord" are used over and over again. They are repeated like a chorus. We proceed in the narrative, see another part of the story, and then are reminded again that the ark was the external sign of the oath and promises of God. He was showing that He meant to fulfill His promises.

We do not know what happened to the ark. It is conceivable that it was destroyed when Jerusalem was laid waste by Babylon, or it may have been brought back from Babylon and been in the Temple when Titus demolished it in A.D. 70. Perhaps the ark did not come to an end. It is not farfetched to think it exists somewhere and will one day reappear. Whatever happened to it, we must understand that what it represented did not end. The covenant and the oath of God (which reaches all the way back to Genesis 3:15) has come up to today through different forms. From the times of Noah and Abraham, sweeping on through the Old Testament into the New, the promises of God will continue right up to the end of this era and beyond it into eternity.

As we see what happened in Joshua's day, we can take heart in the midst of our struggles. The God who kept His oath and promise to the children of Israel at the dramatic moment of their walking over the Jordan and entering the land will keep His word to the very end. As Bunyan's Pilgrim crossed another river, the river Death, the oath and promises of God gave him absolute assurance. Not only in the river Death, but in the whole of life, we can count on God to keep His living promises.

The Second Kind of Memorial: Two Living Signs

Not long after the two piles of stones were in place, a second kind of memorial was established at this crucial moment in Jewish history.

> And it came to pass, when all the kings of the Amorites, who were on the side of Jordan westward, and all the kings of the Canaanites, who were by the sea, heard that the LORD had dried up the waters of Jordan from before the children of Israel, until we were passed over, that their heart melted, neither was there spirit in them any more, because of the children of Israel. At that time the LORD said unto Joshua, Make thee sharp knives, and circumcise again the children of Israel the second time. And Joshua made him sharp knives, and circumcised the children of Israel at the hill of the foreskins. And this is the cause why Joshua did circumcise: all the people who came out of Egypt, who were males, even all the men of war, died in the wilderness by the way, after they came out of Egypt. Now all the people who came out were circumcised, but all the people who were born in the wilderness by the way as they came forth out of Egypt, them they had not circumcised. For the children of Israel walked forty years in the wilderness, till all the people who were men of war, who came out of Egypt, were consumed, because they obeyed not the voice of the

LORD; unto whom the LORD swore that he would not show them the land, which the LORD swore unto their fathers that he would give us, a land that floweth with milk and honey. And their children, whom he raised up in their stead, them Joshua circumcised; for they were uncircumcised, because they had not circumcised them by the way. And it came to pass, when they had done circumcising all the people, that they abode in their places in the camp, till they were whole. And the LORD said unto Joshua, This day have I rolled away the reproach of Egypt from off you. Wherefore the name of the place is called Gilgal unto this day. (Josh. 5:1-9)

Along with the two piles of stones, God gave two living signs, two sacraments. The emphasis in the above quote is on *circumcision*. God commanded Joshua to circumcise the children of Israel, and Joshua carried this out. All those born during the wilderness wanderings—in other words, all those forty years old and younger—had to be circumcised. This was a huge number.

When the circumcision actually occurred, they called the place where they camped that night *Gilgal,* which means in Hebrew "a rolling." A rolling in what way? God said that with the circumcision there was a rolling away of the "reproach of Egypt" which was upon them.

This circumcising was a strange thing for Joshua, a keen military commander, to do. He was incapacitating his whole fighting force, an absolutely unmilitary act. It is silly to march your men right into the teeth of the enemy and then disable your own people. Joshua did it, nevertheless, because God told him to.

From a human viewpoint Joshua was jeopardizing everything. Why was circumcision so important? In Stephen's speech in the book of Acts we get an answer. Stephen said about Abraham that God "gave him the covenant of circumcision" (Acts 7:8). Circumcision was not just an abstract religious rite, but was rooted in what Stephen properly called "the covenant of circumcision," which originated with Abraham. The reason Joshua's act was so crucial is that before the Israelites began their battles, every man was to have upon his body the mark of the Abrahamic covenant.

We have seen that God repeated the covenant to Abraham a number of times. In one of the last repetitions, God added something new:

Thou shalt keep my covenant therefore, thou, and thy seed after thee in their generations. This is my covenant, which ye shall keep, between me and you and thy seed after thee: Every man child among you shall be circumcised. And ye shall circumcise the flesh of your foreskin; and it shall be a token of the covenant between me and you. And he that is eight days old shall be circumcised among you, every man child in your generations, he that is born in the house, or bought with money of any stranger, which is not of thy seed. He that is born in thy house, and he that is bought with thy money, must needs be circumcised: and my covenant shall be in your flesh for an everlasting covenant. And the uncircumcised man child whose flesh of his fore-skin is not circumcised, that soul shall be cut off from his people; he hath broken my covenant. (Gen. 17:9-14)

God told Abraham to mark himself and every man-child of his household with a covenant token. Previously they had not been marked with an external sign; now they were to take one upon themselves at the command of God. So circumcision had a real meaning. It was the mark of the covenant—God's promises placed on the bodies of the Jewish men.

Notice how fitting this was. The covenant sign to Noah (Gen. 9) was in the sky—the rainbow. Why? Because it was a covenant not only with Noah, but with all of nature. It was a covenant with the earth itself. Therefore, the sign was in the proper place. When the covenant of grace flowed on to Abraham, an appropriate sign was again given. To Abraham the covenant was highly personal-ized; so the sign was placed on his own body and the bodies of his children. God said it was a token of the covenant "between me and you."

Abraham circumcised his household immediately, for Abraham believed God.

And Abraham took Ishmael, his son, and all that were born in his house, and all that were bought with his money, every male among the men of Abraham's house, and circumcised the flesh of their fore-skin in the selfsame day, as God had said unto him. And Abraham was ninety years old and nine, when he was circumcised in the flesh of his foreskin. And Ishmael, his son, was thirteen years old, when he was circumcised in the flesh of his foreskin. (Gen. 17:23-25)

Immediately after Isaac was born, he was circumcised as well (Gen. 21:4).

It was not, then, only those who believed personally or who would believe that were circumcised. Ishmael, for example, was circumcised as well as Isaac. The servants, too, were circumcised. There was an external portion of the covenant represented in the circumcision. In other words, the circumcision was related to the national, natural blessings. It marked the Jew as a Jew. This is the first thing we must understand about circumcision.

Five hundred years later, the Passover was established. When it was first performed, there was an exact repetition of what happened at the time of Abraham:

> And the LORD said unto Moses and Aaron, This is the ordinance of the passover: There shall no stranger eat thereof: But every man's servant that is bought for money, when thou hast circumcised him, then shall he eat of it. . . . A foreigner and an hired servant shall not eat thereof. In one house shall it be eaten; thou shalt not carry forth ought of the flesh abroad out of the house; neither shall ye break a bone of it. All the congregation of Israel shall keep it. And when a stranger shall sojourn with thee, and will keep the passover to the LORD, let all his males be circumcised, and then let him come near and keep it; and he shall be as one that is born in the land; for no uncircumcised person shall eat thereof. (Ex. 12:43-48)

How did a person gain entrance to Passover? Through circumcision. The two sacraments were blended here.

The Passover, of course, involved the tremendous promise of the coming redemption of Christ, on which all the blessings of the covenant rest—both the national and spiritual. They all rest upon Christ's death because they are all rooted in the covenant of grace. For as man turned from God in his rebellion, God immediately promised the Messiah; and every good thing that comes to man rests upon God's grace and upon what He promised to do in Jesus Christ. But there is also an external blessing, seen in the fact that Ishmael was circumcised as well as Isaac. It is the same when a person comes into a Christian church and shares in the Christian situation. He may or may not be saved; nevertheless, here he is in the midst of the worship service and the ongoing life of the church. He is raised in the family of God or he comes in from the outside, and he shares certain blessings because of his association. Back in the Old Testament there was also an emphasis on the external blessing of the circumcision.

But circumcision was not only connected with the external, national blessing to the Jews as Jews. It also had a strong spiritual overtone. Deuteronomy 10:16 reminds us that circumcision was intended to mean something in the flow of the spiritual side of the Abrahamic covenant: "Circumcise, therefore, the foreskin of your heart, and be no more stiff-necked." Deuteronomy 30:6 has the same emphasis: "And the LORD thy God will circumcise thine heart, and the heart of thy seed, to love the LORD thy God with all thine heart, and with all thy soul, that you mayest live."

This teaching was reiterated years later by the prophets. Jeremiah told the people, "Circumcise yourselves to the LORD, and take away the foreskins of your heart" (Jer. 4:4). Speaking to people all of whom were circumcised, Jeremiah was saying, "Don't you understand? There's a spiritual side to circumcision. It is not just your body that is to bear this mark. There is to be a spiritual reality in your life as well."

Jeremiah gave another striking expression of this. He mentioned the various nations that were uncircumcised, those about whom the Jews would proudly say, "You see, we are circumcised; they're not." Then he declared, "All the house of Israel is uncircumcised in the heart" (Jer. 9:26). "Don't forget," Jeremiah warned the people, "circumcision is to be spiritual. It is not only to indicate physically that you are a Jew."

So the circumcision did two things: it marked the Jew as a Jew in the natural flow of history, but it also marked the spiritual side of the covenant, recalling the tremendous fact that Abraham believed God and it was counted to him for righteousness. God gave not only natural promises to Abraham, but spiritual promises to the whole world (Gen. 12). Likewise, there were two aspects to uncircumcision. On the national side, if a person was uncircumcised, he was outside the Jewish people. On the spiritual side, he could have the physical circumcision and yet have an uncircumcised heart. As such, he had no part of the spiritual blessing.

Prior to the campaign against Jericho, it was important for Joshua to circumcise the men so they bore the external sign of the covenant. In the book of Exodus we find an exact parallel. Moses was on his way to lead the Israelites out of bondage. He had been away from his people for forty years. He had married a wife who was not a Jew and had male children who were not circumcised. Before he could begin his leadership, something had to happen: "And it came to pass by the way in the inn, that the LORD met him, and sought to kill him. Then Zipporah took a sharp stone and cut off the foreskin of her son, and cast it at his feet, and said, Surely a bloody husband art thou to me. So he let him go: then she said, A bloody husband thou art, because of the circumcision" (Ex. 4:24-26).

What does this story mean? Simply this: God actually pointed out to Moses that Moses was not ready to lead God's people until the body of his own son was marked with the sign of the covenant of grace. Moses could not bring himself to do it, and so there was a momentary struggle between husband and wife. When Zipporah had performed the rite, Moses could lead the people.

At Gilgal, because the males were uncircumcised, the Israelites were not ready to fight the battle of the Lord. They must first bear the mark of the covenant. As soon as the people were circumcised, they were ready to proceed.

The Passover
Immediately after the men were circumcised, the second of the sacraments was observed: "And the children of Israel encamped in Gilgal, and kept the passover on the fourteenth day of the month at evening in the plains of Jericho" (Josh. 5:10). The two sacraments were brought together again at this moment of history.

And once more we have a strong parallel with Moses. A short time after the mark of circumcision was placed on him, Moses, under God's hand, was the instigator of the Passover. The parallels between Moses and Joshua are amazing and teach us an important lesson. "Years pass," God seems to say, "but throughout history there is a continuity in My dealings with My people. This continuity is rooted in Myself—My character, My promises, My covenant."

As with all the other continuities, the continuity of the Passover did not end with Joshua. The Passover is continued in the Lord's Supper. Both signify the same reality:

> Now the first day of the feast of unleavened bread, the disciples came to Jesus, saying unto him, Where wilt thou that we prepare for thee to eat the passover? And he said, Go into the city to such a man, and say unto him, The Master saith, My time is at hand; I will keep the passover at thy house with my disciples. And the disciples did as Jesus had appointed them, and they made ready the passover. Now when the evening was come, he sat down with the twelve. . . . And as they were eating, Jesus took bread, and blessed it, and brake it, and gave it to the disciples, and said, Take, eat; this is my body. And he took the cup, and gave thanks, and gave it to them, saying, Drink ye all of it; for this is my blood of the new testament, which is shed for many for the remission of sins. But I say unto you, I will not drink henceforth of this fruit of the vine, until that day when I drink it new with you in my Father's kingdom. And when they had sung an hymn, they went out into the mount of Olives. (Matt. 26:17-20, 26-30)

Jesus was saying, "I'm taking the Passover because although the time is changing, there is a continuity." Though there was a change in the external form, there was no change in the flow of the covenant and no change in the fact of having an external token. The Passover became the Lord's Supper. Paul says we are to keep the Lord's Supper until Jesus returns. The Lord's Supper looks back to Christ's death and forward to His second coming.

What, then, was the Passover? The Passover also looked two ways—back to the liberation from Egypt and forward to the first coming of the Lord as Savior. The Bible clearly indicates that the Passover was a prophecy of what Jesus would do. For instance, the Passover lamb had no bone broken, and John says that no bone of Jesus was broken while he was on the cross, "that the scripture should be fulfilled" (John 19:36). Paul says, "Christ, our passover, is sacrificed for us" (1 Cor. 5:7).

Remember that in Joshua 5 the sign of circumcision was given before the Passover was celebrated. We have a similar continuity today. We have seen in Deuteronomy and Jeremiah that circumcision related to the spiritual portion of the covenant. Paul picks this up in Romans: "But he is a Jew who is one inwardly; and circumcision is that of the heart" (Rom. 2:29). Of course! All the little bells ring! This is exactly what Jeremiah said! This is what Deuteronomy says! Real circumcision is related not just to the natural blessings in the body, but to the spiritual blessings as well. True circumcision is of the heart. So just as a circumcised Israelite could eat the Passover at Gilgal, a person today who is circumcised in heart is one who can go on to the Lord's Supper.

Later on in Romans Paul speaks about this even more strongly. Discussing the blessing that came to Abraham on the basis of his faith, he says, "How was it then reckoned? when he was in circumcision, or in uncircumcision? Not in circumcision, but in uncircumcision. And he received the sign of circumcision, a seal of the righteousness of the faith which he had yet being uncircumcised, that he might be the father of all them that believe, though they be not circumcised" (Rom. 4:10, 11). Abraham did not have to be circumcised in order to be saved. There may have been as many as twenty-five years between Abraham's first belief in God and his circumcision. In all those years, Abraham was not separated from God. He had believed God, and God had counted it to him for righteousness. "That's just like your justification," Paul is saying.

Yet that does not mean circumcision was unimportant when the right time came. Being uncircumcised, he had been declared righteous; he had become a child of God. But years later a sign and seal was applied to him. In Genesis 17:11, God told Abraham, "Ye shall circumcise the flesh of your foreskin; and it shall be a token of the covenant between me and you." In other words, "You're already Mine, Abraham, but I'm going to give you a token in your flesh." In Romans 4 we find exactly the same thing. What the Hebrew means by *token,* the Greek means by *seal.*

There is a flow between the circumcision of the Old Testament and the baptism of the New. The New Testament speaks of baptism as the Christian's circumcision. "In whom also ye are circumcised with the circumcision made without hands, in putting off the body of the flesh in the circumcision of Christ; having been buried with him in baptism" (Col. 2:11, 12). The main flow of the sentence is clear: "In whom also ye are circumcised in the circumcision of Christ, having been buried with him in baptism." We could say it this way (though the previous quote is the literal translation), "You are circumcised by Christian circumcision, being baptized."

Abraham was not saved by circumcision; he was already saved. And the New Testament argues, especially in various Pauline sections, that a person does not have to be either circumcised or baptized to be saved. You can be saved without the sign. The book of Romans argues that neither the Jews nor the Gentiles needed the sign of circumcision for their redemption. First Corinthians also argues it. Galatians, strongest of all, argues against any legality that would add an external sign such as circumcision or baptism to the way of salvation. Salvation is all by grace, all on the finished work of Jesus Christ. You can add nothing to it—nothing at all.

Nevertheless, Abraham was commanded to take the covenant sign. Moses, too, learned how important the covenant sign was. And God told Joshua, "You have entered the land; now place the covenant sign on the men before they march against Jericho."

So while Rahab was waiting, God was leading his people to establish at Gilgal two kinds of memorials—two piles of stones and two living memorials. When they were in place, Joshua was ready to march toward Jericho.

Jericho, Achan and Ai

This is the story of Jericho. To appreciate its force, we must deliberately put ourselves into the frame of mind that we are looking at space-time history. These events were real happenings; these people were real people, and the book of Joshua portrays the people involved with psychological depth.

Likewise, the geography is real space-time geography. It is especially important for us to picture the geography of the promised land because we are now studying a period of war. Geography has always been important in warfare, even more in those days than in our own. In warfare armies try to take the commanding points, especially the peaks of mountains, because from there they can control the roads, the rivers, the railroads or whatever may be the main way of transporting supplies.

We can think of three campaigns in World War II in which geography affected tactics. When the Germans entered France, their tactic was to drive a wedge into the middle of France and then expand in both directions. When the Greeks were fighting the Italians, the Italians took the plain and the Greeks took the hills. As a result the Greeks controlled the situation, even with less well-armed forces. The English smashed strongholds first and then fanned out into weaker areas. If we combine these three tactics of warfare, we have a picture of the God-given strategy for Joshua's campaign to take the land.

Let us consider, then, some of the geography of the promised land. Standing at the Jordan River, which flows down into the Dead Sea which is far below sea level, one sees in the west steep hills which rise quickly from the valley. Gilgal was somewhere on the river valley, between the river and Jericho. Jericho controlled the way of ascent into the mountains. At the head of the ascent was another fortress, Ai. The descents and ascents were made by old riverbeds which had carried the torrents down these steep hills. Swiss mountain climbers understand this well because the oldest roads and trails in the Alps follow old riverbeds. These are steep because the hills are steep. From a military viewpoint, the old riverbeds in that day were exactly what the railroads were up through the Second World War. If the Israelites were going to capture the hill country from which they could control the rest of the land, they would have to press past Jericho, which controlled the lowest part, go up the ascent, and take Ai. Then they would be on top of the hill country, able to expand their wedge and control the various parts of the country from here.

God's Strategy Against Jericho
First, the Israelites had to defeat Jericho. Through archaeological digs we have a better idea of what Jericho was like than those who read the Bible in years past. Jericho was not a big city; it was only about seven acres in its entirety. What it really was was a fortress—a very strong fortress prepared to resist siege.

Joshua did not take the city merely by a clever, human military tactic. The strategy was the Lord's.

Now Jericho was straitly shut up because of the children of Israel: none went out, and none came in. And the LORD said unto Joshua, See, I have given into thine hand Jericho, and its king, and the mighty men of valor. And ye shall compass the city, all ye men of war, and go round about the city once. Thus shalt thou do six days. And seven priests shall bear before the ark seven trumpets of rams' horns; and the seventh day ye shall compass the city seven times, and the priests shall blow with the trumpets. And it shall come to pass, that when they make a long blast with the ram's horn, and when ye hear the sound of the trumpet, all the people shall shout with a great shout; and the wall of the city shall fall down flat, and the people shall ascend up, every man straight before him. And Joshua, the son of Nun, called the priests, and said unto them, Take up the ark of the covenant, and let seven priests bear seven trumpets of rams' horns before the ark of the LORD. And he said unto the people, Pass on, and compass the city, and let him that is armed pass on before the ark of the LORD. (Josh. 6:1-7)

The people were to march for six days around the city, going around it once each day with the priests leading the way. On the seventh day everyone was to march around the city seven times. Then the priests were to blow the rams' horns and the people were to cry out. When this was done, God said, the walls of the city would fall down flat, and everyone could ascend up "straight before him."

Since Jericho was a small city, as was normal for the walled cities of that time, the Israelite army was large enough to completely encircle it. So by the time the first troops had marched around the walls, the last troops would just be starting. On the seventh day when the army cried out and the walls fell, all that the soldiers would have to do is march straight ahead to the center of the city and thus capture it from all sides at once.

"You won't even have to scale the wall," God said. "Every fighting man will be able to draw his sword and march straight forward. You will take the whole city with one blow."

Joshua's obedience revealed Joshua's faith.

And it came to pass, when Joshua had spoken unto the people, that the seven priests bearing the seven trumpets of rams' horns passed on before the LORD, and blew with the trumpets; and the ark of the covenant of the LORD followed them. And the armed men went before the priests that blew with the trumpets, and the rereward came after the ark, the priests going on, and blowing with the trumpets. And Joshua had commanded the people saying, Ye shall not shout, nor make any noise with your voice, neither shall any word proceed out of your mouth, until the day I bid you shout; then shall ye shout. So the ark of the LORD compassed the city, going about it once; and they came into the camp, and lodged in the camp.

And Joshua rose early in the morning, and the priests took up the ark of the LORD. And seven priests bearing seven trumpets of rams' horns before the ark of the LORD, went on continually, and blew with the trumpets; and the armed men went before them, but the rereward came after the ark of the LORD, the priests going on, and blowing with the trumpets. And the second day they compassed the city once, and returned into the camp; so they did six days.

And it came to pass on the seventh day, that they rose early about the dawning of the day, and compassed the city after the same manner seven times; only on that day they compassed the city seven times. And it came to pass at the seventh time, when the priests blew with the trumpets, Joshua said unto the people, Shout; for the LORD hath given you the city. (Josh. 6:8-16)

Because of the promise of God, because of his experience over the past forty years, Joshua expected the walls to fall. So "Joshua said unto the people, Shout; for the LORD hath given you the city." They had marched for six days in complete silence, but now they were to shout. When the fighting men did shout, the walls fell down and the men marched in.

Was this a direct act of divine intervention? Or did God simply use a principle of vibration, the principle which explains why an opera singer can break a glass by hitting the right note? We do not know, because God has not told us, but it does not matter which is the case. This was God's strategy, and there was a complete miracle in what occurred. God had made a promise, God had given the strategy, and the victory was accomplished.

At this particular moment Joshua remembered Rahab. All this time Rahab had been sitting in her house, surrounded by the power of the Amorite king. Now her deliverance was at hand. On the basis of the promises she had been given, in faith she had felt safe. Now she was to experience her safety in the midst of judgment. "The city shall be accursed," Joshua said (Josh. 6:17). "Accursed" represents only a part of what this word means. The Hebrew word means both "accursed" or "devoted" (that is, "given to God"). Here it clearly means the latter: "The city shall be devoted, even it, and all that are in it, to the LORD; only Rahab, the harlot, shall live, she and all who are with her in the house, because she hid the messengers that we sent." In this way, Joshua gave the command for her protection.

Joshua's commands to the people make clear that the city was devoted: "But as for you, only keep yourselves from the devoted thing, lest when you have devoted it ye take of the devoted thing, so would ye make the camp of Israel accursed, and trouble it. But all the silver and gold, and vessels of bronze and iron, are holy unto Jehovah; they shall come into the treasury of Jehovah" (Josh. 6:18, 19, American Revised). The city of Jericho was a sign of the first fruits. In all things the first fruits belonged to God. Jericho was the first fruits of the land; therefore, everything in it was devoted to God.

The tithe, the first fruits, goes back at least to Abraham. It is another continuity which stretches through the Old Testament to us in New Testament times (in the sense that the New Testament commands proportional giving). Just as Abraham brought his tithes, so Jericho was to be the first fruits.

As Jericho was being overrun, Rahab's great moment came. "But Joshua had said unto the two men that had spied out the country, Go into the harlot's house, and bring out from there the woman, and all that she hath, as ye swore unto her. And the young men that were spies went in, and brought out Rahab, and her father, and her mother, and her brethren, and all that she had; and they brought out all her kindred, and left them without the camp of Israel" (Josh. 6:22, 23). Here Rahab became completely identified with the people of God. Just as Noah went into the ark and was safe in the midst of the flood, just as Lot was led out of Sodom, just as the Israelites in Egypt marked their houses with the blood of the Passover lamb, so Rahab, on the basis of her belief, was safe in the midst of the judgment of the city of Jericho.

The city was totally burned (Josh. 6:24). It was neither spoiled nor plundered. Nothing was removed. Everything was burned as it stood because Jericho was devoted to God. Utensils and jars stayed in the houses. The grain remained in the grain pits. To give themselves stores during siege, the inhabitants of Jericho had carved huge grain bins out of the center of the rock on which the city stood. Since the Israelites simply burned the city, the fire scorched the top of the grain while the rest remained. As a matter of fact, such grain from very ancient times has been found, has been planted, and has grown.

Joshua gave a prophecy about what it would mean to try to build the city again: "Cursed be the man before the LORD, that riseth up and buildeth this city, Jericho; he shall lay the foundation thereof in his firstborn, and in his youngest son shall he set up the gates of it" (Josh. 6:26). Later in the Old Testament we find that it was rebuilt, and with just such a tragedy as Joshua prophesied, but we will not deal with that here. (See 1 Kings 16:34.)

Achan's Sin

The people had destroyed Jericho, and the bottom portion of the ascent was completely open. What remained was to take the smaller fortress, Ai, at the top, for then the Israelites would hold the hill country and could begin to expand their wedge. The greater place had fallen with ease; the lesser place stood before them. The seventh chapter of Joshua begins with the word "But," and stands in antithesis to the sixth, for it tells a tale of defeat.

We can well understand the psychological condition of these people. Everything must have seemed wide open before them. What was coming must have seemed simple. The men who were sent out to look at Ai reported to Joshua: "Let not all the people go up, but let about two or three thousand men go up and smite Ai; and make not all the people to labor there; for they are but few" (Josh. 7:3). So only 3,000 men went up.

The way the story is presented, we cannot be certain whether the people were motivated by pride or faith. "God can do it with a smaller number," they might have said in faith. Or, "It's a small city. We can do it," they could have said in pride. From what follows, pride seems to have been the motive, for there was a tremendous defeat. Thirty-six men were killed, and the rest were chased down the descent. They had gone up to this steep place above Jericho, and suddenly they were overwhelmed. Those who climb in the mountains can picture the difficulty of making haste down a steep mountain road, falling all over oneself in trying to get down in a hurry.

How could there be defeat? Didn't they have the book? Didn't they have the supernatural power? Didn't they have the supernatural leader? Wasn't it true that the national aspect of the Abrahamic covenant was being fulfilled? Wasn't it true that the spiritual portion of the Abrahamic covenant had functioned in Rahab's life? Didn't the Israelites have the ark of God with which the Jordan River had rolled back? Hadn't they commemorated this marvelous happening with two piles of stones? Hadn't they been circumcised and put themselves under the external sign of the covenant? Hadn't they celebrated the Passover? Hadn't Jericho fallen? How, then, could there be defeat?

We must feel the tremendous upheaval in the mind of these people. If we do, we can understand Joshua's lament:

> And Joshua rent his clothes, and fell to the earth upon his face before the ark of the LORD until the eventide, he and the elders of Israel, and put dust upon their heads. And Joshua said, Alas, O Lord GOD, wherefore hast thou at all brought this people over Jordan, to deliver us into the hand of the Amorites, to destroy us? Would to God we had

been content, and dwelt on the other side of Jordan! O Lord, what shall I say, when Israel turneth their backs before their enemies! For the Canaanites and all the inhabitants of the land shall hear of it, and shall environ us round, and cut off our name from the earth. And what wilt thou do unto thy great name? (Josh. 7:6-9)

Joshua tore his clothes. Going up to the ark, which represented the presence of God, he fell on his face and cried aloud: "Here are these people, the Amorites. Their iniquity is full. The cup has overflowed. Only judgment will do. Now they have defeated us, and what is this going to do to Your great name, O God?"

God is brusque at times. He is brusque when those who have ample reason to know the answer forget it. So God responded to Joshua in a hard way:

And the LORD said unto Joshua, Get thee up; wherefore liest thou thus upon thy face? Israel hath sinned, and they have also transgressed my covenant which I commanded them; for they have even taken of the accursed thing, and have also stolen, and dissembled also, and they have put it even among their own stuff. Therefore the children of Israel could not stand before their enemies, but turned their backs before their enemies, because they were accursed. Neither will I be with you any more, except ye destroy the accursed from among you. (Josh. 7:10-12)

We find God saying to Joshua, "Don't you understand? There is only one reason for this defeat, and you should know what it is. Sin has come among the people of God." How could the defeat be? What caused the difference between the victory at Jericho and the defeat at Ai? Only one thing, and Joshua, remembering what caused the wandering for thirty-eight years in the wilderness, should have recognized its symptom. "Don't you remember that, Joshua? You should not be here on your face. You should be out dealing with sin among the people. For sin has made the difference."

Soon we learn that Achan had taken some of the things that were devoted to God. God told Joshua that the people "have also stolen" (Josh. 7:11). Stolen from whom? From God. Consequently, what Achan did was no small thing. He had not stolen a possession from another man; he had stolen the first fruits.

Therefore, God ordered Joshua, "Up, sanctify the people, and say, Sanctify yourselves" (Josh. 7:13). When the people first entered the land, before they began the conquest, there had come a call to sanctify themselves in the presence of God. Now, in the midst of defeat, there was only one way to return: the people had to sanctify themselves again.

God himself pointed out the man who had sinned. The people came by tribes, and God pointed out the tribe of Judah. Next he pointed out the family, and the household came, man by man, until the one man, Achan, was indicated.

Then followed Achan's instructive explanation of what he had done and what he had stolen: "Indeed, I have sinned against the LORD God of Israel, and thus and thus have I done: When I saw among the spoils a goodly Babylonish garment [a beautiful robe from Babylonia], and two hundred shekels of silver, and a wedge of gold of fifty shekels weight, then I coveted them, and took them; and, behold, they are hid in the earth in the midst of my tent, and the silver under it" (Josh. 7:20, 21). Achan thought, "With piles of stuff lying around, who'll know?" So he carted off the booty, dug up the earth under his tent, and buried the loot. And he thought nobody knew. But God knew.

While it is wonderful to have an infinite God, this means we must take His omniscience into account in our daily lives. There is nothing we do that God does not know. There is no night so dark, no coal mine so deep, no astronaut so far out in space that God does not know it. God knows every single thought, every single action. He knew when Achan first coveted, and He knew when he carried out his covetousness.

Achan expressly said, "I coveted them." Sin always begins in the mind. As a work of art begins in the mind and then is externalized, so also does sin. It is from the heart, Jesus said, that sin comes. The last commandment of the Ten Commandments is "Do not covet" because coveting precedes every other sin. Before we break any of the other nine, we have coveted internally something either of God's or of another man's. Then we externalize the sin. Achan coveted; then he stole.

As a result, thirty-six men were killed. Just imagine: here was a man going up the hill, perhaps in pride but nevertheless in expectancy, and all of a sudden an Amorite took a spear and thrust him through. In the moments before his death he must have been filled with the realization that something had gone wrong. Achan thought he could hide his sin, but these thirty-six men knew when they had been struck down. Soon the whole camp of the Jews knew that the blessing had stopped. At the judgment of Achan, everybody knew he had sinned. Jesus said that the things that are done in darkness will be known in the light (Luke 12:3).

What Achan took is also instructive. He took two kinds of things. First, he took two hundred shekels of silver and a wedge of gold of fifty shekels weight. We can understand easily why he took something which had monetary value. But he also took a "goodly Babylonish garment" or "a beautiful robe from Babylonia." Why did he bother with this? The Hebrew literally calls it, "a mantle of Shinar." Because Shinar is Babylonia, the Authorized Version translates it "Babylonian garment." Babylon was one of the great cities of the world Babylon became the cultural leader of Mesopotamia. It was the mark of success and power. Anything from Babylon was chic. Even in Assyrian times, Babylon was a great place. As far as military might was concerned, Babylon was strong in Hammurabi's time and again in Neo-Babylonian times, but it kept its cultural prestige even throughout its periods of weakness. In 606 B.C. it returned to military greatness and soon overflowed the Jewish nation. At the period of the Israelites' conquest of the promised land, Babylon was weak militarily, but still tremendously great in everybody's mind.

So this mantle of Shinar was not just an old shepherd's cloak, but a very stylish garment. It marked somebody as being "in," as really being "a man of the world." This Babylonian garment, therefore, becomes important for understanding the story. Achan bothered to take it because he wanted to be marked with success, to be chic. Achan's sin, then, had two parts: simple theft and prideful desire deep in his heart. What should this teach Christians? Do we struggle against the danger of stealing from God because we want a mantle of Shinar? Does it teach us to beware of grasping for affluence, for prestige, of trying to be a VIP?

When judgment came upon Achan, all the people of God joined in the judgment which God directed. All the people had seen the results, so all the people applied the discipline. They stoned Achan and his family (Josh. 7:25). After the nation was cleansed, all the people moved against Ai.

God now sent out the many to defeat Ai for the same reason he sent out Gideon's few—so that men could not boast, but had to credit God for the victory. In Gideon's time God emphasized "take just a few" so that the victors could not boast. The people under Joshua had boasted, "We need only a few," and they had lost. So now God said, "You need everybody to take the city." It was the opposite approach, but the same lesson was learned: man must look to God for the victories, and not boast, or there will be no victories.

The sequence of events at the fall of Ai was completely different from what had happened at Jericho. At Jericho there had been a miracle: the walls had fallen. At Ai there was no miracle. The Israelites had to take the city through the normal processes of war. God is not mechanical but personal. He is not going to deal with every situation in a mechanical way, and we must not reduce Him to a series of mechanical acts, as though because God acts one way in one moment He will act the same way in another. We must allow God to be free. God uses many methods. At Jericho there was a miracle; at Ai, none.

We Christians should not be surprised when the Holy Spirit leads us in different ways at different times. He will not contradict His own principles or character as set forth in the Scripture, but He will not act like a machine, always responding to similar situations in exactly the same ways. When a Christian falls into the idea that because Jericho has been taken one way Ai must be taken the same way, he has stopped thinking of God as personal.

There is another interesting contrast between the destruction of Ai and of Jericho. Jericho, as we saw, was the first fruits to God; therefore, the men were not to touch anything in it. Achan was punished because he had stolen from God. At Ai, this was reversed. The tithe had already been given, so the people were free to take spoil from this city. Tragedy came to Achan and to the people of God because Achan had been impatient. Had he waited obediently, he could have had the blessing.

Ai, like Jericho, was completely overthrown. So now the people controlled both the top and bottom of the gorge. The whole land was open before them.

The Principle of Judgment
As we think of Jericho, Achan and Ai, let us notice a principle. There is a sequence of factors which is relevant to the people of God in all ages. First, Achan stole from God just as a man today might steal by promising to give a tithe and failing to do so. Second, though only one man sinned, the blessing stopped for the people of God corporately. Third, when judgment was applied, victory came. This simple yet profound process explains all the rest of the Old Testament. It explains the period of the judges, the

period of kings, the captivities under Assyria and Babylon, the Jews' return from Babylon, and the Jews' dispersion in A.D. 70 under Titus. It explains Romans 9—11, which speaks of the Jews turning away from God and yet at a future day coming back to God and once more, as a nation, being the people of God. First comes blessing; then if sin enters, judgment comes. If the people of God return to him after the judgment, the blessing begins again and flows on.

This process is as much a universal as any continuity we have studied so far. It is the principle of God's judgment of His people. It is unchanging throughout Scripture because God really is there. God is a holy God, God loves His people, and God deals with His people consistently. God blesses His people, and one thing can spoil the blessing—sin, either individual or corporate. When either life in the Church or doctrine is not cared for, this stops the blessing as much as when an individual sins. Sin among the people of God either diminishes the blessing or brings the blessing to a halt until it is confessed, judged and removed.

Does this continuity really flow into the New Testament, to this side of the cross and Pentecost? Or is this something that applies only in the Old Testament? Achan's sin, we recall, came at the beginning of a new era. The people had received the law of God and a new order of worship; the race had become the nation; the nation was possessing the land. It was important that the people learn at the beginning of this new era that sin is not to be dealt with lightly.

Another new era began at Pentecost. The Holy Spirit was given to all the people of God. In John 7:39 we are told that the Holy Spirit was not given before Pentecost because Christ was not yet glorified. This does not mean that there was no Holy Spirit, that He had not previously worked in regeneration, that He had not come upon prophets, kings and priests in the Old Testament. The Holy Spirit is the third person of the Trinity. He has always existed and has always been active. But at Pentecost all the believers became priests of God, all the believers were indwelt by the Holy Spirit, and a new era began.

A little later we read:

> And when they had prayed, the place was shaken where they were assembled together; and they were all filled with the Holy Ghost, and they spoke the word of God with boldness.
>
> And the multitude of those that believed were of one heart and of

one soul; neither said any of them that ought of the things which he possessed was his own; but they had all things common. And with great power gave the apostles witness of the resurrection of the Lord Jesus; and great grace was upon them all. Neither was there any among them that lacked; for as many as were possessors of lands or houses sold them, and brought the prices of the things that were sold, and laid them down at the apostles' feet; and distribution was made unto every man according as he had need. And Joseph, who by the apostles was surnamed Barnabas, (which is, being interpreted, The son of consolation), a Levite of the country of Cyrpus, having land, sold it, and brought the money, and laid it at the apostles' feet.

But a certain man named Ananias, with Sapphira, his wife, sold a possession, and kept back part of the price, his wife also being privy to it, and brought a certain part, and laid it at the apostles' feet. But Peter said, Ananias, why hath Satan filled thine heart to lie to the Holy Ghost, and to keep back part of the price of the land? While it remained, was it not thine own? And after it was sold, was it not in thine own power? Why hast thou conceived this thing in thine heart? Thou hast not lied unto men, but unto God. And Ananias, hearing these words fell down, and gave up the ghost; and great fear came on all them that heard these things. And the young men arose, wound him up, and carried him out, and buried him.

And it was about the space of three hours after, when his wife, not knowing what was done, came in. And Peter answered her, Tell me whether ye sold the land for so much? And she said, Yea, for so much. Then Peter said unto her, How is it that ye have agreed together to tempt the Spirit of the Lord? Behold, the feet of them who have buried thy husband are at the door, and shall carry thee out. Then fell she down straightway at his feet, and yielded up the ghost; and the young men came in, and found her dead, and, carrying her forth, buried her by her husband. And great fear came upon all the church, and upon as many as heard these things. (Acts 4:31—5:11)

At the beginning of this even greater period of God's redemptive activity, exactly the same thing occurred as in the story of Achan. Achan stole and Joshua reprimanded him, "You've stolen from God." Peter said to the sinning couple, "You have lied to God." Ananias and Sapphira were not lying to the church; they were lying to the Holy Spirit. Money was involved and, in its own way, a Babylonian garment was too. Achan wanted to be like the world, so he took the Babylonian garment. Ananias and Sapphira wanted a different kind of garment—social acceptance in the church of God. They wanted to have the mark of the elite, the mark of the most spiritual and consecrated. They didn't want to be generous; "We sold this possession, and we're giving you such and such a percentage." Everybody in the church would have said, "That's fine," and God would have said, "Thank you." But they did not. They put on their own kind of Babylonian garment. This desire can easily become a sin in any Christian's heart. It is wrong to perform an action merely to be accepted in our own Christian group. It does not matter how good the act is in itself or how good it looks.

The sin of Ananias and Sapphira was followed by judgment, because sin would have stopped the church's advance. The church had just experienced a second great filling of the Holy Spirit. Power was there—power to face the lost Graeco-Roman world. If this sin of acting from bad motivation in order to be superficially accepted by the church had been allowed to grow in the church's heart, the whole advance would have been endangered. But after the judgment, the early church went on in power.

We are not in the beginning of a new era (that beginning was almost 2,000 years ago). Can we breathe easily then? Can we count sin lightly, whether individual or corporate, just because this is no longer the opening thrust of the church, as it was after the resurrection of Christ, His ascension and the giving of the Holy Spirit? Can we now have quiet hearts about sin? "No!" the Scripture answers.

We must be careful here. First, not *all* weakness comes because of sin. Our physical or mental weaknesses do not prove that we have sinned. Second, we must avoid falling into a new legalism, either for salvation or for the Christian life. Equally bad, however, is falling into the mentality of antinomianism—the notion that because we are saved by grace on the basis of the finished work of Christ, it does not matter how we live. We must resist always equating weakness with sin; we must resist creating a new kind of legalism. But the Word of God makes plain that we equally must oppose all forms of antinomianism.

Thus in the book of Joshua we have one more great flowing continuity: the principle of the judgment of the people of God. It runs like this: (1) When we sin, God knows (because He exists and is infinite). (2) When we sin, the blessing slows or stops. It can even stop for a whole group on the basis of the sin of one or a few. (3) There will be judgment either from ourselves in confessing our sin or judgment from God. (4) If we return, the blessing rolls on again.

CHAPTER SEVEN

Mount Ebal and Mount Gerizim

The victorious Israelites now controlled the northern end of the ridge highway that went south by Jerusalem to Hebron. Below them on the east the Jordan River ran parallel to these mountains. Having defeated Ai, the people marched northward on a road which ran over the top of the mountains toward Shechem. They did not have to press through a forest where there was no trail. There was a well-established road. A real culture had been in this land for a long, long time.

Let us imagine ourselves among this great crowd of people marching northwest along the road, the Jordan River on our right. After we have traveled about twenty miles, we see two mountains on our left, Mount Ebal and Mount Gerizim. The former stands north of the latter. One road branches off the main road and runs through the valley between the two mountains, heading toward the city of Samaria, which is approximately seven miles beyond.

Between the two mountains is the city of Shechem. Shechem already had a long history and was important to the Jews. Approximately 600 years before, Abraham stopped there as he came from Ur and built his first altar to the living God. Jacob, when he was fleeing from Laban, carried to this city the teraphim, his

241

father-in-law's family gods which Jacob's wife had stolen. Joseph sought his brothers here just before going on to Dothan where his brothers sold him into slavery; and Joseph eventually was buried there. Jacob dug a well near Shechem, and at this well Jesus would one day speak to a Samaritan woman (John 4). Later yet, Justin Martyr would be born near here. Space-time history had already begun to weave a web around this place.

Ebal and Gerizim are about a mile and a half apart at the top, but only about five hundred yards apart at the bottom. Gerizim reaches to approximately 2,895 feet above sea level, Ebal to 3,077 feet. This means that Gerizim stands about 800 feet above the valley and Ebal about 1,000 feet. The names *Gerizim* and *Ebal* have the same meaning: "barren."

There are two interesting things about these mountains. First, from the top of Ebal or Gerizim we can see a great deal of the promised land. Second, at one place a natural amphitheater exists and as we stand on the top or on the sides of these mountains, we can see and hear everything that is occurring on both of the mountains and in the valley below. Through the years many people have tested this. They have stood on one of the mountains and had other people stand on other parts of the two mountains or in the valley. As they read something in a loud voice but without amplification, the other persons were able to hear all that was spoken. It is God's own amphitheater.

The Altar on Mount Ebal

Moses, before he died, gave an express command that after the Israelites were in the land, they were to go to Ebal and Gerizim. At this place were to occur certain events which were to remind them of their relationship to God. So the people came up the road from the south, turned westward, and swarmed over these mountains:

> And all Israel, and their elders, and officers, and their judges, stood on this side of the ark and on that side before the priests the Levites, who bore the ark of the covenant of the LORD, as well as the strangers, as he that was born among them; half of them over against Mount Gerizim, and half of them over against Mount Ebal; . . . with the women, and the little ones, and the strangers among them. (Josh. 8:33, 35)

This was the whole congregation of the people of God, not just the fighting men. None were left at their camp in Gilgal.

God had commanded that Mount Gerizim be marked the mountain of blessing and that the taller mountain, Mount Ebal, be marked as the place of warning, or the place of the curse. God was giving the people a huge object lesson: what happened to them in the land was going to depend, as it were, on whether they were living on Mount Gerizim or Mount Ebal. The people were to hear from Mount Gerizim the blessings which would come to them if they kept God's law and from Mount Ebal the curses which would fall upon them if they did not.

On Ebal and Gerizim the people would be confronted with the law in a very striking fashion, as we shall see; but before the law could be read to them, an altar had to be raised to remind them of an important truth. Speaking in the plain of Moab before his death, Moses had instructed,

> Therefore, it shall be when ye be gone over Jordan, that ye shall set up these stones, which I command you this day, in Mount Ebal, and thou shalt plaster them with plaster. And there shalt thou build an altar unto the LORD thy God, an altar of stones; thou shalt not lift up any iron tool upon them. Thou shalt build the altar of the LORD thy God of whole stones, and thou shalt offer burnt offerings thereon unto the LORD thy God. And thou shalt offer peace offerings, and shalt eat there, and rejoice before the LORD thy God. (Deut. 27:4-7)

The people followed the command of God:

> Then Joshua built an altar unto the LORD God of Israel in Mount Ebal, as Moses, the servant of the LORD, commanded the children of Israel, as it is written in the book of the law of Moses, an altar of whole stones, over which no man hath lifted up any iron; and they offered thereon burnt offerings unto the LORD, and sacrificed peace offerings. (Josh. 8:30, 31)

It is significant that the altar was not built on Gerizim, the mountain of blessing, but on Ebal, the mountain from which was declared what would happen when the people sinned. This was a strong reminder to the people that they were not going to be perfect and that they would therefore need an altar. In this we should hear God saying, "You shouldn't sin. But when you do sin, I will give you a way to return to Me, through the altar." So while the people were warned of what would occur when they sinned, they were also taught from the very beginning that there would be a way of return.

We have seen many parallels between the time when Moses

began to lead the children of Israel out of Egypt and the beginning of the ministry of Joshua, and here is one more. After the law was given on Sinai, God told the people to build an altar: "An altar of earth thou shalt make unto me, and shalt sacrifice thereon thy burnt offerings, and thy peace offerings, thy sheep, and thine oxen; in all places where I record my name I will come unto thee, and I will bless thee. And if thou wilt make me an altar of stone, thou shalt not build it of hewn stone; for if thou lift up thy tool upon it, thou hast polluted it" (Ex. 20:24, 25). This special altar was not to have any works of man upon it. In this way, it was different from the brass altar that was commanded for the tabernacle. When He gave the Ten Commandments, God wanted the people to understand and never to forget that an altar does not have value because of what people do to it. In other words, this was a complete negation of all humanism. God was teaching the people, "Build an altar at this crucial moment, and it has to be a special kind. Make it of earth and of stones taken right out of the field. Don't carve beautiful designs on them. Don't even square them. There is to be no human mark upon this altar."

When the Israelites were entering into the land under Joshua, they already had built the brazen altar. Nevertheless, they were returned to the earlier lesson made by the rough altar. On Ebal was to be "an altar of whole stones, over which no man hath lifted up any iron" (Josh. 8:31). "Learn the lesson well," God was saying. "I'm bringing you here into the heart of the land. And I am giving you again a special altar so that you will never forget that you cannot come to Me on a humanistic level." We are reminded in both Exodus and Joshua that the approach to God must always be through sacrifice and not through the keeping of the law or any other work man may himself do.

According to Paul, the Jews should have understood their lesson. Abraham understood: "For what saith the scripture? Abraham believed God, and it was counted unto him for righteousness. Now to him that worketh is the reward not reckoned of grace, but of debt" (Rom. 4:3, 4). Abraham did not try to come to God on the basis of his works, because he understood that he was a sinner. He came, rather, on the basis of what God supplied. Paul's argument in Romans 4 is that the Old Testament people of God had to come to God exactly as we do, even though Christ had not yet died. If they tried to come on the basis of humanistic works, they could never make it. God is infinite; man is finite. Man has deliberately sinned; therefore, an infinite chasm of moral guilt exists between God and man. How can man with his good works or his worship cross the gap? He cannot. So Abraham's return to God was not by works, but by the way God prescribed.

Paul speaks even more strongly when he explains why the Jews missed the way. Why did the Old Testament people not come to God? What stood in their way?

> But Israel, following after a law of righteousness, did not arrive at that law. Wherefore? Because they sought it not by faith, but as it were by works. They stumbled at the stone of stumbling; even as it is written,
>
> > Behold, I lay in Zion a stone of
> > stumbling and a rock of offence:
> > And he that believeth on him shall
> > not be put to shame.
>
> Brethren, my heart's desire and my supplication to God is for them, that they may be saved. For I bear them witness that they have a zeal for God, but not according to knowledge. For being ignorant of God's righteousness, and seeking to establish their own, they did not subject themselves to the righteousness of God. For Christ is the end of the law unto righteousness to every one that believeth. (Rom. 9:31—10:4, ASV)

The reason many of the Old Testament Jews missed their way while Abraham found it is that Abraham came to God on the basis of God's promises of what God Himself would do. Because he did not keep the law perfectly, Abraham, as it were, did not try to come to God through Mount Gerizim. He came through Mount Ebal, for he was looking forward to what Christ would do. Paul maintains that the entire series of Old Testament tragedies occurred because the Jews kept trying to come to God through Gerizim, the mountain of blessing—through the works of the law, rather than through Mount Ebal. They did not understand that the only way to come to God is not trusting in works, but coming only through sacrifice. Much indeed has been told to the Jews: "Remember, the important thing is the altar!"

When the Assyrians carried away the northern kingdom into captivity, they transported all kinds of people into the promised land. This mixed group became the Samaritans. The Samaritans hated the Jews. The Samaritans set up their own worship and, following the thinking of men, made the center of it (amazingly)

Mount Gerizim. They were the humanists. When the Samaritans came into the land and were figuring out for themselves how to worship God, they must have thought, "We won't choose Mount Ebal. Who wants to say we're sinners? We'll worship on Mount Gerizim." In other words, they stood in the place of Cain who tried to please God in his own way. And the Samaritans, from that day to this, have worshiped on Mount Gerizim, trying to come to God on the basis of their own works. The only sacrifice going on anywhere in the world today that has any relationship to the Old Testament is carried out each Passover season on Mount Gerizim. The leading Jewish priests from Israel travel to watch the non-Jews, the Samaritans, sacrifice there. They watch with great care because there is some parallel between this and what the Jews did before the Temple was destroyed. Undoubtedly, there is a question in many of their minds: "When are we going to begin the sacrifices again?"

Now we can better understand Jesus' conversation at the well with the Samaritan woman. The well stood between Mount Ebal and Mount Gerizim. The woman must have turned and pointed to Mount Gerizim when she said, "Our fathers worshipped in this mountain; and ye say that in Jerusalem is the place where men ought to worship" (John 4:20). Jesus did not reply, "Yes, you should worship in Jerusalem rather than in Mount Gerizim." He did exactly the opposite. He pointed her away from both Gerizim and Jerusalem, and toward Himself. Without going into a big explanation, Jesus implied, "You can't come to God by keeping the law. On the other hand, true worship isn't in Jerusalem either. It's in Me. I am the way, the truth and the life. I am the Savior of the world." What Jesus actually did to her, without her realizing all that was involved, was to lift her from Mount Gerizim, where she was trying to come to God on the basis of her own good works (and, like all people, her works were not very good, as you will remember), and to put her on Mount Ebal, where she could come to God in the proper way through Him.

The Law on the Mountains
After the altar was built on Ebal, Joshua "wrote there upon the stones a copy of the law of Moses, which he wrote in the presence of the children of Israel" (Josh. 8:32). The account in Joshua 8 does not tell us by what means the Ten Commandments were copied there, but if we look back into Deuteronomy, we can find out.

The words were not carved with a hammer and chisel; they were put on the stones in a much faster way. When Moses gave this command about Ebal and Gerizim,

> Moses, with the elders of Israel, commanded the people, saying, Keep all the commandments which I command you this day. And it shall be on the day when ye shall pass over Jordan unto the land which the LORD thy God giveth thee, that thou shalt set thee up great stones, and plaster them with plaster; and thou shalt write upon them all the words of this law, when thou art passed over, that thou mayest go unto the land which the LORD thy God giveth thee, a land that floweth with milk and honey, as the LORD God of thy fathers hath promised thee. Therefore, it shall be when ye are gone over Jordan, that ye shall set up these stones, which I command you this day, in Mount Ebal, and thou shalt plaster them with plaster. . . . And thou shalt write upon the stones all the words of this law very plainly. (Deut. 27:1-4, 8)

The stones were to be covered with some kind of calcium solution on which the Ten Commandments could be carefully copied. Therefore, the whole process went quickly. The Israelites just picked up field stones and piled them together. Then somebody covered these big stones with a coating that could be easily etched, or painted quickly with a brush as was done on the shards. Someone carefully wrote the Ten Commandments in this coating.

You must see what was involved. You are on Mount Ebal, O humanist man, and here is the law of God. Nobody keeps that, do they? Consequently, what are you going to do? The altar gives you the key. It tells you that the whole approach to God is present in these first and second steps: the remembering of the Ten Commandments and the reality of the altar.

Not only was the altar built and the commandments written, but next a section of the writing of Moses was read to all the people, as they crowded onto the sides of the mountain in this natural amphitheater. They could see what was occurring on the tops of the mountains. Now they were going to hear with their ears what would occur if they kept the commandments of God and what would occur if they did not. This was not for salvation, because God had already said, "Salvation is to be through the way of the altar." Nevertheless, God had given the people of Israel commandments which were a representation of His character, which is the eternal law of the universe.

Moses had charged the people to have certain tribes stand on

Mount Gerizim to bless the people and the remaining tribes stand on Mount Ebal to curse (Deut. 27:11-13). Then the Levites were to read the curses and blessings. Joshua followed the command exactly. After the building of the altar and the copying of the law, "he read all the words of the law, the blessings and cursings, according to all that is written in the book of the law. There was not a word of all that Moses commanded, which Joshua read not before all the congregation of Israel, with the women, and the little ones, and the strangers among them" (Josh. 8:34, 35).

When Achan sinned, judgment came upon him. We have seen that this is a universal principle: the blessing of God stops when sin enters and flows on again only after the sin is judged. The reading of the blessings and curses forms, therefore, a continuity with the lesson of Achan. Undoubtedly as the people were on Ebal and Gerizim, that recent event with Achan was very much on their minds. On these mountains it was clearly stated as a general principle that sin must be judged if the blessing is to go on.

Another factor was involved, too: the people needed to be reminded that the blessings of God would be dependent upon their obedience to Him. While the Old Testament is full of blessings to the Jews, these blessings were divided into two parts—the unconditional portion and the conditional portion. When God first gave Abraham the Abrahamic covenant, he made it absolutely unconditional: "Now the LORD had said unto Abram, Get thee out of thy country, and from thy kindred, and from thy father's house, unto a land that I will show thee; and I will make of thee a great nation, and I will bless thee, and make of thee a great nation, and I will bless thee, and make thy name great; and thou shalt be a blessing. And I will bless them that bless thee, and curse him that curseth thee: and in thee shall all families of the earth be blessed" (Gen. 12:1-3). God has taken the Jews; He has made a covenant with them, and He is going to keep it no matter what. As Paul said, looking into the future beyond his day and even beyond our own, "The gifts of God are without repentance."

In the midst of the unconditional promise, however, God put conditional portions. God was not going to turn away from the Jews, but the kind of blessing they would have in the land depended on the extent to which they lived in the light of God's commands. God was pointing this out to the people on Mounts Ebal and Gerizim. He was teaching them, "The whole people must remember this. Many of the blessings, as well as judgments, are conditional. The continuance of the blessings depends upon your keeping My law."

We must remember that God's commands are His propositional statements about His character. They are not arbitrary. God has a character, and His character is the law of the universe. The law is grace in that it reveals what the fulfilling of His character is. God was telling the people that if they lived in the light of His character, then would come the blessing. If they failed to do this, then it would stop.

The Blessings and Curses

We see in the reading of the blessings and curses not only a continuity of the authority of the written, propositional Scriptures, but also an emphasis on the fact that bare knowledge is not enough. It was not that the Pentateuch gave these people knowledge, and that was the end of it. This knowledge demanded action. When Joshua took up his leadership, he was told the same thing: "This book of the law shall not depart out of thy mouth; but thou shalt meditate therein day and night, that thou mayest observe *to do* according to all that is written therein; for then thou shalt make thy way prosperous, and then thou shalt have good success" (Josh. 1:8). The normative standard was the law of God; it was not an existential experience (as is often emphasized in the twentieth century), not a nonpropositional religious experience (as is said by almost all contemporary liberal theologians). Not at all. What was involved was a propositional, written statement.

The conditional portion of the covenant was being emphasized. It is wonderful for God's people to have the law, but we are then called upon "to do." Our understanding of the rest of the Scriptures turns on our grasp of this point. In the time of the judges, the people did not keep the law of God; so God removed the conditional blessings from them. In the time of the kings, the same thing occurred. The people's disobedience finally caused the captivity of the northern kingdom by the Assyrians and the southern kingdom by the Babylonians. Later, when the people repented, God returned them to the land and the conditional promises again became operative. Later—even with the witness of Jesus—most of the Jews turned completely away, and in A.D. 70 Titus destroyed Jerusalem; so the conditional blessing was once more removed. In the future, as we have seen, God will deal with the Jews as a nation again (Rom. 11).

If we understand this, we understand the ebb and flow of history. The Jews remain Jews—they are not wiped out—for God's unconditional promise stands. When people violate the character of God, this is not only sin but stupidity. It is like rubbing your hand over a rough board and getting splinters. For it opposes what we are made to be and what the universe really is. God has revealed His character, and if God's people live in accordance with His character, the conditional blessings stand. Once we understand this, we really understand the flow of history for the Jews.

Moses, speaking before his death, said, "Behold, I set before you this day a blessing and a curse: a blessing, if ye obey the commandments of the LORD your God, which I command you this day; and a curse, if ye will not obey the commandments of the LORD your God, but turn aside out of the way which I command you this day, to go after other gods, which ye have not known" (Deut. 11:26-28). *If!* Both the blessings and the curses are conditional. O man, made in the image of God, O man, who is not merely determined by chemistry, society or psychology, O man, who is a man—you have a choice. Choose!

Hear some of the blessings and curses that were read on the two mountains:

> Cursed be the man who maketh any graven or molten image, an abomination unto the LORD, the work of the hands of the craftsman, and putteth it in a secret place. And all the people shall answer and say, Amen.
> Cursed be he who setteth light by his father or his mother. And all the people shall say, Amen.
> Cursed be he who removeth his neighbor's landmark. And all the people shall say, Amen.
> Cursed be he who maketh the blind to wander out of the way. And all the people shall say, Amen.
> Cursed be he who perverteth the judgment of the stranger, fatherless, and widow. And all the people shall say, Amen.
> Cursed be he who lieth with his father's wife, because he uncovereth his father's skirt. And all the people shall say, Amen.
> Cursed be he who lieth with any manner of beast. And all the people shall say, Amen.
> Cursed be he who lieth with his sister, the daughter of his father, or the daughter of his mother. And all the people shall say, Amen.
> Cursed be he who lieth with his mother-in-law. And all the people shall say, Amen.

Cursed be he who smiteth his neighbor secretly. And all the people shall say, Amen.

Cursed be he who taketh reward to slay an innocent person. And all the people shall say, Amen.

Cursed be he who confirmeth not all the words of this law to do them. And all the people shall say, Amen.

And it shall come to pass, if thou shalt hearken diligently unto the voice of the LORD thy God, to observe and to do all his commandments which I command thee this day, that the LORD thy God will set thee on high above all nations of the earth; and all these blessings shall come on thee, and overtake thee, if thou shalt hearken unto the voice of the LORD thy God. Blessed shalt thou be in the city, and blessed shalt thou be in the field. Blessed shall be the fruit of thy body, and the fruit of thy ground, and the fruit of thy cattle, the increase of thy kine, and the flocks of thy sheep. Blessed shall be thy basket and thy store. Blessed shalt thou be when thou comest in, and blessed shalt thou be when thou goest out.

The LORD shall cause thine enemies that rise up against thee to be smitten before thy face; they shall come out against thee one way, and flee before thee seven ways. The LORD shall command the blessing upon thee in thy storehouses, and in all that thou settest thine hand unto; and he shall bless thee in the land which the LORD thy God giveth thee. The LORD shall establish thee an holy people unto himself, as he hath sworn unto thee, if thou shalt keep the commandments of the LORD thy God, and walk in his ways. And all people of the earth shall see that thou art called by the name of the LORD, and they shall be afraid of thee. And the LORD shall make thee plenteous in goods, in the fruit of thy body, and in the fruit of thy cattle, and in the fruit of thy ground, in the land which the Lord swore unto thy fathers to give thee. The LORD shall open unto thee his good treasure, the heaven to give the rain unto thy land in its season, and to bless all the work of thine hand; and thou shalt lend unto many nations, and thou shalt not borrow. And the LORD shall make thee the head, and not the tail; and thou shalt be above only, and thou shalt not be beneath, if that thou hearken unto the commandments of the LORD thy God, which I command thee this day, to observe and to do them. And thou shalt not go aside from any of the words which I command thee this day, to the right hand or to the left, to go after other gods to serve them. (Deut. 27:15—28:14)

These conditions were, of course, addressed to the Jews as a nation in the land, but they reveal a general principle as well: the people of God must choose whether or not they are going to keep the law. As I have stressed, the whole history of the Jews from this point on turns on their decisions. When they kept the law, the blessings were there. When they turned away, the blessings came to a close until they returned.

Keeping God's Commands

The altar was on the mount of cursing, for salvation cannot come by man's keeping the law. Each one of us must see this. We cannot come to God on the basis of humanistic, religious, or moral works. God is an infinite God, and we have sinned against Him. There was only one way for the Israelites to come, and that was through the altar. The New Testament says this in regard to the work of Christ. Those of us living on this side of Christ must not be foolish like the Samaritans who tried to come through Gerizim. The only one way to come is through Ebal. We must acknowledge that we have not kept the law.

According to Old and New Testament alike—according to the unconditional spiritual portions of the Abrahamic covenant, the prophecies in the Old Testament which looked forward to Christ, the teaching of Christ Himself, and the teaching of Paul and the rest of the apostles—once we have come to God in the proper way, we stand in unconditional blessing. There is an unconditional portion to me and to you. It reaches all the way back to the beginning of the Bible and is emphasized in the Abrahamic covenant. If we come in the way that God has directed—namely, through the work of Christ—we will never be lost again. We rest in the hands of God. Jesus promises to hold us fast (John 10:28, 29). Because Christ is God, His death has infinite value. God's promises are Yea and Amen. Once we have become Christians, we have entered, by faith, by the grace of God, into the spiritual portion of the Abrahamic covenant; and the unconditional promise applies to us—we will never, never, never be lost again.

While this is true, the New Testament makes plain that for the Christian, as for the Old Testament Jew, there is also a conditional aspect. The moral law is the expression of God's character, and we are not to set it aside when we become Christians. Our obedience to it will make a difference in what happens to us both in this present life and in the believers' judgment in the future. So much of Jesus' teaching emphasizes the importance of keeping the law of God! So much of the New Testament emphasizes that we should *think* and then *live* in a conditional as well as an unconditional framework!

How a Christian lives is very important. A Christian should put himself into the arms of his Bridegroom, Christ, and let Christ produce His fruit through him. Just as a bride cannot produce natural children until she puts herself into the arms of the bridegroom, so a Christian cannot produce real spiritual fruit except he put himself into the hands of Christ. I can have real spiritual power to the extent that I look to the finished work of Christ and allow Him to produce His fruit through me into the external world.

In the Sermon on the Mount Jesus taught much about how a Christian should live. Notice the parallel with the way the Israelites were taught on Mounts Ebal and Gerizim. Jesus was saying to us, the children of God who stand in a spiritual continuity with the Jews, "Yes, I'm going to tell you about an unconditional justification, but there is a conditional portion as well. Think about it because it is important." Important to whom? To the unsaved man? Yes, because it shows him he cannot come by himself; he must come through Christ. To the saved man? Yes, because there is a conditional promise.

I suggest you read this out loud so you can feel it on your own lips and hear it with your own ears:

> Take heed that ye do not your alms before men, to be seen by them: otherwise ye have no reward of your Father, who is in heaven.
>
> Therefore, when thou doest thine alms, do not sound a trumpet before thee, as the hypocrites do in the synagogues and in the streets, that they may have glory from men. Verily I say unto you, They have their reward. But when thou doest alms, let not thy left hand know what thy right hand doeth, that thine alms may be in secret; and thy Father, who seeth in secret, shall reward thee openly.
>
> And when thou prayest, thou shalt not be as the hypocrites are; for they love to pray standing in the synagogues and in the corners of the streets, that they may be seen by men. Verily I say unto you, They have their reward. But thou, when thou prayest, enter into thy closet, and when thou hast shut thy door, pray to thy Father, who is in secret; and thy Father, who seeth in secret, shall reward thee openly.
>
> But when ye pray, use not vain repetitions, as the heathen do; for they think that they shall be heard for their much speaking. Be not ye, therefore, like unto them; for your Father knoweth what things ye have need of, before ye ask him. After this manner, therefore, pray ye: Our Father, who art in heaven, Hallowed be thy name. Thy kingdom come. Thy will be done in earth, as it is in heaven. Give us this day our daily bread. And forgive us our debts, as we forgive our debtors. And lead us not into temptation, but deliver us from evil. For thine is the kingdom, and the power, and the glory, forever. Amen. For if ye

forgive men their trespasses, your heavenly Father will also forgive you; but if ye forgive not men their trespasses, neither will your Father forgive your trespasses.

Moreover when ye fast, be not, as the hypocrites, of a sad countenance; for they disfigure their faces, that they may appear unto men to fast. Verily I say unto you, They have their reward. But thou, when thou fastest, anoint thine head, and wash thy face, that thou appear not unto men to fast, but unto thy Father, who is in secret, and thy Father, who seeth in secret, shall reward thee openly. Lay not up for yourselves treasures upon earth, where moth and rust doth corrupt, and where thieves break through and steal, but lay up for yourselves treasures in heaven, where neither moth nor rust doth corrupt, and where thieves do not break through nor steal; for where your treasure is, there will your heart be also. (Matt. 6:1-21)

We do not keep these commands to earn our salvation. Salvation comes only on the basis of the altar, which represented Christ's death in space and time. We must accept salvation with the empty hands of faith. Rather, the commands are the conditional statement in the midst of the unconditional promises. For example, do you as a Christian want to be forgiven existentially by God? Then have a forgiving heart toward other men. That is what Jesus was saying.

Finally, I would remind us of God's command to Joshua about the book:

This book of the law shall not depart out of thy mouth, but thou shalt meditate therein day and night, that thou mayest *observe to do* according to all that is written therein; for then thou shalt make thy way prosperous, and then thou shalt have good success. (Josh. 1:8)

Notice how this parallels the way Jesus ended the Sermon on the Mount:

Therefore, whosoever heareth these sayings of mine, and *doeth them,* I will liken him unto a wise man, who built his house upon a rock. And the rain descended, and the floods came, and the winds blew and beat upon that house, and it fell not; for it was founded upon a rock. And every one that heareth these sayings of mine, and doeth them not, shall be likened unto a foolish man, who built his house upon the sand. And the rain descended, and the floods came, and the winds blew and beat upon that house, and it fell; and great was the fall of it. (Matt. 7:24-27)

On what does successful building depend? It depends first of all upon *hearing* Jesus' words. But if we have heard them and declare them to be the Word of God, what then? Then we must *do* them.

CHAPTER EIGHT

The Gibeonites

After the reading of the blessings and the curses, the conquest of the land continued. The Israelites were now on top of the mountains; the wedge had been driven in. From this time on the wedge was expanded, first to the south, then to the north.

The Israelites' opponents banded together to oppose this campaign: "And it came to pass, when all the kings who were on this side Jordan, in the hills, and in the valleys, and in all the coasts of the Great Sea over against Lebanon, the Hittite, and the Amorite, the Canaanite, the Perizzite, the Hivite, and the Jebusite, heard thereof, that they gathered themselves together, to fight with Joshua and with Israel, with one accord [literally, with one mouth]" (Josh. 9:1, 2). The leaders mounted a united campaign against the people that now stood in such an advantageous position on the mountains. Part of the warfare itself is described in Joshua 10. It can be easily summarized: in a short span of time all the strongholds of the south fell.

The Defeat of the Southern Confederation

The first battle began this way. Jerusalem was the key city in a confederation of five southern city-states. The king of Jerusalem called together the other four kings to attack Gibeon, a city related to the confederation: "Adoni-zedek, king of Jerusalem, sent unto Hoham, king of Hebron, and unto Piram, king of Jarmuth, and unto Japhia, king of Lachish, and unto Debir, king of Eglon, saying, Come up unto me, and help me, that we may smite Gibeon; for it hath made peace with Joshua and with the children of Israel" (Josh. 10:3, 4). As the confederation moved against Gibeon, the Gibeonites gave a call for help to the Israelites. (Why Joshua had made peace with Gibeon we will see in a moment.) They sent to Gilgal, the Israelites' permanent base in the valley, to which the women, children and animals had probably returned while the soldiers fought in the highlands, and said, "Slack not thy hand from thy servants; come up to us quickly, and save us, and help us; for all the kings of the Amorites that dwell in the mountains are gathered against us" (Josh. 10:6). So Joshua departed quickly from Gilgal, and the war was on.

"And the LORD said unto Joshua, Fear them not; for I have delivered them into thine hand. There shall not a man of them stand before thee" (Josh. 10:8). The Israelites had the Word of the Lord with them. They were not functioning on their own without listening to God, as they had in the case of Ai. God said, "This is of Me; so go forward without fear and with courage."

They fought a great pitched battle against the confederacy of the five nations, broke the strength of this united army, and put the Amorites to flight. Joshua 10:10 speaks of their fleeing by a way that "goeth up to Beth-horon," while Joshua 10:11 talks about the Amorites' going "down to Beth-horon." At first sight this might seem to be contradiction, but we know from archaeological studies that there were two Beth-horons, an upper and a lower.

The battle was not won only by the Israelites' valiant fighting. God had said He would be with the people, and, as we pointed out earlier, there should be no stereotypes about how God will act. The fall of Jericho was different from the fall of Ai. The fall of the five kings was again different. God intervened directly through two acts of nature. First, hailstones fell upon the enemy. This added to their confusion in the midst of battle. Second, Joshua spoke to the Lord "in the day when the LORD delivered up the Amorites before the children of Israel, and he said in the sight of Israel, Sun, stand thou still [literally, be silent] upon Gibeon; and thou, Moon, in the valley of Ajalon. And the sun stood still, and the moon stayed, until the peoples had avenged themselves upon their enemies" (Josh. 10:12, 13). Joshua spoke and God heard him.

"Is not this written in the book of Jasher?" the text then asks. The "book of Jasher" is not part of the inspired Bible, though this portion of it was put into the Bible. The rest of the book is lost. It was apparently not named for a man. As best we can tell, it was a book of poetry that recounted the great acts of God and informed the Jewish people about their heroes. The book of Jasher was mentioned again about 400 years later, at the time of David. So though not inspired, it continued to be popular.

When the Israelites came out of Egypt, another poem, "the song of Moses," was recited. "I will sing unto the LORD, for he hath triumphed gloriously," it began (Ex. 15:1). In Exodus (14:21-29), as in Joshua (10:13), the message is given in prose as well as in poetry. There is no conflict in this. Both texts are talking about a historic event, whether in poetry or prose.

What the text from Joshua is actually saying is that there was a long day. We cannot use the phrase "the sun stood still" to prove that the Jews were ignorant cosmologically. Whether they were or not, the use of this term does not demonstrate that the text is inaccurate, for the simple reason that we today use the same kind of expression. I have never heard a twentieth-century person say when the sun came up in the morning, "The earth has turned far enough to allow me to see the sun." If you said, "The sun is rising" and someone suddenly responded, "How ignorant you are! The earth has turned far enough for you to see the sun," everyone would laugh. The comment would be ridiculous because it is outside the forms in which we normally speak.

I find it strange that some people are upset by the long day. It is not difficult to visualize it. In Switzerland during the summer I can count on light till 9:00 at night. In the middle of winter, however, I must be out of the forest by 6:00, or I am in trouble. In Norway on the longest day of the year, the sun does not go down at all! In the North, for days the sun never sets. So we know that the lengths of daylight vary.

How did God do it? We do not know. We might visualize it either of two ways: the earth could have slowed or the earth could have tilted, making the conditions in Israel like those in the North where the sun does not set. There could be other ways that we might not be able to visualize. However it was accomplished, the Bible says that God worked into space-time history to fight for the Israelites.

After the main resistance was broken, the Israelite forces swept on. Throughout the day, one after another of the small city-states fell: Makkedah, Libnah, Lachish, Gezer, Eglon, Hebron and Debir. The whole south fell in one united campaign. The armies were broken, the cities overthrown, and the five major kings killed.

> So Joshua smote all the country of the hills, and of the south, and of the vale, and of the springs, and all their kings; he left none remaining, but utterly destroyed all that breathed, as the LORD God of Israel commanded. And Joshua smote them from Kadesh-barnea even unto Gaza, and all the country of Goshen, even unto Gibeon. And all these kings and their land did Joshua take at one time, because the LORD God of Israel fought for Israel. And Joshua returned, and all Israel with him, unto the camp to Gilgal. (Josh. 10:40-43).

The wedge was now spread in one direction. The whole southern portion of the land had fallen. This does not mean that all these cities were permanently occupied, but the confederacy was broken and the south was in the hand of the Israelites.

The Deception of the Gibeonites

Having seen the southern campaign successfully completed, let us turn our attention back to Joshua 9. As the Amorite confederacy had prepared for its fight against the Israelites, the inhabitants of Gibeon had taken a drastic step:

> And when the inhabitants of Gibeon heard what Joshua had done unto Jericho and to Ai, they did work wilily, and went and made as if they had been ambassadors, and took old sacks upon their asses, and wine bottles, old and rent, and bound up; and old shoes and clouted upon their feet, and old garments upon them; and all the bread of their provision was dry and moldy. And they went to Joshua unto the camp at Gilgal, and said unto him, and to the men of Israel, We have come from a far country; now, therefore, make ye a league with us. And the men of Israel said unto the Hivites, Peradventure ye dwell among us; and how shall we make a league with you? And they said unto Joshua, We are thy servants. And Joshua said unto them, Who are ye? and from where come ye? And they said unto him, From a very far country thy servants have come because of the name of the LORD thy God; for we have heard the fame of him, and all that he did in Egypt, and all that he did to the two kings of the Amorites, that were beyond Jordan, to Sihon, king of Heshbon, and to Og, king of Bashan, who was at Ashtaroth. Wherefore our elders and all the inhabitants of our country spoke to us, saying, Take victuals with you for the journey, and go to meet them, and say unto them, We are your servants;

therefore, now, make ye a league with us. This our bread we took hot for our provision out of our houses on the day we came forth to go unto you; but now, behold, it is dry, and it is moldy; and these bottles of wine which we filled, were new; and, behold, they are rent; and these our garments and our shoes have become old by reason of the very long journey. And the men took of their victuals, and asked not counsel at the mouth of the LORD; and Joshua made peace with them, and made a league with them, to let them live; and the princes of the congregation swore unto them.

And it came to pass at the end of three days, after they had made a league with them, that they heard that they were their neighbors, and that they dwelt among them. And the children of Israel journeyed, and came unto their cities on the third day. Now their cities were: Gibeon, and Chephirah, and Beeroth, and Kiriath-jearim. And the children of Israel smote them not, because the princes of the congregation had sworn unto them by the LORD God of Israel. And all the congregation murmured against the princes. But all the princes said unto all the congregation, We have sworn unto them by the LORD God of Israel; now, therefore, we may not touch them. This we will do to them: we will even let them live, lest wrath be upon us, because of the oath which we swore unto them. And the princes said unto them, Let them live, but let them be hewers of wood and drawers of water unto all the congregation; as the princes had promised them.

And Joshua called for them, and he spoke unto them, saying, Wherefore have ye beguiled us, saying, We are very far from you; when ye dwell among us? Now, therefore, ye are cursed, and there shall none of you be freed from being bondmen, and hewers of wood and drawers of water for the house of my God. And they answered Joshua, and said, Because it was certainly told thy servants, how that the LORD thy God commanded his servant, Moses, to give you all the land, and to destroy all the inhabitants of the land before you; therefore, we were sore afraid of our lives because of you, and have done this thing. And now, behold, we are in thine hand; as it seemeth good and right unto thee to do unto us, do. And so did he unto them, and delivered them out of the hand of the children of Israel, that they slew them not. And Joshua made them that day hewers of wood and drawers of water for the congregation, and for the altar of the LORD, even unto this day, in the place which he should choose. (Josh. 9:3-27)

The Gibeonites performed an act of deception. The "wine bottles," of course, were skins, and the Gibeonites said, "They are torn. The bread which we took from the oven is now old and dried." They knew very well what had happened to Jericho and Ai, but they never mentioned it. They only mentioned what they would have heard about had they left home a long time ago—that is, they only mentioned what had happened on the east side of the Jordan. And Joshua made a league with them.

The text specifically says that the Israelites did not ask God's counsel. "They received the men by reason of their food" is actually a better translation of the Hebrew; in other words, the Israelites looked at the Gibeonites' food. We can hear the Israelites buzzing among themselves, "Of course, they're telling the truth. Look how old the food is. Look at the bread." We can picture somebody going up and feeling the hard loaves. They did not bother talking to God about the situation, and so they were fooled.

Three days later they found out that they had been taken in, that instead of coming from a far country the Gibeonites lived nearby. So the congregation murmured against the princes: "Why did you do this? You made the oath, and you shouldn't have." Joshua and the other leaders responded that though it was made in deception, the oath nevertheless held, because it had been made in the name of the Lord. Then Joshua turned to the Gibeonites and said, "There shall none of you be freed from being bondmen, and hewers of wood and drawers of water for the house of my God." "You have asked to be servants; now you will be servants," Joshua told them. They were indeed made servants, but in a special capacity—in the house of God.

The end of this narrative explains the reason for the Gibeonites' action: "It was certainly told thy servants, how that the LORD thy God commanded his servant, Moses, to give you all the land" (Josh. 9:24). The Gibeonites had understood that God had made a promise to Moses. We can see the force of this when we connect it with the fact that they came "because of the name of the LORD thy God; for we have heard the fame of him" (Josh. 9:9). They had heard about God and what He had done.

Let us quickly put all this together. The Gibeonites sought the Israelites' protection. The Israelites made a league with them without consulting God. Nevertheless, once the oath was made in God's name, it had to be kept. The five-member confederacy said, "Now we're in real trouble. Jericho has fallen; Ai has fallen; and Gibeon, one of the great royal cities, has gone over to the other side." So the confederacy tried to destroy the Gibeonites in order to warn everyone else not to desert to the enemy. The people of Gibeon cried to the Israelites, "You've made a promise to us. This is the moment to fulfill it. Come quickly, or we will be destroyed!" They must have held their breath as they waited to see if the Israelites would honor the oath which had been given because of their own duplicity. But the Israelites did honor the oath (Josh. 10:2-7).

And this was completely right with God. Once the oath was made, God expected the people to keep it. And Joshua did. Many years later, however, the oath was broken. In the days of David there was a three-year famine, and David asked the Lord why. The Lord answered: "It is for Saul, and for his bloody house, because he slew the Gibeonites" (2 Sam. 21:1). When Saul killed the Gibeonites, thereby transgressing the oath made by Joshua about 400 years before, God responded, "This is serious. Saul broke an oath made in My name, and I hold him accountable."

In the time of Ezekiel, God's people swore in the name of the Lord that they would serve the king of Babylon. Later, because it seemed expedient, they broke their oath. Through the prophet Ezekiel God spoke into the situation:

> As I live, saith the Lord GOD, surely in the place where the king dwelleth who made him king, whose oath he despised, and whose covenant he broke, even with him in the midst of Babylon he shall die. . . . Seeing he despised the oath by breaking the covenant, when, lo, he had given his hand, and hath done all these things, he shall not escape. Therefore, thus saith the Lord GOD; As I live, surely mine oath that he hath despised, and my covenant that he hath broken, even it will I recompense upon his own head. And I will spread my net upon him, and he shall be taken in my snare, and I will bring him to Babylon, and will plead with him there for his trespass that he hath trespassed against me. (Ezek. 17:16, 18-20)

The king despised an oath made in God's name. In so doing, he did not transgress against the king of Babylon (though that is what the king of Babylon said), but he transgressed against God. God said, "I don't take lightly a king of the Jews making an oath in My name and then breaking it." What was done in the book of Joshua fits into the whole structure of Scripture: an oath made in the name of the God of holiness is to be kept with holy hands.

Psalm 15 states this as a universal principle: "Lord, who shall abide in thy tabernacle? Who shall dwell in thy holy hill? . . . He that sweareth to his own hurt, and changeth not" (Psa. 15:1, 4). One who swears in the name of God, even if he swears to his own hurt, must keep the oath in order to represent God's character.

God is a holy God, and to break an oath made in His name is to transgress, to blaspheme, to caricature the God in whose name the oath is made. Because the Jews were the people of God, they were to have a morality that was not only individual but national. The nation itself was required to keep oaths made in God's name. In light of this principle, we can understand Jesus' warning: "Don't swear lightly, because when you swear in the name of God God expects you to be faithful" (Matt. 5:33-37).

Rahab and the Gibeonites

Rahab was a harlot. The Gibeonites were liars. As far as we can tell, they dealt in duplicity without any motion of conscience at all. Bringing their heathen heritage with them, they lied with ease. Why did the Gibeonites come to Joshua? Because they had heard about the Lord and what He had done. And this fact alerts us to the truly important parallels between Rahab and the Gibeonites.

Rahab said this to the spies: "For we have heard how the LORD dried up the water of the Red Sea for you, when ye came out of Egypt; and what ye did unto the two kings of the Amorites, that were on the other side Jordan, Sihon and Og, whom ye utterly destroyed. And as soon as we had heard these things, our hearts did melt, neither did there remain any more courage in any man, because of you" (Josh. 2:10, 11). The inhabitants of Gibeon, too, were fearful when they heard "what Joshua had done unto Jericho and to Ai . . . and all that he did to the two kings of the Amorites, that were beyond Jordan, to Sihon, king of Heshbon, and to Og, king of Bashan, who was at Ashtaroth" (Josh. 9:3, 10).

In the midst of pagan Jericho, Rahab believed on the living God: "And she said unto the men, I know that the LORD hath given you the land" (Josh. 2:9). Strikingly, she affirmed, "For the LORD your God, he is God in heaven above, and in earth beneath" (Josh. 2:11). When she heard what had happened in Egypt and on the other side of Jordan, she said, "This is the living, universal God!" She made a decision on what to her was an adequate testimony. This high and holy expression was something one would never have heard in the heathen world, for there the gods were limited. It does not strike our ears as a surprise because this is the way we think about God, but she was making a declaration of faith which was startling: "I know He isn't a limited god. He's a different kind of a god. He is the LORD your God" She used the Tetragrammaton—God's high and holy name.

Though the Gibeonites' testimony was not as clear as Rahab's. it is apparent that they did believe what they had heard. They said they came "because of the name of the LORD thy God." In Semitic usage a name is a verbalization which represents one's entire character. What the Gibeonites were really saying was, "We came because of who the LORD your God is." Similarly, they spoke of "how that the LORD thy God commanded his servant, Moses" (Josh. 9:24). So in the cases of both Rahab and the Gibeonites, what they had heard was sufficient to convince them.

Rahab left the kingdom of the enemies of God for the kingdom of the Jews. In making her decision, she pitted herself against her king and her culture. The Gibeonites did likewise. They broke with the confederacy and came over to the people of God. Further, Rahab's act meant that if her old king had found out what she had done, he would undoubtedly have killed her. The Gibeonites were actually caught in their defection. The confederacy knew well what they had done. The confederacy, therefore, did in fact come against the Gibeonites to exterminate them.

Rahab the harlot became a part of the people of God: "And Joshua saved Rahab, the harlot, alive, and her father's household, and all that she had; and she dwelleth in Israel even unto this day" (Josh. 6:25). The whole group of Gibeonites stood in a like circumstance: "And Joshua made them that day hewers of wood and drawers of water for the congregation, and for the altar of the LORD, even unto this day" (Josh. 9:27).

Both Rahab and the Gibeonites proved their loyalty. Rahab helped the spies escape and hung out the scarlet cord. The Gibeonites were faithful to their oath. The Gibeonites were Hivites, a people who remained the enemies of the Israelites, fighting them throughout the period of the judges. And though the Hivites fought against the Israelites, we find no note that the Gibeonites were unfaithful. So the Gibeonites not only left the confederacy, they broke their normal line. They joined neither their former allies nor their blood relations in the wars that followed. They remained, by an act of choice, in the midst of the people of Israel.

Rahab not only remained a part of the people of God; she married a son of a prince of Judah and became an ancestor of Christ. The Gibeonites, too, had a special place. They remained close to the altar of God. Though they were only hewers of wood and drawers of water, their activity was on behalf of worship of the living God, and it led gradually to a place of religious privilege.

When the land was divided, Gibeon was one of the cities given to the line of Aaron. It became a special place where God was known. Approximately 400 years later, David put the tabernacle in that city. This meant that the altar and the priest were in Gibeon as well. At least one of David's mighty men, those who were closest to him in battle, was a Gibeonite. At that important and solemn moment when Solomon, David's son, ascended the throne, Solomon made burnt offerings at Gibeon. It was there he had his vision, when God spoke to him about his coming rule. Much later still, about 500 years before Christ, in the time of Zerubbabel, the genealogies of those Jews who returned from captivity under the Babylonians included a list of the Gibeonites. This is especially striking because the names of some who claimed to be Jews were not found in the registry, and they were not allowed to be a part of the Jewish nation. In the days of Nehemiah, the Gibeonites were mentioned as being among the people who rebuilt the walls of Jerusalem. The Gibeonites had come in among the people of God, and hundreds of years later they were still there.

Both Rahab and the Gibeonites stood under the spiritual portion of the covenant of grace. We know from the book of Hebrews that Rahab had salvation. Whether these people who came to Joshua as a group all had individual salvation, we have no way of knowing. But the way God honored these people's faith suggests a tremendous implication: if God, on the basis of the spiritual portion of the covenant of grace, so dealt with Rahab and the Gibeonites when they believed, what would have happened if others had believed? We can also think about the judgment of Nineveh being lifted when its people repented through the preaching of Jonah.

So there really are exact parallels between Rahab (the individual) and the Gibeonites (the corporate unit). Rahab (plus her family) was the only individual saved out of Jericho. The Gibeonites were the only people saved out of the land. Rahab believed, left Jericho, and came among the people of God. The Gibeonites were the only people in the land who turned to God, and they flowed on through all the years of Jewish history.

Rahab, the Gibeonites, and Us

Every Christian, no matter who he is, was once, like Rahab (a prostitute) and the Gibeonites (liars), under the wrath and judgment of God. We were all rebels. Not one of us was born good. Not one of us who was raised a Christian automatically became a Christian.

Those who are not Christians remain where Rahab and the Gibeonites stood prior to their identification with the people of God. But Rahab and the Gibeonites believed, and they were accepted. If it is true that God accepted them, how much more true can it be for us who have an open invitation from God. Jesus said, "Whosoever will may come" (see, for instance, John 3:15, 16). "Come unto me, all ye that labor and are heavy laden," Jesus invited, "and I will give you rest" (Matt. 11:28).

Let us remember that God insisted that the Israelites keep their oath, even though it was made because of the Gibeonites' deception. If God will not tolerate the breaking of an oath made in His name, how much more will He never break His own oath and covenant made to us on the basis of the shed blood and infinite value of Jesus Christ. How secure are we who have cast ourselves upon Christ as our Savior!

For God has made an oath:

> For when God made promise to Abraham, because he could swear by no greater, he swore by himself, saying, Surely, blessing I will bless thee, and multiplying I will multiply thee. And so, after he had patiently endured, he obtained the promise. For men verily swear by the greater: and an oath for confirmation is to them an end of all strife. Wherein God, willing more abundantly to show unto the heirs of promise the immutability of his counsel, confirmed it by an oath, that by two immutable things, in which it was impossible for God to lie, we might have a strong consolation, who have fled for refuge to lay hold upon the hope set before us, which hope we have as an anchor of the soul, both sure and steadfast, and which entereth into that within the veil, where the forerunner is for us entered, even Jesus, made an high priest forever after the order of Melchizedec. (Heb. 6:13-20)

Here is described the establishment of the Abrahamic covenant, both its natural and spiritual sides. When men make an oath, they swear by God. When God made His promise to Abraham, He swore by Himself. There is no one else by whom God can swear because there is no one greater. He "confirmed it by an oath," the Authorized Version translates, but the Greek is much stronger: "He interposed Himself by an oath." His oath was Himself. It rested upon His existence and character. Therefore, to the heirs of the promise he brought two things to bear: the unchangeableness of the act of His will (His counsel), and the fact that He interposed Himself by an oath in His own name. And God will not lie. Why? Because God is a holy God. Men may draw back from the idea of judgment, but if God is going to be worth anything He must be holy. Therefore, the very justice of God should reassure us. He will never break His oath and word. Never!

Notice the word *we:* " . . . *we* might have a strong consolation, who have fled for refuge to lay hold upon the hope set before us." The book of Hebrews is not just talking about the Jews. It is talking about believers of all ages, going back to the time of Abel and flowing on to all who will come under the promises of God. I love this picture—"we who have fled"—for it carries us back to the Gibeonites and Rahab. Rahab fled from her place in the kingdom of Jericho to the name of God. The Gibeonites fled from their race, the Hivites, and they fled from the confederacy. And we who have come to Christ have done the same thing; we have fled from Satan and the world to lay hold of the hope that is set before us.

Like a boat with an anchor wedged in a rock, we have an anchor who already stands in the presence of God within the veil. Who is this anchor? Jesus Himself. He is the forerunner. We will follow Him because we have believed in Him. He is within the veil, so we will be within the veil.

If the Gibeonites could rely on an oath the Israelites made in the adverse circumstance of the Gibeonites' deception, when the Israelites did not even ask God's counsel, how much more confident can we be in God's oath to us. May we rely upon it. May we cast ourselves upon Christ and be those of a completely quiet heart.

CHAPTER NINE

Caleb's Faithfulness

After the Israelites had overthrown the southern strongholds in one mighty effort, they turned to the north. Since the king of Hazor headed the confederacy of the north, he called on the northern kings to do battle, and the Israelites defeated them at the waters of Merom. The north, too, the Israelites took in one campaign, as Joshua 11 describes. In the sense that the strongholds had been broken, the land belonged to them.

The campaigns took seven years, as we see if we study Joshua 14 carefully. Joshua 14:7 says Caleb was forty years old when Moses sent him to spy out the land. The wilderness wanderings lasted thirty-eight years. This is a total of seventy-eight years. Joshua 14:10 says that Caleb at the end of the campaigns was eighty-five years old. Therefore, the campaigns must have taken seven years. Verse 10 confirms this, for the thirty-eight years of the wandering plus the seven years of the campaigns equal the forty-five years of which Caleb speaks. If the Israelites had entered the land when they could have entered, they would have spent one year coming out of Egypt and seven years fighting west of Jordan. Thus, in a bit more than eight years after leaving Egypt they could have had the land. Instead of that, they wasted thirty-eight years.

Chapter 11, like earlier chapters, insists on the continuity of the law of Moses: "As the LORD commanded Moses, his servant, so did Moses command Joshua, and so did Joshua; he left nothing undone of all that the LORD commanded Moses. . . . So Joshua took the whole land, according to all that the LORD said unto Moses; and Joshua gave it for an inheritance unto Israel according to their divisions by their tribes. And the land rested from war" (Josh. 11:15, 23). This insistence is important because liberal theologians try to drive a wedge between the Pentateuch and the rest of the Bible. It cannot be done. The rest of the Bible, beginning with Joshua, stands in total continuity with the Pentateuch. Joshua was acting on the basis of God's revelation through Moses.

Joshua 12 is a summary of the total campaign. The summary is divided into two parts: verses 1-6 describe the campaign under Moses on the east side of the Jordan; verses 7-24, the campaign under Joshua on the west side of the Jordan. When we reach the end of the twelfth chapter, we are halfway through the book, for the book of Joshua is divided into two parts: first, the conquest of the land (chapters 1—12), and then the settlement of the land and the division to the tribes (chapters 13—24).

Possessing the Possessions

We turn now to the division of the land among the tribes. The major campaigns were past, but land still remained to be secured: "Now Joshua was old and stricken in years; and the LORD said unto him, Thou art old and stricken in years, and there remaineth yet very much land to be possessed" (Josh. 13:1). There was land to be taken to the north, south, east and west (Josh. 13:2-6). The Israelites had broken the main force of the opposition, but they were still an island in the midst of those who were not the people of God.

Concerning the unconquered people, the Israelites had a promise from God: "Them will I drive out from before the children of Israel; only divide thou it by lot unto the Israelites for an inheritance, as I have commanded thee" (Josh. 13:6). The major campaigns had proven that God indeed is great and that the Israelites, in this supernatural way, could break the heart of the enemy force. Now God promised, "Go on. Divide the land, because I'm going to give you the strength to clear it up and to *possess your possession.*"

Suddenly, however, comes a new note: the failure of the people of God to possess their possessions. Though it lay open before them, they simply did not take hold of that which was theirs to hold. Later Joshua said to the children of Israel, "How long are ye slack to go to possess the land, which the LORD God of your fathers hath given you?" (Josh. 18:3). In other words, "It's yours! Why don't you go and get it?"

There were two reasons for the people's failure. The first was not their fault. For a time they could not. For instance, "As for the Jebusites, the inhabitants of Jerusalem, the children of Judah could not drive them out; but the Jebusites dwell with the children of Judah at Jerusalem unto this day" (Josh. 15:63). And, "The children of Manasseh could not drive out the inhabitants of those cities; but the Canaanites would dwell in that land" (Josh. 17:12). But this was not the primary problem, for Joshua 17:13 says, "Yet it came to pass, when the children of Israel were waxen strong, that they put the Canaanites to tribute, but did not utterly drive them out." Though there was a time when they could not vanquish them, when they did become strong enough to drive them out, they did not do so. Rather, they put them under tribute. This was their own fault.

The people of God did not go on to do what God told them to do for two reasons. First, they wanted peace at any cost and in spite of God's commands; second, they wanted wealth. They were practical materialists. For the sake of ease and money, they did not go forward and do what God told them to do. "Tribute! Tribute! Tribute!" they demanded. And they let the people stay in the land. And through the time of the judges and beyond, instead of gaining ground the Israelites slowly lost it, because they had not possessed their possessions on the basis of God's promise.

Does that sound up to date? These were people who would rather have affluence than possess their possessions under the promises of God. Had God lost His power? Had God reneged on the promise? Was he unable to keep it? Not a bit. God's power was still there. The iron chariots of the enemy should have been no detriment. In Deborah's day the battle was won in the valley plain where the chariots were most useful. All the land was theirs, but through their lack of faith and their disobedience they did not make it theirs. The desire for peace and tribute stood in the way. Therefore, on the basis of the conditional portion of the covenant of God, the blessings stopped.

Caleb Remains Faithful

In contrast, happily, somebody did possess his possessions:

> Then the children of Judah came unto Joshua in Gilgal; and Caleb, the son of Jephunneh the Kenezite, said unto him, Thou knowest the thing that the LORD said unto Moses, the man of God, concerning me and thee in Kadesh-barnea. Forty years old was I when Moses, the servant of the LORD, sent me from Kadesh-barnea to spy out the land; and I brought him word again as it was in mine heart. Nevertheless my brethren who went up with me made the heart of the people melt; but I wholly followed the LORD my God. And Moses swore on that day, saying, Surely the land whereon thy feet have trodden shall be thine inheritance, and thy children's forever, because thou hast wholly followed the LORD my God. And now, behold, the LORD hath kept me alive, as he said, these forty and five years, even since the LORD spoke this word unto Moses, while the children of Israel wandered in the wilderness; and now, lo, I am this day fourscore and five years old. As yet I am as strong this day as I was in the day that Moses sent me; as my strength was then, even so is my strength now, for war, both to go out, and to come in. Now, therefore, give me this mountain, which the LORD spoke in that day; for thou heardest in that day how the Anakim were there, and that the cities were great and fenced; if so be the LORD will be with me, then I shall be able to drive them out, as the LORD said.
>
> And Joshua blessed him, and gave unto Caleb, the son of Jephunneh, Hebron for an inheritance. Hebron, therefore, became the inheritance of Caleb, the son of Jephunneh the Kenezite, unto this day, because he wholly followed the LORD God of Israel. (Josh. 14:6-14)

Caleb said, "In the past I followed the Lord God." What was he talking about? He and Joshua were the spies under Moses who years earlier had believed God's promises. While the rest of the spies had said, "We are afraid," and had turned the people aside, Caleb and Joshua had said, "We can take the land because God says we can."

When the campaigns had broken the heart of the land, Caleb (now eighty-five) came to Joshua and said, "Now by faith I'm going to do what I said all along could be done." What a man! Here he was, out of step among a people who, for the sake of peace and wealth, were not continuing the warfare. In that moment, as in the past, Caleb followed the Lord. Caleb actually went up and claimed his land—he fought for it and won it (Josh. 15:13-19) and proved what he had believed for many long years. Apparently the city he captured was one of the great fortresses.

When the spies had seen it, they thought it would be extremely difficult to take; but Caleb had maintained, "We can take it under God." Now he proved this by faith. This was Caleb!

Caleb was not following a new principle. This was the principle of his life. When he was a spy, he was faithful to God, saying the conquest could be achieved. Under Joshua, we can be sure, he continued in battle with confidence. When the heart of the land was broken, he reaffirmed his principle of trusting God by not turning aside into these cul-de-sacs. So a section of the promised land fell into Caleb's hands, while the others were sitting in the midst of peace and tribute and not possessing the promises of God.

Promises to Christians

Caleb's faithfulness speaks to us today. If you and I have cast ourselves upon Christ, if we have believed in Him in the biblical way, if we have been justified, the central battle has been won, just as when the Israelites' southern and northern campaigns broke the heart of the resistance. But there are also promises made to Christians. We are called upon to *possess our possessions*. Was God, who gave the people the power to break the strongholds, not able to give them the possessions? Was God's power ended? If we are Christians, we have believed that Christ in the infinite value of His death takes away our guilt and opens the way to God for us. Has Christ lost His power since we were justified? Have God's promises to us diminished?

What are God's promises to Christians? We could follow several veins, but I would like to follow this one: the promises of the fruit and power of the Holy Spirit. As Jesus was preparing to leave His disciples, He promised, "I will not leave you orphans. I will come to you" (John 14:18). Here is the promise of God: "I am going to send the Holy Spirit, the third person of the Trinity, to live within every true Christian from Pentecost on." Romans 8 emphasizes that the Holy Spirit is the agent through which the power of the victorious, resurrected Christ brings forth fruit in a Christian's life.

Christ has not left us orphans. The Holy Spirit dwells within us. And this fact has great implications. Jesus promised His followers, "But ye shall receive power [from the same Greek word which gives us our word *dynamite*], after that the Holy Ghost is come upon you; and ye shall be witnesses unto me both in Jerusalem, and in all Judea, and in Samaria, and unto the uttermost part of the earth" (Acts 1:8). The Holy Spirit will be Christ's agent in us—producing dynamite-power so we can witness to this rebellious world.

The Holy Spirit also gives us the fruit of the Spirit, which is described in Galatians: "But the fruit of the Spirit is love, joy, peace, long-suffering, gentleness, goodness, faith, meekness, temperance; against such there is no law. And they that are Christ's have crucified the flesh with the affections and lusts. If we live in the Spirit, let us also walk in the Spirit" (Gal. 5:22-25). If we have accepted Christ as our Savior, we are indwelt by the Holy Spirit. Isn't that fine? All right, then, let us walk in the Spirit. Let us possess our possessions.

What was the Israelites' trouble? Why did they not possess their possessions? Very simple: they wanted their peace and materialism. These things always stand in the way of the people of God. There is an intriguing parallel in the parable of the sower: "And that which fell among thorns are they who, when they have heard, go forth, and are choked with cares and riches and pleasures of this life, and bring no fruit to perfection" (Luke 8:14). There are people who hear the gospel and turn away because of the cares of life, and there are people who turn away because of their fears of losing riches and pleasure. But Christians, too, can be so caught up in the cares and riches and pleasures of this world that they bring little or no fruit to perfection.

What Jesus desires is this: "That on the good ground are they who, in an honest and good heart, having heard the word, keep it, and bring forth fruit with patience" (Luke 8:15). Hold it fast! Bring forth fruit with patience! Patience in what? First, patience in enduring the cares of this world and the trouble that Christianity brings. Does Christianity bring you any troubles? If it does not, you have not been active enough. As Christians, we are in the midst of war. If we never have any troubles, if we have nothing but peace, we have not been involved in this war in the midst of a generation that has rebelled against God. Second, we need patience in resisting the riches and pleasures which can also stop fruitbearing.

What was the first reason why the Israelites did not possess their possessions? They wanted peace. Doesn't this exactly parallel the "cares"? What was the second reason? They wanted tribute. Because of riches and pleasures, a Christian can also be distracted from continuing God's conquest. That which stood in the way of blessing in the time of Joshua is exactly what today stands in the way of a Christian's bearing fruit.

With the Israelites, the master conquest was over. With us, the master conquest ended at two great historic points: a cross in space and time (where Jesus said, "It is finished"—the propitiatory work was complete) and the moment we personally were justified (when God, the Judge of all the universe, declared, "Your guilt is gone. You are returned to Me").

Back in Joshua's day, when the master conquest was over God was the same, His promise was the same, His power was the same. But the people did not possess their possessions because of their desire for peace and for tribute. We Christians stand in the same danger. It is all too easy to fail to possess the possessions God has promised because we either draw back out of fear of the troubles that being a Christian will bring us or we become caught up in the affluent society where people sail their little boats upon this plastic culture.

CHAPTER TEN

East and West of Jordan

After the three successful campaigns, God commanded the children of Israel to divide the land in faith even before it was completely conquered. "Only divide it by lot unto the Israelites for an inheritance, as I have commanded thee," He said (Josh. 13:6). Jacob, of course, had twelve sons. And God had made a covenant with Abraham, Isaac, and Jacob that all twelve would have an inheritance in the land of promise.

The land was divided in three steps. The first took place under Moses on the east side of Jordan, the second and third under Joshua on the west side, first at Gilgal, then at Shiloh. Moses gave two and a half tribes—Reuben, Gad and half of the tribe of Manasseh—an inheritance on the eastern side of the Jordan before he died. After the major campaigns, Joshua divided the land west of the Jordan among the remaining tribes. As we shall study later, the Levites received no land as a capital possession, though they were given land to live in.

Joshua 13:15-31 reminds us of the inheritances received on the east side of Jordan and then Joshua 13:32 summarizes, "These are the countries [the portions of the land] which Moses did distribute for an inheritance in the plains of Moab, on the other side of Jordan, by Jericho, eastward."

The final verse of Joshua 13 reminds us that Levi did not receive a normal share of the land because the Levites would live on the sacrifices: "But unto the tribe of Levi, Moses gave not any inheritance; the LORD God of Israel was their inheritance, as he [God] said unto them." The Levites did not receive any land because Moses had said so, and Moses said so because the Lord God of Israel had said so. Thus Joshua 13 also emphasizes that the Pentateuch was already completely normative. It was the Word of God to these people. Was this because Moses was a great or wise man? Not at all. It was because Moses was the mouthpiece of God. The Levites received no land because of a propositional statement which called forth a specific action in history.

Joshua 14 describes the beginning of the division of the land on the west side of Jordan. The people were at Gilgal, which had remained their central camp throughout the warfare. There the second phase of the allotment occurred: "And these are the countries which the children of Israel inherited in the land of Canaan, which Eleazar, the priest, and Joshua, the son of Nun, and the heads of the fathers of the tribes of the children of Israel, distributed for inheritance to them. By lot was their inheritance, as the LORD commanded by the hand of Moses, for the nine tribes, and for the half tribe" (Josh. 14:1, 2). Who oversaw the distribution? The priests, Joshua, and the elders. How were the portions determined? By lot. So it was God who made the division. The men only supervised the distribution under the hand of God through the lot.

The Division to Judah

First on the west side of Jordan, land was given to Judah. Caleb was of Judah, and so his act of faith is discussed in the second half of Joshua 14. Then Joshua 15:1-12 tells us the boundaries of Judah's territory. This portion began at the shore of the Dead Sea and ended at the river of Egypt (not the Nile, but a little wadi, Wadi el Arish)—that is, at the bend of the Mediterranean between Palestine and Egypt. This area contained Jerusalem, which became important as David's city and the capital of the southern kingdom. Verses 20-63 provide a detailed list of the cities and towns in Judah's inheritance.

Why did Judah, who was not the oldest son, receive the first of the land on the west side of the Jordan? You must remember the continuity of history and the continuity of prophecy which are interwoven in the Scripture. God knows and sometimes tells the future. As a matter of fact, Isaiah and other writers insist that this knowledge is one of the marks which distinguishes God from other gods. Because He is a living, infinite God, and not just an idol or a projection of man's mind, He can tell us the future course of history, just as we can read a history of the past.

Long before the land was divided, the dying Jacob gave a prophecy (Gen. 49). It is sometimes called a blessing, but it was really a foretelling about Jacob's sons.

Jacob spoke first of all to Reuben, the firstborn, the one who should have had preeminence: "Reuben, thou art my first-born, my might, and the beginning of my strength, the excellency of dignity, and the excellency of power. Unstable as water, thou shalt not excel, because thou wentest up to thy father's bed; then defiledst thou it: he went up to my couch" (Gen. 49:3, 4). What had Reuben done? This boy, growing into manhood, had had sexual relations with Bilhah, his father's concubine (Gen. 35:22). Because of this, Jacob set aside his preeminence.

The next two sons were Simeon and Levi. Jacob dealt with them like this:

> Simeon and Levi are brethren; instruments of cruelty [swords of violence] are in their habitations. O my soul, come not thou into their secret; unto their assembly, mine honor, be not thou united; for in their anger they slew a man, and in their selfwill they digged down a wall. Cursed be their anger, for it was fierce; and their wrath, for it was cruel: I will divide them in Jacob, and scatter them in Israel. (Gen. 49:5-7)

This prophecy referred to an incident which had involved Shechem, a prince in a neighboring land, and Dinah, a daughter of Jacob (Gen. 34). Shechem found Dinah in the field, had sexual relations with her, and then wanted to marry her. These two boys, Simeon and Levi, through a strategy which included a colossal lie, weakened Shechem's whole people and then killed them all. Because the brothers had lied, Jacob isolated himself from their act; and because of their act, they were not going to receive the first place either. Rather, they were to be scattered. They were not to have a fixed location like the rest of the tribes.

This has a lot to say, does it not, to the existential mentality that history is going nowhere. The biblical emphasis is constantly the reverse. History does have meaning; the past brings forth the present, and the present influences the future. Something happens in history because of a previous effect. Hume was wrong. Cause and effect does exist, not only in science but in meaningful, significant human events.

Jacob prophesied that Simeon and Levi were to be scattered in the land. Something happened, however, to modify this. The prophecy was still fulfilled, yet it was divided into two halves. It stood as Jacob had given it concerning Simeon, but it shifted in the case of Levi. In the midst of the orgies around the golden calf, Moses gave a call: Who is on the Lord's side? Who will speak for God? Who will act for God against a rebellious people? Then "all the sons of Levi gathered themselves together unto him" (Ex. 32:26) and went forward to end this revolt. Therefore, though the scattering stood, it was turned into a blessing. The Levites, along with the descendants of Aaron (who were of the tribe of Levi), were given a special closeness to the altar and to the Jewish worship.

Now we know why Judah received his place first in the giving of the land on the west of the Jordan, the heart of the promised land. Reuben, Levi and Simeon had all been set aside.

Jacob continued his prophecy by turning to Judah:

> Judah, thou art he whom thy brethren shall praise: thy hand shall be in the neck of thine enemies; thy father's children shall bow down before thee. Judah is a lion's whelp: from the prey, my son, thou art gone up: he stooped down, he crouched as a lion, and as an old lion. Who shall rouse him up? The sceptre shall not depart from Judah, nor a staff [or lawgiver] from between his feet, until Shiloh come; and unto him shall the gathering of the peoples be. (Gen. 49:8-10)

So Judah was awarded the preeminence among the people of God. Judah received the first share of the land on the west of the river, which included Jerusalem. This is important because Judah is the one out of whom David comes, and David is the one out of whom the truly great Ruler, Christ, comes.

The emphasis in Jacob's prophecy was that Judah would rule, and whether one translates the word in verse 10 as "lawgiver" or "staff," this emphasis is not changed. In Judges 5:14 the word is used to mean "a ruler" who symbolizes his authority by holding a sceptre. In other words, in Genesis 49:10 a double emphasis is being given through the parallel meaning of the words *sceptre* and *staff.*

David, Solomon and their successors came as partial fulfillments of this prophecy that Judah would rule, but the whole truth is far deeper. A greater reign was being prophesied here than the secular regimes of the later Jewish kings. Jacob spoke of Judah as a lion, and in Revelation this symbol is applied to one special Person: "One of the elders saith unto me, Weep not; behold, the Lion of the tribe of Judah, the Root of David, hath prevailed to open the book [of redemption], and to loose the seven seals thereof" (Rev. 5:5). The final rule that Jacob was describing was the rule of Christ, who shall be the great King of Israel as well as its Redeemer.

Numbers 21:18 speaks of Moses as "the lawgiver" or "staff" or "sceptre." Deuteronomy describes Moses as a "prophet" and records Moses' great prophecy about the coming Messiah: "The LORD thy God will raise up unto thee a Prophet from the midst of thee, of thy brethren, like unto me; unto him ye shall hearken" (Deut. 18:15). As we have seen, the New Testament expressly relates this to Christ. The idea of the ruler has shifted from Levi (Moses) to Judah (Christ)—an important change. Moses was "the lawgiver" or "ruler," but a time would come when the ruler would not be from the tribe of Levi but from the tribe of Judah, just as the great prophet when he would come would not come from Levi but from Judah. Interestingly, the last phrase of Psalm 60:7 uses the same word: Judah is my sceptre or ruler.

Also in Jacob's prophecy we find the term *Shiloh.* When the southern kingdom's rebellion against God came to the full and the kingly line from Solomon became totally corrupt, God made a striking statement through the prophet Ezekiel:

> And thou, profane wicked prince of Israel, whose day is come, when iniquity shall have an end, thus saith the Lord GOD: Remove the diadem, and take off the crown; this shall not be the same; exalt him that is low, and abase him that is high. I will overturn, overturn, overturn it: and it shall be no more, until he come whose right it is; and I will give it him. (Ezek. 21:25-27)

"I'm done with you!" God said. "But I'm not done totally because somebody is going to come—somebody 'whose right it is'—and then He will rule." Some believe *Shiloh* means "The Coming One." One was coming who was going to be the real ruler of the Jews.

It is important that the division of the land occurred by the God-directed lot and not by the wisdom of men. Joshua and the other Jewish leaders did not read the prophecy and then deliberately fulfill it. God fulfilled it through the throwing of the lot. He guided the lot because Christ would fulfill all of Jacob's prophecy: He, the Lion of Judah, would come to be Israel's ruler.

Who is this Christ, this King of the Jews? The Gospel of John portrays the Coming One for us. At the beginning of Jesus' ministry, Nathanael identified him: "Rabbi, thou art the Son of God; thou art the King of Israel" (John 1:49). Here was a double emphasis: Jesus is deity, but he is also the Old Testament-prophesied King. In Matthew, the wise men came asking, "Where is he that is born King of the Jews?" (Matt. 2:2). They asked this of Herod, who was king of the Jews by the grace of Caesar, and his wrath was stirred up because he was threatened by Christ's kingship. In Luke, Christ's kingship was strikingly proclaimed at His triumphal entry. As Jesus rode into Jerusalem just before His death, the people strewed His path with palm branches and with their clothes, saying, "Blessed be the King who cometh in the name of the LORD" (Luke 19:38).

This same Jesus is coming again in a space-time moment future to us. Just as Joshua stood in judgment against the Amorites when their iniquity was full, Jesus will come in flaming judgment on the world when the iniquity of the era of the Gentiles is full. What is His name? "KING OF KINGS, AND LORD OF LORDS" (Rev. 19:16).

Jacob prophesied finally that "unto him shall the gathering of the peoples be" (Gen. 49:10). This is one of the many Old Testament prophecies that say that the Gentiles will have a place among the people of God. The Coming One is not only the King of the Jews, but also the Gatherer of the Peoples. And those of us who are Gentiles redeemed by the work of Christ are part of the fulfillment of that prophecy.

The Division to Joseph

After the division to Judah came the division to Joseph (Josh. 16:1—17:18). Joseph had two sons, Manasseh and Ephraim, and each son's tribe was given a share. Though Ephraim was the younger, he received his place in the giving of the land on the west of Jordan before Manasseh. Why? Once more prophecy entered in:

And Israel (Jacob) said unto Joseph, I had not thought to see thy face; and, lo, God hath shown me also thy seed. And Joseph brought them out from between his knees, and he bowed himself with his face to the earth. And Joseph took them both, Ephraim in his right hand toward Israel's left hand, and Manasseh in his left hand toward Israel's right hand, and brought them near unto him. And Israel stretched out his right, and laid it upon Ephraim's head, who was the younger, and his left hand upon Manasseh's head, guiding his hands wittingly; for Manasseh was the first-born. And he blessed Joseph, and said, God, before whom my fathers, Abraham and Isaac, did walk, the God who fed me all my life long unto this day, The Angel who redeemed me from all evil, bless the lads; and let my name be named on them, and the name of my fathers, Abraham and Isaac; and let them grow unto a multitude in the midst of the earth.

And when Joseph saw that his father laid his right hand upon the head of Ephraim, it displeased him; and he held up his father's hand, to remove it from Ephraim's head unto Manasseh's head. And Joseph said unto his father, Not so, my father; for this is the first-born; put thy right hand upon his head. And his father refused, and said, I know it, my son, I know it; he also shall become a people, and he also shall be great; but truly his younger brother shall be greater than he, and his seed shall become a multitude of nations. And he blessed them that day, saying, In thee shall Israel bless, saying, God make thee as Ephraim and as Manasseh: and he set Ephraim before Manasseh. (Gen. 48:11-20)

God, working through the lot, preserved the continuity of this prophecy given all those long years previously.

After Ephraim was given his place, the half-tribe of Manasseh that had not received land on the east side of the Jordan was allotted its inheritance. Usually the land was given to sons, but in this case daughters also received it because there were no sons (Josh. 17:3, 4). Once more we are reminded that these people regarded the Pentateuch as normative in every detail, for when the women presented their case they argued, "The LORD commanded Moses to give us an inheritance among our brethren. Therefore, according to the commandment of the LORD, he gave them an inheritance among the brethren of their father" (Josh. 17:4). They regarded the Pentateuch as the Word of God and as something which not only conveyed some sort of religious feeling, but also gave specific commands which were to be obeyed in detail. They were referring to Numbers 27:1-11 and to Numbers 36.

The Final Divisions at Shiloh
Prior to the final divisions of the land, the Israelites moved permanently from Gilgal to Shiloh (Josh. 18:1). Shiloh was in the hill country, just off the highway to the north of Bethel and Ai as one travels toward Gerizim and Ebal. The Israelites left the plain and established themselves in the mountains. They took the tabernacle with them, which means they removed everything from their former camp.

Although the big campaigns were finished, much land remained to be taken. Therefore, they sent spies to map out the territory so that the lots could be thrown for this piece of geography. "And the men went and passed through the land, and described it by cities into seven parts in a book, and came again to Joshua to the host at Shiloh" (Josh. 18:9). Writing was so common that the spies were able to write their report and present it to Joshua.

The fall of the lot located Benjamin right next to Judah: "And the lots of the tribe of the children of Benjamin came up according to their families; and the coast of their lot came forth between the children of Judah and the children of Joseph" (Josh. 18:11). As a matter of fact, their land came together at the city of Jerusalem. Moses had made this prophecy concerning Benjamin: "The beloved of the LORD shall dwell in safety by him; and the LORD shall cover him all the day long, and he shall dwell between his shoulders" (Deut. 33:12). Benjamin was going to have a special closeness to the Lord. When the northern tribes later turned away from God, the tribes that stood fast were Judah and Benjamin; so Moses' prophecy was fulfilled.

In the second lot thrown at Shiloh, the remaining tribes received their land. Simeon did not receive a separate inheritance because, as you remember, Jacob said he was going to be scattered. He was given a place in the midst of Judah. So while in the fulfilling of the prophecy of Genesis 49:5-7 the Levites became the special servants of God scattered throughout the people, the Simeonites had no real share of the land.

Next, Zebulun's place was designated. Jacob had prophesied concerning Zebulun: "Zebulun shall dwell at the haven of the sea; and he shall be for an haven of ships" (Gen. 49:13). He was the only person related to seafaring. And when the land was divided, Zebulun's "border went up toward the sea" (Josh. 19:11).

Places were designated, too, for Issachar (Josh. 19:17), Asher (Josh. 19:24), Naphtali (Josh. 19:32), and Dan (Josh. 19:40). Finally, Joshua was given a special inheritance, the city of Timnath-serah. Every tribe now had its land. The divisions were complete. The entire matter is summarized like this:

> These are the inheritances, which Eleazar, the priest, and Joshua, the son of Nun, and the heads of the fathers' houses of the tribes of the children of Israel, divided for an inheritance by lot in Shiloh before the LORD, at the door of the tabernacle of the congregation. So they made an end of dividing the country. (Josh. 19:51)

The Conclusion of the Era of Conquest

We need to look at one more chapter, Joshua 22, in order to bring the era of the campaigns to a close.

When the two and a half tribes were given their land east of the Jordan, Moses said to them, "The west side still has to be taken. Are you going to stay here in peace while your brothers who fought for you have to go on in war?"

The fighting men from these tribes responded, "We'll go with the rest and fight as long as the war is on."

To which Moses replied, "Good. Then all is well."

These men built cities and left some of their people on their land. This means that for the seven years of campaign, these soldiers were separated from their wives, their families, their inheritance. Now that the campaigns were over and the land divided, it was time to go home.

> Then Joshua called the Reubenites, and the Gadites, and the half tribe of Manasseh, and said unto them, Ye have kept all that Moses, the servant of the LORD, commanded you, and have obeyed my voice in all that I commanded you. Ye have not left your brethren these many days unto this day, but have kept the charge of the commandment of the LORD your God. And now the LORD your God hath given rest unto your brethren, as he promised them; therefore, now return ye, and get you unto your tents, and unto the land of your possession, which Moses, the servant of the LORD, gave you on the other side of Jordan. But take diligent heed to do the commandment and the law, which Moses, the servant of the LORD, charged you, to love the LORD your God, and to walk in all his ways, and to keep his commandments, and to cleave unto him, and to serve him with all your heart and with all your soul. So Joshua blessed them, and sent them away; and they went unto their tents. (Josh. 22:1-6)

If we use a little imagination, we can feel the tremendous emotion involved in the parting of these comrades at arms. We can picture the men going through the camp, finding the friends with whom they had fought side by side, and saying good-bye to some who had even saved their lives. They shook hands and they parted, as worshipers of God, as friends and as fellow-companions in war. There is a comradeship among men in titanic moments that is one of the great "mystiques" of life. It is the explanation of the mystique of the rope—two men on a mountain battling nature together, depending for their very lives on a common rope.

As the comrades left, they took with them much spoil. Joshua commanded them to divide the spoil with those who had remained on the east side to guard the possessions (Josh. 22:8). Then "the children of Reuben and the children of Gad and the half tribe of Manasseh returned, and departed from the children of Israel out of Shiloh, which is in the land of Canaan" (Josh. 22:9).

The men of the two and a half tribes traveled east and put the Jordan between themselves and the majority of the people. Then came a new note: "And when they came unto the borders of Jordan, that are in the land of Canaan, the children of Reuben and the children of Gad and the half tribe of Manasseh built there an altar by Jordan, a great altar to see" (Josh. 22:10). They built a huge altar, one that could be seen a long way off. And suddenly the complexion of the situation changed. The men who were with Joshua and the priests on the west side of the river spread the word through the camp: "The people who have left us have built a new altar! They've built a new altar!" You can hear this bubbling through the camp. The men with whom they had been shaking hands just a few days before seemed to be establishing a rival worship. And these people said, "Something must be done about this! This is rebellion against God!"

Joshua 22:12 is one of the most touching verses we will ever find, if we do not just read it as words, but see the human content in it: "And when the children of Israel heard of it, the whole congregation of the children of Israel gathered themselves together at Shiloh, to go up to war against them." That is just terrific! We ought to play the bagpipes! These men had just parted as companions of war. I do not know whether they shook hands as we do or rubbed noses like the Eskimos or, like the Brazilians, slapped each other on the back until they could not breathe any longer, but whatever it was, they said good-bye in the strongest, heartiest sense imaginable. But now they thought the holiness of God was being threatened. So these men, who were sick of war, said, "The holiness of God demands no compromise." I would to God that the church of the twentieth century would learn this lesson. The holiness of the God who exists demands that there be no compromise in the area of truth. Tears? I am sure there were tears, but there had to be battle if there was rebellion against God.

The leaders on the west side did their best, however, to straighten the matter out. They did not go off to war without first attempting reconciliation. This is a good example of the simultaneous exhibition of both the holiness and the love of God. It is a biblical example of truth and beauty. Because of their concern for God's holiness, they were ready for battle; but the fact that they did not attack immediately was a practical demonstration of love. Instead, they chose a prince from each of the tribes and sent them along with Phinehas, the high priest, to see if this matter could be straightened out. When they confronted the two and a half tribes on the east, they did not beat around the bush. I am convinced that what we see here is the kind of thing that Jesus later commanded concerning a practical relationship among the people of God. They came without compromise, talked face to face, and made an honest charge.

> And they came unto the children of Reuben, and to the children of Gad, and to the half tribe of Manasseh unto the land of Gilead, and they spoke with them, saying, Thus saith the whole congregation of the LORD, What trespass is this that ye have committed against the God of Israel, to turn away this day from following the LORD, in that ye have builded you an altar, that ye might rebel this day against the LORD? Is the iniquity of Peor too little for us, from which we are not cleansed until this day, although there was a plague in the congregation of the LORD, but that ye must turn away this day from following the LORD? And it will be, seeing ye rebel today against the LORD, that tomorrow he will be wroth with the whole congregation of Israel. Notwithstanding, if the land of your possession be unclean, then pass ye over unto the land of the possession of the LORD, wherein the LORD's tabernacle dwelleth, and take possession among us; but rebel not against the LORD, nor rebel against us, in building you an altar beside the altar of the LORD our God. Did not Achan, the son of Zerah, commit a trespass in the accursed thing, and wrath fell on all the congregation of Israel? And that man perished not alone in his iniquity. (Josh. 22:15-20)

Notice that the whole congregation agreed with the charges. This was not a political issue, the two and a half tribes talking rebellion against the rest. Rebellion against God was the issue. The representatives reminded the others of the seriousness of this, not only for the people who had sinned, but for all the people of God. They reminded them of the iniquity of Peor, which was a corporate sin that had occurred approximately eight years before (see Num. 25:1-3, 18). They said, "Because the people of the congregation were involved, everybody suffered" (Josh. 22:18). And they reminded them of what happened when Achan sinned. They said, "You can't sin with impunity and the people of God not be injured. When either a group or one man sins, the whole people is injured. Consequently, we are here to prevent that." This illustrates the practicality of love. It is no use talking about love if there is no action to it. What was the practicality in this case? It was shown in the willingness of the tribes west of Jordan to sacrifice money and land to resolve the situation properly.

Once more, here is the tragedy of the modern church. Our spirituality and our brotherhood often stop at the point of material possessions. In the early church this was not so. The Christians had things in common not because there was a law to this effect, not because this was an enforced Marx-Engels communism, but because they loved each other. And a love that does not go down into the practical stuff of life, including money and possessions, is absolute junk! To think that love is talking softly rather than saying something sharply and that it is not carried down into the practical stuff of life is not biblical. We must say with tears that the orthodox evangelical church in our generation has been poor at this point.

This generation of Jews was not. They were willing to go to battle, but they were dialoguing in love to try to find a solution. The solution even came to this: "If you don't want to live over here, bring everything into our land. Bring your herds, bring your sheep. We'll move over in our pasturelands. We'll move out of the villages. We'll give you some of the cities. You can share it with us, but don't rebel against God." How many would have come? Probably the total number who had entered the land had been about two and a half million. Thus those on the east side of Jordan would have been many, many thousand. What a practical lesson for the people of God—a generous, loving offer was made at material cost!

The people being confronted could have gotten angry and responded, "What are you getting so worked up for?" But they did not. We see here the interplay that should characterize discipline in the church of Christ. The majority thought a trespass had been committed. They did not gloss it over; indeed, they were ready to go to battle in order to preserve the holiness and the commands of God. In reply, the other side did not just stalk out of the church door, as it were. They gave an honest, open answer.

> Then the children of Reuben and the children of Gad and the half tribe of Manasseh answered, and said unto the heads of the thousands of Israel, The LORD God of gods, the LORD God of gods, he knoweth, and Israel he shall know; if it be in rebellion or if in transgression against the LORD (save us not this day,) that we have built us an altar to turn from following the LORD, or if to offer thereon burnt offering or meat offering, or if to offer peace offerings thereon, let the LORD himself require it; and if we have not rather done it for fear of this thing, saying, In time to come your children might speak unto our children, saying, What have ye to do with the LORD God of Israel? For the LORD hath made Jordan a border between us and you, ye children of Reuben and children of Gad; ye have no part in the LORD; so shall your children make our children cease from fearing the LORD. Therefore we said, Let us now prepare to build us an altar, not for burnt offering, nor for sacrifice, but that it may be a witness between us, and you, and our generations after us, that we might do the service of the LORD before him with our burnt offerings, and with our sacrifices, and with our peace offerings; that your children may not say to our children in time to come, Ye have no part in the LORD. Therefore said we, that it shall be, when they should so say to us or to our generations in time to come, that we may say again, Behold the pattern of the altar of the LORD, which our fathers made, not for burnt offerings, nor for sacrifices; but it is a witness between us and you. God forbid that we should rebel against the LORD, and turn this day from following the LORD, to build an altar for burnt offerings, for meat offerings, or for sacrifices, beside the altar of the LORD our God that is before his tabernacle. (Josh. 22:21-29)

I love this: "We know in our hearts right now that God is satisfied; and we are going to tell you the facts, and we know you will then be satisfied." They did not have to convince God. God already knew. But they were going to point out the situation lovingly so that the rest of the people of God would know.

This statement, it seems to me, is the key: "If it be in rebellion or if in transgression against the LORD, save us not this day." They agreed that if they were worshiping another god or rebelling against God and His commands (including the commands about how to worship), they deserved judgment. This is the basis of the marvelous results which we will see shortly. These results were rooted and grounded in an agreement that God is holy, that God's commands must not be breached, and that if God's commands are breached this deserves judgment. There was no accommodation of relativism, no Hegelian synthesis, no compromise with truth. The reason these people were able to have a real unity and a real peace was that they were locked into the truth and commandments of God. Without the concept that is laid down here, any right unity is impossible. Any unity, any peace, that is not rooted in truth is nothing!

The two and a half tribes protested that their action was not sinful. They did not build this altar for the purpose of rebellion, nor even for the purpose of worship. Why then did they build it? They intended it to be a pattern, a replica of the true altar by the tabernacle. They wanted this large copy of the real altar to stand as a witness that they, too, had a right to cross the Jordan and worship.

So we come to the marvelous conclusion:

> And when Phinehas, the priest, and the princes of the congregation and heads of the thousands of Israel who were with him, heard the words that the children of Reuben and the children of Gad and the children of Manasseh spoke, it pleased them. And Phinehas, the son of Eleazar, the priest, said unto the children of Reuben, and to the children of Gad, and to the children of Manasseh, This day we perceive that the LORD is among us, because ye have not committed this trespass against the LORD; now ye have delivered the children of Israel out of the hand of the LORD. And Phinehas, the son of Eleazar, the priest, and the princes, returned from the children of Reuben, and from the children of Gad, out of the land of Gilead, unto the land of Canaan, to the children of Israel, and brought them word again. And the thing pleased the children of Israel; and the children of Israel blessed God, and did not intend to go up against them in battle, to destroy the land in which the children of Reuben and Gad dwelt. And the children of Reuben and the children of Gad called the altar Ed; for it shall be a witness between us that the LORD is God. (Josh. 22:30-34)

First, the ten princes from the west of Jordan along with Phinehas, the priest, turned to the rest and said, "We're agreed. It's tremendous! Everything is in place. We see there is no rebellion here. We give you the right hand of fellowship." Then they returned to the other side of the Jordan and reported to the remainder of the people. The land was at peace, and there was a happy ending indeed. On both sides of the river, the witness of this altar stood, and as it were there came a cry from the entire people of God, "The Lord, He is God! The Lord, He is God!"

Why was there this happy ending? Because of the two steps I have mentioned. First, there was a clear agreement on importance of doctrine and truth, an understanding that the holiness of God demands bowing before Him and obeying His commands. Remember Joshua's words as he sent the people away to the other side of the Jordan: "Take diligent heed . . . to love the LORD your God, and to walk in all His ways, and to keep His commandments." There was a happy ending because the people did this.

Second, those who were courageous in standing for truth were also courageous in acting in love. If there had only been a stand for truth, there would never have been a happy ending. There would have only been war, because the ten tribes would have torn across the river and killed the other Israelites without talking to anybody. There would have been sadness in the midst of misunderstanding. But because of the love of God, the tribes talked to each other openly, and the love and holiness of God were able to come together. Psalm 85 speaks of the righteousness of God and the love of God kissing each other (v. 10). This was what happened here.

What is a Christian's duty in life? He has only one basic duty: to exhibit the existence of God and to exhibit His character in the midst of a rebellious world. What is the character of God? God is holy and God is love. Christians—both individually and corporately—have a duty to stand for God's truth with no compromise while simultaneously dealing in love with brothers and sisters in Christ—yes, and with men and women outside the Church. Joshua 22 is not just history; it is a rule in the continuity of God's commands to His people through the flow of history. It is an example for the people of God in dealing with each other for all time.

This chapter has emphasized two things: (1) the continuity of prophecy in the flow of history (the very opposite of modern man's not being able to tell the difference between fantasy and reality); and (2) the importance of right action among the people of God. When the people of God are acting as they should, they manifest the unity of the holiness and the love of God.

Whenever church leaders ask us to choose between the holiness of God and the love of God, we must refuse. For when the love of

God becomes compromised, it is not the love of God. When the holiness of God becomes hardness and a lack of beauty, it is not the holiness of God. This is the calling to us who live in the New Testament era too—to practice the holiness and love of God with no compromise to either. If anything, it is an even greater responsibility for us than for those who practiced it so beautifully in Joshua's tme, for we live on this side of the cross, the open tomb, the ascension and Pentecost.

CHAPTER ELEVEN

The Cities of Refuge

As we have seen, the Levites were given special cities scattered throughout the other tribes' portions. It was at Shiloh that the Levites came forward to claim that inheritance, referring, as we have seen the Jews so frequently do, to the Pentateuch as an authoritative canon which should be consciously obeyed.

> Then came near the heads of the fathers of the Levites unto Eleazar, the priest, and unto Joshua, the son of Nun, and unto the heads of the fathers of the tribes of the children of Israel, and they spoke unto them at Shiloh in the land of Canaan, saying, The LORD commanded by the hand of Moses to give us cities to dwell in, with the suburbs thereof for our cattle. And the children of Israel gave unto the Levites out of their inheritance, at the commandment of the LORD, these cities and their suburbs. (Josh. 21:1-3)

Numbers 35 records the command to which the Levites referred Eleazar and Joshua.

> And the LORD spoke unto Moses in the plains of Moab by Jordan near Jericho, saying, Command the children of Israel, that they give unto the Levites of the inheritance of their possession cities to dwell in; and ye shall give also unto the Levites suburbs for the cities round

about them. And the cities shall they have to dwell in; and the suburbs of them shall be for their cattle, and for their goods, and for all their beasts. (Num. 35:1-3)

Moses himself followed this command when he was dividing the land on the east side of the Jordan: "Only unto the tribe of Levi he gave no inheritance; the sacrifices of the LORD God of Israel made by fire are their inheritance, as he said unto them" (Josh. 13:14; see also v. 33). Speaking of the division of the land at Shiloh, Joshua said, "But the Levites have no part among you; for the priesthood of the LORD is their inheritance" (Josh. 18:7). God had spoken: the Levites were to be a special case.

We saw that Simeon and Levi were given no normal inheritance because of their sin. Simeon was scattered in the midst of Judah. On the other hand, Levi's faithfulness at the time of the golden calf turned his scattering from a confusion into a blessing. At that moment, the Levites became the servants of God. They had no separate territory, but they had cities throughout the land.

The Levites' allotment, of course, raises a question. Men need not only a place to live, but also food to eat. The economy of the Israelites was rooted in agriculture, which meant that land was crucial. Having land gave a person his basic economic possibilities. The Levites, therefore, had no such possibilities because while they had villages, they did not have an extensive territory upon which to grow crops or raise sheep and cattle. Where were they going to get their food? The answer is that they did not need a regular portion because they were to receive the tithes of the rest of the Jews. While other people had large territories for sheep, cows, or grain as a pay crop, the basic income for the Levites was the tithes which the others gave. When the Lord said to Aaron, "Thou shalt have no inheritance in their land, neither shalt thou have any part among them: I am thy part and thine inheritance among the children of Israel" (Num. 18:20), he did not mean that Aaron was only to stand in a special relationship to Him, but that Aaron and the Levites were to be recipients of the gifts made to God. God commanded, "Thus speak unto the Levites, and say unto them, When ye take of the children of Israel the tithe which I have given you from them for your inheritance, then ye shall offer up an heave offering of it for the LORD, even a tenth part of the tithe" (Num. 18:26). The Levites' tithes were then passed on to Aaron and the other priests (Num. 18:28). It was a double tithe:

the people tithed and gave to the Levites, and the Levites tithed and gave to the priests.

This continuity of the tithe, which began at least with Abraham and continued in the story of Jericho, Achan and Ai, came down to the Israelites in the land; and the command of proportional giving passed on eventually into the New Testament. Paul wrote to the Corinthian Christians, "Upon the first day of the week let every one of you lay by him in store, as God hath prospered him" (1 Cor. 16:2). So the command to the Church is the same as the command to God's people in the Old Testament—proportional giving. Giving to God proportionately is not optional. God specifically commands it.

The Distribution of the Levites' Cities

How were the Levites' cities distributed? The distribution was based on the fact that Levi, the son of Jacob, had three sons: Gershon, Kohath and Merari (Gen. 46:11). Each of the sons was consistently dealt with as a unit throughout the centuries that followed. For example, when the people made camp during the wilderness wanderings the Levites were always divided into three sections. The Gershonites pitched their tents "behind the tabernacle westward" (Num. 3:23), and this one family had a special task: "And the charge of the sons of Gershon in the tabernacle of the congregation shall be the tabernacle, and the tent, the covering thereof, and the hanging for the door of the tabernacle of the congregation, and the hangings of the court, and the curtain for the door of the court, which is by the tabernacle, and by the altar round about, and the cords of it for all the service thereof" (Num. 3:25, 26). In other words, they had charge of the tent itself. When the Israelites broke camp, the Gershonites carried this material with them.

The family of Kohath pitched "on the side of the tabernacle southward" (Num. 3:29). They, too, had a special task: they dealt with all the instruments of worship that were used outside the Holy of Holies (Num. 3:31). (The priests themselves took care of the instruments of worship within the Holy of Holies.)

Finally, the third family, the family of Merari, pitched "on the side of the tabernacle northward" (Num. 3:35). They dealt with the hardware of the tabernacle—the wooden frames, the bars, the sockets of metal and so forth (Num. 3:36, 37). Moses and the priests, incidentally, pitched on the east side of the tabernacle (the side to which the opening of the tabernacle faced), thus completing the square.

We should not be at all surprised, therefore, that the Levites' cities were allotted on the basis of these three family units. The Kohathites got the first lot. The priests themselves (the children of Aaron who belonged to this family) received thirteen cities (Josh. 21:19). The rest of this family received ten cities (Josh. 21:26). Gershon then received thirteen cities (Josh. 21:33) and Merari twelve (Josh. 21:40). All in all, forty-eight cities out of the land were given to the tribe of Levi (Josh. 21:41). God had commanded through Moses, "So all the cities which ye shall give to the Levites shall be forty and eight cities; them shall ye give with their suburbs" (Num. 35:7). Joshua's generation carried this out perfectly in the flow of continuity. To tamper with the unity of the Old Testament is to deal with it unfairly, not according to its own claims. The result is to make it intellectually meaningless.

The Cities of Refuge

The Levites' cities were divided into two parts: six of the forty-eight cities were *cities of refuge*. God had commanded in the Pentateuch, "Among the cities which ye shall give unto the Levites there shall be six cities for refuge, which ye shall appoint for the manslayer, that he may flee there; and to them ye shall add forty and two cities" (Num. 35:6). "The LORD also spoke unto Joshua, saying, Speak to the children of Israel, saying, Appoint out for you cities of refuge, which I spoke unto you by the hand of Moses" (Josh. 20:1, 2). So Joshua set up the cities of refuge when he divided the land.

On Mount Sinai God gave the moral law. "God spoke all these words . . ." and then came the Ten Commandments (Ex. 20:1-17). Immediately after this the civil law was given. As the race became a nation they needed a civil law; so God gave them one. The civil law for the Jews was based as much on the command of God as was the moral law.

One of the civil laws God gave was this: "He that smiteth a man, so that he die, shall be surely put to death. And if a man lie not in wait, but God deliver him into his hand; then I will appoint thee a place to which he shall flee" (Ex. 21:12, 13). If a man was a real murderer, he was to die; but a system was to be set up whereby a man who had slain somebody by mistake would not be put to death, but would have a place of escape.

These cities of refuge are next mentioned in Numbers 35, to which I will return in a moment, and then in Deuteronomy 4:41-43, which names the three cities of refuge Moses established on the east side of Jordan. The next mention is in Deuteronomy 19. Since there is an interplay between Deuteronomy 19 and Joshua 20, I want to cite first some verses from that chapter of Joshua.

The LORD also spoke unto Joshua, saying, Speak to the children of Israel, saying, Appoint out for you cities of refuge, of which I spoke unto you by the hand of Moses, that the slayer who killeth any person unawares and unwittingly may flee there; and they shall be your refuge from the avenger of blood. And when he who doth flee unto one of those cities shall stand at the entering of the gate of the city, and shall declare his cause in the ears of the elders of that city, they shall take him into the city unto them, and give him a place, that he may dwell among them. And if the avenger of blood pursue after him, then they shall not deliver the slayer up into his hand, because he smote his neighbor unwittingly, and hated him not beforetime. And he shall dwell in that city, until he stand before the congregation for judgment, and until the death of the high priest that shall be in those days; then shall the slayer return, and come unto his own city, and unto his own house, unto the city from where he fled. . . . These were the cities appointed for all the children of Israel, and for the stranger who sojourneth among them, that whosoever killeth any person at unawares might flee there, and not die by the hand of the avenger of blood, until he stood before the congregation. (Josh. 20:1-6, 9)

This section obviously takes a lot for granted. If we only had Joshua 20, we would wonder about much of the detail. Why didn't God tell Joshua to give the people more information? He did not have to because the people knew Deuteronomy 19, and there the details are enumerated with great clarity and care:

When the LORD thy God hath cut off the nations, whose land the LORD thy God giveth thee, and thou succeedest them, and dwellest in their cities, and in their houses, thou shalt separate three cities for thee in the midst of thy land, which the LORD thy God giveth thee to possess it. Thou shalt prepare thee a way [that is, you shall build a road], and divide the coasts of thy land, which the LORD thy God giveth thee to inherit, into three parts, that every slayer may flee there.

And this is the case of the slayer, who shall flee there, that he may live: whoso killeth his neighbor ignorantly, whom he hated not in time past; as when a man goeth into the wood with his neighbor to hew wood, and his hand fetcheth a stroke with the axe to cut down the tree, and the head slippeth from the helve and lighteth upon his neighbor, that he die; he shall flee unto one of those cities, and live, lest the avenger of the blood pursue the slayer, while his heart is hot, and overtake him, because the way is long, and slay him; whereas he was not worthy of death, inasmuch as he hated him not in time past. Wherefore I command thee, saying, Thou shalt separate three cities for thee. And if the LORD thy God enlarge thy coast, as he hath sworn unto thy fathers, and give thee all the land which he promised to give unto thy fathers; if thou shalt keep all these commandments to do them, which I command thee this day, to love the LORD thy God, and to walk ever in his ways, then shalt thou add three cities more for thee, beside these three, that innocent blood be not shed in thy land, which the LORD thy God giveth thee for an inheritance, and so blood be upon thee.

But if any man hate his neighbor, and lie in wait for him, and rise up against him, and smite him mortally that he die, and fleeth into one of these cities, then the elders of his city shall send and fetch him from there, and deliver him into the hand of the avenger of blood, that he may die. Thine eye shall not pity him, but thou shalt put away the guilt of innocent blood from Israel, that it may go well with thee. (Deut. 19:1-13)

The cities of refuge did not help a real murderer. They pertained only to the man who had, unhappily, killed someone unintentionally. They were to aid the one who had committed an accidental homicide—and no one else. The text tells us why such a man had to flee. The state didn't kill in the case of a homicide; it was the dead man's family who killed. The Bedouins follow the same practice to this day. If somebody kills a member of a family, someone is appointed by the family to be the avenger of blood. It is his right to go out and take the other man's life. But when a man has committed an accidental murder, and another man is coming to take his life, what shall he do? He shall run to a city of refuge. The city of refuge was for the accidental killer fleeing from the avenger of blood.

Now we turn back to Numbers 35:

And the suburbs of the cities, which ye shall give unto the Levites, shall reach from the wall of the city and outward a thousand cubits round about. And ye shall measure from without the city on the east side two thousand cubits, and on the south side two thousand cubits, and on the west side two thousand cubits, and on the north side two thousand cubits; and the city shall be in the midst: this shall be to them the suburbs of the cities. . . .

These six cities shall be a refuge, both for the children of Israel, and for the stranger, and for the sojourner among them: that everyone who killeth any person unawares may flee there. And if he smite him with an instrument of iron, so that he die, he is a murderer: the murderer shall surely be put to death. And if he smite him with throwing a stone, wherewith he may die, and he die, he is a murderer: the murderer shall surely be put to death. Or if he smite him with an hand weapon of wood, wherewith he may die, and he die, he is a murderer: the murderer shall surely be put to death. The revenger of blood himself shall slay the murderer; when he meeteth him, he shall slay him.

But if he thrust him from hatred, or hurl at him by laying of wait, that he die, or in enmity smite him with his hand, that he die; he that smote him shall surely be put to death; for he is a murderer: the revenger of blood shall slay the murderer, when he meeteth him. But if he thrust him suddenly without enmity, or have cast upon him anything without laying of wait, or with any stone, wherewith a man may die, seeing him not, and cast it upon him, that he die, and was not his enemy, neither sought his harm; then the congregation shall judge between the slayer and the revenger of blood according to these judgments. And the congregation shall deliver the slayer out of the hand of the revenger of blood, and the congregation shall restore him to the city of his refuge, whither he was fled; and he shall abide in it unto the death of the high priest, which was anointed with the holy oil. But if the slayer shall at any time come without the border of the city of his refuge, to which he was fled, and the revenger of blood find him without the borders of the city of his refuge, and the revenger of blood kill the slayer; he shall not be guilty of blood: because he should have remained in the city of his refuge until after the death of the high priest: but after the death of the high priest the slayer shall return into the land of his possession.

So these things shall be for a statute of judgment unto you throughout your generations in all your dwellings. Whoso killeth any person, the murderer shall be put to death by the mouth of witnesses, but one witness shall not testify against any person to cause him to die. (Num. 35:4, 5, 15-30)

It is really beautiful that the cities were available not only for the children of Israel, but also for both the non-Israelites who were living permanently in the land and those who were merely passing through. This was entirely new to the heathen world. Here was real justice—a universal civil code that pertained equally to the citizen and the stranger. This justice was not rooted in the notion of a superior people, but in the character of God; therefore, it pertained to all men.

Moses told how to distinguish between an intentional murderer and an unwitting killer. A deliberate homicide involved a prepared instrument, a clear intent and a clear motive. Such a murderer had no place of refuge. But if a man thrust a victim "suddenly without enmity" or "cast any thing upon him without lying in wait," he had a place. For example, if a man was prying out a big rock and it accidentally fell on somebody coming along the path, this was not murder. It was without preparation and without motive.

In our jurisprudence, we follow in general the same procedure. In considering whether a man is guilty, our trials take into account the same questions. Moses clearly outlined the procedure. If a man killed somebody without premeditation, he was to run to a city of refuge! He was kept there until the facts were gathered (more than one witness was needed) and then he was tried, as in our jury system, by his peers. Not some great person but the assembled congregation decided whether he had committed murder or not. If he had, he was pushed outside the city where the avenger of blood could take his life. If he had not, he was returned to the city of refuge. He then had to remain in the city until the death of the current high priest; otherwise the protection was gone.

Law in a Post-Christian Culture
We can now begin to understand why it may be emphasized that in Reformation countries, the Old Testament civil law has been the basis of our civil law. We are not a theocracy, it is true; nevertheless, when Reformation Christianity provided the consensus, men naturally looked back to the civil law that God gave Israel, not to carry it out in every detail, but to see it as a pattern and a base.

But we have changed, of course. We are no longer a Christian culture. And because of that we are seeing a change in our concept of law. The differences between past and present fall into two areas.

The first difference involves the foundation of law. The cities of refuge were Levitical cities—that is, they had something to do with God. The person taking refuge had to stay in the city until the death of the high priest; so he would be reminded that the civil laws were related to God. They did not just exist in a sociological vacuum. Unlike modern man, the people of the Old Testament and of Christian communities after the Reformation did not view civil law as basically sociological. To them, it was not founded primarily on a social contract. Civil law was related to society, but not only to society. It was ultimately related to the existence and character of God. This is important. Law which comes from God can provide something fixed. Today's sociological law is relativistic.

The *moral* law is rooted in the fact of the existence and character of God. It has validity because God is there. "And God spoke all these words, saying, I am the LORD thy God, who have brought thee out of the land of Egypt, out of the house of bondage. Thou shalt have no other gods before me" (Ex. 20:1-3). The *civil* law is also based upon the reality of God's existence; so it, too, has an absolute base. Reformation law was like this—one can think of Samuel Rutherford's *Lex Rex*—and so was in total contrast to the post-Christian, sociological law which is developing in the Western world.

Paul Robert, who lived at the end of the last century, was a wonderful Christian and a great Swiss painter of his era. He painted huge murals, one of which is on the stairwell of the old supreme court building in Lausanne, Switzerland. Paul Robert placed it there so the justices would never forget the basis of law. He knew what he was doing in every detail, including the title, "Justice Instructing the Judges." We may not completely like his technique, because it is marked by the conventions of the period, but the mural has a strong thrust. Several litigants stand in the foreground of the painting: wife against husband, builder against architect. The question is, On what basis are the judges able to judge? Justice points with her sword so that the judges can follow it and see what should be the basis. Justice points to a book on which Robert has carefully lettered the phrase, *The Law of God*. That is tremendous! There was a foundation for civil law, fixed in the existence and character of God and His revelation of that character to men.

The second difference between the civil law of the theocracy and the law of the post-Christian world is the former's emphasis on the seriousness of murder. God commanded, "He that smiteth a man, so that he die, shall be surely put to death" (Ex. 21:12). Nothing could change this. No bribe or satisfaction—common practices in those days—could be taken for the murderer (Num. 35:31, 32). As far back as the covenant with Noah, God said, "Whoso sheddeth man's blood, by man shall his blood be shed; for in the image of God made he man" (Gen. 9:6). The Bible says that though man is fallen, he is still the image-bearer of God. Human worth does not rest on the fact that man can breed with others of the same biological species. Rather, it rests on the fact that man is unique; he is made in the image of God.

Man is a significant creature. He is not part of the machinery. And this has many implications. One which society must understand is that murder isn't trivial but extremely serious. It is not merely a breach of social custom or mores, or even that which upsets society. The Bible's great outcry against the murderer is, "You have slain an image-bearer of God." When a person deliberately murders an image-bearer of God, he has done a serious thing indeed.

Because God exists and because He has a character, we live in a true moral universe. Murder breaks the law of the universe. This means that the murderer has true moral guilt before God—something our modern generation knows nothing or little about—and this guilt must be taken seriously.

We must keep saying to our generation that men are guilty with true moral guilt before a holy God, for the existential theologians who now control the theological thinking among both progressive Roman Catholics and liberal Protestants have no real sense of the importance of God's being there and His giving propositional truth in the Bible.

We must, therefore, respond forcefully that everything hangs not upon "God words," but upon the fact that God is really there and really has a character. He is really a holy God. Therefore, when I sin, my guilt is real. And because God is infinite, and infinitely holy, my guilt when I sin is total. The value of the guilt does not rest upon my value, but upon the value of the One against whom I have sinned. Therefore, because I have sinned against the One who is infinitely holy, my guilt comes up to this level. True moral guilt has nothing to do with our finitude. If we see the tension as modern theologians and philosophers do between man (finite) and God (infinite), we can never derive true moral guilt. The law does not stand behind God, because the final thing is God. And it is God's character which *is* the law of the universe.

Christ and the Cities of Refuge
If we begin to tamper with the truth about true moral guilt, we will not be able to understand the death of Christ any more than we can understand

the cities of refuge. In fact, we will understand it less. We would not want to take the cities of refuge as a type, but they certainly are a strong illustration of the work of Christ. It seems to me that the New Testament itself relates the work of Christ to these cities. Hebrews says,

> For men verily swear by the greater, and an oath for confirmation is to them an end of all strife. Wherein God, willing more abundantly to show unto the heirs of promise the immutability of his counsel, confirmed it by an oath, that by two immutable things, in which it was impossible for God to lie, we might have a strong consolation, *who have fled for refuge to lay hold upon the hope set before us,* which hope we have as an anchor of the soul, both sure and steadfast, and which entereth into that within the veil, where the forerunner is for us entered, even Jesus, made an high priest forever after the order of Melchizedek. (Heb. 6:16-20)

In our study of the Gibeonites, we discussed this passage's teaching about how seriously God takes an oath given in His name and about the surety of our safety in Christ. Now I would like us to consider the phrase, "who have fled for refuge to lay hold upon the hope set before us." In my opinion, although there is no way to be final about it, the writer of Hebrews, who is writing to Jews and is constantly referring to the Old Testament, is referring here to the cities of refuge and paralleling them to Christ's work.

Let us notice some facts about the cities of refuge. First, they were in central places on both sides of the Jordan, so they were easy to reach from any place in the country. God expressly commanded that roads were to be made to these cities (Deut. 19:3). From nonbiblical sources we can add some further detail about the highways. They were carefully repaired every spring, after the rains and bad weather of winter. Further, bridges were built where needed so that a man did not have to run down into a ravine but could go straight across, taking the shortest possible route to the city. At every crossroad were special signs which said, "Refuge!" and pointed in the direction of the city. They had to be large enough so that a man running hard could easily read them.

We can picture a man coming up the road. Another man is pursuing him, sword out. The first man, having no time to use a magnifying glass, approaches the sign and sees the big words, "Refuge!" He runs to the city and is safe.

Second, the cities of refuge were open to all—to the Israelite, the stranger, and sojourner.

Third, from nonbiblical sources we hear that the great doors of these cities were never locked. We can see why. Otherwise a man might die while beating on the door.

Fourth, these sources also tell us that each city of refuge was stocked with food. It was a sufficient refuge, then, not only providing legal protection, but also meeting a man's needs once he was inside.

Fifth, we know from the Bible itself, of course, that if a killer did not flee to a city of refuge there was no help for him.

The similarities between the cities of refuge and Christ, our refuge, are striking. We can compare them point for point. First, Christ is easy to reach. We may cast ourselves upon Christ at any time, in any place. The Church is to be the teller of this good news. The Church is to cry, "Refuge! Refuge!" to the lost world. This emphasis is made at the very end of the Bible in the book of Revelation: "And the Spirit and the bride say, Come. And let him that heareth say, Come. And let him that is athirst come. And whosoever will, let him take the water of life freely" (Rev. 22:17).

Second, Christ is open to all—the Jew and the Gentile, the Greek and the barbarian, to all people.

Third, Christ never locks His gates. There is no need to wake Him. He is infinite; He is God; He is never asleep. We do not have to beat upon the door and die because He does not open it. Many times I have stood by a deathbed and seen men believe in the last moments of life. It is good that there is no gate to unlock and that men can enter quickly.

Fourth, Christ is a totally sufficient refuge. Christ's death in space-time history is completely adequate to meet our need for refuge from the true moral guilt which we have. It is final because of who He is. He is the infinite second person of the Trinity; therefore, His death has infinite value. Furthermore, the cities of refuge were not only a legal protection, but also had a supply of food. So Christ not only makes a Christian legally safe through His propitiatory death, but He supplies the believer with great riches. God the Father is now his father, and the Holy Spirit indwells him and is the agent by which the whole Trinity produces Christ's fruit through him.

Fifth, if we do not flee to the refuge which God has given to us at such a great price, there is no help for us. Hebrews relates this negative emphasis to the Old Testament: "He that despised Moses' law died without mercy under two or three witnesses; of how much sorer punishment, suppose ye, shall he be thought worthy, who hath trodden under foot the Son of God, and hath counted the blood of the covenant, with which he was sanctified, an unholy thing, and hath done despite unto the Spirit of grace?" (Heb. 10:28, 29). There isn't one of us who does not stand in that situation. We have heard the gospel, and if in the Old Testament ignoring God's law brought death, what about us if we despise the work of Christ and the grace which He showers upon us?

But there are differences between the cities of refuge and Christ our refuge. The biggest difference is that the cities protected only the innocent. They were only for the man who killed by mistake. Christ died for the guilty, for the deliberate sinner. Who is that deliberate sinner? Every one of us can say, "It is I!"

How is it possible that the holy God would accept those that are guilty? It is not by giving up His holiness. He does not devalue that, or we would have no moral absolute in the universe. Rather, the reason Christ is able to be our Redeemer is that He is a high priest and the sacrifice He gave was His own death. A man stayed in a city of refuge until the death of the high priest. Christ is our high priest. He has died once for all, and He lives forever. So though we are legally guilty before the God who is there, when we cast ourselves upon Him we are free forever. Hebrews says this strongly:

> And they, truly, were many priests, because they were not suffered to continue by reason of death; but this man, because he continueth ever, hath an unchangeable priesthood. Wherefore, he is able also to save them to the uttermost that come unto God by him, seeing he ever liveth to make intercession for them. For such an high priest became us who is holy, harmless, undefiled, separate from sinners, and made higher than the heavens; who needeth not daily, as those high priests, to offer up sacrifice, first for his own sins, and then for the people's; for this he did once, when he offered up himself. (Heb. 7:23-27)

Hebrews also speaks of Christ as "the forerunner [who] is for us entered" (Heb. 6:20). That means that He has entered into God's presence and that we can enter, too. When do we enter this refuge? I would suggest we enter at three different times. First, we enter in once for all at the moment we cast ourselves upon Christ and accept Him as our Savior. We are declared justified by God the Judge on the basis of Christ's finished work. In Romans 5:11 Paul uses the aorist tense, indicating our justification is a past thing, completed forever. If we are saved, we are saved. Second, we enter into this refuge as Christians in every existential moment when we claim the blood of Christ to cover a specific sin. Third, at that great moment when we die or when the Lord returns, we will enter in perfectly and completely.

The second difference between Christ and a city of refuge is that, happily, Christ is nearer than any city of refuge. A runner could fail, but a man who looks to Christ can never fail. The Bible makes a specific promise: "Him that cometh to me I will in no wise cast out" (John 6:37). In fact, Jesus says, "I stand at the door and knock" (Rev. 3:20). He Himself seeks us.

We are not like a man who runs to a city of refuge and is acquitted after a trial because he is innocent. We are guilty. If you are still a non-Christian, run to Christ, for God's own promises say, "Refuge! Refuge!" If we are Christians, we should take Christ as our sufficient refuge in bringing specific sins under the work of Christ and in all the vicissitudes of life, this moment and moment by moment, through the whole of our lives.

CHAPTER TWELVE

Joshua's Farewell: Choose!

The major campaigns of conquest were over. The land had been divided and the cities of refuge established. "And it came to pass a long time after that the LORD had given rest unto Israel from all their enemies round about, that Joshua waxed old and stricken in age. And Joshua called for all Israel, and for their elders, and for their heads, and for their judges, and for their officers" (Josh. 23:1, 2).

What would Joshua say to the people at such a time? What was his word to them as they were about to continue without his leadership? He began like this:

> I am old and stricken in age; and ye have seen all that the LORD your God hath done unto all these nations because of you; for the LORD your God is he who hath fought for you. Behold, I have divided unto you by lot these nations that remain, to be an inheritance for your tribes, from Jordan, with all the nations that I have cut off, even unto the great sea in the west. And the LORD your God, he shall expel them from before you, and drive them from out of your sight; and ye shall possess their land, as the LORD your God hath promised unto you. (Josh. 23:2-5)

Joshua gave a promise for the future which was rooted in a

space-time past. He did not ask the people to make a Kierkegaardian leap of faith. This stress on God's action in history recurs
throughout his farewell:

> And, behold, this day I am going the way of all the earth; and ye know
> in all your hearts and in all your souls, that not one thing hath failed of
> all the good things which the LORD your God spoke concerning you;
> all are come to pass unto you, and not one thing hath failed there-
> of. . . . And when they cried unto the LORD, he put darkness be-
> tween you and the Egyptians, and brought the sea upon them, and
> covered them, and your eyes have seen what I have done in Egypt;
> and ye dwelt in the wilderness a long season. . . . For the LORD our
> God, he it is who brought us up and our fathers out of the land of
> Egypt, from the house of bondage, and which did those great signs in
> our sight, and preserved us in all the way wherein we went, and
> among all the people through whom we passed. (Josh. 23:14; 24:7, 17)

Joshua appealed to what some of the people had seen themselves. The former generation had died, but some who heard
Joshua's farewell had been children when the Israelites crossed the
Red Sea. He reminded them of the historical realities on which
their faith rested. Biblical faith is rooted in what may be seen by
the eye and heard by the ear. The difference between Greek and
Hebrew thinking is not that the Greeks were rationalists while the
Hebrews were existentialists. Quite the contrary. The Jews insisted on a tougher reality than the Greeks. They demanded not
only that which was reasonable, but also that which was rooted in
space and time.

This emphasis continues in the New Testament, which insists,
for instance, that the first eleven chapters of Genesis describe
actual history. Every New Testament reference to these chapters
in Genesis indicates that the event mentioned was space-time history. The New Testament also assumes that that history is stated
in ordinary literary forms. Scripture never suddenly confronts us
with a heavenly language which carries us into a contentless religious experience.

Believers have been given good and sufficient reasons for believing. This was not only true in Joshua's days; it has been true
throughout God's redemptive program. When John explains why
he wrote his Gospel, he says that "many other 'space-time proofs'
did Jesus in the presence of his disciples, which are not written in
this book" (John 20:30). "Space-time proofs" is exactly what the

Greek word means in the terminology of our own day. John's statement parallels what Joshua said. What happened at the Red Sea was done in the Israelites' presence. Jesus' actions, recorded in John's Gospel, were done in the presence of the disciples. These space-time proofs were written, John continues, "that ye might believe that Jesus is the Christ, the Son of God; and that believing ye might have life through his name" (John 20:31). So whether it is in Joshua's exhortation or through the cry of John's Gospel, the Bible claims that there are good and sufficient reasons for faith that may be considered and acted upon.

Joshua was saying to the people as he was about to leave them, "Remember the past! Remember these things that are rooted in history and open to reason!"

Remember the Standard

The promises for the future were not, however, unconditional. Joshua confronted the people with a set of categories within which they had to live if the promises were to come to pass: "Be ye therefore very courageous to keep and to do all that is written in the book of the law of Moses, that ye turn not aside therefrom to the right hand or to the left" (Josh. 23:6). This hearkens back to Joshua 1 and its emphasis upon the book: "This book of the law shall not depart out of thy mouth; but thou shalt meditate therein day and night, that thou mayest observe to do according to all that is written therein; for then thou shalt make thy way prosperous, and then thou shalt have good success" (Josh. 1:8). The statement God made to Joshua at the beginning of his leadership, Joshua passed on to the people at the end of his life—namely, "live within the categories of the book and you will be blessed."

At the end of Joshua's life we see once more the growth of the canon: "And Joshua wrote these words in the book of the law of God" (Josh. 24:26). Moses' books were accepted as normative at the time of his death; and by the time Joshua died, he had written another book and added it to the canon, which was the authority for God's people. This is in complete contrast to the new theology with its focus in contentless, existential experience. God gave the people a set of moral categories in verbalized form, categories that God Himself declared to be absolute. Joshua said, "This is the standard! If you depart from it, the conditional portions of the promise will come to an end." God Himself gave a written, objective, propositional authority by which to judge in moral matters.

Joshua contrasted what would happen if the people lived within these categories with what would happen if they did not:

> One man of you shall chase a thousand; for the LORD your God, he it is that fighteth for you, as he hath promised you. Take good heed, therefore, unto yourselves, that ye love the LORD your God. Else if ye do in any wise go back, and cleave to the remant of these nations, even these who remain among you, and shall make marriages with them, and go in unto them, and they to you, know for a certainty that the LORD your God will no more drive out any of these nations from before you; but they shall be snares and traps unto you, and scourges in your sides, and thorns in your eyes, until ye perish from off this good land which the LORD your God hath given you. (Josh. 23:10-13)

This carries us back to Ebal and Gerizim, where Joshua "read all the words of the law, the blessings and cursings, according to all that is written in the book of the law. There was not a word of all that Moses commanded, which Joshua read not before all the congregation of Israel, with the women, and the little ones, and the strangers among them" (Josh. 8:34, 35). These commands, considered simple and straightforward enough for everyone, young or old, Israelite or non-Israelite, to understand, highlighted the conditional aspects of the Abrahamic covenant. So at the end of his life Joshua was insisting, as he had practiced, that the blessings depended upon whether or not the people kept God's commands. Once we depart from this mentality, we are on totally shifting sand. God's Word, the Bible, is a rock, something solid and immovable. It gives us moral absolutes rather than situation, relativistic ethics.

An Ungodly Heritage

Joshua gathered all the tribes at Shechem, one of the cities of refuge. He began by reminding them, "Thus sayeth the LORD God of Israel, Your fathers dwelt on the other side of the flood [that is, the Euphrates River] in old time, even Terah, the father of Abraham, and the father of Nahor; and they served other gods" (Josh. 24:2). We know that Ur and Haran were centers of moon worship. Joshua was telling the people, "Your past heritage is a people that were not God's people."

Ezekiel likewise points this out: "Thus saith the Lord GOD unto Jerusalem: Thy birth and thy nativity are of the land of Canaan; thy father was an Amorite, and thy mother, an Hittite"

(Ezek. 16:3). No compliment to a Jew, certainly! Nevertheless, Ezekiel told the people, "That's what you were. The only reason you are something else is that God in His grace reached down and did something with you."

God does not allow Christians, either, to go on in pride. He constantly reminds us of our heritage—a heritage of those who have turned aside from Him. In Ephesians Paul says to believers, "In times past ye walked according to the course of this world, according to the prince of the power of the air, the spirit that now worketh in the children of disobedience; among whom also we all had our conversation in times past in the lusts of our flesh, fulfilling the desires of the flesh and of the mind; and were by nature the children of wrath, even as others" (Eph. 2:2, 3). Who does he say we were? He says to us, "Remember, at one time Satan was your god and your father. This is who you were."

Whether studying the Old Testament or the New, we are reminded that we are not where we are because of a long, wise and godly heritage. We come from rebellion. Individually, we are children of wrath. After we are Christians, we must look at others who are still under God's wrath and always say, "I am essentially what you are. If I am in a different place, it is not because I am intrinsically better than you, but simply because God has done something in my life." There is no place for pride.

Three Sets of Gods
In reminding the Israelites of their ungodly heritage, Joshua spoke of three sets of false gods and called upon the people to choose against them:

> And Joshua said unto all the people, Thus saith the LORD God of Israel, Your fathers dwelt on the other side of the flood in old time, even Terah, the father of Abraham, and the father of Nahor; and they served other gods. And I took your father, Abraham, from the other side of the flood, and led him throughout all the land of Canaan, and multiplied his seed, and gave him Isaac. And I gave unto Isaac, Jacob and Esau. And I gave unto Esau Mount Seir, to possess it; but Jacob and his children went down into Egypt. I sent Moses also, and Aaron, and I plagued Egypt, according to that which I did among them; and afterward I brought you out. And I brought your fathers out of Egypt, and ye came unto the sea; and the Egyptians pursued after your fathers with chariots and horsemen unto the Red Sea. And when they cried unto the LORD, he put darkness between you and the Egyp-

tians, and brought the sea upon them, and covered them, and your eyes have seen what I have done in Egypt; and ye dwelt in the wilderness a long season. And I brought you into the land of the Amorites, which dwelt on the other side of Jordan, and they fought with you; and I gave them into your hand, that ye might possess their land; and I destroyed them from before you. (Josh. 24:2-8)

Interestingly, the three sets of gods were related to three different waters. On the other side of the Euphrates were the gods of the Sumerian and Babylonian culture. On the other side of the Red Sea were the gods of ancient Egypt. On both sides of the river Jordan were the gods of the Amorites.

Now, therefore [Joshua challenged], fear the LORD, and serve him in sincerity and in truth; and put away the gods which your fathers served on the other side of the flood, and in Egypt, and serve ye the LORD. And if it seem evil unto you to serve the LORD, choose you this day whom ye will serve, whether the gods which your fathers served that were on the other side of the flood, or the gods of the Amorites, in whose land ye dwell; but as for me and my house, we will serve the LORD. (Josh. 24:14, 15)

"Choose," he said, "between the Sumerian gods, the Egyptian gods, the Amorite gods—and the LORD. Choose!"

Joshua's own choice was emphatic: "But as for me and my house, we will serve the Lord." The English uses a future tense here, but the Hebrew tense has a fuller meaning. It expresses continuous action. It involves the future, but it also can point to the past. Joshua was undoubtedly affirming, "I have chosen, and I will choose."

His words were not just an empty boast, because the people standing in front of him knew his past choices. Not long after the crossing of the Red Sea, Joshua had stood as the general against the Amalekites. When the people worshiped the golden calf, Joshua, by choice, did not identify with them. When the spies entered the land, he had stood with Caleb against his own people when they were wrong. He chose to affirm that God's word was valid and that they could conquer the land. When God's leader, Moses, died outside the promised land, Joshua knew it was because God had clearly told Moses to do one thing and Moses had done another. He saw the result of Moses' bad choice.

This was the character of Joshua. He chose, and he chose, and he chose, and he kept right on choosing. He understood the dynamics of choice—once-for-all choice and existential choice as well. Thus, this word to the people was not an affirmation puffed up on the spur of the moment. It was deeply embedded in Joshua's comprehension of what is required of a person made in the image of God—one called upon not to obey God like a machine or an animal, but to obey God by choice.

The people responded positively to Joshua's challenge:

> God forbid that we should forsake the LORD, to serve other gods; for the LORD our God, he it is that brought us up and our fathers out of the land of Egypt, from the house of bondage, and which did those great signs in our sight, and preserved us in all the way wherein we went, and among all the people through whom we passed. And the LORD drave out from before us all the people, even the Amorites which dwelt in the land. Therefore will we also serve the LORD; for he is our God. (Josh. 24:16-18)

Because of what the people had seen in the past, they made the same choice as Joshua. Yet theirs was in one respect different. Joshua's choice was rooted in a series of continuous choices. These people had been like a weathervane. Consequently, Joshua warned them not to choose lightly:

> And Joshua said unto the people, Ye cannot serve the LORD; for he is an holy God, he is a jealous God, he will not forgive your transgressions nor your sins. If ye forsake the LORD, and serve strange gods, then he will turn and do you hurt, and consume you, after he hath done you good. And the people said unto Joshua, Nay; but we will serve the LORD. And Joshua said unto the people, Ye are my witnesses against yourselves that ye have chosen you the LORD, to serve him. And they said, We are witnesses. Now, therefore, put away, said he, the strange gods which are among you, and incline your hearts unto the LORD God of Israel. And the people said unto Joshua, The LORD our God will we serve, and his voice will we obey. (Josh. 24:19-24)

Despite Joshua's warning, the people continued to insist. So Joshua stressed that their choice (which was, of course, the right choice) had to be total and have practical repercussions in their lives.

The Extension of the Covenant

In response to the people's affirmation, the covenant was extended another step: "So Joshua made a covenant with the people that day, and set them a statute and an ordinance in Shechem" (Josh.

24:25). This covenant was a part of the ongoing covenant. You will remember, it had been established immediately after the Fall and was continued in the times of Noah, Abraham and Moses. At the end of Joshua's life it was again extended. This extension of the covenant was related to the book: "And Joshua wrote these words in the book of the law of God, and took a great stone, and set it up there under an oak, that was by the sanctuary of the LORD. And Joshua said unto all the people, Behold, this stone shall be a witness unto us; for it hath heard all the words of the LORD which he spoke unto us: it shall be, therefore, a witness unto you, lest ye deny your God" (Josh. 24:26, 27).

Notice Joshua put up a stone as a testimony. Now, in addition to the stones at Gilgal and the altar on Ebal, another memorial in stone was established so that in years to come the children of coming generations would be able to walk through the land and be reminded of what occurred in that place and of the promises their fathers had made to God.

Sometime after the covenant was extended, Joshua died.

> And it came to pass after these things, that Joshua, the son of Nun, the servant of the LORD, died, being an hundred and ten years old. And they buried him in the border of his inheritance in Timnath-serah, which is in Mount Ephraim, on the north side of the hill of Gaash. And Israel served the LORD all the days of Joshua, and all the days of the elders who overlived Joshua, and which had known all the works of the LORD, that he had done for Israel. (Josh. 24:29-31)

The faithfulness of Joshua's generation is also extolled in the book of Judges, but it is followed by a shift:

> And the people served the LORD all the days of Joshua, and all the days of the elders that outlived Joshua, who had seen all the great works of the LORD, that he did for Israel. . . . And also all that generation were gathered unto their fathers: and there arose another generation after them, who knew not the LORD, nor yet the works which he had done for Israel. (Judg. 2:7, 10)

We come to a group of people who did not imitate Joshua's continual choice. The children of Israel remembered for a time the choice they had made at Joshua's farewell, but they then forgot it. And thus came the confusion, the sorrow, and the total lawlessness of the period of the judges.

We are seeing exactly the same shift in our own generation. Those of us from the Reformation countries have experienced a

Christian consensus. (This does not mean that every individual was a Christian, but that society was strongly influenced by Christian values.) But my generation and the generations immediately preceding my generation made a bad choice, and so we now live in a post-Christian world. The choices of faith have been set aside and forgotten, and accordingly the confusion, sorrow and lawlessness of the time of the judges is occurring in our generation. If you are a member of the younger generation, you are a recipient of the consequences of this bad choice. This is who you are. To understand yourself, you must understand that you have grown up in a post-Christian world.

Choices

The element of personal choice stands out as a key theme in the book of Joshua.

In Chapter 2 of this study, we saw that the captain of the host of the Lord stood before Joshua, and Joshua had to choose. The people of God had the opportunity to follow their own wisdom, but Joshua made a different decision for them. He fell down and said, "It's Your leadership." And he removed his shoes in the presence of the One who had now come as the captain of the host of the LORD.

In Chapter 3 we considered the blessings to the Jews under the national portion of the Abrahamic covenant. Under Joshua the people chose to enter the land (a complete contrast to the choice they made thirty-eight years before) and suddenly, after all the decades of waiting, the complex of the Abrahamic covenant fell into place. We also saw that, as Romans 9—11 make clear, the Jews' whole history, from that time to this and into the future, rests on their choices. If they continued in disobedience and unbelief, they did not have God's blessing. If they obeyed, they came into the blessing of the people of God.

Rahab and the Gibeonites (Chapters 4 and 8) chose to step over among the people of God and entered into the spiritual portion of the Abrahamic covenant. Rahab the harlot became an ancestor of Jesus Christ. The Gibeonites, down to the time of David and beyond, worked close to the altar. All this because they had decided to step over from the kingdom of darkness to the kingdom of the living God!

Chapter 5 concerned two kinds of memorials, the stones and the sacraments. The Israelites chose to cross the river Jordan, enter the land, and establish the stone memorials as God commanded. Joshua—foolishly from a human military point of view—observed the sacrament of circumcision. Then he observed the Passover. But we also saw that the external signs, like the sacraments of baptism and the Lord's Supper today, mean nothing unless there is a choice to be in a proper relationship with God. They are not mechanical.

In Chapter 6 we saw Achan's titanic choice. This one man decided to take silver and gold and the mantle of Shinar. He coveted within; then he acted. Soon he saw the terrible results of his choice. He himself died, but others died too. His choice led to a temporary defeat for the whole people of God.

On Mounts Ebal and Mount Gerizim (Chapter 7) a choice was set before the people: "Obey the propositional moral absolutes of God, and you'll receive blessing within the covenant. If you don't, the blessing will come to an end."

In Chapter 9 we saw how Caleb chose to stand against the rest of the Israelites. We saw how the people failed to take the totality of the land because they lacked faith. But Caleb went in and took the territory he had been promised. The faith which he had exhibited through thirty-eight years of wandering plus seven years of conquest he continued to practice.

In Chapter 10 we saw that the two and a half tribes that returned to the east side of Jordan chose to serve the true, living God. They even raised a great altar of testimony to show that they intended to continue to worship Him properly even though they had left the west side of the river. The remaining tribes chose to practice both truth and love as they dealt with what they feared was rebellion.

The cities of refuge involved two sorts of choices (Chapter 11). The first sort of choice was made by the man who really chose to murder; the second was made by the innocent man who chose to flee to a city of refuge to escape the avenger of blood.

So we find throughout the entire book of Joshua an emphasis on choice—choice that makes a tremendous difference in history, for individuals, for groups, for future generations. The Bible insists, "Don't forget who you are. You are not a puppet or a machine. You do not obey a universal law of cause and effect in a closed system. Rather, you are made in the image of God, and, as such, you must choose, and choose rightly, at every point." Adam chose wrongly, and we all bear the marks of his error. Abraham believed God, and his choice was counted to him for righteousness. Joshua chose rightly, too. For those of us today, the situation is the same. Whether Christian or non-Christian, we are called upon to make choices which will have significant results.

If you are not a Christian, remember that you are faced with a choice which will make total differences to you. God says to you concerning that choice,

> And, as Moses lifted up the serpent in the wilderness, even so must the Son of man be lifted up, that whosoever believeth in him should not perish, but have eternal life. For God so loved the world, that he gave his only begotten Son, that whosoever believeth in him should not perish, but have everlasting life. For God sent not his Son into the world to condemn the world, but that the world through him might be saved. He that believeth on him is not condemned; but he that believeth not is condemned already, because he hath not believed in the name of the only begotten Son of God. . . . He that believeth not the Son shall not see life, but the wrath of God abideth on him. (John 3:14-18, 36)

Your choice is not a piece of theater. You are not thistledown in the wind. There are good and sufficient reasons in history to know that this is the choice you should make, and you are called upon to make it. Choose once for all for justification.

If you are a Christian, having made the once-for-all choice that was involved in your justification, remember that your choices do not end. You do not enter a static situation. Paul gives this imperative: "If we live in the Spirit, let us also walk in the Spirit" (Gal. 5:25). We must continually choose to live within the commands of God.

In Romans Paul describes himself as "a slave of Jesus Christ" (Rom. 1:1). In Philippians he pictures both Timothy and himself as "the slaves of Jesus Christ" (Phil. 1:1). Did Paul have to be a slave? No. A Roman slave could not escape, for he had a hard, heavy band of iron riveted around his neck. He could not remove it. Paul, by a continual act of choice, held the slave-band in place.

Joshua's great call, "Choose! Choose!" is as meaningful to us today as to the people of God when Joshua was preparing to leave them. If you are a Christian, I urge you to continue to make this choice:

> Now, therefore, fear the LORD, and serve him in sincerity and in truth; and put away the gods which your fathers served on the other side of the flood, and in Egypt; and serve ye the LORD. And if it seem evil unto you to serve the LORD, choose you this day whom ye will

serve, whether the gods which your fathers served that were on the other side of the flood, or the gods of the Amorites, in whose land ye dwell; but as for me and my house, we will serve the LORD. (Joshua 24:14, 15)

What are your gods of Ur? What are your gods of Egypt? What are your gods of the Amorites? *What are your gods?* What gods did you leave when you made the great first choice to become a Christian? God says, "You chose once for all to be a Christian. Fine. Continue to choose, continue to choose, continue to choose— moment by moment, existentially. You must continue to choose between the old gods and Me, the living God." And, as Joshua said, we must not choose lightly.

When the people affirmed their commitment to God, Joshua insisted, "Remember how you have chosen" (Josh. 24:22). Joshua affirmed, "As for me and my house, we will serve the Lord." Like Joshua, any Christian who wishes to be of any help to this poor sinful world, especially to a confused generation like ours, must be one who continues to choose to serve the LORD in the here and now. Let us say as we face the choices of life: As for me and my house, by God's grace, we will serve the Lord!

Volume Two ● Book Four

BASIC BIBLE STUDIES

Introduction

These twenty-five basic Bible studies are meant to give an understanding of the whole system of teaching given in the Bible. Very often when people begin to study the Scripture, they do not see the relationship of all its parts. However, because one of the wonderful things about the Bible is its unity, Bible study without keeping this unity in mind is a real loss.

Thus, each individual lesson should be studied with the whole table of contents consciously in mind, so that each lesson can be seen in relationship to the whole Bible's teaching.

These twenty-five studies are not meant to be read as a book. If they were, a much more detailed text would have been given. Rather, they are to be followed to be a help in a study of the Bible itself. When one begins to go through these studies, he or she should have both the Old and New Testaments at hand.

The best way to use these studies is to look up each individual verse in the Bible, to read the verse with care, and then to read the statement which is made in the studies about that verse. The statements are not supposed to be complete explanations of any of the verses. Instead, they point out one specific thing that is taught in the verse, as that one specific thing bears on the teaching of that particular lesson. For example, the first Bible reference given (Ephesians 1:4) has many rich things in it which are not mentioned in the statement following it. But attention is called to just one of the things that Ephesians 1:4 teaches—that God, being a personal God, thinks. Thus, each verse should be looked up and considered in the light of the statement that immediately follows it—not merely as an isolated statement, but in the light of that whole lesson, and in the light of the flow of the unity of the biblical teaching as it is set forth in the complete twenty-five studies. The Bible is not just an unrelated group of verses. It is a unit. And it has content that can be studied as one studies other books.

Studied in this way, the Bible will be seen to have many things to say in answer to the questions which people are asking in our generation about the meaning and purpose of life. It tells us who Man is, Man's purpose, the source of Man's problems, and the solution to those problems. Of course, this study is just a beginning to help us to begin studying the Bible. The Bible is a unit and eventually we should read it all and see the relationship of each part to the whole. The unity of the Bible begins at the beginning, Genesis, and goes to the end, the book of Revelation.

Using verses as I have used them in these twenty-five *Basic Bible Studies* has a danger that must be recognized and leaned against. That danger is choosing certain "proof texts" isolated from the context, and forcing all the rest of the Bible's teaching into our understanding of that one text. This is a danger. No one verse can give the whole Bible's richness. Each verse is to be taken in context if it is to be rightly understood. There are three contexts of each verse we study: (1) the immediate context; (2) the whole book in which the verse is located, and this includes the careful consideration of the purpose of that book; (3) the whole Bible and its teaching.

The whole Bible's teaching gives us a series of balances that no one verse can give. This takes a lifetime of careful study.

However, as I have used the verses I have tried to use them fairly—using my lifetime of study of the whole Bible as the background of the use of each verse as I have used it here.

Thus, these *Basic Bible Studies* are just that: basic teaching to open the door for a lifetime of studying the Bible. With the entire table of contents in mind as you study, it is hoped that these studies will provide a framework to understand the wonder of the flow of the whole Bible, from Genesis to Revelation. Then a lifetime of careful and prayerful study will show that these twenty-five studies are indeed only a beginning. I do think though that you will find that as I have used the verses I have taken into account the whole Bible's teaching.

As you do these studies it is not necessary to do a whole study at a time. If desired, one may spend a specific amount of time each day. When that time is reached, simply draw a line and start at that point the next day.

It would be my advice that each time you do these studies, you speak to God and ask Him to give you understanding through the use of the Bible and the study together. If someone pursues these studies who does not believe that God exists, I would suggest that you say aloud in the quietness of your room: "O God, if there is a God, I want to know whether You exist. And I ask You that I may be willing to bow before You if You do exist."

Francis A. Schaeffer

CHAPTER ONE

God

1. The God of the Bible

The God of the Bible is personal.

Ephesians 1:4   Notice here that God has a plan, that He thinks.

Genesis 1:1   God not only thinks; He acts.

John 3:16   God not only thinks and acts, God feels. Love is an emotion. Thus the God who exists is personal. He thinks, acts, and feels, three distinguishing marks of personality. He is not an impersonal force, nor an all-inclusive everything. He is personal. When He speaks to us, He says "I" and we can answer Him "You."

Deuteronomy 6:4   The Old Testament teaches there is only one God.

James 2:19   The New Testament also teaches there is only one God.

But the Bible also teaches that this one God exists in three distinct persons.

Genesis 1:26   "Let *us* make." Here it is shown that there is more than one person in the Godhead.

Genesis 11:7   Here again is an emphasis on there being more than one person in the Godhead. In this verse, as in 1:26, the persons of the Trinity are in communication with each other.

Isaiah 6:8 Again we see that there is more than one person in the Godhead.

Matthew 3:16, 17 Each of the three persons is shown clearly here. Also read Matthew 28:19; John 15:26; 1 Peter 1:2.

Matthew 9:2-7 Jesus Christ claims the power of forgiving sins as His natural right, thus showing that He claims to be God.

Matthew 18:20 Jesus said He was everywhere at once, another claim to deity.

Matthew 28:20 As Jesus is through all space, He is through all time.

John 5:22 Jesus Christ is to be Judge of all mankind. Only God could do this.

John 8:58 Jesus said He was living before the time of Abraham. Abraham lived at 2,000 B.C.

John 17:5, 24 Jesus said that He lived with the Father and that the Father loved Him before the world was made.

2 Corinthians 5:10 Here again we are told Christ will judge the world.

John 1:1-3 These verses say that the person called "the Word" is God and made all things. Verses 14 and 15 of this same chapter show that "the Word" is Jesus Christ.

John 20:28 Thomas affirms that Jesus is God.

Thus, the second person of the Trinity is not only distinct from the first person, but He is equally God.

Luke 12:10, 12 Let us now think about the third person of the Trinity. These two verses show that He is God and just as much a person as the first and second persons of the Godhead.

John 15:26 The Spirit is again said to do something only a person can do.

John 16:7-14 The Spirit, or Comforter, is distinct from the second person and does things only a person can do. The Spirit is "He," not "it."

Acts 8:29 Only a person can speak.

Acts 13:2; 15:28; 16:6, 7 The Holy Spirit is a person.

Ephesians 4:30 The above passages show that the Holy Spirit thinks and acts; this verse shows He also feels.

2 Peter 1:21   The Holy Spirit is the person of the Trinity who gave us the Bible.

It is central and important to our Christian faith to have clearly in mind the facts concerning the Trinity.

Genesis 1:26; John 17:24   Communication and love existed between the persons of the Trinity before the creation.

2 Corinthians 13:14   The work of each of the three persons is important to us. Jesus died to save us, the Father draws us to Himself and loves us, and the Holy Spirit deals with us.

Romans 8:11, 14, 26, 27   The Holy Spirit is a person, and He indwells and leads the Christian and prays for him when the Christian does not know what to pray for himself.

2. Creation

In our last study, we saw that the Bible sets forth God as one God but in three persons. We are not worshiping the Christian God unless we worship this God, who is one but three persons.

Likewise, a person is not worshiping the Christian God as he should unless he recognizes that God is sovereign.

When we speak of God's sovereignty, two thoughts are in mind—His work of creation and His work of providence. When we speak of providence, we mean His dealings in the world now.

The following Bible study deals with the Bible's teaching on creation.

Revelation 4:11   God created all things of His own free will. He did not have to create. Before creation the triune God stood complete, and there was love and communication between the persons of the Trinity. Revelation 4:11 reads: "You are worthy, our Lord and our God, to receive glory and honor and power, for You created all things, and by Your will they were created and have their being."

Colossians 1:16, 17   Before God created, He dwelt alone.

Psalm 33:9   God created out of nothing. He created by fiat: He spoke and it was.

Genesis 1:1   The word "create" used here means to create out of nothing. God created matter out of nothing. He did not just shape preexistent matter, but brought it into being. He did not make only the world, but the heavens and the earth—everything there is.

He created all things out of nothing. They now have objective existence; they are not an extension of Himself or His essence.

Genesis 1:31   After God had created all things, He pronounced it good. All things were good as they were originally made. They were not only good in man's judgment, but in God's absolute judgment.

If God made us, then we have a responsibility to obey Him.

CHAPTER TWO

God's Dealing with Man

3. God and Man

With this study we begin considering what the Bible tells us of the relationship between God and man.

Genesis 2:7 In this verse we are told that God formed the body of man out of the dust of the ground. However, man is more than a body.

Genesis 1:26 Man was made in God's image. This is man's glory, and it is this which sets him off from other creatures. What does it mean that man is made in God's image? Well, among other things it certainly means this: man is moral. This means he can make moral choices. Also, man is rational. This means that he can think. It also means that man is creative—we find that men everywhere make works of art. It is also the reason why man loves.

Genesis 1:31 As God made man, man was good, both in body and soul.

Genesis 3:8a Notice the first phrase in this verse. Man is here shown to be in perfect harmony with God, so that man and God could walk together in the cool of the day. Being in harmony with God, man was also in full harmony with his wife, with nature, and with himself. There was no place for divided personality or schizophrenia in man as he was originally made. He had power to love and obey God, but as a free agent he could also transgress.

Genesis 2:16, 17   Here stand two parties—God and man. In this verse God states the condition, in order for man to continue in fellowship with God. The condition is simple. Man must show his love for God by obeying Him. If man disobeys God, death would be the result. This is more than physical death. Spiritual death, or separation from God, came immediately. Physical death means that which we usually speak of as "death." Eternal death comes at the Judgment. As man was faced with the choice of obedience or disobedience, he had these gracious provisions from God:

(a) He was made in the image of God (Genesis 1:26).

(b) He had constant fellowship with God (Genesis 3:8a).

(c) He was surrounded by a perfect environment (Genesis 2:8).

(d) He had a truly free choice, with power to obey or power to transgress. He was not a deterministically conditioned being. He was not programmed (Genesis 2:16, 17).

(e) The test was most simple, with both the command and penalty clearly stated (Genesis 2:16, 17).

Genesis 3:1-20   Adam and Eve willfully chose to disobey God.

Genesis 3:7   By trying to cover themselves with the work of their own hands, they showed that guilt had come upon them.

Genesis 3:24   They lost communion with God and were put out of the Garden. Both the body and soul felt the effects of sin.

Genesis 3:17, 18   The external universe is now abnormal. It is not as God made it. It was changed because of man's sin. All that was under man's dominion was affected.

Romans 5:12, 17   Since Adam's fall, all men are sinners. Each time we look upon the body of one who has died, it should remind us that man is a sinner.

Isaiah 53:6

Jeremiah 17:9

Romans 3:10-12, 23

Galatians 3:10

The following two passages point out to us that those who are now Christians were "children of wrath" before they accepted Christ as their Savior.

Ephesians 2:2, 3

Colossians 1:21

It would be well to close our consideration with the fact that each of us personally has sinned in God's sight (1 John 1:10).

In conclusion, God made man. Man's body and soul were good. Man had a true, unprogrammed choice by which he could show his love for God by obedience. Man had continued fellowship with God. He was in a perfect environment. He was given a simple test so that he could demonstrate his love and obedience. Adam and Eve sinned. Since then all people, you and I, have personally sinned.

John 3:18, 36 Having sinned, we are under the judgment of God, under his condemnation, *now*.

4. God's Grace (A)

Romans 6:23 Every one of us has earned only one thing at the hand of God, and that is judgment. As far as God's holiness and justice are concerned, He owes us nothing but judgment. He has made us and we have sinned. But the last part of this verse tells us that in spite of this, because of His love, God has provided us with a way of approach to Him. It is not because God owes it to us; it is a gift based on His love. Adam and Eve were given a way of work which could please God. However, they sinned and we also have all sinned, and thus this new approach which God gives us cannot be on the basis of our work, but on God's grace.

John 3:15, 16 Here we have the triune God standing with His arms open, telling us that even though we are sinners He has provided a way through which "whosoever will" may come.

Philippians 2:7, 8 How can the holy God say "whosoever" to sinners? God cannot just overlook our sin, because He is holy. If He did that, no moral absolute would exist. We can come to God through grace, because Christ worked for us. This finished work is His death upon the cross.

Romans 3:24-26 Because Christ died in substitution, God remains righteous, there is a moral absolute, and yet we do not need to come under His judgment.

John 3:15; 17:4 It is a gift to us, but only on the basis of Christ's perfect work.

1 Peter 1:18,19 We are purchased with an infinite price.

John 6:29 Christ had to work for us, in His death. But because of His perfect work, we now can approach God simply by faith, without works.

John 3:15, 16 God's promise is clear. If we accept Jesus as our Savior, then on the basis of Christ's finished work (which we accept by faith alone), we have God's promise of an eternal life. Faith is the empty hand which accepts the gift.

John 3:18, 36 God's penalty is also clear. Because we are sinners, we are already under the condemnation and judgment of God. If we refuse God's gift, if we do not accept Christ's work for us, we remain under the condemnation and judgment of God.

Hebrews 2:3 Adam was commanded to obey God and he sinned. We have all sinned. Therefore, we have earned spiritual, physical, and eternal death. Now God in His love has given us another opportunity. This is not of works, but of grace, in which we partake if we accept His gift. If we accept Christ as our Savior and trust Him only for our salvation, if we believe on Him and accept His death for us, then we have eternal life. If we refuse God's gracious provision, we stay where we are, under the condemnation and judgment of God.

5. God's Grace (B)

Genesis 3:15, 21 As soon as man sinned, God gave the promise of the coming Savior. He did this in words in verse 15 and by illustration in verse 21. After man sinned, he tried to cover himself with the works of his own hands (verse 7). God took this away and provided a covering of skins. To do this, an animal had to be slain. This was an immediate picture that the way man could come to God, now that he had sinned, was not by the humanistic works of his own righteousness, but by that which God would provide through the death of the coming Messiah.

Genesis 4:3-5 It would seem that God told Adam and Eve how He wanted them to worship in the future, through the presentation of a lamb as a picture of the coming Messiah. Abel did this, but Cain tried to come on the basis of his own works. Hebrews 11:4 tells us that Abel believed God; Cain did not.

Genesis 12:1-3 The promise which was given to Abraham, 2,000 years before Christ came, was twofold—national but also personal. The national promises were and are to the Jews. The spiritual promises were and are to all who would believe God and thus be in the right relationship to the coming Messiah. This Messiah would be one of Abraham's descendants, humanly speaking.

Genesis 22:1-18 Here we have a clear picture in space-time history of the coming Messiah and His substitutionary work. The Old Testament saints had a much clearer concept of Christ's work than we usually attribute to them. Verse 14 ties the events of this chapter at 2,000 B.C. into the coming death of Christ 2,000 years later. This geographical location was later the geographical location of Jerusalem, where Jesus died. Compare verse 14 with 2 Chronicles 3:1.

Exodus 20:24, 25 Immediately after the Ten Commandments were given, God, in anticipation of man's inability to keep them, provided a way of approach to Him. This building of an altar without man's work on it looked forward to the promise of the Messiah, whose work would have none of man's work added to it. No man has ever kept the Ten Commandments perfectly.

Isaiah 53 Now, 700 years before Christ, we see again that the Jews were informed explicitly concerning the work of the coming Messiah. Incidentally, the whole sacrificial system of the Old Testament was a preview of the work of the coming Messiah. The Messiah would come and die for us.

Luke 2:25-32, 36-38 When Jesus was brought to the Temple as a baby, Simeon recognized Him for who He was: the Messiah prophesied in the Old Testament. There was a remnant in that day who had their personal faith fixed in the coming Messiah. Notice that Anna not only recognized Jesus as the Messiah, for whom she had been looking throughout her life, but she immediately went to tell others in Jerusalem who also had their personal faith fixed in the coming Messiah.

Romans 4:1-3 This states that Abraham, 2,000 years before Christ, was saved exactly as we are saved—through faith, without works.

Romans 4:6-8 David (1,000 years before Christ) was saved by faith, just as we are saved. The Ten Commandments had been given through Moses 500 years before David's time. Yet David is clearly said to have been saved not of works, but by faith. No man has ever been saved by his own humanistic works.

Romans 4:10, 11 After Abraham was saved by faith, he was later circumcised. Circumcision did not save him. It was merely an external sign of the fact that he had already been accepted by

God through faith alone. No *religious* good works on our part can help us before the perfect God.

Romans 4:20, 22-25 Abraham was accepted by God because of faith, his believing what God had promised. The same is true of us.

Galatians 3:13, 14 When we receive Christ as our Savior by faith, we receive the same blessing of God Abraham received by faith.

Galatians 3:24 If all this is true, what good then is the law of God, the Ten Commandments, and the other eternal commandments given by God in the Old and New Testaments? The law is meant by God to show us that we are sinners, so that we see our need of accepting Christ as our Savior.

Hebrews 11:1—12:2 A long list is given of those who in the Old Testament times had faith in God. We who have these to look back upon are told to have the same faith in God, through the acceptance of Christ as our Savior.

Thus through all the ages, before Christ and after Christ alike, there is one way of salvation. All men have sinned. Salvation is available only through faith on the basis of the Messiah's finished work for us.

6. Old Testament Prophecies of the Coming Messiah

After Christ was raised from the dead, He met a number of disciples on the road to Emmaus, but they did not recognize Him. We are told that before He made Himself known to them, He talked to them, and this is what the Bible says about it:

"And beginning at Moses and all the prophets, he expounded unto them, in all the scriptures, the things concerning himself" (Luke 24:27).

In other words, on the way to Emmaus He went back into the Old Testament and told them many things that the Old Testament had said concerning Him, which He had fulfilled in His life, death, and resurrection. The following are some of the Old Testament passages that foretold the coming of the Messiah. The word *Messiah* in Hebrew is the same as the word *Christ* in Greek, and so one is merely the Old Testament word and the other the New.

The following does not exhaust these Old Testament references. They are only a cross section.

Genesis 3:15 Man has just sinned. God made man perfect and gave him opportunity to obey God and show his love for Him. Instead of that, man disobeyed. God then gave a promise to mankind that a Messiah would come, One who would win the victory. This Messiah would come "born of a woman" (see Galatians 4:4).

Genesis 9:26 Time has passed. We are now in the days of Noah. Now the promise which in Genesis 3:15 was given to the whole human race is narrowed down to one portion of the human race—the Semitic peoples. The Semitic people today include such races as the Assyrians, Babylonians, Egyptians, Hebrews, Arabians, and a number of others.

Genesis 12:3 More time has passed again. Now, of all the Semitic people, the promise of the coming Messiah is given to one man, Abraham. The coming Savior would be born from his family—i.e., of the Jews.

Genesis 49:10 After Abraham there came Isaac, then Jacob, who had twelve sons. In this passage we are told from which of these twelve families the Messiah would come. He would be born of the tribe of Judah.

Exodus 12:46 We now enter another phase of the picture which is being drawn of the coming Messiah. This was written about 1,500 years before Christ. The passages given above occurred even before that time. Here Moses is saying that in regard to the passover lamb, which prefigured the coming of the Messiah, none of its bones should be broken. Notice how carefully John 19:36 points out that no bones of Christ were broken, even though He was crucified and even though this was not the case with the two thieves who were crucified with Him.

Deuteronomy 18:15 We are still about 1,500 years before Christ. Moses here gives a different line again concerning the Coming One. We are told here something of His work. When He comes, He will be an unusual and unique prophet. A prophet, according to Scripture, is not basically one who tells the future, but rather one who speaks for God to men.

2 Samuel 7:16 The line is now narrowed down again. Of all the tribe of Judah, the Christ must come from a certain family. That family is the royal family of David. See Matthew 1:1 and 22:42.

Psalm 2:2 The picture of the coming Christ has grown more clear—what He must be, how He must act, what He must do if

He is to be really the Messiah, the Savior of the world. In verse 7 we are told that this One is to be more than a man; God calls Him His Son. See Acts 13:33; Hebrews 1:5. Verse 12 urges each to come into right personal relationship with this Messiah.

Psalm 16:8-11 Here we are told another thing about the Messiah. He will die, but His body will not remain in the grave. He will be raised from the dead. See Acts 2:25-31.

Psalm 22:1-18 This is a tremendous picture of the crucifixion of Christ. The Jews did not crucify; they stoned to death. The only nation that would crucify as a general practice would be the Romans. This passage in the book of Psalms was written about 1,000 years before Jesus lived and died, and long before the Romans came to prominence. Yet the picture given here of Jesus' death is a perfect picture of crucifixion. Notice too the many other details fulfilled at Christ's death.

Psalm 41:9 When this Messiah would come, he would be betrayed by one who had been close to Him. Jesus was so betrayed, of course, by Judas. See John 13:18; Acts 1:16.

Psalm 69:9 This is quoted of Jesus when He cleansed the Temple of those who had turned it into a place of commerce. See John 2:17.

Psalm 69:21 When Jesus was dying, this is exactly what happened to Him. See Matthew 27:34.

Psalm 110:1-4 Moses, 500 years before this psalm was written, said that the Messiah would be a prophet. This passage tells us he would also be a priest. A priest is very different from a prophet. A prophet speaks for God to men; a priest represents men before God. See Acts 2:32-35.

Isaiah 7:14 Here we have a stupendous sign. When the Messiah came, He would have a human mother but no human father. See Matthew 1:23.

Isaiah 9:6, 7 Notice the names given to the coming Messiah. Obviously He is to be more than a man; He is also to be God.

Isaiah 42:1-3, 6, 7 We have already seen that this Messiah would be born of a woman, without a human father, and would be God. But He would also be a servant, and this servant would open the way of blessing for Jews and Gentiles as well. See Matthew 12:17-21; Luke 2:32.

Isaiah 50:6 Here we are told something of the things that Jesus would suffer. The New Testament says this is exactly what happened to Him. They hit Him. They beat Him. They did everything, not only to hurt, but to humiliate Him. See Matthew 26:67; 27:26.

Isaiah 52:13 to the end of Isaiah 53   The Coming One was to be a priest in a very special way. He was to be a priest by Himself bearing our sins. He was to be a suffering Messiah, to die for us.

Jeremiah 31:15   The New Testament says this was fulfilled literally when the little children were killed by King Herod at the time of Jesus' birth, in Herod's attempt to kill the coming Messiah who the wise men said had been born. See Matthew 2:17, 18.

Micah 5:2   Here we are told the exact city where the Messiah would have to be born: the town of Bethlehem. This verse also says that he has existed from the days of eternity. See Matthew 2:6.

Zechariah 9:9   Now we come to the third part of the work of Christ. Moses said He would be a *prophet.* Psalms and Isaiah designated Him as a *priest.* Zechariah clearly says He is to be a *king.* Jesus literally fulfilled this passage when He came in triumphal entry into Jerusalem just before His death. See Matthew 21:5.

Zechariah 11:11-13   We are told here exactly how much Judas would receive for betraying Christ. See Matthew 26:15.

Jesus fulfilled each of these literally. The possibility of any one man having done all these things, let alone being all that was designated, was impossible as a matter of coincidence. Jesus fulfilled them all because He is what the Bible says He would be. He is God, and man born of a virgin, the One promised for thousands of years. When He came, all these things came to pass. These, then, are just a few of the things that Jesus must have talked about with the disciples on the road to Emmaus.

7. Christ the Mediator—His Person

1 Timothy 2:5   Notice that this verse says there is only one mediator between God and man. That one mediator is the man, Christ Jesus. There are not several possible mediators; Jesus Christ is the *only* one. He is the only possible intercessor between God the Father and man.

a) First of all, let's review some of our observations in a previous study, "The God of the Bible." You will remember that in this we saw that the Bible teaches that Jesus Christ is God, equally God as is God the Father. We saw that the second person of the Trinity was God before He was born to Mary; He was God while

He was on the earth; and He is God now. We also saw that the second person of the Trinity is distinct from the first person of the Trinity, the Father, and from the third person of the Trinity, the Holy Spirit.

b) The Bible also teaches that Jesus Christ is truly man. In our day most heresies deny the true deity of Christ, but in the early church the common heresy was the denial of the true humanity of Christ. We should remember that from God's viewpoint, it is far more wonderful that the second person of the Trinity became a man than that He is God. He had been God for eternity—He became a man when He was born.

Matthew 4:2   Christ became hungry.

Matthew 8:24   He slept.

Matthew 26:38   Jesus Christ had a soul as well as a body.

Luke 1:32   On His human side, Christ descended from a human family.

Luke 2:40, 52   He grew physically and mentally.

Luke 22:44   Christ suffered anguish.

Luke 23:46   He died.

Luke 24:39   After His resurrection, He still had a true body.

John 11:33, 35   Jesus wept.

John 19:28   Christ suffered thirst.

John 19:34   He had blood in His veins.

Romans 5:15   Adam was a man, and Christ was a man.

Galatians 4:4   This verse tells us that God the Father sent His Son, and that He, the Son, was born of a woman—as we all are born.

1 Timothy 3:16   This verse tells us that God revealed Himself in the flesh.

When men looked at Jesus Christ, they saw only one person, but He had two natures. He is truly God and truly man.

Hebrews 2:14, 18   God became man in order to become our mediator.

Hebrews 4:15   Our mediator knows how we feel, even in our temptations.

1 John 4:1, 2   The Bible says that it is most important to believe that Jesus had preexistence and that at a point of history He came as a man. In this verse, we are told that it is upon this point that we are to test religious teachers, spirits, and systems. If they do not teach Jesus' preexistence and that He became truly a man, they are not Christian.

c) How did the unique Son of God become a man?

Isaiah 7:14 Seven hundred years before Jesus was born, it was prophesied that He would be born of a virgin. See Matthew 1:23. The Greek word used in Matthew can only mean "virgin" in its normal sense of the word.

Galatians 4:4 Notice that Paul says that Christ was born of a woman. In this important verse, dealing with the incarnation, no father is mentioned, and this would have been against Jewish usage if he had had a father.

Genesis 3:15 In this first promise of the coming Savior, the seed of the woman is mentioned. No father is mentioned.

Luke 1:27-38 It is interesting that Luke was a doctor, and that he gives the most detail about the virgin birth of Christ. Note verse 34.

Matthew 1:18-25 Joseph had the most to lose if Jesus was not virgin-born. But he was convinced that Mary had not been unfaithful, that the child to be born to Mary would have no human father, and that God alone was the child's father. The fact that Joseph was convinced after his original suspicion of Mary is strong testimony of the virgin birth.

Thus, concerning the person of Christ the mediator, He has always been God. Ever since He was born to Mary in the virgin birth, the incarnation, He has been one person with two natures. He is truly God and truly man forever.

This is the one who is our mediator. There is no other.

8. Christ the Mediator—His Work: Prophet

When we think of the work of Christ as mediator, we usually think of His death. This is especially true in our day because many people who have departed from the teaching of the Bible put all their emphasis on the moral facets of Christianity. Therefore, we in reaction are apt to speak only of the death of Christ. However, the Bible teaches us that there are three parts to Christ's work.

First, Christ is a prophet. A prophet is one who reveals the things of God to men. It is the giving of true knowledge, propositional knowledge.

Luke 13:33 Christ here says that He is a prophet.

Deuteronomy 18:15, 18 The Old Testament said the coming Messiah would be a prophet. Compare this passage with Acts 3:22, 23, which states that Christ fulfilled this.

John 1:18   However, Christ is not just *a* prophet. He is a *unique* prophet. He is the person of the Godhead who reveals the triune God to man.

John 1:1, 2   Here Christ is called the Word (see verses 14, 15). This signifies the fact that He is the one who reveals truth to men. Verses 14 and 15 make clear that "the Word" is Jesus Christ.

Colossians 2:9   While on the earth, Christ revealed the triune God to men. By considering Christ, we can learn about the character of God, and Christ taught men facts concerning the past, present, and future by His spoken words.

1 John 5:20   Christ came in the incarnation to give us true knowledge.

John 14:26; 16:12-14   Here Christ promises that after His death, resurrection, and ascension He will still continue to give knowledge to men through the Holy Spirit who will be coming.

9. Christ the Mediator—His Work: Priest

Since man has fallen into sin, he needs more than knowledge. He also needs holiness and righteousness. Thus, Christ not only acts as a prophet, in giving us knowledge, but also acts as a priest. As priest, He removes the guilt of sin from us and provides for us true holiness and righteousness.

Psalm 110:4   This Old Testament prophecy predicted that when the Messiah came, He would do a priestly work.

Mark 10:45   Christ came to die. This was His great priestly work.

John 1:29   John called Christ the Lamb of God, thus signifying that Christ would die to take away the guilt which is ours because of sin. By the term "Lamb of God," John also showed that the Old Testament sacrificial system was a type or illustration of the work Christ would do for us in a complete and final way by His death. That death was the act which the Old Testament sacrifices had foreshadowed.

1 Corinthians 5:7   Christ is here called our Passover lamb, and He died for us. The Passover lamb of Exodus 12 was a type or illustration of the work which Christ would do for those who believe on Him.

Ephesians 5:2   This verse says specifically that Christ gave Himself in His death as an offering and a sacrifice.

Hebrews 3:1   The book of Hebrews gives more detail on the priestly work of Christ than any other biblical writing. This verse says Christ is our High Priest.

Hebrews 4:14; 6:20 Christ is our High Priest not only when He was on earth, but now and forever.

Hebrews 5:5, 6 As a priest, Christ fulfilled the prophecy of Psalm 110:4.

Hebrews 7:26, 27 Christ's high-priestly work is different in three ways from that of the Old Testament priests:

(1) He is perfectly sinless.

(2) He made a sacrifice that will never need to be repeated.

(3) The sacrifice He offered was Himself.

Hebrews 8:1 Since His ascension Christ, our high priest, is on the right hand of God the Father.

Hebrews 9:11-15 Again the Scriptures emphasize that the sacrifice was Christ Himself, and that when the sacrifice was once made, it never needed to be repeated. Being God, Christ's sacrifice (His death) had infinite value.

Hebrews 9:25-28 Again it is emphasized that Christ's sacrifice was once for all. Just as men die only once, just as certainly there cannot be (and does not need to be) any repetition of Christ's sacrifice.

Hebrews 10:11-14 The sacrifice was once for all. Because of who Christ the high priest is, a single offering (His once-for-all death for us) is enough.

Hebrews 10:19-22 Once we have accepted Christ as our Savior, we can have confidence in the presence of the holy God.

1 Peter 3:18 In the Greek the word used clearly means "once for all." So Peter is saying that Christ's sacrifice cannot, and need not, be repeated. From this and preceding verses we have considered, it is clear that Christ as our priest gave Himself as the sacrifice upon Calvary's cross at a point of space-time history, so that He might once for all bear the punishment which we deserve because of the guilt of our sin.

1 John 4:10 Christ's work is substitutionary, the expiation of our sins—it is an atoning sacrifice. In other words, He took the punishment rightly due to us because of our sin.

1 John 2:1 After we accept Christ as our Savior, we should strive not to sin. But if we sin, Christ is on the right hand of God the Father as our advocate. Christ's sacrifice on the cross was complete; but He now continues his high-priestly work by interceding for us in Heaven. Remember Hebrews 4:14; 6:20.

Hebrews 9:24   Christ is in Heaven, in the presence of the Father, for us.

Hebrews 7:25   Christ's sacrifice being perfect, He continues his priestly work and is able to save us completely and forever.

John 17:9   This is the high-priestly prayer of Christ which He prayed shortly before His death. In this verse we see that Christ does not intercede for everyone. He prays for those who, by God's grace, have accepted Him as their Savior.

John 17:20   Christ interceded at that time, and does so now in Heaven. He intercedes for all who have believed on Him on the basis of the testimony of those who were firsthand witnesses. This testimony is given in the New Testament in connection with the Old.

Romans 8:34   Once we have accepted Christ as our Savior, neither Satan nor man can successfully condemn us, because Christ died for us and now intercedes for us.

Christ's intercession in Heaven is based upon the substitutionary atonement which He wrought for us when He died upon the cross. His intercession for us can never fail, because in His death He merits all He asks on our behalf. Christ is our priest; we need no other.

10. Christ the Mediator—His Work: King

Genesis 49:10   Here we have the first promise that the coming Messiah will be a king.

2 Samuel 7:16   (with *Matthew 1:1; 22:42*) Here the Lord tells David that the coming Messiah will come from among his descendants. Thus the Messiah will be of the kingly line.

Psalm 2:6   Again we see the Messiah as king.

Isaiah 9:6, 7   We usually use this as one of the Christmas verses. But notice that it says specifically that the Messiah will be of the line of David; He will be a king.

Micah 5:2   This verse reaffirms the same point, that the Messiah will be a ruler.

Luke 1:31-33   The angel makes the promise to Mary that the child which will be born to her will be a Savior (His name will be "Jesus"). He will be the Son of the Most High, and on His human side He will be of the family of David. He will be a king.

Matthew 2:2   When the wise men came, they were looking for the King of the Jews. Verse 6 connects this with Micah 5:2.

John 1:49 Nathanael realized that Christ was the Messiah, the King of the Jews.

Luke 19:37, 38 On Palm Sunday, the Sunday before Christ's crucifixion, for one short moment Jesus was proclaimed as king. Verse 40 shows that Christ accepted this.

John 18:37 Christ here acknowledges before Pilate that He is king.

John 19:2, 3, 12, 14, 15, 19, 21, 22 When the people were mocking Jesus, they did it in such a way that they made fun of His kingship. Verse 12 seems to indicate that if He had rejected this claim, the case against Him would have collapsed.

Acts 17:7 After His death and resurrection, Jesus' followers still taught that Jesus was king.

Christ is king in three ways:

a) Christ is head over all things now.

Matthew 28:18 Right now all power is given to Christ in Heaven and earth.

Ephesians 1:20-22 Today Christ, on the right hand of God the Father, is head over all things for the Church.

b) The second coming of Christ.

Hebrews 2:8 There will come a time when Christ will rule in a way that He does not rule now. See also 1 Corinthians 15:24, 25.

Acts 1:6, 7 Just before Christ's ascension, He was asked when He would establish His kingdom upon the earth. He did not say He never would do so, but that the time was not yet come.

1 Timothy 6:14, 15 When Christ comes back again, He will then be King of kings and Lord of lords in a new way.

Matthew 25:31-34 When Christ returns, He will judge as king.

Revelation 17:14; 19:16 Again we see Christ, when He returns as King of kings and Lord of lords. The Bible tells us that at that time every knee shall bow before Him (Philippians 2:10, 11). This does not mean that every knee will wish to bow before Him, but will bow of necessity, even if the individual sinful heart is still in rebellion against Him.

c) Christ, the king of our lives.

Colossians 1:13 When we accept Christ as our Savior, we step from the power of darkness into the kingdom of Christ. Thus, we who have received Christ are in His kingdom now.

Ephesians 5:23, 24 Christ is now head of the Church, which is made up of all who have accepted Him as Savior. Once we have done this, we are to obey Him.

Luke 19:11-27 In this whole passage, Christ teaches us that after we have accepted Him as our Savior, we, as now His servants, are responsible for serving Him and will be held accountable for the way we do serve Him. If we serve Him well, He will then say to us, "Well done, my good servant." Verses 14 and 27 contrast the servants with the citizens, "the subjects." As Creator, everyone is His rightful subject, but there are those who are still in rebellion against Him.

When we have taken Jesus as our Savior, He should be the king and Lord of our lives now.

The story is told that when Queen Victoria was a young girl, she was present at a concert where Handel's *Messiah* was played. Everyone stood when the music rang out, "King of kings, Lord of lords." When Victoria also rose, others who were with her restrained her, saying she should not stand, because she was queen. Victoria answered, "I am Queen of England, but Christ is my King of kings and Lord of lords." After we have accepted Christ as our Savior, then He should in reality be our king, just as He is our prophet and priest.

11. Christ's Humiliation and Exaltation

When we consider Christ's work as a whole, we find that it presents two aspects: His humiliation and His exaltation.

a) *Christ's humiliation.*

John 17:5 Here Christ speaks of the glory which He had had with God from before the creation of the world.

Philippians 2:6, 7 When Christ came into the world, He humbled Himself, so that the Creator of all the universe became the servant.

John 1:14 The Creator (verse 3) took upon Himself the form of a man. He "became flesh."

Luke 2:7 When Christ was born, He was not born of a great human family, but to a very poor one. When He was born, there was not even a home to shelter Him or a room in the public inn; He was born in a stable.

John 7:52 Christ did not even come from a respected portion of the country, but from Galilee, which was looked down upon by the Jews.

Mark 6:3 His family was not one of the great ones of the

community. Joseph, the husband of Mary, was a carpenter, and Jesus followed his trade.

Galatians 4:4 The great Lawgiver placed Himself under the law.

Philippians 2:8 The one who Himself deserved obedience from all creation became obedient.

Galatians 3:13 The righteous Judge of all the universe placed Himself under the curse of the law. He identified Himself with sinful mankind.

Matthew 4:1-11; Hebrews 4:15 The Holy One allowed Himself to suffer every temptation that mankind can know. Consider what pain it must have been for Him to be daily buffeted by the sin that permeates the world in which we live.

John 1:11 The Jews, who were His ancient people, rejected Him.

John 7:3-5 His own half-brothers—i.e., the natural children born to Mary and Joseph after Jesus' birth—rejected Him until after His death and resurrection.

Matthew 27:46 As He hung upon the cross, having taken upon Himself the sin of those who would trust Him as Savior, God the Father turned from Him. His physical sufferings were great, but were not the greatest part of His suffering.

Luke 22:47, 48 Judas, one of His friends, betrayed Him with a kiss.

Matthew 26:56 All His disciples forsook Him in His hour of need.

Matthew 27:11-50 Consider the various forms of humiliation and agony heaped upon Jesus in these hours. Remember that this is God who allowed Himself to be so treated.

2 Corinthians 5:21 The eternally Holy One died as sin for us.

1 Peter 3:18, 19 Like natural man, His spirit and body were unnaturally torn asunder when He died. His body rested in the grave. His soul descended into Hades.

b) *Christ's exaltation.*

Acts 2:25-31 At this point comes a great change. Through Christ's humiliation, His steps have been downward all the way. Now comes the increasing glory. First, while His body lay in the grave, it did not see corruption.

Luke 24:36-43 The human body and the human soul of Christ are reunited. It was not just Christ's spirit which rose from the dead. It was the complete man, with body and spirit reunited.

John 20:25-28   Christ's resurrected body was the same body which the disciples had known before His death. Thomas's conquered skepticism is one proof of the physical resurrection of Christ—of the fact that the body which came out of the garden tomb was the one that had been placed in it.

Acts 1:3   Jesus, with His resurrection body, was seen from time to time over a forty-day period. This is spoken of here as convincing proof.

Acts 1:9-11   After Jesus had showed Himself upon the earth for many days after His resurrection, He was taken up into Heaven. He went from one place, earth, to another, Heaven. His baptism began His public ministry (Matthew 3:13-17). His ascension showed it to be terminated.

John 14:2, 3   In this place called Heaven, Christ is now preparing a place for us.

Acts 2:32, 33   The exaltation of the Lord Jesus Christ continues.

Ephesians 1:20-22   The One who was spat upon and humiliated before the eyes of sinful men is now head over all things.

Revelation 19:9-16   When Christ comes back again to the earth, Gentile and Jew alike will know that the One they humiliated and crucified is what He claimed to be: the Old Testament-prophesied Messiah, the only Savior of men, King of kings, Lord of lords, and indeed truly God.

CHAPTER THREE

Salvation

12. Salvation—How?

With this study we begin a completely new topic. We've already looked at "God," and "God's Dealing with Man." This third topic is "Salvation," how it is received and what it includes.

How do we obtain salvation? The Bible's answer, as we have already partially seen in our study of God's grace, is that salvation is obtained by faith in Christ, plus nothing.

John 3:15, 16, 18 We have used these verses a number of times, but they are worth looking at again to see how clearly Christ says that salvation is received by faith in Him, plus nothing.

John 3:36 John the Baptist emphasizes that salvation is through faith plus nothing.

Romans 3:9-20 By the deeds of the law—that is, by good works—no man is or can be just in the sight of God.

Isaiah 64:6 Even our best works are not good enough in the sight of the holy God. Even when the outward acts are good, who can completely untangle all the mixed and complex motives which move us?

Galatians 3:24 God never gave the law (the Ten Commandments, the Sermon on the Mount, or any other commands) as though salvation would come through the keeping of it. As far as salvation goes, each of God's laws shows us that we need Christ.

Romans 2:1-3 Men do not even keep their own made-up norms, by which they judge others.

Acts 16:30-33 Just as moral good works cannot save us, so also religious good works cannot save us. Baptism is a sign of salvation, not the basis for it.

Romans 4:9-11 It was the same in the Old Testament. Abraham put his faith in God. Circumcision came later. Religious good works cannot save.

Romans 9:6 Not all the Old Testament Jews were true spiritual Israel. Neither today will church membership in itself save. Salvation is indeed ours only on the basis of faith in Christ, plus nothing.

Romans 9:30-33 Those Jews who were not true spiritual Israel were those who tried to come to God on the basis of their religious and moral "good works" instead of by faith.

Galatians 2:16 Salvation is never on the basis of any kind of good works.

Romans 3:21-26 Good works cannot save us, but faith in Christ will. The word "freely" in verse 24 means *"gratis."* There is no cost to us.

John 8:24 There is only one way of salvation. If we do not accept Christ as our Savior, we remain under the judgment of God.

John 14:6 There are not many ways of salvation. There is only one way to come to God the Father. There is no way to come to God the Father except through Christ.

Acts 4:12 It is faith in Christ or nothing.

As you finish looking up these verses, I urge you to consider Christ's invitation: "Whoever comes to me I will never drive away" (John 6:37). *The basis* is the finished, substitutionary death of Christ. *The instrument* by which we accept the free gift is faith. Faith has a double significance: it is believing God's promises, and it is the empty hand which accepts the gift without trying to add humanistic religious or moral good works to it.

13. Justification

Romans 1:16 As the word "salvation" is used here and throughout the New Testament, it has a much wider meaning than is usually given to it today. Today it is often limited to becoming a Christian. The scriptural use of the term includes all those things in the past, present, and future which will come to the man or woman who has accepted Christ as his or her Savior. In this lesson, we will consider the first of these things—that is, justification.

Romans 3:20 We cannot be justified on the basis of our good works.

James 2:10 In order to be justified before God on the basis of our good works, we would have to be perfect, without one sinful act or sinful thought from our birth to our death. The word "gospel" means "good news." Telling a person to be good is not good news. For example, if a person were in jail for some crime and someone rushed up to him and shouted, "Good news!" the person looking through the bars would expect word of possible liberation. If the friend's message were instead, "Be good," it would be foolish and cruel. So it is if we would say, "Be good" to the man already bound by sin and marked with its guilt.

Romans 4:1-9, 22-25 Justification is the declaration on God's part that we are just in His sight because He has imputed to us the obedience of Christ. This means that God charges our sins to Christ's account. It is not an infused righteousness within us. He attributes to us the obedience of Christ. Christ's obedience has two aspects: His death to take away our true moral guilt; and His perfect keeping of the law of God on our behalf.

It is as if a little child enters a store and buys more than he can pay for. Then the parent arrives and says, "Charge that to my account." The child's debt is erased. The parent pays. When we are justified, God charges the punishment due to the guilt of our sin to the account of Christ.

Romans 5:1 Once we are declared just by God, there is peace between God and us.

Colossians 2:13, 14 It is not that God overlooks our sins. God cannot do this, for He is holy. It is that our sins have actually been punished in the sufferings of Christ upon the cross.

Isaiah 38:17; 43:25; Micah 7:19 When we have been declared just by God, it is as though God has dropped the guilt of our sins into the deepest sea. The justification is not merely a pardon, but, as has been said, once we have been justified, it is "just as though we have never sinned."

Isaiah 53:4,5 The ground for our justification is the perfect work of Christ on Calvary.

Romans 5:8, 9   This is the wonder of the love of God—that while we were sinners, Christ died for us. Because Christ has died for us (Romans 3:26), God can be just and yet declare our sins forgiven.

Acts 13:38, 39   The instrument by which we lay hold of this great gift of God is faith in Jesus Christ.

Romans 3:28   Justification is by faith, plus nothing.

Galatians 2:16   There is only one way to be justified before the holy God, and that is by faith in Christ.

What is faith in Christ? A missionary when seeking a native word for *faith* could not find it. Finally, he sat in a chair and raised his feet from the ground, putting his full weight on the chair and bearing none of his weight himself. He then asked what word described his fact, and used that word for faith. This is an accurate picture.

Faith in Christ is resting totally on Him and His finished work.

14. The New Relationship: Adoption

When we accept Christ as our Savior, we are immediately justified. Another aspect of the salvation which is immediately ours is a new relationship—adoption by God the Father.

John 1:12   When we accept Christ as our Savior, we become the children of God. This indicates that we are not God's children until we do accept Christ. Before we accept Christ as our Savior, we are separated from God by our moral guilt. God made us all, but we are the children of God only as we come through Jesus Christ.

2 Corinthians 6:18   In most Bible verses men and women together are spoken of as "the sons of God." But here we have a very significant passage where God speaks of the women who come to him through Christ as "his daughters."

John 20:17   Christ is very careful to make a clear distinction between His unique and eternal Sonship and our becoming the children of God.

Galatians 4:4, 5   Christ is the eternal Son of God. He is unique. He is the only begotten Son. But when we take Christ as our Savior, we receive the adoption of sons. These verses say that on the basis of Christ's finished work, we receive the full rights of sons.

Ephesians 1:3-5   Once we have taken Christ as our Savior and so are God the Father's children, we may come into His presence with all boldness. As the child of a king may come into the king's presence as his child, so we may come into the presence of Almighty God, the Creator. We may rightfully say to Him, "Thou art our Father," and He says to us, "You are My children."

1 John 3:1   This is the consummation of God's love, that when we accept Christ as our Savior we are the sons of God.

Matthew 6:32   When I am a child of God, He is concerned about my material needs.

Romans 8:15   When God is our Father, we may call Him "Abba"—i.e. "Daddy," or "Papa."

Romans 8:17   When God is our Father, we are joint-heirs with Christ. Think what this means. The riches of Heaven are ours, not only after death but in this life as well.

Galatians 4:6, 7   As soon as God becomes our Father, these blessings are ours, including the indwelling of the Holy Spirit. As sons of God, these blessings are ours in the present life.

Hebrews 12:5-11   Once God has become our Father, many blessings are ours, and among them is this: as a human father who deeply loves his child chastens his child when he is naughty, so God our Father brings things into our lives to keep us close to Himself. After we have taken Christ as our Savior, and God is our Father, our sins have been all punished on Calvary. But the Father at times allows hard things to come into our lives when we wander away from Him, so our lives may experience "the peaceable fruit of righteousness," which is not only righteousness but peace.

15. The New Relationship: Identified and United with God the Son

After we have put our faith in Christ, we enter a second new relationship—we are identified and united with Christ.

Romans 8:1   After we have accepted Christ as Savior, we are in Christ.

1 Corinthians 6:17   We are joined to, united with, Christ.

Galatians 2:20   Christ lives in me.

Ephesians 1:3   We are in Christ.

Ephesians 1:6, 7; 2:1-6, 13   These verses all restate this glorious truth—we are in Christ. See also Colossians 2:10.

Christ is the *Bridegroom;* we are the *bride.*

Matthew 22:2-14; 25:10   Our union with Christ is like a marriage. Christ is the Bridegroom.

Romans 7:4   When we accept Christ as Savior, we are married to Christ. As natural marriage brings forth children, so our union with Christ should produce fruit for God.

2 Corinthians 11:2   A bride who loves her husband has her mind only on him and is faithful to him. So we should have our minds fixed on Christ and be faithful to Him.

Ephesians 5:31, 32   Marriage is a picture of the believer's union with Christ.

Revelation 19:7-9   At the second coming of Christ, there will be a great event known as "the marriage supper of the Lamb (Christ)."

Revelation 22:17   The bride, those who have taken Christ as Savior, should be busy inviting others to partake in this high privilege and honor. As a bride talks very naturally about her beloved, so our conversation should be much about Christ.

Christ is the *vine;* we are the *branches.*

John 15:1-5   The life of the vine flows into the branches to bring forth fruit. In the same way, those who have accepted Christ as Savior have a vital union with Christ. If we "abide" in him moment by moment, His life flows into us to bring forth spiritual fruit.

Christ is the *Head;* the Church (those who have received Christ as Savior) is the *body.*

Romans 12:5   As the body has many parts, yet is one body, so we who have accepted Christ as Savior are many, yet we are one body, the Church, the body of Christ.

1 Corinthians 12:11-27   As the body's health depends on the condition of all its parts, so it is important for all the Christians to be in good spiritual condition. As the body is subject to the direction of the head, so we should constantly do the bidding of Christ.

Ephesians 1:22, 23; 4:15, 16; 5:30; Colossians 1:18   The Church (all who have accepted Christ as Savior) is Christ's body.

Christ is the *foundation;* we are the *spiritual house* built on it.
1 Peter 2:2-6   We are living stones.

The only begotten Son of God is called our brother, as we become the adopted children of God.
Hebrews 2:16-18   As the natural son of a household is the

brother of the adopted child, so Christ is our wonderful Elder Brother when we take Him as our Savior. As our Elder Brother, He understands us in all the portions of our lives.

In our studies of Christ as mediator we have seen that when we take Christ as our Savior, God the Son is our prophet, priest, and king. Christ is our prophet, and in fellowship with Him the believer is a prophet.

John 16:13; 1 John 2:27 Through Christ we have true knowledge, knowledge that we should give to a dying world which is in confusion, intellectually lost in unrelatedness. God has given us the Bible to give us true knowledge, and it is our calling to give this true knowledge to others.

Christ is our priest, and in fellowship with Him every believer is a priest.

1 Peter 2:5, 9; Revelation 1:6; 5:10; 20:6 Every believer has the privilege of coming immediately into the presence of God in prayer. We should diligently avail ourselves of this privilege, including prayer for the non-Christians about us. We should seek to lead those who do not know Christ as Savior to Him, the great High Priest.

Romans 12:1, 2 Every believer has the privilege of offering himself to God as a living sacrifice.

Christ is our king, and with Him the believer is a king.

1 Peter 2:9; Revelation 1:6; 3:21; 5:10; 20:6 We are a *royal* priesthood. We are to praise God now, and we shall reign with Christ on the earth when Christ comes back again.

It is by being united with Christ that we can bring forth fruit in all the phases of our lives.

John 15:5 Abiding in Christ is the secret of fruitbearing.

2 Corinthians 12:9 It is not our strength, but the strength of Christ in the midst of our weakness.

Ephesians 2:10 After becoming united with Christ, we should bring forth good works.

Philippians 1:11 The fruit we should bring forth after we are Christians must be by Christ working in and through us.

Colossians 2:10 We have all we need in Christ, for this life as well as for eternity.

16. The New Relationship: God the Holy Spirit Indwells the Christian

When we accept Christ as Savior we have a third new relationship—God the Holy Spirit dwells within us.

Joel 2:28, 29   The Old Testament prophesied this.

John 14:16, 17; 7:38, 39; 16:7; Acts 1:5   Christ promised this.

Matthew 3:11   John the Baptist so spoke concerning Christ.

Acts 2:1-18   The promise and prophecy were fulfilled after Christ had died, had risen, and had ascended into Heaven.

Romans 8:9   There is no such thing as a person who has accepted Christ as Savior who is not at once indwelt by the Holy Spirit.

1 Corinthians 3:16   The Holy Spirit dwells in all who have received Christ.

1 Corinthians 6:19   The body of the believer is the temple of the Holy Spirit. The temple in Jerusalem was destroyed a few years after this was written. Believers' bodies are now God's temple.

2 Timothy 1:14   The Holy Spirit lives in the Christian.

Here are some examples of the Holy Spirit's activity:

John 16:8   The Spirit reproves the world of sin. Because the Christian is indwelt by the Holy Spirit, his life should reprove the world of sin.

John 3:5, 6   Regeneration is the Spirit's work.

John 15:26; 16:14; Acts 5:32   He bears witness to Christ, not to Himself.

1 Corinthians 12:4, 13; Ephesians 2:22   He builds the Church (those who are real Christians) into a well-balanced whole.

2 Corinthians 13:14   The indwelling Spirit deals with the Christian. He communicates to the believer the benefits of redemption.

John 14:16-18; Romans 8:9-11   When the Holy Spirit dwells in us, Christ dwells in us.

John 14:23   When the Holy Spirit dwells in us, both the Father and the Son come to us, make their home with us. The indwelling Holy Spirit is the agent of the whole Trinity as He indwells us.

John 14:26; 15:26; 16:7; Acts 9:31   The indwelling Holy Spirit is the Christian's counselor. The Greek word translated "counselor" is a hard word to translate. It can also be comforter, advocate, protector, supporter. It means "one called to one's side to help."

John 14:26; 16:13; 1 Corinthians 2:12, 13; Hebrews 10:15, 16;

1 John 2:20, 27   The indwelling Spirit is our teacher, especially in opening our minds to understand the Bible.

Acts 1:8   He is the Christian's source of power.

Luke 12:11, 12   He gives the believer the right words in time of persecution.

Romans 5:5; 14:17; 15:13; 1 Thessalonians 1:6; Galatians 5:22, 23   The indwelling Spirit gives the Christian graces of love, joy, peace, hope, longsuffering, etc. As *all* Christians are indwelt by the Spirit, the fruit of the Spirit is to have meaning for *all* Christians.

> The great distinction of a true Christian is the indwelling of the Holy Spirit. How careful should he be, lest anything in his thoughts or feelings would be offensive to this divine guest!
>
> Dr. Charles Hodge

This new relationship with the triune God is, then, the second of the blessings of salvation, justification being the first. This new relationship, as we have seen, is threefold:

(1) God the Father is the Christian's Father.

(2) The only begotten Son of God is our Savior and Lord, our prophet, priest, and king. We are identified and united with Him.

(3) The Holy Spirit lives in us and deals with us. He communicates to us the manifold benefits of redemption.

17. The New Relationship: The Brotherhood of Believers

We have seen that when we take Christ as Savior we are immediately justified, and we immediately have a new relationship with God the Father, God the Son, and God the Holy Spirit.

When we come into this new relationship with the triune God, all those who have ever trusted Christ as their Savior are our brothers and sisters. This has been usually spoken of as "the communion of saints."

Matthew 23:8   Not all men are brothers, according to the biblical use of that word. We are all created by God. As all are descendants of Adam and Eve, all men are "my kind" and are to be carefully treated as neighbors (Luke 10:27-37). But in the terms of the Bible, we are brothers to those who have Christ as their Savior and therefore have God as their father.

Galatians 6:10   We are to do good to *all* men, but there is a clear line between the "family of believers" and others.

Ephesians 2:19   Before we took Christ as our Savior, we were strangers and foreigners. But when we became Christians, we were made fellow-citizens and members of God's household with all others who had done the same.

1 Thessalonians 5:14, 15   Again we are told to do good to all people, but again it is made clear that there is a distinction between those who are the "family of believers" and others.

1 Peter 2:17   We have a special relationship to those who are brothers in Christ.

1 John 1:3   A person cannot have true spiritual fellowship with Christians until he has heard the facts of the gospel and has acted upon those facts by accepting Christ as his Savior.

Revelation 19:10   The brethren are defined as those who hold to the testimony of Jesus.

John 13:30, 34, 35   Judas, who did not believe on Christ, had left the table before this command for special love among Christians was given.

John 21:23   It is clear that "brethren" as used here speaks of believers.

Acts 9:17   Saul was considered a "brother" only after he had taken Christ as his Savior.

Acts 21:17   Only the fellow-believers were "the brothers."

1 Corinthians 7:12   In this passage the man is a believer and therefore a brother. The wife is not a believer and therefore is not included in this term.

There are three practical aspects of the brotherhood of believers. The first practical aspect is that brothers in Christ should be a *spiritual help* to each other.

Romans 12:10   Christians should love one another and should desire the advancement of their brothers above their own advancement.

1 Corinthians 12:26, 27   Christians should sorrow when other Christians suffer, and should rejoice when other Christians have joy.

Romans 15:30; 2 Corinthians 1:11   Christian brothers are to pray for each other.

Ephesians 4:15, 16   When individual Christians become what they should be, the Church becomes what it should be. Each Christian has something to contribute to this.

Ephesians 5:21—6:9 The brotherhood of believers should be the predominant factor between Christians in all the relationships of life. This is true of husbands and wives, children and parents, servants and masters, employees and employers. In all such relationships we are also brothers and sisters. See Song of Solomon 4:9, 10, 12—there is a double relationship of sister and bride.

Ephesians 6:18 Christians should pray for each other and for all Christians. The brotherhood of believers cuts across the lines of nationality, race, language, culture, social position, and geographical location.

1 Thessalonians 5:11 The two great spiritual helps which brothers in Christ should be to each other are that of encouraging one another and edifying one another. The latter means helping other Christians to be what they should be in doctrine and life.

The second practical aspect is that brothers in Christ should be a *material help* to each other.

Acts 11:29 From the earliest days of the Church, Christians gave of their material goods to help those brothers in Christ who had less materially, even those at great geographical distance.

2 Corinthians 8:4 This is one illustration of many examples given in the New Testament of Christians giving money to help other Christians in material need.

Romans 12:13; Titus 1:8; Philemon 5, 7, 22 One form of practical help is by giving hospitality.

1 John 3:17, 18 There is no use talking about Christian love if we do not help our brothers in Christ when they have material needs.

Acts 5:4 The Christians helped each other materially, but they did it voluntarily. Each man kept the right of personal property and possession.

The third aspect is that brothers in Christ should enjoy the *fellowship and companionship* of each other.

Acts 2:42, 46 From the earliest days of the Church, the Christians had daily fellowship with each other.

Ephesians 4:1-3; Colossians 2:1, 2 True Christians should try to have fellowship together in love and peace.

Hebrews 10:25 It is the direct command of our Lord that after we have become Christians, we should meet together for worship with other Christians. This was not just to be a passing thing in the early days of the Church, but should continue even until Christ comes back again. This verse says we should be especially careful to keep this command as we come toward the time of the second coming of Christ. If we have accepted Christ as our Savior, we have the responsibility to search out a Bible-believing group of God's people, where there is right doctrine and real community in love, and meet with them. We should not join ourselves to just any group that calls itself Christian, but one where the teaching is truly biblical, where discipline is maintained concerning life and doctrine, and where there is true community. If there is *no* such group geographically available (and there are such places), then prayerfully before the Lord we should find even a small number to meet for worship, prayer, study, encouraging one another, and to have community.

We have seen that the brotherhood of believers crosses all the lines of space. It also crosses all the lines of time.

Hebrews 12:22, 23   This brotherhood includes not just Christians on the earth today, but Christians who are in Heaven.

18. Never Lost Again

We have seen that salvation immediately includes justification and new relationship. Now we come to a third consideration: once we accept Christ as Savior, we will never be lost again.

Romans 8:31-34   We will never be lost again, because of the perfection of Christ's priestly work for us. The ground of our salvation is not our good works in the past, present, or future, but the perfect work of Christ. Christ's perfect priestly work includes two things: His perfect death and His perfect intercession for us now.

Hebrews 7:25   This one passage reminds us of everything we studied under Christ's work as priest, including His present intercession for us. You will remember that this verse teaches that the Lord saves us both completely and forever. The Christian could be lost again only if Christ failed as a priest.

Romans 8:28-30; Ephesians 1:3-7   After becoming Christians by accepting Christ, we learn that God the Father has chosen us. The

Christian could be lost again only if the first person of the Trinity, the Father, failed.

Ephesians 1:13, 14 In days gone by when a man bought some land, he was given a handful of earth (an earnest or seal) to signify that all the land was his. The fact that the Holy Spirit now lives in us is a deposit guaranteeing that one day we will have all the benefits of salvation. We will not be lost again.

Ephesians 4:30 In past centuries a king would seal a document with wax and then mark the wax with his ring. No man then dared to break this seal except under the authority of the king. This passage says that God Himself has sealed us with the indwelling Holy Spirit unto the day of redemption—that is, until the day in which Christ will return and we will receive all the benefits of redemption. A rebel might break a human king's seal, but nothing which God has created can break the seal of God.

Romans 8:26 When we do not know how to pray for ourselves as we should, the indwelling Spirit prays for us. The Christian could be lost again only if the Holy Spirit failed.

John 10:27-29 Christ says that when we accept Him as our Savior, we have eternal life. Eternal life could be no shorter than eternity. Christ says we shall never perish; "never" can only mean "never." Christ says that nothing can pluck us out of His hand or the Father's hand. It's not that we hold fast to God; He holds fast to us.

Romans 8:35-39 Here God says specifically that no created thing can separate us from Himself after we have come through Jesus Christ.

Philippians 1:6 "The day of Jesus Christ" is Christ's second coming, when we will receive the full benefits of salvation.

1 John 4:13; 5:13 Notice the use of the word "know." God wants us to have the assurance that we are His and will be forever.

2 Timothy 4:7, 8 Paul had this assurance.

Romans 8:15, 16 The assurance that we are God's children and that we will be His forever is one of the good things God means us to have after we have accepted Christ as Savior. Not all who are true Christians have this assurance; but if they do not, they have not taken advantage of one of the riches in Christ Jesus which it is their privilege to have now.

John 3:36 "Whoever puts his faith in the Son has eternal life." If you know that you have believed in Christ for your salvation and are not trusting in your own moral or religious works, then you have the express promise of God that you do have everlasting life, *now and forever*.

19. Sanctification (A)

We have seen that once we accept Christ as Savior, we are justified. We enter into a new relationship with each of the three persons of the Trinity. We will never be lost again. In this study we begin to consider another part of our salvation—sanctification. While justification deals with the past (once I have become a Christian), sanctification deals with the present. It has to do with the power of sin in the Christian's life. Justification is the same for all Christians, but obviously sanctification has proceeded further in some Christians than in others. For a book-length study of the subject of sanctification, see my book *True Spirituality*.

Romans 8:29, 30 Salvation is not a blank from the time we are justified until we reach Heaven. Rather, it is a flowing stream involving the past (when we became Christians), the present, and into the future. If we have truly taken Christ as our Savior, this has many implications for our present lives, including the fact that our lives should show that we are Christ's.

Colossians 3:1-3 Once we have accepted Christ as personal Savior, it should make a difference in the lives we live.

John 15:1-5 If a man is truly a Christian, there should be some spiritual fruit in his life.

1 Thessalonians 5:23; Hebrews 13:20, 21 God the Father is active in our sanctification.

Ephesians 5:25, 26; Titus 2:11-14 So is God the Son.

1 Corinthians 6:11; 2 Corinthians 3:18; 2 Thessalonians 2:13 God the Holy Spirit is active in our sanctification.

Romans 12:1-19; 2 Corinthians 7:1; Colossians 3:1—4:6 These are just a few of the commands given in the Bible as to how we should walk in this life. As Christians, God's law is our rule of life. In such passages as these, God tells us what conforms to His character and what pleases Him. Being Christians should make a difference in every aspect of our lives.

1 Corinthians 6:20 We were saved by faith, not by good works. But after we are saved, we should show forth our gratitude in our lives by good works.

Matthew 22:37, 38; Revelation 2:1-5 The only proper basic motive for desiring to get over our sins and to grow spiritually is our love for God. Fear of getting caught, etc. will not do. We are to live a Christian life because we love the Lord and wish to glorify Him.

John 15:8   When a believer sins, he is not glorifying the heavenly Father as he should.

Philippians 1:20   When a believer sins, he is not showing forth the glory of Christ in this present life, as a reborn person should.

Romans 8:9; Galatians 5:16-25; Ephesians 5:18; 4:30; 1 Thessalonians 5:19   When a person accepts Christ as Savior, he is indwelt by the Holy Spirit immediately and from then on. But when a believer sins, he is walking after the flesh and not after the Spirit. He is grieving (making sad) the Holy Spirit who indwells him and putting out the Spirit's fire.

1 John 1:3, 7; 2:1   When a Christian sins, he does not lose his salvation. The blood of Christ is enough to cover the sin; and Christ, on the right hand of the Father, intercedes for the Christian. But a Christian does break his fellowship with God when he sins. If a child is disobedient, he does not cease being a child of his parent. But the joy of the child-parent relationship is gone. As long as our fellowship with our heavenly Father is broken because of sin, we cannot expect spiritual power or joy.

Hebrews 12:5-11   When a believer sins, God chastens him in this life, even as a loving human parent chastens his child. God does not do this to punish us, for our sins were punished once for all on Calvary, but to bring forth the peaceable fruit of righteousness in our lives. However, it is most important to remember that all the troubles of life are *not* the result of personal sin. For example, consider the trials of Job.

2 Corinthians 5:9, 10; 1 Corinthians 3:11-15; Luke 19:11-27   In the future life, the Christian will receive rewards, which will depend on the life now lived after he has become a Christian. In Luke notice the distinction between the Christians (servants), who receive rewards, and the non-Christians (subjects and enemies), who are put aside.

1 Corinthians 11:31, 32   When a Christian sins, his fellowship with God can be restored. The first thing necessary is to acknowledge that the thing which we have done is sin. As surely as God the Father is our Father, if we do not do this He will chasten us—not to punish us, but to bring us back to Himself.

1 John 1:9   After self-judgment, acknowledging his sin to be sin, the believer must confess his sin to God—not to a priest or any other man, but directly to God. He is our Father, and in prayer we can come into His presence at any time. We must bring the specific sin under the finished work of Christ. Then our fellowship with God is restored. After this confession, the matter is finished, unless I have injured other people by my sin. Then, of course, if I am repentant, I will desire to make restitution.

1 John 1:8   The process of sanctification goes on until death. By God's grace, the Christian always has new ground to win for Christ.

20. Sanctification (B)

Matthew 5:48   While we will always have new ground to gain for Christ in our lives, our standard for every moment must be no lower than God's command—that is, perfection.

Ephesians 4:12, 13; 2 Peter 3:18   While it is a comforting truth that when a Christian sins he can confess his sins and have his fellowship with God restored, yet our Christian lives should be something more than always sinning and confessing the same old sins.

Romans 6:1-19   If we have partaken of the benefit of Christ's death for justification, we should also be partakers of the power of His life, so that we should no longer serve sin—sin should not reign in us and through us. As we yield to Christ at this one moment, He will bring forth his fruit through us.

2 Corinthians 13:14   As seen in our studies of the "new relationship" we have with God, we have a personal relationship with each of the three members of the Trinity. Our relationship is never mechanical and not primarily legal. It is personal and vital. God the Father is my Father; I am united and identified with God the Son; God the Holy Spirit dwells within me. The Bible tells us that this threefold relationship is a present fact, just as it tells us that justification and Heaven are facts.

We have seen that once we are saved, we always are saved, but that some Christians do not have this confidence, simply because they have never realized what the Bible teaches concerning assurance or, knowing the facts, they have not rested on them.

It is also possible to be a Christian and yet not take advantage of what our vital relationship with the three persons of the Trinity should mean in living a Christian life. We must first intellectually realize the fact of our vital relationship with the triune God and then in faith begin to act upon that realization. At this point I would urge you to glance again over the three studies on our "new relationship" with the Father, Son, and Holy Spirit.

Ephesians 3:14-19; 2 Corinthians 12:9   It is not my weakness but the triune God's strength that counts.

1 John 5:3-5   The victory that overcomes the world is our faith. (It is not that the ground is our faith; in sanctification, as in justification, the only ground is the perfect, finished work of Christ.) The Bible tells us both the fact of justification and the fact of our present vital relationship with the Trinity. But mere intellectual acceptance is not enough in either case. Knowing the facts, we must rest upon them in faith. Justification is an *act;* I throw myself on Christ as Savior once, and God declares me justified forever. Sanctification is a *process* which begins when I take Christ as my Savior and continues until I die. Thus, for my daily walk as a Christian, I must by God's grace rest in faith upon my present vital relationship with the three persons of the Trinity for every moment of my life. In both justification and sanctification I must see that I cannot keep God's law in my own strength. Therefore for my justification I must have rested in faith in Christ as my Savior; in sanctification moment by moment I must throw myself upon the fact of my present vital relationship with Father, Son, and Holy Spirit. The Bible tells me that this vital relationship is a fact. Through faith I lay hold of this fact for this one moment, and all of life is only a succession of moments—one moment at a time. Thus, by God's grace, "his commands are not burdensome." And, by God's grace, I may have spiritual power and the Lord will be my song.

21. Sanctification (C)

1 Peter 2:2; John 17:17; Acts 17:11; Acts 20:32; Ephesians 5:26; 2 Timothy 2:15   There are four practices which help us greatly to grow spiritually. The first is the study of the Bible, which is the Word of God.

Philippians 4:6; 1 Thessalonians 5:17   The second is prayer. We should cultivate the habit of two types of prayer:
  (1) Special times of prayer: for example, morning and evening, grace at meals, and from time to time special days of prayer.
  (2) Praying constantly as we go about our daily tasks.

Acts 1:8   The third is witnessing for Christ. This command is to all Christians. You can do your part, you can be a "teller" no matter where the Lord places you in life.

Hebrews 10:24, 25; Acts 2:46, 47   The fourth is regular attendance at a Bible-believing church. As we saw under "The Brotherhood of Believers," this does not mean just any church or group, but one which is true to the Word of God—that has an orthodoxy of doctrine and an orthodoxy of love and community. To repeat what was said under "The Brotherhood of Believers": If there is *no* such group geographically available (and there are such places), prayerfully before the Lord we should find even a small number to meet for worship, study, prayer, encouraging one another and to have community.

In connection with our attendance at a Bible-believing church, we also have the privilege of partaking in the Lord's Supper.

It is wonderful to know that we are justified and that we will be in Heaven. But our present desire should be to glorify the triune God because we love the Father, because we love the Son, because we love the Holy Spirit.

22. Glorification at Death

As we have previously seen, our salvation includes things past, present, and future. If we have accepted Christ as Savior, justification (God's declaration that our guilt is covered) is past. Sanctification deals with the present. Glorification is that which comes to a Christian at death and afterwards.

2 Thessalonians 1:4-10   The Bible speaks here of that which all of us can observe in the world about us. It is obvious that the accounts of life are not balanced in this life. Christians are often persecuted, while wicked men seem to prosper. This passage of Scripture teaches that the very fact these inequalities take place in this life proves that in the future there will be a judgment by God, who is perfectly just. The books will be balanced.

John 3:36   When we accept Christ as our Savior, we are promised not a salvation which terminates with this life, but an everlasting, an eternal, salvation.

Ecclesiastes 12:7   Notice the clear distinction made here between the body and the soul at death. Physical death is the separation of soul and body.

Luke 23:39-43   When the Christian dies, the body goes into the grave, but the soul is immediately with Christ.

Acts 7:54-59   At the Christian's death the soul is immediately in Christ's presence.

2 Corinthians 5:6, 8   For the Christian, death is not something to fear. It brings us entrance into that which is better than we now possess. This does not change the fact that death is abnormal, caused by the Fall.

Luke 9:28-36   Moses died and was buried about 1,500 years before this event took place. But the disciples recognized him, even though they had never seen him and even though, as far as we know, his body was still in the grave. When we die, we can expect to know our loved ones and other Christians, even though their bodies are still in their graves.

23. Glorification at the Resurrection

Genesis 2:7   God made our bodies as well as our souls.

Genesis 3:1-20   Man's fall into sin involved the complete man, both body and soul. Because man sinned, three deaths came upon him. Spiritual death (separation from God) came immediately. Physical death is what we usually speak of as "death." Eternal death will come at the final judgment. When we take Christ as our Savior, the first and third of the above three deaths are finished for us. Our fellowship with God is restored, and our sins have been punished once for all on Calvary. The second death, the separation of soul and body at death, has yet to be dealt with.

Romans 8:23   We have the "first fruits of the Spirit," but there is still the last step to be realized—"the redemption of our bodies."

1 Corinthians 15:12-26   As Christ rose physically from the dead, so the bodies of Christians will also be raised physically. When this happens, our redemption, our salvation, will be complete. Just as God made the whole man and the whole man fell, so the whole man will be redeemed.

1 Corinthians 15:52-58; 1 Thessalonians 4:13, 14   The bodies of Christians who have died ("them who are asleep") will be raised from the dead when Christ comes back again.

1 Corinthians 15:51, 52; 1 Thessalonians 4:13-18   These verses show us that those Christians still alive when Christ comes back will not go through death. Their bodies will be changed in a twinkling of an eye—as fast as it takes to wink. They will pass immediately from this present life to full glorification.

Philippians 3:20, 21; 1 John 3:2   The glorified bodies of all Christians (whether they have died and have been raised again or have been changed in a twinkling of an eye) will be like Christ's body after His resurrection.

John 20:26   After His resurrection, Christ's body could pass through closed doors. After our glorification we will be able to do the same.

Luke 24:36-43   After His resurrection Christ could and did eat. After our glorification we will be able to do the same.

John 20:27, 28   The conclusion of each of the four Gospels and the beginning of Acts tell us what a wonderful body Christ had after His resurrection. But it is clear from verse 27 and others that this was not a new body that Christ had after His resurrection, but the same body which He had before His death and at His death. After our glorification, we will have the same bodies as we have now, but glorified. They will be changed bodies, glorified bodies, but the same bodies.

CHAPTER FOUR

Things of the Future

24. The External World and the People of God

In this series of Bible studies, we have considered three large
sections: "God," "God's Dealing with Man," and "Salvation."
Now we will finish with a short section of two studies on "Things
of the Future." Of course, what we have already studied of the
Christian's glorification at death and at the resurrection is also
future for us.

In this chapter we will look at the external world and the people
of God.

Luke 17:26-30; 18:8   The world is not going to get better and
better. The Christian's hope is not the gradual betterment of the
world, but that Christ is coming back again.

*Acts 1:10, 11; Mark 13:26; 1 Corinthians 15:23; Philippians 3:20,
21; 1 Thessalonians 1:10; 2:19; 3:13; 4:14, 16, 17; 2 Thessalonians
1:7; 1 Timothy 6:14; Titus 2:12, 13; 2 Peter 3:3-14; Revelation 1:7,
8*   The fact of Christ's coming again is clearly stated. History *is*
going someplace!

*Acts 1:6-9; Matthew 24:36; 25:13; Mark 13:32, 33; Luke 12:35-
40*   The time of Christ's return is not given. These verses teach us

to not set times, saying we know when He is coming. On the other hand, they tell us that Christ may come at any time. The Christian should be constantly awaiting Him. The command is to "watch."

1 Thessalonians 3:13; 4:13-17   True Christians, those who have put their faith in Christ as Savior, shall be caught up to meet Christ in the air and then come with Him. It is at this time that the bodies of Christians who have died will be raised from the dead and that living Christians will be glorified in a twinkling of an eye.

Matthew 24:36-44; Luke 17:26-30, 34-36; 21:36; Isaiah 26:19-21   Noah was out of danger in the ark before the flood came. Lot was safe before the destruction of Sodom began. It would seem that in the same way, true Christians will be taken out of danger before God's wrath is poured out upon the earth. Some Christians will be sleeping when they are taken, some will be awake. But all true Christians will be taken. The unsaved will be left.

Matthew 25:1-13   In this parable the Lord shows that not even all of those who are church members will be taken. Church members who have not put their personal faith in Christ as their Savior will be left.

2 Thessalonians 2:1-12; Revelation 13:1-18   Before Christ's coming visibly and in glory with His saints, there will be a period of great apostasy with a dictator, called the "Antichrist," ruling the world. He is completely opposite and opposed to Christ, completely subservient to Satan, the "dragon." He will control governmental and economic life and will be worshiped as God.

Revelation 6:1-17; 8:7—9:21; 11:13, 14; 15:1   God's wrath is poured out upon the earth during this period.

Revelation 16:13-16; 19:11-21   Here Christ comes visibly and in glory. He overthrows the assembled might of the world organized against Him by the Antichrist and Satan. This is the battle of Armageddon. This is not just a great war between nations; it is the final confrontation between the world's might under Antichrist and Satan, and Christ and the glorified Christians. Armageddon is the plain of Megiddo in Palestine.

Revelation 20:1-6; Romans 8:18-23; Isaiah 11:1-10   The Devil is shut up, and Christ rules the earth for a thousand years. The bodies of all true Christians will have been redeemed and glorified. Then the curse which God put upon the earth (Genesis 3:17, 18) because of man's sin will be removed. The world will, during this period, then be normal again—that is, as God made it.

Revelation 20:6; Luke 19:11-27   The Christians (servants) will reign with Christ during this period. Apparently our place of service in that time will be conditioned by our faithfulness in this present time.

Romans 11:25-29; Isaiah 11:10—12:6; Jeremiah 30:7-11; Zechariah 12:8-10; 13:6; 14:16-21   When Christ comes back in glory, the Jews will see Him as the true Messiah whom they, as a nation, rejected; and they will believe on Him.

Revelation 20:7-15   At the end of the thousand years, Satan will be loosed. There will be a final revolt against Christ, and the judgment of the lost will take place.

Revelation 21:1—22:5   There will be a new Heaven, a new earth, and a heavenly city. It is definite, so that this passage can state the size of the heavenly city, that from which it is constructed, that from which its foundations, gates, and streets are made. It is an objective reality. It is eternal—forever and ever, without end.

> When we've been there ten thousand years,
> Bright shining as the sun,
> We've no less days to sing God's praise,
> Than when we first begun.

25. The Lost

We have studied the present and future of those who have accepted God's gift of salvation by receiving Christ as Savior. This final study is the other side.

Revelation 19:20   This describes the end of the Antichrist and also of the false religious head who led in the worship of him.

Revelation 20:10   Originally created as the angel Lucifer (son of the morning), Satan revolted against God. This is his end.

Jude 6; 2 Peter 2:4; 1 Corinthians 6:3; Matthew 8:28, 29   This is the end of the angels who followed Satan in his revolt.

Romans 2:5, 6; 2 Thessalonians 1:4-9   There is a day of judgment for men and women who follow Satan in his revolt.

Daniel 12:2; John 5:28, 29; Acts 24:15   There will be a future physical resurrection of the lost.

Revelation 20:5, 6   The physical resurrection of the lost takes place a thousand years after the physical resurrection of the Christians. All Christians are raised in the first resurrection, and they need not fear the "second death," the condemnation of the final judgment. Either a person must be twice-born (natural birth and the new birth when he takes Christ as Savior), or he must die twice (the natural death and eternal judgment).

John 8:44; Matthew 25:41, 46; Revelation 20:11-15   The end of the lost is the same as that of the Devil and the angels who follow him. As the complete man (body and soul) of those who put their faith in Christ is redeemed, so the complete man (body and soul) of those who do not accept God's gift of salvation is judged. Hell is prepared for the devil and his angels, and the result of following him is to end up in the same place.

Matthew 3:12; 5:22; 8:12; 13:42, 50; 22:13; 25:30; Mark 9:43-48; 2 Peter 2:17; 3:7; Revelation 19:20; 20:15   In these and many other verses the Bible speaks of this place. Notice how much of this is given by Christ Himself, the One who came and died so that people might escape this by accepting Him as Savior.

Luke 12:48   There are degrees of judgment. As there is a believer's judgment, there are also degrees of judgment of the lost. There is a balancing of the books on both sides of the chasm.

Matthew 25:41, 46; 18:8; 2 Thessalonians 1:9; Jude 13; Revelation 20:10   The same words are used in the original Greek for the eternal quality of the future of the lost as are used for the eternal quality of the future of the redeemed. The two stand parallel.

In concluding this sober study, what should be in our minds?

Romans 5:8, 9; Ephesians 2:1-9; 1 Thessalonians 1:10   If we are Christians, remember that this is what we have been saved from by the death of Christ on Calvary. He suffered there infinitely, so that we might not be separated from God everlastingly.

Matthew 28:19, 20; Romans 10:13-15; Revelation 22:17   If we are Christians, in the light of this study we should give ourselves to the task which Christ has given to the Church in this age—telling others the content of the gospel.

Matthew 11:28-30   If you have not yet taken Christ as your Savior, if you are not a Christian, the triune God invites you to come and accept God's free gift of salvation by accepting Christ as Savior.

John 3:36   If you are not a Christian, you are here told that the judgment of God is upon you. But this same verse tells you as clearly as can be put into human language that there is only one thing necessary to have that other everlasting, eternal life, immediately and without end.

ART AND THE BIBLE

CHAPTER ONE

Art in the Bible

What is the place of art in the Christian life? Is art—especially the fine arts of painting and music—simply a way to bring in worldliness through the back door? We know that poetry may be used to praise God in, say, the psalms and maybe even in modern hymns. But what about sculpture or drama? Do these have any place in the Christian life? Shouldn't a Christian focus his gaze steadily on "religious things" alone and forget about art and culture?

The Lordship of Christ

As evangelical Christians, we have tended to relegate art to the very fringe of life. The rest of human life we feel is more important. Despite our constant talk about the Lordship of Christ, we have narrowed its scope to a very small area of reality. We have misunderstood the concept of the Lordship of Christ over the whole of man and the whole of the universe and have not taken to us the riches that the Bible gives us for ourselves, for our lives, and for our culture.

The Lordship of Christ over the whole of life means that there are no Platonic areas in Christianity, no dichotomy or hierarchy between the body and the soul. God made the body as well as the soul, and redemption is for the whole man. Evangelicals have been legitimately criticized for often being so tremendously interested in seeing souls get saved and go to Heaven that they have not cared much about the whole man.

The Bible, however, makes four things very clear: (1) God made the whole man; (2) in Christ the whole man is redeemed; (3) Christ is the Lord of the whole man now and the Lord of the whole Christian life; and (4) in the future as Christ comes back, the body will be raised from the dead and the whole man will have a whole redemption. Therefore, let us consider more fully what it means now to be a whole man whose whole life is under the Lordship of Christ. It is within this framework that we are to understand the place of art in the Christian life.

The conception of the wholeness of man and the lordship of man over creation comes early in Scripture. In Genesis 1:26, 27 we read, "And God said, Let us make man in our image, after our likeness; and let them have dominion over the fish of the sea, and over the birds of the heavens, and over the cattle, and over all the earth, and over every creeping thing that creepeth upon the earth. So God created man in his own image, in the image of God created he him; male and female created he them." From the very beginning, therefore, man and woman, being created in the image of God (both of them!), were given dominion (lordship) over the whole of the created earth. They were the ones who bore the image of God and, bearing that image, were to be in charge, to tend the Garden, to keep it and preserve it before their own Lord. Of course, that dominion was spoiled by the historic, space-time Fall, and therefore it is no longer possible to maintain that dominion in a perfect fashion.

Yet, when a man comes under the blood of Christ, his whole capacity as man is refashioned. His soul is saved, yes, but so are his mind and body. True spirituality includes the Lordship of Christ over the total man.

There have been periods in the past when Christians understood this better than we have in the last decades. Some years ago when I started to work out a Christian concept of culture, many people considered what I was doing suspect. They felt that because I was interested in intellectual answers, I must not be biblical. But this attitude represents a real poverty. It fails to understand that if Christianity is really true, then it involves the whole man, including his intellect and creativeness. Christianity is not *just* "dogmatically" true or "doctrinally" true. Rather, it is true to what is there, true in the whole area of the whole man in all of life.

The ancients were afraid that if they went to the end of the earth, they would fall off and be consumed by dragons. But once we understand that Christianity is true to what is there, including true to the ultimate environment—the infinite, personal God who is really there—then our minds are freed. We can pursue any question and can be sure that we will not fall off the end of the earth. Such an attitude will give our Christianity a strength that it often does not seem to have at the present time.

But there is another side to the Lordship of Christ, and this involves the total culture—including the area of creativity. Again, evangelical or biblical Christianity has been weak at this point. About all that we have produced is a very romantic Sunday school art. We do not seem to understand that the arts too are supposed to be under the Lordship of Christ.

I have frequently quoted a statement from Francis Bacon, who was one of the first of the modern scientists and who believed in the uniformity of natural causes in an open system. He, along with other men like Copernicus and Galileo, believed that because the world had been created by a reasonable God, they could therefore pursue the truth concerning the universe by reason. There is much, of course, in Francis Bacon with which I would disagree, but one of the statements which I love to quote is this: "Man by the Fall fell at the same time from his state of innocence and from his dominion over nature. Both of these losses, however, can even in this life be in some part repaired; the former by religion and faith, the latter by the arts and sciences." How I wish that evangelical Christians in the United States and Britain and across the world had had this vision for the last fifty years!

The arts and the sciences do have a place in the Christian life—they are not peripheral. For a Christian, redeemed by the work of Christ and living within the norms of Scripture and under the leadership of the Holy Spirit, the Lordship of Christ should include an interest in the arts. A Christian should use these arts to the glory of God—not just as tracts, but as things of beauty to the praise of God. An art work can be a doxology in itself.

Nonetheless, while the concept of the Lordship of Christ over the whole world would seem to include the arts, many Christians will respond by saying that the Bible has very little to say about the arts. More specifically, some people say that the Jews had no interest in art because of what the Scripture says in the Ten Commandments. But that's just what we cannot say if we read the Bible carefully. Still, because many Christians make this challenge, their view deserves to be considered and answered in some detail.

No Graven Image

Those who feel that art is forbidden by the Scripture point first to the Ten Commandments: "Thou shalt not make unto thee any graven image, or any likeness of anything that is in heaven above, or that is in the earth beneath, or that is in the water under the earth; thou shalt not bow down thyself unto them, nor serve them; for I, Jehovah thy God, am a jealous God . . ." (Ex. 20:4, 5). Isn't it clear, they say, that man is forbidden to make likenesses of anything, not just of God but anything in Heaven or on the earth? Surely this leaves no place for art.

But before we accept this conclusion, we should look at another passage in the law, which helps us to understand what the commandment in Exodus actually means. "Ye shall make no idols, neither shall ye rear you up a graven image, or a pillar [that is, a standing image or a statue], neither shall ye place any figured stone in your land, to bow down unto it: for I am Jehovah your God" (Lev. 26:1). This passage makes clear that Scripture does not forbid the making of representational art, but rather the worship of it. Only God is to be worshiped. Thus, the commandment is not against making art, but against worshiping anything other than God and specifically against worshiping art. To worship art is wrong, but to make art is not.

Art and the Tabernacle

One major principle of interpreting Scripture is that Scripture does not contradict itself. This is why it is important to note that on Mount Sinai God *simultaneously* gave the Ten Commandments and commanded Moses to fashion a tabernacle in a way which would involve almost every form of representational art that men have ever known. Let us look at this in more detail.

While Moses was on Sinai, God gave him specific instructions concerning the way in which the tabernacle should be made. He commanded Moses to gather from the Israelites gold and silver, fine cloth and dyed ram skins, fine wood and precious gems, and so forth. Then God said, "According to all that I show thee, the pattern of the tabernacle, and the pattern of all the furnishings thereof, even so shall ye make it" (Ex. 25:9). Where did the pattern come from? It came from God. This is reaffirmed a few verses later, where God said, "And see that thou make them after their pattern, which was shown thee in the mount [or, as the Hebrew says, "which thou wast caused to see"]" (Ex. 25:40). God Himself showed Moses the pattern of the tabernacle. In other words, God was the architect, not man. Over and over in the account of how the tabernacle is to be made, this phrase appears: "And thou shalt make . . ." That is, God told Moses what to do in detail. These were commands, commands from the same God who gave the Ten Commandments.

What were some of them? We will concentrate on those concerned with the art in the tabernacle, the very place of worship itself. First, we find this statement about the art in the Holy of Holies: "And thou shalt make two cherubim of gold, of beaten work shalt thou make them, at the two ends of the mercy seat" (Ex. 25:18). What are cherubim? They are part of the angelic host. What is being commanded? Simply this: a work of art is to be constructed. What kind of art? Representational art in the round. A statuary of representation of angels was to be placed in the Holy of Holies—the place where only once a year one man, the high priest, would go—and it was to be done by the command of God Himself.

Some may say, "Yes, but this is very special because these are angels that are being pictured. There is a sort of religious subject matter. It's not ordinary art representing things on the earth." True enough. But we find that just outside the Holy of Holies lampstands are to be placed: "And thou shalt make a candlestick of pure gold: of beaten work shall the candlestick be made, even its base, and its shaft; its cups, its knobs, and its flowers, shall be of one piece with it: and there shall be six branches going out of the sides thereof; three branches of the candlestick out of the one side thereof, and three branches of the candlestick out of the other side: three cups made like almond-blossoms in one branch, a knob and a flower; and three cups made like almond-blossoms in the other branch, a knob and a flower: so for the six branches going out of the candlestick" (vv. 31-33), and the description goes on. Thus we have another work of art—a candlestick. And how is it decorated? Not with representations of angels, but with representations of nature—flowers, blossoms, things of natural beauty. And these are to be in the tabernacle at the command of God in the midst of the place of worship.

Later in Exodus, we find this description of the priests' garments: "And upon the skirts of it thou shalt make pomegranates of blue, and of purple, and of scarlet, round about the skirts thereof" (Ex. 28:33). Thus, when the priest went into the Holy of Holies, he was to take with him on his garments a representation of nature, carrying that representation into the presence of God. Surely this is the very antithesis of a command against works of art.

But there is something further to note here. In nature, pomegranates are red, but these pomegranates were to be *blue, purple* and *scarlet*. Purple and scarlet could be natural changes in the growth of a pomegranate, but blue isn't. The implication is that there is freedom to make something which gets its impetus from nature but can be different from it, and it too can be brought into the presence of God. In other words, art does not need to be "photographic" in the poor sense of photographic!

It is tempting sometimes to read the Bible as a "holy book," treating the historical accounts as if they were upper-story situations that had nothing to do with down-to-earth reality. But we must understand that when God commanded these works of art to be built, some artist had to make them. There are two sides to art. It is creative, yes, but art also involves the technical details of how things are to be made. In Exodus 37:7 we are given something of these technical details: "And he made two cherubim of gold; of beaten work made he them at the two ends of the mercy seat." The cherubim on the ark didn't suddenly appear out of the sky. Somebody had to get his hands dirty, somebody had to work out the technical problems. The very thing that a modern artist wrestles with, these artists had to wrestle with. We shall see more of this as we discuss the temple.

The Temple

The temple, like the tabernacle, was not planned by man. Once more, the Scripture insists that the plan derived from God. David, the chronicler says, gave Solomon "the pattern of all that he had by the Spirit" for the various parts of the temple (1 Chron. 28:11, 12). And verse 19 reads, "All this, said David, have I been made to understand in writing from the hand of Jehovah, even all the works of this pattern." David's experience with God regarding the temple was not just an upper-story religious experience. Part of his experience involved the propositional revelation of how the temple should be made. David knew how to build the temple because God told him. In fact, David said that God made him understand *in writing* what the temple was to look like. We are not told by what means this writing, this propositional revelation, came, but we are told that David by inspiration of God had such a writing which gave him the pattern of the building.

What, therefore, was to be in the temple? For one thing, the temple was to be filled with art work. "And he (Solomon) garnished (covered) the house with precious stones for beauty" (2 Chron. 3:6). Notice this carefully: the temple was covered with precious stones *for beauty*. There was no pragmatic reason for the precious stones. They had no utilitarian purpose. God simply wanted beauty in the temple. God is interested in beauty.

Come with me to the Alps and look at the snow-covered mountains. There can be no question. God is interested in beauty. God made people to be beautiful. And beauty has a place in the worship of God. Here in the temple which Solomon built under the leadership of God Himself beauty was given an important place.

The chronicler goes on to say that Solomon "overlaid also the house, the beams, the thresholds, and the walls thereof, and the doors thereof, with gold; and graved (carved) cherubim on the walls" (2 Chron. 3:7). We talked above about the cherubim in the Holy of Holies; they were art in the round. Here is carving, bas-relief. There was bas-relief everywhere you looked. And there was also art in the round: "And in the most holy house he made two cherubim of image work" (v. 10).

Then in verses 16 and 17 we read, "And he made chains in the oracle, and put them on the tops of the pillars; and he made a hundred pomegranates, and put them on the chains. And he set up the pillars before the temple, one on the right hand, and the other on the left." Here are two free-standing columns. *They supported no architectural weight and had no utilitarian engineering significance.* They were there only because God said they should be there as things of beauty. Upon the capitals of those columns were pomegranates fastened upon chains—art work upon art work. If we understand what we are reading here, it simply takes our breath away. This is something overwhelmingly beautiful.

In 2 Chronicles 4, we are told how Solomon made a huge altar and also a "molten sea" (a pool or bath) that was about fifteen feet in diameter and, according to some estimates, may have had the capacity of just under 10,000 gallons. Under this sea and holding it up was "the likeness of oxen, which did compass it round about, for ten cubits, compassing the sea round about. The oxen were cast in two rows, cast when it was cast. It stood upon twelve oxen, three looking toward the north, and three looking toward the west, and three looking toward the south, and three looking toward the east; and the sea was set upon them above, and all their hinder parts were inward" (2 Chron. 4:3, 4). Here again is representational art in the round placed in the temple. Angels are represented by the bas-relief of cherubim, inanimate nature is represented in carvings of flowers and pomegranates, and animate nature is represented in the form of cast oxen. Representational art of nonreligious subjects was thus brought into the central place of worship.

To some extent, it could be said that the oxen were functional since they held up the "sea." But what function would the following have? "And it [the molten sea] was a hand-breadth thick; and the brim thereof was wrought like the brim of a cup, like the flower of a lily" (v. 5). The sea was not to be plain, but to be carved with lilies simply to be beautiful.

In 1 Kings 7:29, we have an additional detail. It comes in the description of the panels on the ten bases of brass in the temple: "And on the panels that were between the ledges were lions, oxen, and cherubim." God is saying, "I'll even have lions in my house, carved lions, oxen and cherubim." Not for a pragmatic function, just for beauty.

We could continue to multiply the references to art in relationship to the temple. For example, 1 Kings 6:29 reads, "And he carved all the walls of the house round about with carved figures of cherubim and palm trees and open flowers, within and without." This sounds much like what we have looked at above, but it brings into focus something additional. Here cherubim, palm trees and flowers are put together. In other words, we have representational art of both the seen and the unseen world. I don't believe *cherubim* is a figure of speech. Cherubim have form and are real. In fact, I am looking forward to seeing them some day. Yet, we may well ask, "How can you make a representation of something in the unseen world?" The answer is simple: it's easy if God tells you what they look like. The making of cherubim has something to do with propositional revelation. Ezekiel, for example, saw cherubim twice (Ezek. 1:4-25; 3:12, 13). There is nothing at all problematic in picturing cherubim if God shows you or tells you what they look like.

We saw how with the tabernacle the artist was required to solve certain technical problems. The same is true for the art in the temple: "In the plain of Jordan did the king cast them [the various art works that were to be in the temple], in the clay ground between Succoth and Zeredah" (2 Chron. 4:17). Just as Michelangelo chipped with his hands the marble from the great Italian quarries, so the Hebrew artist cast the bronze in a particular geographical place, a place where the clay was just right to make a good form from his model. These Hebrew artists were not different from men today; both live in the same world and have to deal with all the technical realities of the various forms of art.

Secular Art

So far we have been concerned with art that is involved specifically with the worship of God, whether its subject is angels or nature. And it is clear that since all this art was God-commanded, specifically religious subjects are not necessary for art. The factor which makes art Christian is not that it necessarily deals with religious subject matter.

In 1 Kings 10 we learn something about the secular art of Solomon's day, for here Solomon's throne is described. "Moreover the king made a great throne of ivory, and overlaid it with the finest gold. There were six steps to the throne, and the top of the throne was round behind; and there were stays on either side by the place of the seat, and two lions standing beside the stays. And twelve lions stood there on the one side and on the other upon the six steps; there was not the like made in any kingdom" (1 Kings 10:18-20). Every time I read this description I am intrigued. I would like to have seen this magnificent work of art—"ivory . . . overlaid with the finest gold" and guarded by two lions by the side of the throne and twelve lions on the stairway to the throne.

Some scholars who have wondered why the two lions and the twelve lions are mentioned separately have suggested that the two lions at the top were alive and the other twelve were cast. We cannot be sure whether that is the case or not, but if it is, just imagine it for a moment: Imagine yourself as Solomon, sitting up there with the two lions roaring away on either side of you, chained securely, no doubt, but what a throne! What a piece of secular art!

Jesus' Use of Art

If anyone is still troubled concerning the Bible and representational art, then he should consider what the Bible says about the brazen serpent that Moses lifted up in the wilderness. You will recall that while the children of Israel were wandering in the desert, they complained to Moses about the lack of bread and water. Because of their complaining, God then sent "fiery serpents among the people, and they bit the people; and much people of Israel died" (Num. 21:6). So the Israelites came to Moses, confessing that they had sinned and asking Moses to pray that God would take the serpents away. God then replied to Moses' prayer: "Make thee a fiery serpent, and set it upon a pole; and it shall come to pass, that every one that is bitten, when he looketh upon it, shall live" (v. 8). Moses obeyed this command and those who looked upon the "serpent of brass" lived.

The striking thing is that Jesus used this incident and this work of art as an illustration of his coming crucifixion: "And, as Moses lifted up the serpent in the wilderness, even so must the Son of man be lifted up, that whosoever believeth in him should not perish, but have eternal life" (John 3:14, 15). What was Jesus using as his illustration? A work of art.

But then perhaps someone will say, "Yes, but they smashed it. Hezekiah broke it up in 2 Kings 18:4." That's true. In fact, God was even pleased with its destruction. But why did Hezekiah smash the brazen serpent? "And he [Hezekiah] brake in pieces the brazen serpent that Moses had made; for unto those days the children of Israel did burn incense to it." Did he smash it because it was a work of art? Of course not, because God had commanded Moses to make it. He smashed the work of art because men had made it an idol. What is wrong with representational art is not its existence, but its wrong uses.

Poetry

We have been concerned thus far solely with representational art, but the Bible is concerned with other art forms as well. The most obvious is poetry. When we think of poetry in the Bible, we think immediately of the psalms. But there is much Jewish poetry elsewhere, and not all of it concerns specifically religious subjects. For example, 2 Samuel 1:19-27 is a secular ode, a poem by David to the praise of Saul and Jonathan as national heroes.

Later in 2 Samuel we are told that David wrote his psalms under the leadership and inspiration of the Holy Spirit:

> David, the son of Jesse, said,
> and the man who was raised up on high,
> the anointed of the God of Jacob,
> and the sweet psalmist of Israel, said,
> The Spirit of Jehovah spoke by me,
> and his word was in my tongue. (2 Sam. 23:1, 2)

Acts 2:25-31 confirms the fact that David was a prophet. So we might paraphrase David as follows: "Yes, I was a prophet. I was a forth-teller of God. And how did I write? Well, I wrote my poetry under the leadership of the Holy Spirit." We must not think that David was a prophet only when he wrote prose, for his poetry is just as inspired. How then can we say, or have even the slightest inclination to feel, that God despises poetry?

Interestingly enough, we have in the Septuagint, the Greek version of the Old Testament Scriptures that dates back to the second or third century B.C., a record of a psalm that is not in our Bible. There is a question, of course, whether it is a real psalm of David, but it sounds like David. We do not need to think that everything David wrote was "inspired by God" the way what is in the Bible is inspired. So even if this is a genuine psalm of David, it is probably not inspired in that sense. Certainly not all art is God speaking as a muse through the artist. Rather, it is the "mannishness" of man that creates. The artist as a man does not disappear, leaving the muse alone to speak. We can consider the following psalm from the Septuagint, therefore, to be David writing a piece of poetry as a piece of poetry.

> I was small among my brethren
> and youngest in my father's house.
> I tended my father's sheep.
> My hands formed a musical instrument
> and my fingers tuned a psaltery.
> And who shall tell my Lord?
> The Lord Himself, He Himself hears.
> He sent forth his angel
> and He took me from my father's sheep.

> And He anointed me with the oil of his anointing.
> My brothers were handsome and tall,
> but the Lord did not take pleasure in them.
> I went forth to meet the Philistine
> and he cursed me by his idols.
> But I drew his own sword and beheaded him
> and removed reproach from the children of Israel.

That certainly sounds like David. David pictures himself as a young boy out on the hillside tending his sheep. And what does he do? He is the artist. He takes a piece of wood and shapes it to make a harp; "my hands formed a musical instrument." As we shall see, the Bible says that David as a craftsman later made the instruments that were used in the temple of worship.

But David was also a musician. His "fingers tuned a psaltery." Like a man tuning his violin, David prepared his instrument for playing. The writing of poetry, the making of a beautiful instrument, the tuning of it so that its music can be filled with beauty— David did all these things as a spiritual exercise to the praise of God.

There is something exciting here. Art can be offered up before God. David says, "and who shall tell my Lord?" That is, "Who shall tell my Lord that I made a beautiful instrument, who will tell Him that I tuned the psaltery, who will tell Him that I have written this poetry? Who will tell Him about my song?" Then David responds, "The Lord Himself, He Himself hears." Nobody had to go and tell God. God knew. So the man who really loves God could write his poetry, compose his music, construct his musical instruments, fashion his statues, paint his pictures, even if no man ever saw them. He knows God looks upon them.

So you might say to David, "David, why do you sing? Just to amuse yourself? Only the little white-faced sheep will hear." And David will reply, "Not at all. I'm singing and the God of Heaven and earth hears my song; that's what makes it so worthwhile."

Art can, of course, be put into the temple. But it doesn't have to be put into the temple in order to be to the praise of God.

One of the most striking secular poems in the Bible is the Song of Solomon. Many Christians in the past have felt that this poem represents the love of Christ for his Church. The poem can in fact be interpreted in this way. But we must never reduce it solely to the picture of this relationship. It depicts the relationship between Christ and the Church because every proper relationship between a man and a woman is an illustration of the relationship between Christ and the Church. The fact is that God made the love of a man for a woman to be representational of the love of God for His people, of the Bridegroom for the bride, of Christ for His Church. But in the Song of Solomon God takes a poem that expresses in great antiphonal strength the love of a man for a woman and a woman for a man, and places it in the Word of God. This kind of poetry, just like the psalms, can also represent something wonderful. How beautiful a praise to God this poem is! In one way, its placement in the Bible is parallel to the sort of secular art that we noticed on Solomon's throne, but it is more significant because this poem is put into the Scripture as Scripture itself.

How often do Christians think of sexual matters as something second-rate. Never, never, never should we do so, according to the Word of God. The whole man is made to love God; each aspect of man's nature is to be given its proper place. That includes the sexual relationship, that tremendous relationship of one man to one woman. At the very beginning God brought Eve to man. A love poem can thus be beautiful. So if you are a young man or a young woman and you love a girl or you love a boy, you may indeed write beautiful love poetry. Don't be afraid. And older lovers can love and write love songs as well! This too can be a praise to God.

Before passing on to other art forms, I would like to simply reemphasize that even though it uses a different poetic form than English does, Hebrew poetry demands strict literary discipline. In fact, Hebrew poetry is probably much harder to write than Anglo-Saxon poetry. And just as an artist, a craftsman, was required to work with precision as he cast the bronze statues or carved the bas-relief on the walls of the temple, so the Hebrew poet had to be careful with the technical aspects of his poetry and strive for technical excellence. And in the striving for excellence comes a way to praise God too.

Music
Music is another art form which the Bible does not ignore. One of the most fantastic pieces of musical art must have been the song the Hebrews sang after they were rescued from Pharaoh's army. Exodus 15 gives us that song. Think of this great host of Israelites—hundreds of thousands of people—gathered on the far side of the Red Sea and singing an antiphonal song—a work of art.

"And Miriam the prophetess, the sister of Aaron, took a timbrel in her hand; and all the women went out after her with timbrels and with dances. And Miriam answered them, Sing ye to Jehovah, for he hath triumphed gloriously; the horse and his rider hath he thrown into the sea" (Ex. 15:20, 21). Here we have the men singing the stanza (given in Ex. 15:1-19) and the women led by Miriam singing the chorus. Think of the joy of deliverance from oppression, and think of what a scene this music-making must have been.

But there was also music in the temple. We are told in 1 Chronicles 23:5 that "four thousand praised Jehovah with the instruments which I made, said David, with which to praise." Four thousand! A song rang out from 4,000 at once. And the chronicler adds, "And David divided them into courses [divisions] according to the sons of Levi: Gershon, Kohath, and Merari" (v. 6). In other words, David divided the singers into parts, making what we would call a chorus. And art breaks forth with all its beauty, all its strength, all its communication, and all its glory.

From the time of Hezekiah comes a scene I love to picture. Hezekiah had had the temple cleansed and the worship reformed according to the law of God which had been set aside for so long. And then, while the sacrifices were being offered, Hezekiah "set the Levites in the house of Jehovah with cymbals, with psalteries, and with harps [notice the various instruments], according to the commandment of David, and of Gad, the king's seer, and Nathan, the prophet; for so was the commandment of Jehovah by his prophets. And the Levites stood with the instruments of David, and the priests with the trumpets" (2 Chron. 29:25, 26). Then Hezekiah commanded that the offerings be burnt upon the altar: "And when the burnt offering began, the song of Jehovah began also, and the trumpets, together with the instruments of David, king of Israel. And all the assembly worshipped, and the singers sang, and the trumpeters sounded; all this continued until the burnt offering was finished" (vv. 27, 28). A tremendous use of music and art, again all at the commandment of God through his prophets.

I suppose my favorite piece of music is Handel's *Dettingen Te Deum.* I have a record of this music (Fontana 875-015-CY), in which all the instruments meant to be involved are used, and I want to tell you it is marvelous. I've played the grooves off of it. Every time I read this section in 2 Chronicles, I think of the

Dettingen Te Deum and of the fact that what was going on in the time of Hezekiah must have been ten times greater. Trumpets, cymbals, psalteries, harps, all the various instruments of David—music upon music, art upon art—all pouring forth, all pointing up the possibility of creativity in praise of God, all carried to a high order of art at God's command. And when you begin to understand this sort of thing, suddenly you can begin to breathe, and all the terrible pressure that has been put on us by making art something less than spiritual suddenly begins to disappear. And with this truth comes beauty and with this beauty a freedom before God.

We should note that with regard to the temple, all of the art worked together to form a unity. The whole temple was a single work of architecture, a unified unit with free-standing columns, statuary, bas-relief, poetry and music, great huge stones, beautiful timbers brought from afar. It's all there. A completely unified work of art to the praise of God. Surely this has something to say to us about architecture, and we ought to be asking the Lord how we can produce this kind of praise to God today.

Drama and the Dance
Two more art forms are mentioned in the Scripture. The first is drama. In Ezekiel we read, "Thou also, son of man, take thee a tile, and lay it before thee, and portray upon it a city, even Jerusalem; and lay siege against it, and build a fort against it, and cast up a mound against it; set the camp also against it, and set battering rams against it round about. Moreover, take thou unto thee an iron pan [or, flat plate], and set it for a wall of iron between thee and the city; and set thy face toward it, and it shall be besieged, and thou shalt lay siege against it. This shall be a sign to the house of Israel" (Ezek. 4:1-3). What was this? It was a simple drama. The "tile" had the skyline of Jerusalem drawn upon it as a simple backdrop, so that the people could not miss what Ezekiel was portraying. Jerusalem was to be besieged, and the warning was taught to the people by the command of God, in a drama.

Let us notice: It is not that *every* use of any of these art forms is automatically right, but that they are not wrong per se. Ezekiel was asked to enact this drama each day for over a year. For these long months he portrayed a work of drama before the backdrop in order that Israel would understand that God was going to bring down judgment.

The second art form, the dance, is mentioned in Psalm 149:3, in which Israel is encouraged to praise God: "Let them praise his name in the dance; let them sing praises unto him with the timbrel and harp." Some may reply, "Well, in the margin of my Bible it says that maybe it isn't the dance, but rather the 'pipe,' and I like that better." But that is not the best translation. Psalm 150:4, 5 says, "Praise him with the timbrel and dance; praise him with stringed instruments and pipe. Praise him upon the loud cymbals; praise him upon the high sounding cymbals."

Two historical portions of the Bible show that God was pleased with people dancing. Exodus 15:20 says that Miriam as prophetess went out "with timbrels and with dances." And in 2 Samuel 6:14-16 we are told, "And David danced before Jehovah with all his might; and David was girded with a linen ephod." Imagine David bringing the ark of God into his city—a very high moment indeed among the Jews. The ark which had been outside the city is now being brought in, and David is filled with joy as he worships God. It is interesting, by the way, that David was clothed with an ephod. This means that he was not dancing naked as was common among the heathen. Nonetheless, when David's wife saw it she didn't like it (v. 16). Yet God liked it, and David's wife was reproved for reproving David.

Art and Heaven

Revelation 15:2, 3 reads, "And I saw, as it were, a sea of glass mingled with fire, and them that had gotten the victory over the beast, and over his image, and over his mark, and from the number of his name, standing on the sea of glass, having the harps of God. And they sing the song of Moses, the servant of God, and the song of the Lamb, saying, Great and marvelous are thy works, Lord God Almighty; just and true are thy ways, thou King of the ages." Art does not stop at the gate of Heaven. Art forms are carried right into Heaven. Is there any Platonic separation here? Not a bit.

In the art museum at Neuchatel are three great murals by Paul Robert which for over eighty years have borne testimony to all the people of Neuchatel that Christ is coming again. One of the murals testifies to the fact that Christ has a relationship to agriculture, another to the fact that Christ has a relationship to industry. But the third one is the greatest. It depicts the relationship between Christ, the intellectual life, and the arts. Paul Robert, a Swiss artist who was a real man of God, understood this relationship very well.

In the background of this mural he pictured Neuchatel, the lake on which it is situated, and even the art museum which contains the mural. In the foreground near the bottom is a great dragon wounded to the death. Underneath the dragon is the vile and the ugly, the pornographic and the rebellious. Near the top Jesus is seen coming in the sky with His endless hosts. On the left side is a beautiful stairway, and on the stairway are young and beautiful men and women carrying the symbols of the various forms of art—architecture, music and so forth. And as they are carrying them up and away from the dragon to present them to Christ, Christ is coming down to accept them. Paul Robert understood Scripture a lot better than many of us. He saw that at the second coming the Lordship of Christ will include everything.

But he also knew that if these things are to be carried up to the praise of God and the Lordship of Christ at the second coming, then we should be offering them to God now. In the same picture he portrayed the city of Neuchatel, the beautiful lake, and the art museum itself; the art museum of Neuchatel and its works of art should be to the praise of Christ *now*. The reality of the future has meaning for the present!

Do we understand the freedom we have under the Lordship of Christ and the norms of Scripture? Is the creative part of our life committed to Christ? Christ is the Lord of our whole life, and the Christian life should produce not only truth—flaming truth—but also beauty.

CHAPTER TWO

Some Perspectives on Art

All of us are engaged daily with works of art, even if we are neither professional nor amateur artists. We read books, we listen to music, we look at posters, we admire flower arrangements. *Art,* as I am using the word, does not include just "high art"—that is, painting, sculpture, poetry, classical music—but also the more popular expressions—the novel, the theater, the cinema and popular music. In fact, there is a very real sense in which the Christian life itself should be our greatest work of art. Even for the great artist, the most crucial work of art is his life.

In what follows, I wish to develop a Christian perspective on art in general. How should we as creators and enjoyers of beauty comprehend and evaluate it? There are, I believe, at least eleven distinct perspectives from which a Christian can consider and evaluate works of art. These perspectives do not exhaust the various aspects of art. The field of aesthetics is too rich for that. But they do cover a significant portion of what should be a Christian's understanding in this area.

The Art Work as an Art Work
1. The first is the most important: *a work of art has a value in itself.* For some this principle may seem too obvious to mention, but for

many Christians it is unthinkable. And yet if we miss this point, we miss the very essence of art. Art is not something we merely analyze or value for its intellectual content. It is something to be enjoyed. The Bible says that the art work in the tabernacle and the temple was for beauty.

How should an artist begin to do his work as an artist? I would insist that he begin his work as an artist by setting out to make a work of art. What that would mean is different in sculpture and poetry, for example, but in all cases the artist should be setting out to make a work of art.

As a Christian we know why a work of art has value. Why? First, because a work of art is a work of creativity, and creativity has value because God is the Creator. The first sentence in the Bible is the declaration that the Creator created: "In the beginning God *created* the heavens and the earth." So too the first words of the prologue to the Gospel of John: "In the beginning was the Word, and the Word was with God, and the Word was God. . . . All things were made through him; and without him was not anything made that hath been made" (John 1:1, 3). Therefore, the first reason that creativity has value is that God is the Creator.

Second, an art work has value as a creation because man is made in the image of God, and therefore man not only can love and think and feel emotion, but also has the capacity to create. Being in the image of the Creator, we are called upon to have creativity. In fact, it is part of the image of God to be creative, or to have creativity. We never find an animal, non-man, making a work of art. On the other hand, we never find men anywhere in the world or in any culture in the world who do not produce art. Creativity is a part of the distinction between man and non-man. All people are to some degree creative. Creativity is intrinsic to our "man-nishness."

But we must be careful not to reverse this. Not everything that man makes is good intellectually or morally. So, while creativity is a good thing in itself, it does not mean that everything that comes out of man's creativity is good. For while man was made in the image of God, he is fallen. Furthermore, since men have various gifts and talents, everyone cannot create everything equally well. However, the main point is that creativity as creativity is a good thing as such.

When I was younger, I thought it was wrong to use the word

create in reference to works of art. I thought it ought to be used solely in relation to what God can do. Later, I saw that I was desperately wrong; I am now convinced that it is important to understand that both God and man create. Both make something. The distinction is this: God, because He is infinite, can create out of nothing by His spoken word. We, because we are finite, must create from something else that has already been created. Yet the word *create* is appropriate, for it suggests that what man does with what is already there is to make something new. Something that was not there before, something that began as an unmannish part of reality, is transformed by the mannishness of man and now reflects that mannishness.

I am convinced that one of the reasons men spend millions in making art museums is not just so that there will be something "aesthetic," but because the art works in them are an expression of the mannishness of man himself. When I look at the pre-Columbian silver or African masks or ancient Chinese bronzes, not only do I see them as works of art, but I see them as expressions of the nature and character of humanity. As a man, in a certain way they are myself, and I see there the outworking of the creativity that is inherent in the nature of man.

Many modern artists, it seems to me, have forgotten the value that art has in itself. Much modern art is far too intellectual to be great art. I am thinking, for example, of such an artist as Jasper Johns. Many modern artists do not see the distinction between man and non-man, and it is a part of the lostness of modern man that they no longer see value in the work of art as a work of art.

I am afraid, however, that as evangelicals we have largely made the same mistake. Too often we think that a work of art has value only if we reduce it to a tract. This too is to view art solely as a message for the intellect.

There are, I believe, three basic possibilities concerning the nature of a work of art. The first view is the relatively recent theory of art for art's sake. This is the notion that art is just there and that is all there is to it. You can't talk about a message in it, you can't analyze it, it doesn't say anything. This view is, I think, quite misguided. For one thing, no great artist functions on the level of art for art's sake alone. Think, for example, of the high Renaissance, beginning with Cimabue (c. 1240-1302) and leading through Giotto (1267-1337), Masaccio (1401-28), and all the way up to Michelangelo (1475-1564) and Leonardo da Vinci (1452-1519). All of these artists worked from one of two viewpoints, and sometimes there was a confusion between the two. They worked either from their notion of Christianity (which to us who hold a biblical viewpoint was often deficient) or from a Renaissance form of humanism. Florence, for example, where so many excellent works of art were produced, was a center for the study of Neoplatonism. Some of the artists studied under Ficino (1433-99), perhaps the greatest of the Neoplatonists and influential throughout Europe. These artists showed their viewpoint in their art.

It is true that the great modern artists such as Picasso never worked for only art for art's sake either. Picasso had a philosophy which showed through in his paintings. It is true that many lesser artists now work, or try to work, in the milieu of art for art's sake, but the great masters did not.

The second view, which I spoke of above, is that art is only an embodiment of a message, a vehicle for the propagation of a particular message about the world or the artist or man or whatever. This view has been held by Christians as well as non-Christians, the difference between these two versions being the nature of the message which the art embodies. But, as I have said, this view, Christian or non-Christian, reduces art to an intellectual statement, and the work of art as a work of art disappears.

The third basic notion of the nature of art—the one I think is right, the one that really produces great art and the possibility of great art—is that the artist makes a work of art, and that then the body of his work shows his world-view. No one, for example, who understands Michelangelo or Leonardo can look at their work without understanding something of their respective world-views. Nonetheless, these artists began by making works of art, and then their world-views showed through the body of their work. I emphasize the body of an artist's work because it is impossible for any single painting, for example, to reflect the totality of an artist's view of reality. But when we see a collection of an artist's paintings or a series of a poet's poems or a number of a novelist's novels, both the outline and some of the details of the artist's conception of life shine through.

How then should an artist begin to do his work? I would insist that he begin by setting out *to make a work of art.* He should say to himself, "I am going to make a work of art." *Perspective number one is that a work of art is first of all a work of art.*

Art Forms Add Strength to the World-View
2. *Art forms add strength to the world-view which shows through, no matter what the world-view is or whether the world-view is true or false.* Think, for example, of a side of beef hanging in a butcher shop. It just hangs there. But if you go to the Louvre and look at Rembrandt's painting, *Side of Beef Hanging in a Butcher Shop,* it's very different. It's startling to come upon this particular work because it says a lot more than its title. Rembrandt's art causes us to see the side of beef in a concentrated way, and, speaking for myself, after looking and looking at his picture I have never been able to look at a side of beef in a butcher shop with the superficiality I did before. How much stronger is Rembrandt's painting than merely the label, A Side of Beef.

In literature, there is a parallel. Good prose as an art form has something bad prose does not. Further, poetry has something good prose does not. We may have long discussions on what is added, but the fact that there are distinct differences is clear. Even in the Bible, the poetry adds a dimension not present in the prose. In fact, the effect of any proposition, whether true or false, can be heightened if it is expressed in poetry or in artistic prose rather than in bald, formulaic statement.

Normal Definitions, Normal Syntax
3. *In all forms of writing, both poetry and prose, it makes a tremendous difference whether there is a continuity or a discontinuity with the normal definitions of words in normal syntax.* Many modern writers make a concerted effort to disassociate the language of their works from the normal use of language in which there is a normal definition of words and a normal use of syntax. If there is no continuity with the way in which language is normally used, then there is no way for a reader or an audience to know what the author is saying.

An artist can, of course, use language with great richness, fill his writing with figures of speech and hyperbole or play games with the syntax. The great artist often does this, going far beyond a merely rudimentary use of normal grammar and normal definition of words. And in doing so, he adds depth and dimension.

Shakespeare is the great example. We understand Shakespeare's dramas because he uses enough normal syntax and normal definitions of words so that there is a running story and a continuity between the running story and all of the artistic devices he uses. We know what Shakespeare is saying not because of the far-flung

metaphors and beautiful verbal twists, but because of the continuity they have with the story on the level of normal definition and
normal syntax. There is a firm core of straightforward propositions.

What is true in literature is also true in painting and sculpture.
The common symbolic vocabulary that belongs to all men (the
artists and the viewers) is the world around us—namely, God's
world. That symbolic vocabulary in the representational arts
stands parallel to normal grammar and normal syntax in the literary arts. When, therefore, there is no attempt on the part of an
artist to use this symbolic vocabulary at all, then communication
breaks down. There is then no way for anyone to know what the
artist is saying. My point is *not* that making this sort of art is
immoral or anti-Christian, but rather that a dimension is lost.

Totally abstract art stands in an undefined relationship with the
viewer, for the viewer is completely alienated from the painter.
There is a huge wall between them. The painter and the viewer
stand separated from each other in total alienation, a greater alienation than Giacometti could ever show in his alienated figures.

When Giacometti pictures the awful alienation of man, he
makes figures which are alienated, but he is still living in God's
world and is still using the common symbolic forms, no matter
how he distorts them. He plays with the vocabulary, but the
vocabulary is still there. So there is a communication between
Giacometti and me, a titanic communication. I can understand
what he is saying and I cry.

In contrast to this, there is a distinct limitation to totally abstract
art. Like prose or poetry which has no contact with normal syntax
and the normal definitions of words, it is a quarry out of which the
observer or the hearer has a personal emotional response.

Art and the Sacred
4. *The fact that something is a work of art does not make it sacred.*
Heidegger in *What Is Philosophy?* came finally to the view that
there are small beings (namely, people) who verbalize, and therefore we can hope that Being has some meaning. His great cry at
the end of this book is to listen to the poet. Heidegger is not saying
that we should listen to the content of what the poets say, because
one can find two different poets who give absolutely opposite
content and this doesn't matter. Rather, the poet as a poet became
Heidegger's upper-story optimistic hope.

As Christians, we must see that just because an artist—even a great artist—portrays a world-view in writing or on canvas, it does not mean that we should automatically accept that world-view. Art may heighten the impact of the world-view—in fact, we can count on this—but it does not make something true. The truth of a world-view presented by an artist must be judged on grounds other than artistic greatness.

Four Standards of Judgment
5. What kind of judgment does one apply, then, to a work of art? *I believe that there are four basic standards: (1) technical excellence; (2) validity; (3) intellectual content, the world-view which comes through; and (4) the integration of content and vehicle.*

I will discuss *technical excellence* in relationship to painting because it is easy to point out through this medium what I mean. Here one considers the use of color, form, the texture of the paint, the handling of lines, the balance, composition and unity of the painting, and so forth. In each of these, there can be varying degrees of technical excellence. By recognizing technical excellence as an aspect of an art work, we are often able to say that while we do not agree with such and such an artist's world-view, he is nonetheless a great artist.

We are not being true to the artist as a man if we consider his art work junk simply because we differ with his outlook on life. Christian schools, Christian parents, and Christian pastors often have turned off young people at just this point. Because the schools, the pastors and the parents did not make a distinction between technical excellence and content, the whole of much great art has been rejected with scorn or ridicule. Instead, if the artist's technical excellence is high, he is to be praised for this, even if we differ with his world-view. Man must be treated fairly as man. Creative ability and technical excellence are therefore important criteria.

Validity is the second criterion. By validity I mean whether an artist is honest to himself and to his world-view, or whether he makes his art only for money or for the sake of being accepted. If an artist makes an art work *solely* for a patron—whether that patron is the ancient noble, or the modern art gallery to which the artist wants access, or the modern art critics of the moment—his work does not have validity. The modern forms of "the patron" are more destructive than even that of the old noble.

To bring it down to earth, let's see what happens in the art form of preaching. There is many a pastor who does not have validity. Some preach for material gain and others in order to be accepted by their congregation. It is so easy to play to the audience, to adjust what one says or the way one says it to produce the kind of effect which will be most beneficial to the preacher himself. And when one sees the issue in relationship to the gospel, the force of the dishonesty is especially obvious.

We can think of the contemporary dramatists whose future is in the hands of the critics of the passing moment. In drama, art, music and cinema, we have a set of New York and London critics who can make or break the artist. How easy it is to play to the critic and not to take one's art as a serious expression of what the artist himself wants to say and do.

The third criterion for the judgment of a work of art is its *content*, that which reflects the world-view of the artist. As far as a Christian is concerned, the world-view that is shown through a body of art must be seen ultimately in terms of the Scripture. The artist's world-view is not to be free from the judgment of the Word of God. In this the artist is like a scientist. The scientist may wear a white coat and be considered an "authority" by society, but where his statements impinge upon what God has given us in Scripture, they come under the ultimate authority of His Word. An artist may wear a painter's smock and be considered almost a holy man; yet where his work shows his world-view, the content must be judged by its relationship to the Christian world-view.

I think we can now see how it is possible to make such judgments concerning the work of art. If we stand as Christians before a man's canvas and say that he is a great artist in technical excellence and validity—if in fact he is—*if we have been fair with him as a man and as an artist,* then we can say that his world-view is wrong. We can judge his view on the same basis as we judge the views of anybody else—philosopher, common man, laborer, businessman or whatever.

Let's be more specific. The notion of Bohemian freedom which Jean-Jacques Rousseau promulgated and which has been so prevalent in modern society has no place in Christian thinking. Rousseau was seeking a kind of autonomous freedom, and from him stemmed a group of "supermen" whose lives were lived above reason, as it were, and above the norms of society. For a long time this Bohemian life was taken to be the ideal for the artist, and it has come in the last few decades to be considered an ideal for more than the artist. From a Christian point of view, however, this sort of life is not allowed. God's Word binds the great man and the small, the scientist and the simple, the king and the artist.

Some artists may not know that they are consciously showing forth a world-view. Nonetheless, a world-view usually does show through from the body of their work. Even those works which were constructed under the principle of art for art's sake often imply a world-view—even the world-view that there is no meaning is a message. In any case, whether the artist is conscious of the world-view or not, to the extent that it is there it must come under the judgment of the Word of God.

There is a corollary to this third criterion. We should realize that if something untrue or immoral is stated in great art, it can be far more destructive and devastating than if it is expressed in poor art or prosaic statement. Much of the crude art, the common product of counterculture communities and the underground press, is laden with destructive messages, but the art is so poor that it does not have much force. But the greater the artistic expression, the more important it is to *consciously* bring it and its world-view under the judgment of Christ and the Bible.

The common reaction among many, however, is just the opposite. Many seem to feel that the greater the art, the less we ought to be critical of its world-view. This we must reverse.

An example of the devastating effect of great art with non-Christian content occurs in Zen. In Zen, the world is nothing, man is nothing, everything is nothing; but Zen poetry says it beautifully, so much more beautifully than the counterculture press. Swearing in four-letter words, the counterculture press often declares that man is nothing, the world is nothing, nothing is nothing. And one thinks to himself, "Ah, but if it were said with some beauty, maybe there would be something." And then Zen comes along as a high art form and gives this message with beauty. And now you're dead twice.

There is a second corollary related to judging the content of an art work. It is possible for a non-Christian writer or painter to write and paint according to a Christian world-view even though he himself is not a Christian. To understand this, we must distinguish between two meanings of the word *Christian*. The first and essential meaning is that a Christian is a person who has accepted Christ as his Savior and has thus passed from death to life, from the kingdom of darkness to the kingdom of God, by being born again. But if a number of people really are Christians, then they bring forth a kind of consensus that exists apart from themselves, and sometimes non-Christians paint and write within the framework of that consensus even though they as individuals are not Christians.

There are, therefore, four kinds of people in the realm of art. The first is the born-again man who writes or paints within the Christian total world-view. The second is the non-Christian who expresses his own non-Christian world-view. The third is the man who is personally a non-Christian, but nevertheless writes or paints on the basis of the Christian consensus by which he has been influenced. For example, in another area, if one were to ask whether Benjamin Franklin or Thomas Jefferson personally were Christians, the answer, as best we can judge from what they have said, is no. Nonetheless, they produced something that had some sort of Christian framework because they were producing it out of the Christian consensus of Samuel Rutherford's *Lex Rex*. Thus, from a Christian framework Jefferson and Franklin were able to write that men have certain inalienable rights, a notion derived from a specifically Christian world-view.

The fourth person is the born-again Christian who does not understand what the total Christian world-view should be and therefore produces art which embodies a non-Christian world-view. In other words, just as it is possible for a non-Christian to be inconsistent and to paint God's world in spite of his personal philosophy, it is possible for a Christian to be inconsistent and embody in his paintings a non-Christian world-view. And it is this latter which is perhaps the most sad.

The fourth criterion for judging a work of art involves how well the artist has *suited the vehicle to the message*. For those art works which are truly great, there is a correlation between the style and the content. The greatest art fits the vehicle that is being used to the world-view that is being presented.

A clear example is found in T. S. Eliot's "The Waste Land." When Eliot published this in 1922, he became a hero to the modern poets, because for the first time he dared to make the form of his poetry fit the nature of the world as he saw it—namely, broken, unrelated, ruptured. What was that form? A collection of shattered fragments of language and images, and allusions drawn seemingly haphazardly from all manner of literature, philosophy and religious writings from the ancients to the present. But modern poets were pleased, for they now had a poetic form to fit the modern world-view of unrelatedness.

The breakthrough in painting came in Picasso's *Demoiselles d'Avignon* (1907), a painting which takes its name from a house of prostitution in Barcelona. Picasso began this work in the vein of other paintings of the period; but as one critic describes it, Picasso ended it as "a semi-abstract composition in which the forms of the nudes and their accessories are broken up into planes compressed into a shallow space." More specifically, Picasso began on the left by painting the forms rather naturally, toward the middle he painted more like Spanish primitives, and finally on the right, as he finished his work, he painted the women as only abstract forms and symbols or masks, and thus succeeded in making monsters of his human subjects. Picasso knew what he was doing, and for a moment the world stood still. It was in fact so strong an expression that for a long time even his friends would not accept it. They didn't even want to look at it. Thus, in his painting of the women Picasso pictured the fractured nature of modern man. What T. S. Eliot did in his poetry, Picasso had already done in painting. Both men deserve high scores for suiting the vehicle to the message.

No art should be judged on the basis of this criterion alone, however. We should ultimately see all art works in the light of their technique, validity, world-view, and suiting of form to content.

Art Can Be Used for Any Type of Message
6. *Art forms can be used for any type of message, from pure fantasy to detailed history.* That a work of art is in the form of fantasy or epic or painting does not mean that there is no propositional content. Just as one can have propositional statements in prose, there can be propositional statements in poetry, in painting, in virtually any art form.

Some years ago a theologian at Princeton commented that he did not mind saying the Creeds, providing that he could sing them. What he meant was that so long as he could make them a work of art, he didn't feel that he had to worry about the content. But this is both poor theology and poor aesthetics. A lyric can contain considerable theological content. An epic can be as emphatically (and accurately) historic as a straight piece of prose. *Paradise Lost,* for example, contains many statements which while artistically expressed are almost straight theology. Just because something takes the form of a work of art does not mean that it cannot be factual.

Changing Styles
7. Many Christians, especially those unused to viewing the arts and thinking about them, reject contemporary painting and contemporary poetry not because of their world-view, but simply because they feel threatened by a new art form. It is perfectly legitimate for a Christian to reject a particular work of art intellectually—that is, because he knows what is being said by it. But it is another thing to reject the work of art simply because the style is different from that which we are used to. In short: *Styles of art form change, and there is nothing wrong with this.*

This sort of change is not only true of art forms; it is true of whole word systems. Chaucer wrote English, and I write English. But surely there is quite a difference between them. Is it wrong for me to speak my kind of English rather than Chaucer's? Would you read what I wrote if I were writing in Chaucerian English?

As a matter of fact, change is one difference between life and death. There is no living language which does not undergo constant change. The languages which do not change—Latin, for example—are dead. As long as one has a living art, its forms will change. The past art forms, therefore, are not necessarily the right ones for today or tomorrow. To demand the art forms of yesterday in either word systems or art is a bourgeois failure. It cannot be assumed that if a Christian painter becomes "more Christian," he will necessarily paint more and more like Rembrandt. This would be like saying that if the preacher really makes it next Sunday morning, he will preach to us in Chaucerian English. Then we'll really listen!

Now, some may say, "Well, I don't want Chaucerian English, but I would certainly like King James English." I personally love King James English. It is still my language because I was educated in a day when it was one of the marks of the educated man to read it and the language of Shakespeare with facility. Reading it endlessly, I made it my own. But must I preach in King James English or be considered a failure? Must I *always* pray using King James English, the *thee's* and *thou's*, for example? To think so is a mark of a bourgeois mind. Christians must absolutely and consciously separate themselves from such thinking.

Not only will there be a change in art forms and language as time progresses, but there will be a difference in art forms coming from various geographical locations and from different cultures. Take, for example, Hebrew poetry. It has alliteration and parallelism and other such rhetorical forms, but it hardly ever rhymes. Does this mean it is not poetry? Or does it mean that most English poetry is wrong because it rhymes? Must all poetry be frozen into the form of Hebrew poetry? Surely not. Rather, each art form in each culture must find its own proper relationship between world-view and style.

For example, I may walk into a museum I have never been in before and enter a room without seeing its identifying plaque, and I may immediately say to myself, "Ah, this is Japanese art." How can I tell? From the style. The crucial question is, of course, should it show its Japaneseness? The answer is obviously yes.

Then what about the Christian's art? Here three things should be stressed. First, Christian art today should be twentieth-century art. Art changes. Language changes. The preacher's preaching today must be twentieth-century language communication, or there will be an obstacle to being understood. And if a Christian's art is not twentieth-century art, it is an obstacle to his being heard. It makes him different in a way in which there is no necessity for difference. A Christian should not, therefore, strive to copy Rembrandt or Browning.

Second, Christian art should differ from country to country. Why did we ever force the Africans to use Gothic architecture? It's a meaningless exercise. All we succeeded in doing was making Christianity foreign to the African. If a Christian artist is Japanese, his paintings should be Japanese; if Indian, Indian.

Third, the body of a Christian artist's work should reflect the Christian world-view. In short, if you are a young Christian artist, you should be working in the art forms of the twentieth century, showing the marks of the culture out of which you have come, reflecting your own country and your own contemporariness, *and* embodying something of the nature of the world as seen from a Christian standpoint.

Modern Art Forms and the Christian Message
8. While a Christian artist should be modern in his art, he does face certain difficulties. First, we must distinguish carefully between style and message. Let me say firmly that *there is no such*

thing as a godly style or an ungodly style. The more one tries to make such a distinction, the more confusing it becomes.

I remember being in Cambridge once at a symposium of Christians who were addressing themselves to the nature of Christian art and art forms. One of the Christian artists—a very fine organist—insisted that there was a Christian style in music. We discussed this at some length, forcing him to say just what the criterion for Christian style would be. He finally replied, "Christian music is music that you can tap your foot to." This is meaningless.

Yet, while there is no such thing as a godly or ungodly style, we must not be misled or naive in thinking that various styles have no relation whatsoever to the content of the message of the work of art. Styles themselves are developed as symbol systems or vehicles for certain world-views or messages. In the Renaissance, for example, one finds distinctively different styles from those which characterize art in the Middle Ages. It does not take much education in the history of art to recognize that what Filippo Lippi was saying about the nature of the Virgin Mary is different from what was being said in paintings done before the Renaissance. Art in the Renaissance became more natural and less iconographic. In our own day, men like Picasso and T. S. Eliot developed new styles in order to speak a new message.

There is a parallel in language itself. Sanskrit, I am told, developed as a perfect vehicle for Hindu philosophy. And I am told it is a very poor vehicle for the Christian message. As a matter of fact, I have heard some Sanskrit scholars say that they don't think Christianity could ever be preached in Sanskrit. I am no authority on this, but they may be right. It is interesting, for example, that both English and German were codified in their modern forms around the Christian message. The German language was made up of various dialectical forms when Luther translated the Bible. At that point, the German language was set down in a form which became standard. Luther's German became the literary German. In England, the early translations of the Bible, summed up supremely in the King James Version, did the same thing for the English language. This meant that Christianity could be easily taught as long as the generally accepted meaning of the words were the Christian meaning of the words.

In Japan, on the other hand, it is very difficult to use the word *guilt* without a long explanation, because in Japan the word *guilt*

grew up as a vehicle for the Japanese concept of ceremonial un-
cleanliness. Now if we have a word that means ceremonial un-
cleanliness as a vehicle and we try to explain true moral guilt in the
presence of a holy, personal God, we have quite a task. We may
have to use the word, but we must then refashion its definition
and be certain that the people to whom we are speaking understand just how we are using the word. It must mean something
different than it did in the symbol system out of which the word
came.

There is the same dilemma in art styles and forms. Think, for
example, of T. S. Eliot's form of poetry in "The Waste Land."
The fragmented form matches the vision of fragmented man. But
it is intriguing that after T. S. Eliot became a Christian—for example, in "The Journey of the Magi"—he did not use quite this
same form. Rather, he adapted it for the message he was now
giving—a message with a Christian character. But he didn't entirely give up the form; he didn't go back to Tennyson. Rather, he
adapted the form that he used in "The Waste Land," changing it to
fit the message that he was now giving. In other words, T. S.
Eliot the Christian wrote somewhat differently than T. S. Eliot
the "modern man."

Therefore, while we must use twentieth-century styles, we
must not use them in such a way as to be dominated by the
world-views out of which they have arisen. Christianity is a message with its own distinctive propositional content, not a set of
"religious" truths in an upper story. The whole man is to be
addressed, and this includes his mind as well as his emotions and
his aesthetic sensitivity. Therefore, an art form or style that is no
longer able to carry content cannot be used to give the Christian
message. I am not saying that the style is in itself wrong, but that
it has limitations. Totally fractured prose or poetry cannot be used
to give the Christian message for the simple reason that it cannot
carry intellectual content, and you can't preach Christianity without content. The biblical message, the good news, is a good news
of content.

It is here that feedback is important in regard to the style the
artist chooses. Let us say, for example, that you are playing in a
Christian rock group, making an art form of rock. Suppose further that at the same time you are going into certain coffeehouses
and using rock as a bridge to preach the Christian message. That's
fine. But then you must be careful of the feedback. When you

have finished playing, you must ask whether the people who have heard you play have understood what you have been saying. Have they heard your message clearly because you have used their modern idiom, or have they simply heard again what they have always heard when they have listened to rock because you used their form? Sometimes the content will get through, sometimes it will not. Not all situations will be the same; the immediate situation and what you are trying to do must be kept in mind.

The problem is just as prevalent in folk music as it is in rock. Joan Baez sang so beautifully, "You may call him Jesus, but I call him Savior." But as far as Joan Baez and most of her listeners were concerned, when she said, "I call him Savior," she was not calling him Savior in the way a Christian calls him Savior. She could have been singing southern folk or country and western or a Hindu lyric just as well. So when we come along and say, "My purpose is to sing folk so that I will be understood," we must find a way to make it clear that we are singing folk to convey a world-view and not just to sing folk.

The form in which a world-view is given can either weaken or strengthen the content, even if the viewer or reader does not in every case analyze this completely. In other words, depending upon the vehicle you use, something can come across that an audience does not notice and yet will be moving either in the direction of your world-view or away from your world-view. And as a Christian adopts and adapts various contemporary techniques, he must wrestle with the whole question, looking to the Holy Spirit for help to know when to invent, when to adopt, when to adapt, and when to not use a specific style at all. This is something each artist wrestles with for a lifetime, not something he settles once and for all.

In conclusion, therefore, often we will use twentieth-century art forms, but we must be careful to keep them from distorting the world-view which is distinctively ours as Christians. In one way, styles are completely neutral. But in another way, they must not be used in an unthinking, naive way.

The Christian World-View
9. *The Christian world-view can be divided into what I call a major and a minor theme.* (The terms *major* and *minor,* as I am using them, have no relationship to their use in music.)

First, the minor theme is *the abnormality of the revolting world.* This falls into two parts: (1) Men who have revolted from God and not come back to Christ are eternally lost; they see their meaninglessness in the present, and in this they are right from their own standpoint. Nietzsche can say that God is dead and Sartre must follow along, showing that man is dead, and Sartre is right from his own perspective. (2) There is a defeated and sinful side to the Christian's life. If we are at all honest, we must admit that in this life there is no such thing as totally victorious living. In every one of us there are those things which are sinful and deceiving; and while we may see substantial healing, in this life we do not come to perfection.

The major theme is the opposite of the minor; it is *the meaningfulness and purposefulness of life*. From the Christian viewpoint, this falls into two headings, metaphysics and morals. In the area of metaphysics (of being, of existence, including the existence of every man), God is there, God exists. Therefore, all is not absurd. Furthermore, man is made in God's image and so man has significance. With this comes the fact that love, not just sex, exists. True morals, as opposed to only conditioning, exist. And creativity, as opposed to mechanical construction, exists. So therefore the major theme is an optimism in the area of being; everything is not absurd, there is meaning. But most important, this optimism has a sufficient base. It isn't suspended two feet off the ground, but rests on the existence of the infinite-personal God who exists and who has a character and who has created all things, especially man in His own image.

But there is also a major theme in relation to morals. Christianity gives a moral solution on the basis of the fact that God exists and has a character which is the law of the universe. There is therefore an absolute in regard to morals. It is not that there is a moral law back of God that binds both God and man, but that God Himself has a character and this character is reflected in the moral law of the universe. Thus when a person realizes his inadequacy before God and feels guilty, he has a basis not simply for the feeling but for the reality of guilt. Man's dilemma is not just that he is finite and God is infinite, but that he is a sinner guilty before a holy God. But then he recognizes that God has given him a solution to this in the life, death and resurrection of Christ. Man is fallen and flawed, but he is redeemable on the basis of Christ's work. This is beautiful. This is optimism. And this optimism has a sufficient base.

Notice that the Christian and his art have a place for the minor theme because man is lost and abnormal and the Christian has his own defeatedness. There is not only victory and song in my life. But the Christian and his art don't end there. He goes on to the major theme because there is an optimistic answer. This is important for the kind of art Christians are to produce. First of all, Christian art needs to recognize the minor theme, the defeated aspect to even the Christian life. If our Christian art only emphasizes the major theme, then it is not fully Christian but simply romantic art. And let us say with sorrow that for years our Sunday school literature has been romantic in its art and has had very little to do with genuine Christian art. Older Christians may wonder what is wrong with this art and wonder why their kids are turned off by it, but the answer is simple. It's romantic. It's based on the notion that Christianity has only an optimistic note.

On the other hand, it is possible for a Christian to so major on the minor theme, emphasizing the lostness of man and the abnormality of the universe, that he is equally unbiblical. There may be exceptions where a Christian artist feels it his calling only to picture the negative, but in general for the Christian the major theme is to be dominant—though it must exist in relationship to the minor.

Modern art that does not depend on the Christian consensus has tended to emphasize only the minor theme. We look at the paintings hanging in the modern art galleries, and we are impressed by the pessimistic analysis of contemporary man. There are, of course, some works of modern art which are optimistic. But the basis for that optimism is insufficient and, like Christian art which does not adequately emphasize the minor theme, it tends to be pure romanticism. The artist's work appears dishonest in the face of contemporary facts.

Finally, the Christian artist should constantly keep in mind the law of love in a world that is bent upon destruction. The Christian poet or painter may write or paint emphasizing the minor theme; at other times, and on other days, he may concentrate on the major theme. But our world at the end of the twentieth century already has so much destruction without Christian artists so emphasizing the minor theme in the total body of their work that they only add to the poorness and destruction of our generation. A Christian businessman who does not operate on the basis of compassion does not live within the biblical norms of economics, and the Christian artist who only concentrates on the abnormality of the world is likewise not living by the law of love.

There is a parallel in our conversation with men. We must present both the law and the gospel; we ought not end with only the judgment of the law. Even though we may spend most of our time on the judgment of the law, love dictates that at some point we get to the gospel. And it seems to me that in the total body of his work, the artist somewhere should have a sufficient place for the major theme.

The Subject Matter of Christian Art
10. *Christian art is by no means always religious art—that is, art which deals with religious themes.* Consider God the Creator. Is God's creation totally involved with religious subjects? What about the universe? The birds? The trees? The mountains? What about the bird's song? And the sound of the wind in the trees? When God created out of nothing by His spoken word, he did not just create "religious" objects. And in the Bible, as we have seen, God commanded the artist, working within God's own creation, to fashion statues of oxen and lions and carvings of almond blossoms for the tabernacle and the temple.

We should remember that the Bible contains the Song of Solomon, the love song between a man and a woman, and it contains David's song to Israel's national heroes. Neither subject is "religious." But God's creation—the mountains, the trees, the birds and the bird's songs—are also nonreligious art. Think about that. If God made the flowers, they are worth painting and writing about. If God made the birds, they are worth painting. If God made the sky, the sky is worth painting. If God made the ocean, indeed it's worth writing poetry about. It is worth man's while to create works upon the basis of the great works God has already created.

This whole notion is rooted in the realization that Christianity is not just involved with "salvation," but with the total man in the total world. The Christian message begins with the existence of God forever and then with creation. It does not begin with salvation. We must be thankful for salvation, but the Christian message is more than that. Man has a value because he is made in the image of God, and thus man as man is an important subject for Christian art. Man as man—with his emotions, his feelings, his body, his life—this is an important subject matter for poetry and novels. I'm not talking here about man's lostness but about his mannishness. In God's world the individual counts. Therefore, Christian art should deal with the individual.

Modern art often flattens man out and speaks in great abstractions; sometimes we cannot tell whether the subject is a man or a woman. Our generation has left little place for the individual. Only the mass of men remains. But as Christians, we see things otherwise. Because God has created individual man in His own image and because God knows and is interested in the individual, individual man is worthy of our painting and of our writing.

Christian art is the expression of the whole life of the whole person who is a Christian. What a Christian portrays in his art is the totality of life. If, therefore, Christianity has so much to say about the arts and to the artist, why is it that recently we have produced so little Christian art? I should think the answer would now be clear. We have not produced Christian art because we have forgotten most of what Christianity says about the arts.

Christians, for example, ought not to be threatened by fantasy and imagination. Great painting is not "photographic" in the poor sense of photographic. The Old Testament art commanded by God was not always "photographic." There were blue pomegranates on the robes of the priests when he went into the Holy of Holies. In nature there are no blue pomegranates. Christian artists do not need to be threatened by fantasy and imagination, for they have a basis for knowing the difference between them and the real world "out there." Epistemologically, as I have pointed out in *He Is There and He Is Not Silent,* Christian man has a basis for knowing the difference between subject and object. The Christian is the really free man—he is free to have imagination. This too is our heritage. The Christian is the one whose imagination should fly beyond the stars.

Moreover, a Christian artist does not need to concentrate on religious subjects. After all, religious themes may be completely non-Christian. The counterculture art in the underground newspaper in which Christ and Krishna are blended—here is religious art par excellence. But it is completely anti-Christian. Religious subjects are no guarantee that a work of art is Christian. On the other hand, the art of an artist who never paints the head of Christ, never once paints an open tomb, may be magnificent Christian art. For some artists there is a place for religious themes, but an artist does not need to be conscience-stricken if he does not paint in this area. Some Christian artists will never use religious themes. This is a freedom the artist has in Christ under the leadership of the Holy Spirit.

An Individual Art Work and the Body of An Artist's Work

11. *Every artist has the problem of making an individual work of art and, as well, building up a total body of work.* No artist can say everything he might want to say or build everything he might want to build into a single work. It is true that some art forms, such as the epic and the novel, lend themselves to larger conceptions and more complex treatments, but even there not everything that an artist wants to do can be done in one piece. Therefore, we cannot judge an artist's work from one piece. No art critic or art historian can do that. We must judge an artist's performance and an artist's world-view on the basis of as much of that artist's work as we can.

There is a parallel here with the sermon. No single sermon can say everything that needs to be said. And no one can judge a minister's total theology or the content of his faith on the basis of a single sermon. The man who tries to put everything into one sermon is a very poor preacher indeed. Even the Bible is an extended body of books, and it cannot be read as if any one book or any one chapter included the whole; it must be read from beginning to end. And if that is true of the Word of God, how much more is it true of an artist's work!

If you are a Christian artist, therefore, you must not freeze up just because you can't do everything at once. Don't be afraid to write a love poem simply because you cannot put into it everything of the Christian message. Yet, if a man is to be an artist, his goal should be in a lifetime to produce a wide and deep body of work from which his world-view will show forth.

The Christian Life as a Work of Art

I would suggest that we take all of these perspectives on art and consider how they apply to our own Christian life. Perhaps it would be a good idea to read this essay again and specifically apply it to your life as a Christian. No work of art is more important than the Christian's own life, and every Christian is called upon to be an artist in this sense. He may have no gift of writing, no gift of composing or singing, but each man has the gift of creativity in terms of the way he lives his life. In this sense, the Christian's life is to be an art work. The Christian's life is to be a thing of truth and also a thing of beauty in the midst of a lost and despairing world.

Notes to Volume II

GENESIS IN SPACE AND TIME

Chapter One: Creation
[1] For a much fuller treatment of the material in the next few paragraphs, see *He Is There And He Is Not Silent.*
[2] See *Back to Freedom and Dignity* in which I deal with B. F. Skinner's book, *Beyond Freedom and Dignity* (New York: Alfred A. Knopf, 1971).
[3] The biblical teaching concerning the Trinity is, of course, developed more fully in the New Testament, but for another indication of the Trinity in the Old Testament see Gen. 11:7 and Is. 6:8.
[4] The Greek aorist is a once-for-all past tense.
[5] This verse is sometimes used by those who say faith itself gives knowledge and thus undercuts the necessity of the content of Scripture. However, it is Scripture which gives the knowledge that is referred to here, and then we, on the basis of what the Bible claims is sufficient reason, believe what God has told us in the Bible.

Chapter Two: Differentiation and the Creation of Man
[1] For a discussion of the freedom and limitation in cosmogony as set by the Bible, see Chapter 3 of *No Final Conflict.*
[2] See Chapter 4 of *No Final Conflict.*
[3] For the unity of the Book of Genesis, see Chapter 2 of *No Final Conflict.*
[4] In the earlier passages, up to chapter 5, the word *Adam* is used with a definite article, referring to a specific man. In Genesis 5:1, 2 it is used without the article and thus seems better translated as *mankind.*

Chapter Eight: From Noah to Babel and Abraham
[1] See *No Final Conflict,* Chapters 1 and 5.

List of Translated Editions and Publishers of the Books in Volume Two

GENESIS IN SPACE AND TIME

First United States edition, InterVarsity Press, 1972.
First British edition, Hodder and Stoughton, 1973.
Génesis en el Tiempo y en el Espacio (Spanish), Ediciones Evangélicas Europeas, Barcelona, 1974.
Genesis in ruimte en tijd (Dutch), Buijten & Schipperheijn, Amsterdam, 1974.
Korean edition.
Genesis in Raum und Zeit (German), Brockhaus-Verlag, Wuppertal, 1976.
Kaikki alkoi Luomisesta (Finnish), Suomen Evankelisluterilainen, Ylioppilas, 1975.

NO FINAL CONFLICT

First United States edition, InterVarsity Press, 1975.
First British edition, Hodder and Stoughton, 1975.
Der Schöpfungsbericht (German), Haus der Bibel, 1976

JOSHUA AND THE FLOW OF BIBLICAL HISTORY

First United States edition, InterVarsity Press, 1975.
First British edition, Hodder and Stoughton, 1975.
Josua—Gott will retten (German), Brockhaus Verlag, Wuppertal; Haus der Bibel, Geneva, 1977.

BASIC BIBLE STUDIES

First United States edition, Tyndale House, 1972.
First British edition, Hodder & Stoughton, 1973.
25 Estudios Biblicos Basicos (Spanish), Ediciones Evangélicas Europeas, Barcelona, 1971.
Die Bibel zum Thema (German), Brockhaus Verlag, Wuppertal Haus der Bibel, Geneva, 1973.
Les Grands Thèmes de la Bible (French), Maison de la Bible, Geneva, 1974.
Kannada edition, Scripture Literature Publishers, Bangalore, 1974.
25 Bijbelstudies (Dutch), Buijten & Schipperheijn, Amsterdam, 1974.
Korean edition, Word of Life Press, Seoul, 1974.
Os Grandes Temas da Biblia (Portuguese), Casa da Biblia, Sao Paulo.
Chinese edition, Campus Evangelical Fellowship, Taipei, 1979.
Grundläggande Bibelstudier (Swedish), Normans Förlag, 1979.

ART AND THE BIBLE

First United States edition, InterVarsity Press, 1973.
First British edition, Hodder and Stoughton, 1973.
Arte y Biblia (Spanish), Ediciones Evangélicas Europeas, Barcelona, 1974.
Japanese edition in *Kirisutosha Gakusei Kai,* issues 631-642, Tokyo, 1978.
Kunst und die Bibel (German), Hanssler-Verlag, Neuhausen-Stuttgart, 1981.

DATE DUE

10 Sept 84			